EURIPIDES

VII

LCL 504

EURIPIDES

FRAGMENTS

Aegeus–Meleager

EDITED AND TRANSLATED BY

CHRISTOPHER COLLARD
AND
MARTIN CROPP

HARVARD UNIVERSITY PRESS
CAMBRIDGE, MASSACHUSETTS
LONDON, ENGLAND
2008

Copyright © 2008 by the President and Fellows
of Harvard College
All rights reserved

First published 2008

LOEB CLASSICAL LIBRARY® is a registered trademark
of the President and Fellows of Harvard College

Library of Congress Catalog Card Number 2007043817
CIP data available from the Library of Congress

ISBN 978-0-674-99625-0

*Composed in ZephGreek and ZephText by
Technologies 'N Typography, Merrimac, Massachusetts.
Printed on acid-free paper and bound by
Edwards Brothers, Ann Arbor, Michigan*

CONTENTS

PREFACE   ix

INTRODUCTION   xi

CHRONOLOGY   xxix

ABBREVIATIONS   xxxiii

AEGEUS (ΑΙΓΕΥΣ)   3

AEOLUS (ΑΙΟΛΟΣ)   12

ALEXANDER (ΑΛΕΞΑΝΔΡΟΣ)   33

ALCMEON IN PSOPHIS and
   ALCMEON IN CORINTH   77

ALCMEON IN PSOPHIS (ΑΛΚΜΕΩΝ Ο ΔΙΑ
   ΨΩΦΙΔΟΣ)   79

ALCMEON IN CORINTH (ΑΛΚΜΕΩΝ Ο ΔΙΑ
   ΚΟΡΙΝΘΟΥ)   87

ALCMENE (ΑΛΚΜΗΝΗ)

ALOPE (ΑΛΟΠΗ)   115

ANDROMEDA (ΑΝΔΡΟΜΕΔΑ)   124

CONTENTS

ANTIGONE (ΑΝΤΙΓΟΝΗ) 156

ANTIOPE (ΑΝΤΙΟΠΗ) 170

ARCHELAUS (ΑΡΧΕΛΑΟΣ) 229

AUGE (ΑΥΓΗ) 259

AUTOLYCUS A and B (ΑΥΤΟΛΥΚΟΣ A, B) 278

BELLEROPHON (ΒΕΛΛΕΡΟΦΟΝΤΗΣ) 289

BUSIRIS (ΒΟΥΣΙΡΙΣ) 318

DANAE (ΔΑΝΑΗ) 323

DICTYS (ΔΙΚΤΥΣ) 346

EPEUS (ΕΠΕΙΟΣ) 361

ERECHTHEUS (ΕΡΕΧΘΕΥΣ) 362

EURYSTHEUS (ΕΥΡΥΣΘΕΥΣ) 403

THERISTAE, 'HARVESTERS' (ΘΕΡΙΣΤΑΙ) 413

THESEUS (ΘΗΣΕΥΣ) 415

THYESTES (ΘΥΕΣΤΗΣ) 428

INO (ΙΝΩ) 438

IXION (ΙΞΙΩΝ) 460

HIPPOLYTUS VEILED (ΙΠΠΟΛΥΤΟΣ
  ΚΑΛΥΠΤΟΜΕΝΟΣ) 466

[CADMUS] [ΚΑΔΜΟΣ] 491

CRESPHONTES (ΚΡΕΣΦΟΝΤΗΣ) 493

CONTENTS

CRETAN WOMEN (ΚΡΗΣΣΑΙ)   516

CRETANS (ΚΡΗΤΕΣ)   529

LAMIA (ΛΑΜΙΑ)   557

LICYMNIUS (ΛΙΚΥΜΝΙΟΣ)   560

MELANIPPE WISE and MELANIPPE CAPTIVE   567

MELANIPPE WISE (ΜΕΛΑΝΙΠΠΗ Η ΣΟΦΗ)   569

MELANIPPE CAPTIVE (ΜΕΛΑΝΙΠΠΗ Η
    ΔΕΣΜΩΤΙΣ)   587

MELEAGER (ΜΕΛΕΑΓΡΟΣ)   613

INDEX   633

PREFACE

We were invited to contribute these volumes to the Loeb Classical Library at the generous suggestion of Sir Hugh Lloyd-Jones, whose editions of the Aeschylean and Sophoclean fragments provided a template. We had earlier cut our teeth for such work in two volumes which offer selected fragmentary plays on a much larger scale (*SFP* in our Abbreviations list). We have been immeasurably aided in this new task by two recent and complete major editions of Euripides' fragments by François Jouan and the late Hermann Van Looy (ed. Budé) and Richard Kannicht (*TrGF* 5). We briefly describe and admire the extraordinary achievement of these editions in our Introduction under "Collection and Study of the Fragments"; here we express our warmest gratitude to the editors themselves for their encouragement and help.

Amongst other recent editors of the fragmentary texts we salute especially Colin Austin (Austin, *NFE* in the Abbreviations list), James Diggle (Diggle, *TrGFS*), and Wolfgang Luppe, a prolific editor of papyri whom we cite very frequently. Our bibliographies name the many editors of individual plays on whose work we have drawn, and other scholars who have contributed to the surge in fragment studies on which we remark in the Introduction

PREFACE

(note 23 there mentions some bibliographical surveys of this work).

Martin Cropp's work for these volumes has been facilitated by research grants from the University of Calgary. Jason McClure assisted him in checking refererences and preparing the Index, and Elizabeth Cropp read most of our introductions and translations with improving effect. Thanks for various kinds of personal support and practical help go also to Bill Allan, James Diggle, John Gibert, Doreen Innes, Jim Neville and Peter Toohey. We happily record appreciation of a quite different kind, not least for much wondering patience, to our wives, Jean Collard and Elizabeth Cropp.

Lastly, Christopher Collard would like it known how much is owed to Martin Cropp's expertise in preparing the copy for publication.

Christopher Collard, Oxford
Martin Cropp, Calgary

INTRODUCTION

Evidence for the Lost Plays

Euripides first produced plays at the Athenian Dionysia in 455 when he was probably in his late twenties; his dramatic career continued for almost fifty years.[1] Our knowledge of his plays depends almost entirely on the texts collected and edited two centuries later by scholars at Alexandria, who may have relied largely on the official Athenian collection commissioned by Lycurgus around 330; but so little is known about the earlier history of the original scripts, and particularly about the processes of authorial revision, circulation, and adaptation for reperformance at Athens and elsewhere, that we cannot know how exactly these were reproduced in what became the standard texts; we can only assume that what we read for the most part represents Euripides' work.[2]

The Alexandrian scholars seem to have known of ninety-two titles but could find and edit texts of only sev-

---

[1] On Euripides' life and the evidence for it see David Kovacs in the Loeb *Euripides* I.1–21.

[2] For a survey of the ancient and medieval transmission of tragic texts see D. Kovacs in J. Gregory (ed.), *A Companion to Greek Tragedy* (Malden, Mass., and Oxford, 2005), 379–93.

enty tragedies and eight satyr plays.[3] These included five plays whose authenticity was disputed or confused: *Pirithous, Rhadamanthys, Tennes,* a *Sisyphus* (perhaps displacing or confused with Euripides' own *Sisyphus* of 415 B.C.) and the extant *Rhesus* (certainly displacing Euripides' own *Rhesus*). Adding three more satyr plays whose texts seem to have been lost before the Alexandrian editions (*Epeus, Theristae, Lamia*), we have a total of eighty-one known Euripidean or possibly Euripidean titles, of which eighteen are extant and sixty-three are fragmentary or lost almost without trace. All of the latter are included in this edition.[4] Their chronology, so far as it can be known or estimated, is detailed in the Chronology.

Euripides was amongst the most widely read authors of the Greek and Roman world, and many of his plays seem to have remained in circulation at least until the middle of the 3rd century A.D. The fragments of those that were lost after that time or earlier come partly from excerpts and quotations found in the extant or fragmentary texts of other authors (collectively known as 'book fragments') and partly from papyri, i.e. the remains of actual ancient books recovered in the late 19th and 20th centuries, mostly in

---

[3] The satyr plays were *Autolycus A* and *B, Busiris, Eurystheus, Cyclops, Sisyphus, Sciron, Syleus*. For details, computation and lists see R. Kannicht in C. Mueller-Goldingen (ed.), ΛΗΝΑΙΚΑ: *Festschrift für C. W. Müller* (Stuttgart–Leipzig, 1996), 185–201 (sources and list also in *TrGF* 5.77–80, 149–50); H. Van Looy in ed. Budé VIII.1.xi–xvi; Pechstein 19–29.

[4] We also include the negligible evidence for a *Cadmus*. *Pirithous, Rhadamanthys, Tennes* and the disputed *Sisyphus* fragment are printed at the end of our edition.

Egypt.[5] About seventy-five papyri representing some thirty plays are listed in the Index of Sources in Kannicht's recent edition of the fragments (*TrGF* 5; this total includes the papyrus 'hypotheses' mentioned below). Nearly half of them are from the deserted site of Oxyrhynchus, excavated in the 1890s.[6] The papyri include nothing so spectacular as those of Menander, or of Aristotle's *Constitution of Athens*; the most we have for a play of Euripides is about 500 lines (many incomplete) representing less than one-third of *Hypsipyle*. They have nevertheless transformed our knowledge of the lost plays.

The second category mentioned above, the 'book fragments', was the basis for virtually all knowledge of the plays before the discoveries of papyri. These fragments come from a great variety of sources ranging from literary, philosophical, historical and scientific works to anthologies, commentaries on the works of Euripides himself and other authors, mythological handbooks, encyclopedias, dictionaries, and other scholarly and educational books.[7] Among these sources (some of which have themselves been amplified through papyrus discoveries) the comic

[5] A few remnants are actually written on parchment, notably *Cretans* F 472e, *Melanippe Captive* F 495, and the *Phaethon* palimpsest. A few brief quotations are scratched on pottery sherds (*ostraca*), e.g. *Aegeus* F 11.

[6] Information and images of the Oxyrhynchus papyri are easily accessible on the website of Oxford University's Papyrology Project. On the city's history and life as learned from the papyri: Peter Parsons, *City of the Sharp-nosed Fish* (London, 2007).

[7] What follows is a brief sketch. For a fuller survey of the book fragments see H. Van Looy in ed. Budé VIII.1.xxxvii–liv.

playwright Aristophanes is of special importance as a younger contemporary of Euripides who actually saw the first productions of many of his plays. The eleven extant plays of Aristophanes include many quotations and comic adaptations of Euripidean verses, and some extensive parodies of Euripidean scenes; the scholia on them, especially those derived from Alexandrian scholarship, are a rich further source of information (far richer in fact than the scholia on the extant plays of Euripides himself) on provenances and original wordings, contexts and speakers. From the 4th century the philosopher Aristotle, who initiated the systematic study of tragedy as a genre, provides insights into the reception of Euripides in the period following his death. Hellenistic sources are sadly lacking except through citations by later authors, but the continuing importance of Euripides for cultured readers in the Greco-Roman world is evident in (for example) the quotations in Cicero's letters and philosophical works, the rhetorical works of Dio Chrysostom and Aelius Aristides, the learned trivia of Lucian and Athenaeus, and the essays and biographies of Plutarch which make him the most abundant source of Euripidean quotations after Stobaeus and Aristophanes with his scholia. The anthology of Stobaeus (John of Stobi in Macedonia, 5th c.) is by far the most abundant of all, with nearly six hundred Euripidean excerpts from the fragmentary plays occupying about fifteen per cent of the Index of Sources in Kannicht's edition. Stobaeus clearly relied on earlier collections, as did his contemporary anthologist Orion of Thebes in Egypt, most of whose forty excerpts from the lost plays are also found in Stobaeus; such collections were in fact assembled and widely used throughout Hellenistic and Roman times, and their use is evident in such sources as the *Stromata* ('*Miscellanies*') of the Christian convert Clement of Alexandria, composed about 200 A.D.[8] Alongside this excerpt tradition ran the traditions of literary commentary, grammatical analysis and reference books which supplied the Euripidean material in some important late antique and medieval sources, most notably the scholia on the extant works of Euripides, Aristophanes and others, the *Lexica* of Hesychius (5th c., but transmitted in an abridgement) and the patriarch Photius (9th c.), the *Etymologicum Genuinum* (9th–10th c.) in its various manifestations, the Byzantine encyclopedia known as the *Suda* (10th c.), and the voluminous Homeric commentaries of Eustathius, Bishop of Thessalonica (12th c.).[9]

Many of the book sources convey piecemeal information about plots and dramatic situations, although many others (especially anthologies, dictionaries and so on) do not. The fullest such information, however, comes from the remains of an ancient collection of 'narrative hypotheses' sometimes known as the 'Tales from Euripides' (but

---

[8] Euripides was particularly valued in antiquity as a source of the *gnōmai* or ethical judgments and observations which abound in the anthologies: on this aspect of his plays see G. W. Most in M. S. Funghi (ed.), *Aspetti di letteratura gnomica nel mondo antico*, I (Florence, 2003), 141–66. Most rightly emphasizes the dramatic and characterizing functions of the *gnōmai* in their original contexts, which are of course evident in the extant plays. *Gnōmai* excerpted from fragmentary plays often seem banal, especially when considered *en masse*, but their possible dramatic contexts should always be kept in mind.

[9] Eleanor Dickey, *Ancient Greek Scholarship* (London–New York, 2007) provides a useful guide to such sources.

one or two Sophoclean examples are known), which is now represented in some twenty papyri.[10] These are not detailed dramatic outlines but rather summaries of the stories told in the plays, so they generally omit or blur many important details of the plays as such. Neverthless these papyri are of major importance for the reconstruction of *Aeolus, Alexander, Theseus* and *Scyrians*, and of lesser—sometimes minimal—value, according to their degree of physical damage, for about twenty others. For *Melanippe Wise* and *Stheneboea* narrative hypotheses from very damaged papyri are supplemented by more complete texts which happen to be quoted in late rhetorical sources, and the latter add a briefer summary of *Pirithous*. The same or similar collections are probably reflected—but abbreviated, sometimes heavily, and subject to contamination—in book sources which give narrative summaries attributed to Euripides, such as the astronomical sources for *Andromeda*, Hyginus' *Fables* for *Antiope* and *Ino*, Apollodorus for *Alcmeon in Corinth*, John Malalas of Antioch for *Danae*, and the Armenian Moses of Chorene for *Auge* and *Peliades*; and the same may be true of many that do not name him, including those summaries of Hyginus which are our basis (for better or worse) for reconstructing *Alope*, *Archelaus, Cresphontes, Polyidus* and the conclusion of

---

[10] Van Rossum-Steenbeek (1998) provides a thorough introduction with references to previous studies and texts of most of the now known papyri. On style and probable date (2nd c. B.C.–1st c. A.D.) see further J. Diggle in Bastianini–Casanova, *Euripide e i papiri* 27–67. Summaries of this kind are known from as early as the 3rd c. B.C., for example the *Tragoidoumena* ('*Stories from Tragedy*') of Asclepiades of Tragilos, *FGrH* 12 F 1–15.

Telephus.[11] Where such resources are lacking—as for example for *Antigone, Thyestes, Cretan Women, Licymnius, Oenomaus, Peleus, Pleisthenes, Chrysippus* and most of the satyr plays—we are generally reduced to educated guesswork supplemented in some cases by incidental ancient comments which may illuminate some aspect or part of the play.

Pictorial representations are a further but rather limited source of evidence for the precise content of the plays, although they are of greater importance as documenting the reception of Euripides' work. It is clear that Euripides created many highly distinctive dramatic plots, inventing or heavily adapting myths for this purpose, and that some of these fed into the iconographic traditions of the classical world. But the correlation between iconographic representation and dramatic original is seldom if ever simple or exact, even when the lapse of time between the two is brief. The extant *Iphigenia in Tauris* is an obvious example of a distinctly Euripidean subject adopted but also adapted in the iconographic tradition. For the fragmentary plays there are a few cases where works of art—especially Attic and South Italian vase paintings from the two or three generations after Euripides' death—clearly reflect Euripidean scenes, whether staged (*Melanippe Wise, Telephus, Hypsipyle*) or reported (*Antiope*). But in these cases confident identification of the artwork with the play

[11] On the limitations of the summaries in Hyginus and Apollodorus as evidence for reconstructing the plays see van Rossum-Steenbeek 25–30 and more fully M. Huys, *APF* 42 (1996), 168–78 and 43 (1997), 11–30 and *RhM* 140 (1997), 308–27.

and interpretation of its details depends on our already knowing the relevant content of the play from other sources—and even then unanswered questions may remain (such as the possible role of Cretheus in *Melanippe Wise*). Where such confirmation is lacking, identification and interpretation of a Euripidean subject in a work of art remain speculative, and plausible to varying degrees (see for example our introductions to *Aegeus, Aeolus, Alcmene, Dictys, Theseus, Cretans, Meleager, Oeneus, Stheneboea*).[12] The same kind of caution applies to reflections of Euripidean subjects in later poetry, especially the Latin tragedians (themselves preserved only in tenuous fragments: see for example on *Alexander, Alcmeon in Psophis, Antiope, Thyestes, Meleager, Telephus, Philoctetes, Phoenix*) and such tradition-conscious but eclectic and innovative poets as Ovid (see on *Aeolus, Protesilaus, Scyrians, Phaethon*) and Statius (*Protesilaus, Scyrians, Hypsipyle*).

[12] The relationship between art-works (especially vase-paintings) and plays is a subject of continuing controversy, discussed for example by L. Giuliani, *BICS* 41 (1997), 71–86; J. P. Small, *The Parallel Worlds of Classical Art and Text* (Cambridge, 2003), 37–78 (a sceptical approach; abridged in Gregory [note 2 above], 103–18); and now Taplin 1–46. For a survey of the material evidence see J. R. Green, *Theatre in Ancient Greek Society* (London, 1995), 16–88, and for collections of relevant vase-paintings Trendall–Webster (1971, cf. Trendall's survey of South Italian vases in T. Rasmussen and N. Spivey eds., *Looking at Greek Vases* [Cambridge, 1991], 151–82), Todisco (2003), and Taplin 47–267. For earlier systematic uses of vase-paintings for reconstruction of the plays see L. Séchan, *Études sur la tragédie grecque dans ses rapports avec la céramique* (Paris, 1926), and Webster (1967).

Our impressions of the lost plays are of course deter-
mined and potentially distorted by the selection of frag-
ments and testimonies that we happen to have for each of
them. Only the papyri (and the parchments mentioned in
note 5 above) provide texts that extend beyond a single
speech. These are highly illuminating for a few plays (*Alex-
ander*, *Antiope*, *Erechtheus*, *Hypsipyle*, *Phaethon*) and
offer flashes of illumination for others (*Cresphontes*,
Cretans, *Telephus*), but even in the best of these cases
large segments of the play's action remain obscure. Where
extensive papyri and narrative summaries are both lacking,
our sense of the enacted plays and their dramatic charac-
ter is usually still more limited, but often not entirely
deficient. Aristophanes' parodies offer vivid insights into
the opening of *Andromeda* with its captive heroine and her
heroic rescuer's arrival, Bellerophon's flight on the winged
horse Pegasus in *Bellerophon*, and the debate and hostage
scenes in *Telephus*. The special interest of Euripides to
orators, teachers of rhetoric and anthologists has pre-
served extensive speeches from *Autolycus*, *Erechtheus*
and *Melanippe Captive* (F 494 is from a papyrus anthol-
ogy) along with the openings of *Bellerophon*, *Melanippe
Wise*, *Stheneboea* and (in paraphrase) *Philoctetes*. The
comments of a reader such as Plutarch can restore the im-
pact of a particular dramatic moment such as Merope's at-
tack on her own son in *Cresphontes* (F 456).

Even the many fragments transmitted without explana-
tory comment may be more informative than they seem at
first sight. Some groups of anthologized excerpts seem to
have originated in particular scenes of argument and de-
bate which no doubt helped to make their plays notable (or
notorious), especially *Aeolus* F 19–24 on the merits of in-

cestuous marriage, *Alexander* F 48–60 on the status of
slaves, *Antiope* F 183–202 on the choice between lives of
action and contemplation (here the anthologies comple-
ment the accounts of Plato and others), *Archelaus* F 231–
244 on the prerequisites for noble achievement, *Dictys* F
333–7 on nobility and political power, *Meleager* F 520–8
on women's roles and behaviour, *Oedipus* F 542–8 on mar-
riage, and *Palamedes* F 578–85 (the arraignment and trial
of Palamedes). Twenty of the thirty fragments of *Bellero-
phon* (F 285–304) are transmitted through anthologies
(chiefly Stobaeus) and reflect a debate on human worth,
fortune and divine dispensation that must have extended
thematically through the play. Similarly the almost wholly
sententious fragments of *Ino* suggest a play comparable
with *Medea* in its contemplation of female misfortune, ri-
valry and criminality. Sometimes a chance assemblage of a
few brief testimonia and fragments from anthologies and
other sources can provide vivid insights into a play's char-
acteristic scenes, as for example Auge's predicament and
peril and Heracles' saving return in the late and melodra-
matic *Auge*.

In sum, the fragments are an invaluable complement to
the understanding of Euripides and his immense contri-
bution to the development of Athenian drama that we have
from the extant plays. The subjects of the latter are, as it
happens, heavily biased towards the Trojan War and its
aftermath (ten of nineteen, including *Cyclops* and the
inauthentic *Rhesus*) and stories linked with Athens
(*Children of Heracles, Hippolytus, Suppliant Women,
Heracles, Ion*); only *Alcestis, Medea, Phoenician Women*
and *Bacchae* fall outside this range. The fragmentary plays

supplement the first two groups to some extent[13] but greatly enlarge the overall scope, embracing in particular the mythical histories of the Cretan royal family, Thessaly, Aetolia, Thebes and the legend of the Seven, Perseus, Bellerophon, Heracles and his descendants, and the Pelopid dynasty before the Trojan War.[14] At the same time the repertoire of Euripides' tragic subjects is enlarged and diversified. Some of these are well represented in the extant plays: heroes succumbing to divine retaliation, heroines rescued from perils, tragedies of revenge and self-sacrifice.[15] Others are much less so, although no less important: youthful heroes proving themselves against opposition, older heroes isolated amongst their peers, divine rape and its consequences, and other sexually charged

[13] Trojan subjects: *Alexander, Palamedes, Scyrians, Telephus, Philoctetes*. Athenian subjects: *Alope, Erechtheus, Theseus, Hippolytus Veiled*.

[14] Crete: *Cretan Women, Cretans, Polyidus*. Thessaly: *Ino, Melanippe Wise, Peliades, Peleus, Protesilaus, Phrixus A* and *B*. Aetolia: *Meleager, Oeneus*. Thebes etc.: the two *Alcmeons, Antigone, Antiope, Oedipus*. Perseus: *Andromeda, Danae, Dictys*. Bellerophon: *Bellerophon, Stheneboea*. Heracles and Heraclids: *Alcmene, Archelaus, Cresphontes, Licymnius, Temenidae, Temenus*. Pelopid dynasty: *Thyestes, Oenomaus, Pleisthenes, Chrysippus*.

[15] Heroes cast down: *Alcmeon in Psophis, Bellerophon, Ixion* (compare the extant *Andromache, Bacchae, Heracles, Hippolytus*). Heroines rescued: *Andromeda, Antiope, Dictys, Melanippe Captive, Hypsipyle* (cf. *Helen, Iphigenia in Tauris*). Revenge: *Ino, Cresphontes, Oeneus, Stheneboea* (cf. *Hecuba, Electra, Medea*). Self-sacrifice: *Erechtheus, Phrixus A* or *B*(?) (cf. *Heraclidae, Iphigenia at Aulis*).

conflicts;[16] the last two of these in particular are notable for
having inspired many of the plots of New Comedy a cen-
tury later. There is also enrichment in matters of dra-
matic design and structure such as debates and trials,
dramatic reversals, 'messenger' scenes, recognitions and
divine interventions,[17] and in other less neatly classifiable
features—for example, the bizarre scenes of Pasiphae de-
fending her mating with the bull (*Cretans*), Clymene con-
cealing the smouldering remains of her son (*Phaethon*), or
Andromeda exposed as 'fodder for the sea-monster'.

These categories and catalogues could be multiplied,
but they can hardly do justice to Euripides' infinite creativ-
ity in varying and combining the elements of his drama. To

[16] Heroes proving themselves: *Aegeus, Alexander, Archelaus,
Theseus, Oenomaus, Stheneboea*. Isolated heroes: *Palamedes,
Telephus, Philoctetes*. Divine rape: *Alcmene, Alope, Auge, Danae,
Melanippe Wise* (cf. *Ion*). Sexual conflicts: *Aeolus, Antigone,
Hippolytus Veiled, Cretan Women, Cretans, Meleager, Oedipus,
Peleus, Stheneboea, Scyrians, Phoenix, Chrysippus* (elements of
this, of course, in the extant *Hippolytus, Medea* and *Andromache*).

[17] Debates and trials: *Aeolus, Alexander, Alcmene, Antiope,
Cretans, Erechtheus, Melanippe Wise, Melanippe Captive,
Meleager, Oedipus, Palamedes, Protesilaus, Scyrians, Telephus,
Hypsipyle, Philoctetes, Chrysippus*. Reversals: *Antiope, Arche-
laus, Ino, Cresphontes* (twice), *Melanippe Captive, Phrixus A* or
B. 'Messenger' scenes: *Alexander, Andromeda, Antiope, Bellero-
phon, Erechtheus, Melanippe Captive, Meleager, Stheneboea,
Phaethon*. Recognitions: *Aegeus, Alexander, Alcmeon in Corinth,
Antiope, Auge, Cresphontes, Melanippe Captive, Hypsipyle*. Di-
vine interventions: *Alcmene, Antiope, Erechtheus, Phrixus A* and
B (divine 'wrap-ups' in many others).

appreciate this fully, readers must immerse themselves in what we have of the plays themselves.[18]

Collection and Study of the Fragments

The process of collecting the book fragments which culminated in Nauck's editions of 1856 and 1889 was begun in the 1570s by Dirk Canter (Theodorus Canterus), younger brother of Willem Canter whose 1571 edition of the extant plays had included a selection of Euripidean *sententiae* gathered from both extant and lost plays.[19] D. Canter col-

---

[18] For surveys complementing this brief sketch of dramatic content in the lost plays see *SFP* I.5–10, ed. Budé VIII.1.xxv–xxxi, M. Cropp in Gregory (note 2 above), 280–6, and (for Trojan subjects) R. Kannicht in A. Bierl and others, *Antike Literatur in neuer Deutung* (Munich, 2004), 185–201. Huys, *The Tale* analyses exhaustively the plays about heroes exposed at birth (*Alope, Auge, Danae, Melanippe Wise*) and later reunited with their mothers (*Alexander, Antiope, Melanippe Captive, Oedipus*, and the extant *Ion*; Huys excludes *Hypsipyle* where the heroes have been separated from their mother in infancy but not exposed to die).

[19] On the collecting and editing of tragic fragments from the 16th to the mid-19th c. see R. Kassel in H. Hofmann and A. Harder (eds.), *Fragmenta Dramatica* (Göttingen, 1991), 243–53 (translated and supplemented by H. and D. Harvey in McHardy, *Lost Dramas* 7–20) and D. Harvey in McHardy, *Lost Dramas* 21–6; for Euripides in particular, R. Kannicht in G. W. Most (ed.), *Collecting Fragments: Fragmente Sammeln* (Göttingen, 1997), 67–77, and H. Van Looy in ed. Budé lviii–lxxii (previously in *AC* 32 [1963], 170–84). On D. Canter's collection and its subsequent history: J. A. Gruys, *The Early Printed Editions of Aeschylus, 1518–1664* (The Hague, 1981), 277–309, 342–6; C. Collard, *AC* 64 (1995), 243–50; Kannicht (above) 72–5.

lected and documented 837 fragments, three-quarters of
the 1132 that Nauck included in his second edition. His
comprehensive approach distinguished him from other
early collectors who were interested primarily in present-
ing excerpts from classical authors for their moral and
educational value.[20] Canter's collection was unfortunately
never published, although a few scholars used it in the
17th century, and so the first published collection aiming
at comprehensiveness was the philologically inferior one
which Joshua Barnes attached to his pretentious edition of
Euripides in 1694. J. C. Valckenaer later treated the frag-
ments at length in a monograph on the lost dramas of
Euripides (*Diatribe in Euripidis perditorum dramatum
reliquias*, 1767), and increasingly large collections were
included in the complete Euripidean editions of S.
Musgrave (1779), A. Matthiae (1829) and F. Wagner
(1844). Valckenaer also discussed the reconstruction of
some of the lost plays, but the first comprehensive (if over-
imaginative) attempts at reconstruction came more than
seventy years later from F. G. Welcker and J. A. Hartung.[21]

   Much nineteenth-century scholarship remained pre-
occupied with the textual problems of the book fragments,

---

   [20] For example, H. Grotius' collection of poetic excerpts from
Stobaeus (1623, supplemented from other sources in 1626) which
was organized like its model by topics. These contrasting ap-
proaches to the study of the fragments are discussed by Kassel and
Kannicht (see previous note). A collection of *testimonia* for Aes-
chylus, Sophocles and Euripides was published by J. Meursius in
1619 (Kassel 243 [Eng. tr. 7], Kannicht 72).

   [21] F. G. Welcker, *Die griechischen Tragödien mit Rücksicht
auf den epischen Cyclus geordnet* (3 vols., Bonn, 1839–41); J. A.
Hartung, *Euripides Restitutus* (2 vols., Hamburg, 1843–4).

and Nauck's second edition (1889) still relied almost entirely on them while presenting *testimonia* only summarily and generally without comment.[22] Textual work remains of course an essential (especially in the editing of the papyri), but since the time of Welcker and Hartung scholarly interest has increasingly turned to the reconstruction of the lost plays, their place in Euripides' work and in the development of Athenian drama, and (more recently) their continuing role in the culture of the Greek and Roman worlds. This broadening of interest has been motivated by general trends in the historical study of the ancient world, and propelled by archaeological discoveries of both papyri and visual evidence. The resulting proliferation of work in the 20th century need only be briefly noted here; much of it, especially from the 1960s onwards, will be cited in our introductions to the individual plays.[23] By now we have one or more editions with commentary for twenty-four of the known tragedies and all of the satyr plays,[24] and compre-

---

[22] For a brief account of Nauck's work see D. Harvey in McHardy, *Lost Dramas* 26–31.

[23] For surveys see Van Looy in ed. Budé VIII.1.lv–lviii (papyri) and lxxii–lxxx; Harvey in McHardy, *Lost Dramas* 31–46 (papyri, 31–7). Van Looy published detailed bibliographical surveys in *AC* 32 (1963), 162–99, 60 (1991), 295–311, 61 (1992), 280–95, and H. J. Mette a series of surveys and collected *testimonia* in *Lustrum*, especially vols. 13 and 14 (1967–8) and 23–24 (1981–2).

[24] See our bibliographies for *Alexander, Alcmeon in Psophis, Alcmeon in Corinth, Andromeda, Antiope, Archelaus, Autolycus, Bellerophon, Danae, Dictys, Erechtheus, Cresphontes, Cretans, Melanippe Wise, Melanippe Captive, Oedipus, Palamedes, Stheneboea, Telephus, Hypsipyle, Phaethon, Philoctetes, Phrixus A and B*. Satyr plays: Pechstein (1998), Krumeich (1999).

hensive editions of all the fragmentary plays both in the Budé edition of F. Jouan and H. Van Looy (1998–2003) and in R. Kannicht's *Tragicorum Graecorum Fragmenta, Vol. 5* (2004). The Budé edition is particularly valuable for its extensive general introduction and its introductions to each of the plays; we cite the latter routinely in our own bibliographies. Kannicht's edition definitively replaces Nauck's, and mercifully brings together (and in many cases re-edits) the papyrus fragments, previously scattered in dozens of publications. It is also fuller and more systematic in its presentation of numbered *testimonia* both for Euripides' life, works and art (pp. 39–145) and for each of the plays, where ancient references to the play and its content, and to related mythographic and iconographic material, are followed by brief summary paragraphs on plot reconstruction, dramatic location and characters, special historical information as needed, major editions and discussions, chronology, other ancient plays on the same subject, and other fragments sometimes ascribed to the play. Kannicht's textual apparatus for the individual fragments adds a wealth of concise explanatory and illustrative comment. In preparing our own introductions and notes we have assumed as a matter of course that readers wanting fuller information will consult Kannicht's edition.

This Edition

We reproduce Kannicht's numbering of the testimonia and fragments (itself based on Nauck's) and likewise the established ordering of the plays alphabetically by their Greek rather than Latin/English titles; thus the numerical sequence of the fragments is maintained, but those titles be-

ginning with C, Ch, H, Ph and Th in Latin and English
appear 'out of order' since these letters represent K, X, as-
pirated I, Φ and Θ in Greek (and there are other minor dis-
crepancies). The fragments of *Pirithous, Rhadamanthys,
Tennes* and *Sisyphus* which are assigned to Critias in *TrGF*
1 are here added at the end of the edition. We preface each
play with a select bibliography, usually divided between
editions and other studies and discussions, and a brief in-
troduction surveying so far as possible (and with varying
emphases according to the nature of the evidence) the
play's mythical background, its plot and reconstruction,
and its general character, chronology, and impact on sub-
sequent literary and artistic traditions. These introduc-
tions also list 'Brief fragments' (single contextless words or
phrases, or incomprehensible papyri, which we have omit-
ted from the main series) and 'Other ascriptions' (i.e. other
fragments which scholars have assigned inconclusively to
the play). The introductions are followed by a selection of
Kannicht's testimonia (including only those which contrib-
ute substantially to our knowledge of the play's content)
and all of the play's fragments other than the 'Brief frag-
ments' just mentioned. The apparatus accompanying the
Greek texts lists the principal sources (excluding those
which are derivative or otherwise of little importance) and
notes only those textual uncertainties, with a very limited
number of conjectural suggestions, which have a substan-
tial bearing on the sense; most such points are explained
briefly in the notes to the translations. For complete infor-
mation on the sources, history and constitution of the texts
the reader should in all cases consult Kannicht's edition
and those specialized editions of individual plays which
are mentioned in our introductions to the plays.

INTRODUCTION

The following markers are used in Greek texts:

[ ]	gaps in papyri due to physical damage (text within square brackets, if any, is editorial reconstruction)
... ...	dots beneath spaces represent letters missing or illegible in papyri (incomplete letters printed with reasonable confidence are not so marked in this edition)
⟨ ⟩	text or speaker identifications omitted in the source(s) and supplied or left incomplete by editors
{ }	text judged inauthentic
† †	text judged incurably corrupt
—	unidentified speaker
*	fragment (F) or testimony (test.) identified as Euripidean but attributed conjecturally to this play
**	fragment (F) or testimony (test.) attributed conjecturally to Euripides

The English translation uses the last five markers similarly, but parenthesis marks enclose all editorial supplements and completions of sense as well as actual parentheses, and all gaps and omissions are represented by three dots on the line. Translations of papyrus texts occasionally reflect supplements not included in the facing Greek text but recorded in the apparatus below it.

CHRONOLOGY

Exact or near-exact dates of production derived from Athenian public records are available for the nine extant and fourteen fragmentary plays listed in section (*a*) below. Those listed in section (*b*) can be dated more or less closely from several kinds of evidence, of which two are of special importance. First, quotation or parody by Aristophanes and other contemporary comic playwrights provides latest dates for a dozen tragedies in this group, although these are not necessarily close approximations—there are for example parodies of *Telephus* (438) in Aristophanes' *Acharnians* (425) and again in his *Women at the Thesmophoria* (411). Secondly, close or distant approximations for the dates of nearly twenty more tragedies can be estimated from metrical features of the fragments, especially the increasing frequency over time of 'resolutions' (substitutions of two short for one long or *anceps* syllable) in Euripides' iambic trimeters, the increasing variety of word-shapes accommodated by these resolutions, and his use of trochaic tetrameters in dialogue scenes, of which the earliest dated instance is in *Trojan Women* (415).[1]

---

[1] Further chronological details are given in the introductions to the plays. For general guidance on the estimates from metrical data see Cropp–Fick 1–30, 60–1, 66, 69. Several factors make the

»   preceding a date = 'before', following = 'or later'

m   dates inferred mainly or wholly from metrical evidence

q   dates inferred mainly or wholly from quotations or parodies in Comedy (usually Aristophanes)

Capital letters (*ALCESTIS* etc.) denote extant plays.

(a) Dates Derived from Athenian Public Records

455	*Peliades*
438	*Cretan Women, Alcmeon in Psophis, Telephus, ALCESTIS*
431	*MEDEA, Dictys, Philoctetes, Theristae*
428	*HIPPOLYTUS*
415	*Alexander, Palamedes, TROJAN WOMEN, Sisyphus*
412	*Andromeda, HELEN*
411–407	*Hypsipyle, PHOENICIAN WOMEN, Antiope* (?)[2]
408	*ORESTES*
posthumous	*Alcmeon in Corinth, BACCHAE, IPHIGENIA AT AULIS*

statistical estimates necessarily tentative and inexact (see especially Cropp–Fick 2, 23); they are however accurate for most of those plays whose dates can be confirmed from other evidence (*ibid.* 18–19, 23).

[2] Metrical evidence suggests an earlier date for *Antiope* (427–419).

CHRONOLOGY

(b) Approximate Dates

c. 450?	*Rhesus* (lost)
» 431	*Aegeus, Cretans* (m), *Hippolytus Veiled*
c. 430	*CHILDREN OF HERACLES*
» 425	*Bellerophon* (q), *Danae* (m), *Thyestes* (q), *Ino* (q), *Oeneus* (q), *Phoenix* (q), *Protesilaus* (m)
426–412	*Melanippe Captive* (m, q)
c. 425	*Cresphontes, ANDROMACHE*
» 423	*Aeolus* (q), *HECUBA* (q)[3]
c. 423	*SUPPLIANT WOMEN*
423 »	*Temenidae* (m)[4]
» 422	*Stheneboea* (q), *Theseus* (q)
422?	*Erechtheus*[5]
c. 420	*Phaethon* (m), *ELECTRA* (m)
420 »	*Antigone* (m), *Ixion* (?)
419 »	*Meleager* (m), *Oedipus* (m)
c. 417	*HERACLES* (m)
» 414	*Pleisthenes* (q)

[3] *Aeolus* and *Hecuba* are quoted in Aristophanes' *Clouds* which was produced in 423, but the extant text of *Clouds* shows signs of revision. *Aeolus* might therefore be as late as 421 (the date of *Peace* which also quotes it), and *Hecuba* as late as 417 (the latest possible date for the revision of *Clouds*).

[4] If *Temenus, Temenidae* and *Archelaus* formed a trilogy, all should be dated after the accession of Archelaus in 413. See Introduction to *Archelaus*.

[5] The date 422 for *Erechtheus* is inferred uncertainly from Plutarch. Metrical evidence suggests 421–410.

414 »	*Auge* (m), *Polyidus* (m)
c. 413	*IPHIGENIA IN TAURIS* (m), *ION* (m)
412 »	*Archelaus* (and *Temenus, Temenidae*?)[4]
» 411 (421–411?)	*Melanippe Wise* (q)
» 410 (421–410?)	*Alcmene* (m)

(c) Unknown Dates

TRAGEDIES. *Alope, Licymnius* (» 448?), *Oenomaus, Peleus, Scyrians* (» 431?), *Temenus,*[4] *Phrixus A* and *B, Chrysippus,* and the doubtfully ascribed *Pirithous, Rhadamanthys, Tennes.*

SATYR PLAYS. *Autolycus A* and *B, Busiris, Epeus, Eurystheus, CYCLOPS* (c. 408?), *Lamia, Sciron, Syleus* (437–424?)

ABBREVIATIONS

AC	*L'Antiquité Classique*
Aélion (1983)	R. Aélion, *Euripide héritier d'Eschyle*, 2 vols. (Paris, 1983)
Aélion (1986)	R. Aélion, *Quelques grands mythes héroiques dans l'oeuvre d'Euripide* (Paris, 1986)
AJA	*American Journal of Archaeology*
AJP	*American Journal of Philology*
APF	*Archiv für Papyrusforschung*
Austin, *NFE*	C. Austin, *Nova Fragmenta Euripidea in Papyris Reperta* (Berlin, 1968)
Bastianini–Casanova, *Euripide e i papiri*	G. Bastianini, A. Casanova (eds.), *Euripide e i papiri: atti del Convegno Internazionale di Studi, Firenze, 10–11 giugno 2004* (Florence, 2005)
BICS	*Bulletin of the Institute of Classical Studies* (London)
CAG	*Commentaria in Aristotelem Graeca*, 23 vols. (Berlin, 1882–1909)
CCC	*Civiltà Classica e Cristiana*

CPG — *Corpus Pareomiographorum Grae-corum*, ed. E. von Leutsch, F. Schneidewin, 2 vols. (Göttingen, 1839, 1851)

CQ — *Classical Quarterly*

CRAI — *Comptes rendus de l'Académie des Inscriptions et Belles-Lettres* (Paris)

Cropp–Fick — M. Cropp, G. Fick. *Resolutions and Chronology in Euripides: The Fragmentary Tragedies* (London, 1985: BICS Suppl. 43)

Diggle, *TrGFS* — J. Diggle, *Tragicorum Graecorum Fragmenta Selecta* (Oxford, 1998)

DK — H. Diels, W. Kranz, *Die Fragmente der Vorsokratiker* (Berlin, 1951–2⁶)

ed. Budé — F. Jouan, H. Van Looy, *Euripide, Tome VIII: Fragments*, 4 vols. (Paris, 1998–2003)

FGrH — *Die Fragmente der griechischen Historiker*, ed. F. Jacoby, 3 vols. in 15 (Berlin, 1923–58)

Gantz — T. Gantz, *Early Greek Myth: a Guide to Literary and Artistic Sources* (Baltimore, 1993)

Gramm. Gr. — *Grammatici Graeci*, ed. G. Uhlig and others, 4 vols. in 6 (Leipzig, 1867–1910)

GRBS — *Greek, Roman and Byzantine Studies*

ABBREVIATIONS

HSCP	*Harvard Studies in Classical Philology*
Huys, *The Tale*	M. Huys, *The Tale of the Hero Who Was Exposed at Birth in Euripidean Tragedy: A Study of Motifs* (Leuven, 1995)
ICS	*Illinois Classical Studies*
IEG	*Iambi et Elegi Graeci*, ed. M. L. West (Oxford, 1989–91²)
IG	*Inscriptiones Graecae*
JHS	*Journal of Hellenic Studies*
Jouan (1966)	F. Jouan, *Euripide et les légendes des chants cypriens* (Paris, 1966)
Krumeich	R. Krumeich, N. Pechstein, B. Seidensticker (eds.), *Das griechische Satyrspiel* (Darmstadt, 1999)
LIMC	*Lexicon Iconographicum Mythologiae Classicae*, 8 vols., each in two parts (Zürich, 1981–98)
LSJ	H. G. Liddell, R. Scott, *A Greek-English Lexicon,* revised by H. Stuart-Jones, with Supplement (Oxford, 1968⁹)
Matthiessen	K. Matthiessen, *Die Tragödien des Euripides* (Munich, 2002)
McHardy, *Lost Dramas*	F. McHardy, J. Robson, D. Harvey (eds.), *Lost Dramas of Classical Athens: Greek Tragic Fragments* (Exeter, 2005)
MDAI(A)	*Mitteilungen des Deutschen Archäologischen Instituts, Athenische Abteilung*

Nauck *or* N   A. Nauck, *Tragicorum Graecorum Fragmenta* (Leipzig, 1889²: reprinted with *Supplementum continens nova fragmenta Euripidea etc.*, ed. B. Snell, Hildesheim, 1964)

Nauck–Snell   Supplement to Nauck (see above)
or N–Sn

OGCMA   *The Oxford Guide to Classical Mythology in the Arts, 1300–1990s*, ed. J. D. Reid, 2 vols. (Oxford, 1993)

Page, *GLP*   D. L. Page, *Select Papyri, III: Literary Papyri, Poetry* (London and Cambridge, MA, 1941: Loeb Classical Library no. 360)

PCG   *Poetae Comici Graeci*, ed. R. Kassel, C. Austin, 8 vols. in 10 (Berlin, 1983–)

Pechstein   N. Pechstein, *Euripides Satyrographos: Ein Kommentar zu den Euripideischen Satyrspielfragmenten* (Stuttgart–Leipzig, 1998)

P.   Papyrus (followed usually by the name of the place or the collection with which the papyrus is associated, and by the number assigned to the papyrus)

P. Oxy.   Oxyrhynchus Papyrus

PG   *Patrologiae cursus completus . . . series Graeca*, ed. J.-P. Migne, 161 vols. (Paris, 1857–66)

PMG	*Poetae Melici Graeci*, ed. D. L. Page (Oxford, 1962)
PMGF	*Poetarum Melicorum Graecorum Fragmenta*, ed. M. Davies (Oxford, 1991–)
PSI	Pubblicazioni della Società italiana per la ricerca dei papiri greci e latini in Egitto
RAAN	*Rendiconti dell'Accademia di Archeologia, Lettere e Belle Arti di Napoli*
Rau, Paratragodia	P. Rau, *Paratragodia: Untersuchung einer komischen Form des Aristophanes* (Munich, 1967: Zetemata 45)
RFIC	*Rivista di Filologia e di Istruzione Classica*
Rhet. Gr.	*Rhetores Graeci* ed. C. Walz, 9 vols. (Stuttgart, 1832–6); ed. L. Spengel, 3 vols. (Leipzig, 1853–6)
RhM	*Rheinisches Museum*
SFP	*Euripides: Selected Fragmentary Plays*, Vol. 1 ed. C. Collard, M. J. Cropp, K. H. Lee (Warminster, 1995: corrected reprint with Addenda, Oxford, 2008); Vol. 2 ed. C. Collard, M. J. Cropp, J. Gibert (Oxford, 2004)
SIFC	*Studi Italiani di Filologia Classica*
Sourvinou-Inwood	C. Sourvinou-Inwood, *Tragedy and Athenian Religion* (Lanham, 2003)

TAPA	*Transactions of the American Philological Association*
Taplin	Oliver Taplin, *Pots and Plays: Interactions between Tragedy and Greek Vase-painting of the Fourth Century B.C.* (Los Angeles, 2007)
Todisco	L. Todisco and others, *La Ceramica figurata a soggetto tragico in Magna Grecia e in Sicilia* (Rome, 2003)
Trendall–Webster	A. D. Trendall, T. B. L. Webster, *Illustrations of Greek Drama* (London, 1971)
TrGF	*Tragicorum Graecorum Fragmenta*, ed. B. Snell, R. Kannicht, S. Radt, 5 vols. in 6 (Göttingen, 1971–2004)
Van Looy (1964)	H. Van Looy, *Zes verloren Tragedies van Euripides* (Brussels, 1964)
Van Rossum-Steenbeek	M. van Rossum-Steenbeek, *Greek Readers' Digests: Studies on a Selection of Subliterary Papyri* (Leiden, 1998: *Mnemosyne* Suppl. 175)
Voelke	P. Voelke, *Un théâtre en marge: aspects figuratifs et configurationels de drame satyrique dans l'Athènes classique* (Bari, 2001)
Webster	T. B. L. Webster, *The Tragedies of Euripides* (London, 1967)

ABBREVIATIONS

Wilamowitz, *Analecta*	U. von Wilamowitz-Moellendorff, *Analecta Euripidea* (Berlin, 1875)
Wilamowitz, *Kleine Schriften*	U. von Wilamowitz-Moellendorff, *Kleine Schriften*, 6 vols. in 7 (Berlin, 1935–72)
ZPE	*Zeitschrift für Papyrologie und Epigraphik*

EURIPIDES

AEGEUS

H. Van Looy in ed. Budé VIII.1.1–13.

B. B. Shefton, *AJA* 60 (1956), 159–63; Webster 77–80, 297–8; Trendall–Webster III.3.1–3 (cf. Taplin no. 55); *LIMC* I.i.359–67 'Aigeus'; Aélion (1986), 220–2; S. Mills, *Theseus, Tragedy and the Athenian Empire* (Oxford, 1997), 234–45 and in A. Sommerstein (ed.), *Shards from Kolonos* (Bari, 2003), 219–32; C. Hahnemann, *Hermes* 127 (1999), 385–96 and in *Shards from Kolonos* 203–18.

According to the legend elaborated at Athens, Theseus was born and raised in Troezen by his mother Aethra without the knowledge of his father, Aegeus of Athens. On reaching maturity he obtained the tokens of his paternity—a sword and a pair of sandals—by lifting the rock under which Aegeus had concealed them. He then journeyed to Athens, slaying monsters and brigands as he went, in order to claim his heritage. Before he could do this he was recognized by the Colchian sorceress Medea, now living with Aegeus after fleeing from Corinth (cf. Medea 663–758). In what became the standard version of the story (see for example Plutarch, Theseus 12) Medea warned Aegeus that the heroic stranger was a dangerous rival and persuaded him to offer Theseus a poisoned cup, but at the last moment the king recognized the sword his son was carrying and dashed

*the cup from his lips; after their reunion Medea fled from
Athens, and Theseus later undertook to subdue the sav-
age Bull of Marathon. In a variant version found only in
Apollodorus (Epit. 1.5–6 = test. *ii (a)) and the Vatican
Mythographer (1.48 = test. *ii (b)), Medea first persuaded
Aegeus to send Theseus against the Bull in the hope that it
would kill him, and only attempted the poisoning after he
had subdued it.*

*The sparse fragments of Sophocles' and Euripides'
Aegeus show that both plays told the story of Theseus' re-
turn in some form, but it is not clear how the 'standard' and
'variant' versions mentioned above relate to their plots.
Sophocles' plot, which included the capture of the Bull
(Soph. F 25), will have been close to the 'variant' version
unless (as Mills suggests) it did not involve Medea at all.
Euripides' plot is often reconstructed along the lines of the
'variant' version, F 1–2 coming from an early scene in
which the arriving Theseus is questioned about his iden-
tity, F 3–4 referring to Medea, F 7a representing her warn-
ing to Aegeus about Theseus, and F 10–11 referring to
Theseus' campaign against the Bull; but this last group
could refer to other exploits, and Euripides' plot could
in that case have approximated to the 'standard' version
(as Hahnemann argues, attributing the 'variant' version
to Sophocles). Inferences from the iconographic tradition
are also difficult. Between 460 and 430 a series of vase
paintings of Theseus with the captured Bull includes both
Aegeus and a discomfited woman equipped with a jug and
libation dish. After 430 the woman is usually marked by
her oriental clothing as Medea, and in the earlier vases
too she is more likely to be Medea than some other charac-
ter. The change of style might be due to the production*

of Euripides' Aegeus *with an orientalized Medea in the late 430s, or to the orientalizing presentation of Medea in* Medea *(of 431). Euripides'* Aegeus *probably preceded his* Medea, *but neither it nor Sophocles' play can be closely dated.*

Brief fragments: F 11b 'man-killing', F 11c 'having endured the contest', F 12 'Panactus' (a border fortress on the road from Eleusis to Thebes), F 12a (a reference to Medea killing her brother), F 13 'cave-dwelling'. Other ascriptions: Auge *F 271,* Theseus *F **386b; F 858, F 905.*

Theseus' journey to Athens had been popular in Athenian art from about 520 B.C. *onwards. His arrival and Aegeus' anxious reaction are the subject of a dithyramb of Bacchylides (Bacchyl. 18, probably earlier than Euripides' first production in 455). No other Greek tragedies on the subject are known. Ennius appears to have produced both a version of Euripides'* Medea *(distinguished by some sources as* Medea in Exile*) and a* Medea *set at Athens (see fr. 112 Jocelyn) which could have been a version of Euripides'* Aegeus.

ΑΙΓΕΥΣ

1

ποίαν σε φῶμεν γαῖαν ἐκλελοιπότα
πόλει ξενοῦσθαι τῇδε; τίς πάτρας ὅρος;
τίς ἐσθ᾽ ὁ φύσας; τοῦ κεκήρυξαι πατρός;

Clement of Alexandria, *Miscellanies* 6.2.11.3

2

<ΧΟΡΟΣ?>

τί σε μάτηρ ἐν δεκάτᾳ τόκου ὠνόμαζεν;

Schol. on Aristophanes, *Birds* 494 (similarly Suda δ 181)

3

δειλῶν γυναῖκες δεσποτῶν θρασύστομοι.

Stobaeus 4.22.161

4

πέφυκε γάρ πως παισὶ πολέμιον γυνὴ
τοῖς πρόσθεν ἡ ζυγεῖσα δευτέρα πατρί.

Stobaeus 4.22.157

2 δευτέρα πατρί Dindorf (δευτέρα Elmsley): δευτέρῳ πατρί
Stob. ms. M and probably others (δευτε.. πατρί ms. A, δευτέρῳ
πόσει ms. S after alteration)

6

AEGEUS

1

What land shall we say you have left to visit this city? What
is your homeland's border? Who begot you, as whose son
are you proclaimed?

2
<CHORUS?>

What did your mother name you on the tenth day after
your birth?[1]

[1] The sources cite this verse to illustrate the custom of naming
children at a Tenth Day Feast.

3

Weak masters have outspoken wives.

4

A woman is naturally somewhat hostile towards the chil-
dren of a previous marriage when she is their father's sec-
ond wife.

5

εἰ μὴ καθέξεις γλῶσσαν, ἔσται σοι κακά.

Stobaeus 3.34.3

6

τί γὰρ πατρῴας ἀνδρὶ φίλτερον χθονός;

Stobaeus 3.39.6

7

κρεῖσσον δὲ πλούτου καὶ βαθυσπόρου χθονὸς
ἀνδρῶν δικαίων κἀγαθῶν ὁμιλίαι.

Orion 6.1 Haffner; Stobaeus 3.9.5 attributes a largely similar
excerpt to Euripides' *Theseus*.

1 βαθυσπόρου χθονὸς Orion: πολυχρύσου χλιδῆς Stob.
2 ὁμιλίαι Orion: παρουσίαι Stob.

7a (= *Theseus* F 389 N)

ἀνὴρ γὰρ ὅστις χρημάτων μὲν ἐνδεής,
δρᾶσαι δὲ χειρὶ δυνατός, οὐκ ἀνέξεται·
τὰ τῶν ἐχόντων χρήμαθ᾽ ἁρπάζειν φιλεῖ.

Stobaeus 4.4.1, with attribution to Euripides' *Theseus* (cod. S)
or "Euripides' *Theseus Aegeus*" (mss. MA)

2–3 οὐκ ἀνέξεται . . . ἁρπάζειν φιλεῖ: οὐκ ἀφέξεται . . .
ἁρπάζειν βίᾳ Nauck   3 τῶν Valckenaer: τῶν δ᾽ codd.

8

ἀνδρὸς ⟨δ᾽⟩ ὑπ᾽ ἐσθλοῦ καὶ τυραννεῖσθαι καλόν.

Stobaeus 4.6.6

5

If you don't restrain your tongue, it will be the worse for you.

6

What is dearer to a man than his ancestral land?

7

The company of just and virtuous men is worth more than wealth and fertile land.[1]

[1] Cf. *Erechtheus* F 362.21 with note.

7a (= *Theseus* F 389 N)

A man who lacks possessions but has the ability to act forcefully will not hold back; he likes to seize[1] the possessions of those who are well off.

[1] Nauck smoothed the slightly abrupt sequence from v. 1 to v. 2 with 'will not refrain from seizing by force . . .'.

8

It is a fine thing even to be ruled by a noble man.

9
⟨ΧΟΡΟΣ⟩
ἦ που κρεῖσσον τῆς εὐγενίας
τὸ καλῶς πράσσειν.

Stobaeus 4.29.9

10
⟨ΘΗΣΕΤΣ?⟩
κατθανεῖν δ᾽ ὀφείλεται
καὶ τῷ κατ᾽ οἴκους ἐκτὸς ἡμένῳ πόνων.

Stobaeus 4.51.6

11
⟨ΧΟΡΟΣ⟩
ἔστι καὶ πταίσαντ᾽ ἀρετὰν ἀποδείξασθαι θανάτῳ.

Stobaeus 3.1.61; P. Berlin 12311 (ostracon, ed. P. Viereck in
Raccolta . . . G. Lumbroso, 1925)

11a
κρήνης πάροιθεν ἀνθεμόστρωτον λέχος

Photius, *Lexicon* α 1949 Theodoridis

9
⟨CHORUS⟩

Assuredly fine conduct is worth more than noble birth.

10
⟨THESEUS?⟩

Death is due even to a man who sits at home avoiding adversity.

11
⟨CHORUS⟩

Even if one falls, one can exhibit virtue in death.

11a

. . . in front of the spring, a flower-strewn bed . . . [1]

[1] Possibly from a description of Theseus seducing the daughter of one of his brigand victims, Sinis or Kerkyon (Plutarch, *Theseus* 8.3–5; 29.1).

AEOLUS

H. Van Looy in ed. Budé VIII.1.15–37.

Webster 157–60, 303; M. Labate, *Annali della Scuola Normale Superiore di Pisa* 3.7 (1977), 583–93; S. Jaekel, *Grazer Beiträge* 8 (1979), 101–18; *LIMC* I.i.398–9 'Aiolos'; Gantz 169; C. Mülke, *ZPE* 114 (1996), 37–55, esp. 53–5; S. Casali, *Mnemosyne* 51 (1998), 700–10.

Aeolus (son of Hippotes), master of the winds, lived on remote islands in the western Mediterranean; he had six sons and six daughters: see Homer, Odyssey *10.1–12 with Scholia, where his life's story is idyllic. In Euripides, however, one of his sons, Macareus, fell in love with a sister, Canace, and made her pregnant. With the complicity of her nurse she alone, or Macareus too, concealed the imminent birth; and Macareus further deceived Aeolus by proposing that his children should intermarry. Aeolus agreed, but ruled that their unions should be decided by lot. Macareus did not draw Canace as wife; and she had now given birth to a son. An attempt to hide the child from Aeolus failed; he ordered its death by exposure and sent Canace a sword with which to kill herself. Macareus may have considered, or been offered, exile as punishment, but preferred suicide upon Canace's body. The baby boy seems nevertheless to have survived; named Triopas, he founded a house of the Aeolids (but myth confuses this Aeolus and Macareus with the Thessalian Aeolus son of Hellen and his sons and dynasty, for whom see our Introduction to* Melanippe Wise *with F 481).*

The narrative hypothesis in P. Oxy. 2457 (test. ii below) takes us just beyond Macareus' failure in the lottery; F 13a–25 lie within its span. The play's ominous first line (F 13a) was probably spoken by the nurse, already aware of Canace's pregnancy and probably helping to conceal it (as in Cretans *F 472e.47, cf. 472f.29–30); F 14 may also come from her prologue. Hopes by Aeolus for a brilliant dynasty (F 15, 16) may have followed with ironic effect, perhaps before the parodos of the chorus, who are unidentifiable girls (F 17 + 18). Macareus' proposal to Aeolus and his agreement no doubt made an agôn scene; the issues were wealth, nobility and morality (F 19–22) in marriage, and the power of sex (F 23, 24)—all favourite 'social' topics for Euripides. The Chorus's F 24b hints at danger from man's ingenuity (Macareus' proposal?), and may have contained fear for the lottery's outcome (F 24a). Probably the lots were drawn off-stage (but would have made good theatre, like the voting scene in Aeschylus'* Eumenides). *By F 25 Aeolus is disillusioned, so that he must have discovered the baby (cf. the end of the hypothesis). How, and how quickly, Canace's death followed cannot be known: her long 'monologue' in Ovid before her suicide need not reflect a monologue (or a monody) in Euripides, although such a stage moment would be typical of the poet. F 26 may be a report of her death, perhaps also that of Macareus; F 30 (Macareus rejecting exile?) and F 31 (Aeolus advised against vindictiveness) may both be earlier; F 36 (Aeolus?, Chorus?) appears to condemn the Nurse's complicity.*

Most of F 28–39 are gnomic, expressing the aftermath of disaster (F 32–35) or fate's and the gods' cruel unpredictability (F 37, 38: cf. F 13a). In the theatre a god (Athena?) perhaps vouchsafed the baby's future (cf. Lloyd-Jones [app. to test. ii below], Webster), comforted Aeolus, and warned men to avoid incestuous marriage (Mülke, who documents its proscription in contemporary Athens). F 28 and 29 defy location.

Brief fragments: F 40 'strengthless', F 41 'to be fully grown' (a metaphor from horses' shedding milk-teeth, possibly referring to Aeolus' complete misery?). Other ascriptions: F 989 (= *41a N–Sn) 'lottery (is) the child of chance': cf. F 24a.

Aeolus is parodied in Aristophanes' Clouds of 423 B.C. (vv. 1370–3 with Scholia = test. iva) and Peace of 421 (see F 17–18). The metrical style is characteristic of the first half of Euripides' career (Cropp–Fick 72), and in subject-matter Aeolus resembles several other plays from that period which treated women's delinquent or perverse sexual behaviour (Cretan Women, Cretans, Hippolytus Veiled, Stheneboea).

The shape Euripides gave this story was definitive; almost all other accounts are later and derivative (Gantz 169): artistic (Canace's suicide is identified on a Lucanian hydria of 425–400 B.C. = test. vi, LIMC no. 1, Trendall–Webster III.3.4, Todisco L 4, Taplin no. 56), poetic (Ovid, Heroides 11 = test. viib), or scholarly (Sostratus FGrH 23 F 3 = test. iiia, cf. [Plutarch], Moralia 312c–d). Lycophron (3rd c. B.C.) wrote an Aeolus and an Aeolides; both are mere titles, the second ('Grandson of Aeolus') may refer to Canace's baby; but both may have treated rather the Thessalian Aeolids. Euripides' play provided repeated fun

14

for Aristophanes in Peace *(above)*, Frogs *1475 (= F 19) etc., and around 390* B.C. *in two plays called* Aeolosicon ('Aeolus the Cook'?). *In the 4th century Antiphanes and Eriphus each wrote a comic* Aeolus; *but no Latin derivatives are known. Ovid's* Heroides *11 seems to reflect much of Euripides' incident and perhaps his depiction of Canace (Labate, Casali). Suetonius,* Nero *21 alleges that the emperor performed 'Canace giving birth'.*

ΑΙΟΛΟΣ

test. ii (Hypothesis)
Αἴολος, οὗ [ἀρ]χή·
ἡ δεινὰ καὶ δύσγνωστα βουλεύει θεός·
20   ἡ δὲ ὑπόθεσις·
Αἴολος παρὰ θεῶν ἔχων τὴν τῶν ἀνέμων δ[υνάστει-
αν ᾤκησεν ἐν ταῖς κατὰ Τυρρηνίαν νήσο[ις υἱοὺς ἓξ
καὶ θυγατέρας τὰς ἴσας γεγεννηκώς· τ[ούτων δ᾽ ὁ
νεώτατος Μακαρεὺς μιᾶς τῶν ἀδελ[φῶν   ἐ-
25   ρασθεὶς διέφθειρεν· ἡ δ᾽ ἔγκυος γενη[θεῖσα
τὸν τόκον ἔκρυπτεν τῷ νοσεῖν προ[σποιη-
τῶς· ὁ δὲ νεανίσκος ἔπεισε τὸν πατέρα [τὰς θυ-
γατέρας συνοικίσαι τοῖς υἱοῖς· ὁ δὲ συνκα[λεσά-
μενος κλῆρον τοῦ γάμου πᾶσιν ἐξέθη[κεν
30   πταίσας δὲ περὶ τὸν πάλον ὁ ταῦτα μ[ηχα-
νησάμενος ἠτύχει· τὴν γὰρ ὑπὸ τούτου [διεφθαρ-
μένην κλῆρος πρὸς ἄλλου συμβίωσ[ιν ἐνυμ-
φαγώ[γ]ει· συνδραμόντες δ᾽ εἰς τὸ αὐτ[ὸ
κουτ.[..].ι τὸ μὲν γεννηθὲν ἡ τροφὸς [

P. Oxy. 2457.18–34, ed. E. Turner (1962); cf. H. Lloyd-Jones,
Gnomon 35 (1963), 443–4, Austin, *NFE* 88–9.

21–2 δ[υνάστει]αν Diggle: δ[εσποτεί]αν Kassel: δ[ιοίκησιν ǀ

AEOLUS

test. ii (Hypothesis)

Aeolus, which begins 'The designs of heaven are indeed frightening and inscrutable'. The plot is this: Aeolus, who had   20
the mastery of the winds from the gods and lived on the islands off Etruria, had fathered six sons and as many daughters. The youngest of these,[1] Macareus, fell in love with one of his sisters and violated her; she became pregnant and hid the birth   25
by pretending illness. The young man persuaded his father to marry his daughters to his sons; calling them together, Aeolus made them draw lots for their marriage. But the one who had contrived this was unlucky and so failed, for the lot betrothed   30
the daughter he had violated into living with another son. They[2] ran to the same (place?) to meet each other . . . the nurse . . . the newborn child . . .

[1] Macareus is 'youngest' also in [Plutarch], *Moralia* 312c, 'oldest' in Stobaeus 4.20.72.   [2] Reference not clear, but probably Macareus and Canace.

ἀνῴκησεν Turner   24 ἀδελ[φῶν Κανάκης ἐ- van Rossum
29 ἐξέθη[κεν Snell: ἐξεφα[ίνετο Turner

EURIPIDES

13a (= 947 N)

ἦ δεινὰ καὶ δύσγνωστα βουλεύει θεός.

P. Oxy. 2457.19 (see Hypothesis above); also Orion, Euripidean Appendix 3 Haffner

14

Ἡ δὲ Σαλμώνη πλησίον ἐστὶ τῆς ὁμωνύμου κρήνης, ἐξ ἧς ῥεῖ ὁ Ἐνιπεύς . . . τούτου δ᾽ ἐρασθῆναι τὴν Τυρώ φασιν . . . ἐνταῦθα γὰρ βασιλεῦσαι τὸν πατέρα αὐτῆς τὸν Σαλμωνέα, καθάπερ καὶ Εὐριπίδης ἐν Αἰόλῳ φησί.

Strabo 8.3.32

15

⟨ΑΙΟΛΟΣ⟩

ἴδοιμι δ᾽ αὐτῶν ἔκγον᾽ ἄρσεν᾽ ἀρσένων·
πρῶτον μὲν εἶδος ἄξιον τυραννίδος·
πλείστη γὰρ ἀρετὴ τοῦθ᾽ ὑπάρχον ἐν βίῳ,
τὴν ἀξίωσιν τῶν καλῶν τὸ σῶμ᾽ ἔχειν.

Stobaeus 4.21.1; v. 2: Athenaeus 13.566b and (without attributions) in many later authors

16

⟨ΑΙΟΛΟΣ?⟩

λαμπροὶ δ᾽ ἐν αἰχμαῖς Ἄρεος ἔν τε συλλόγοις,
μή μοι τὰ κομψὰ ποικίλοι γενοίατο,
ἀλλ᾽ ὧν πόλει δεῖ μεγάλα βουλεύοντες εὖ.

Stobaeus 4.4.13; vv. 2–3: Aristotle, *Politics* 1277a19 (μή μοι τὰ κόμψ᾽, ἀλλ᾽ ὧν πόλει δεῖ)

3 μεγάλα suspect: χρηστὰ Kannicht

18

AEOLUS

13a (= 947 N)

The designs of heaven are indeed frightening and inscrutable.

14

Salmone is near the spring of the same name, from which flows the river Enipeus . . . they say Tyro fell in love with the river . . . for the king there was her father Salmoneus, as Euripides too says in *Aeolus*.[1]

[1] Strabo is describing Pisa in the western Peloponnese. For Tyro see especially Homer, *Odyssey* 11.235–59 and the remains of Sophocles' two *Tyro* plays; Gantz 171–3.

15

<AEOLUS>

May I see children from them, sons for my sons! In the first place, (may I see in them) good looks worthy of kingship; for excellence in life is greatest when this underlies it, a body indicative of fine qualities.[1]

[1] Beauty of body, beauty of deeds done (not only athletic): Pindar, *Olympians* 9.94, *Nemeans* 3.19 etc.

16

<AEOLUS?>

May they be brilliant amid the spears of War and in debates, not devious I hope with sophistries but good with counsel needed by the city upon great matters.

17 + 18

⟨ΧΟΡΟΣ⟩

17 ἆρ' ἔτυμον φάτιν ἔγνων ⟨ . . . ⟩
Αἴολος εὐνάζειν τέκνα φίλτατα . . .

⟨—⟩

18 δοξάσαι ἔστι, κόραι· τὸ δ' ἐτήτυμον οὐκ ἔχω
εἰπεῖν.

Aristophanes, *Peace* 114–9 with Schol. on 114 (F 17) and
119 (F 18)

17.1 ⟨ . . . ⟩ Collard   17.2 Αἴολος omitted by ms. R:
Αἴολον Dindorf: Αἴολος with e.g. ὡς μέλλει Kannicht

19

⟨ΜΑΚΑΡΕΥΣ⟩

τί δ' αἰσχρὸν ἦν μὴ τοῖσι χρωμένοις δοκῇ;

Aristophanes, *Frogs* 1475 (parodied with τοῖς θεωμένοις 'to
the spectators') and Schol.; Plutarch, *Moralia* 33c; Machon 410
Gow; anthologists.

20

μὴ πλοῦτον εἴπῃς· οὐχὶ θαυμάζω θεόν,
ὃν χὠ κάκιστος ῥᾳδίως ἐκτήσατο.

Stobaeus 4.31.61, cf. 3.3.1; Athenaeus 4.159c; Plutarch, *Moralia* 34d; and others.

AEOLUS

17 + 18
⟨CHORUS⟩

Is the report that I learned true . . . Aeolus . . . to mate his own dearest children to . . . ?[1]

⟨ — ⟩

It may be conjectured, girls; but I cannot tell what is true.

[1] The text is ungrammatical and probably defective: 'that Aeolus is mating' Dindorf; '(that) Aeolus (intends) to mate' suggested by Kannicht.

19
⟨MACAREUS⟩

What is shameful, if it does not seem so to those practising it?[1]

[1] Aristophanes' parody of this line made it a notorious example of Euripides' moral equivocation. Macareus may be arguing his proposal (so Kannicht) rather than defending his rape after it has been revealed.

20

Don't mention wealth: I do not admire a god of whom even the basest man can easily get possession.[1]

[1] Probably Macareus: cf. F 22.

21

⟨ΑΙΟΛΟΣ⟩

δοκεῖτ᾽ ἂν οἰκεῖν γῆν ἐν ᾗ πένης ἅπας
λαὸς πολιτεύοιτο πλουσίων ἄτερ;
οὐκ ἂν γένοιτο χωρὶς ἐσθλὰ καὶ κακά,
ἀλλ᾽ ἔστι τις σύγκρασις, ὥστ᾽ ἔχειν καλῶς.
5 ἃ μὴ γάρ ἐστι τῷ πένητι, πλούσιος
δίδωσ᾽· ἃ δ᾽ οἱ πλουτοῦντες οὐ κεκτήμεθα,
τοῖσιν πένησι χρώμενοι τιμώμεθα.

Stobaeus 4.1.20; vv. 3–4: Plutarch, *Moralia* 369b and 474a and
(οὐκ ἂν . . . σύγκρασις) 25c; v. 3: Theophrastus, *Metaphysics* 18

1 γῆν ἐν ᾗ Cropp: γᾶν εἰ Stob.   7 τιμώμεθα suspect:
θηρώμεθα Bergler

22

⟨ΜΑΚΑΡΕΥΣ⟩

τὴν δ᾽ εὐγένειαν πρὸς θεῶν μή μοι λέγε,
ἐν χρήμασιν τόδ᾽ ἐστί· μὴ γαυροῦ, πάτερ.
κύκλῳ γὰρ ἕρπει· τῷ μὲν ἔσθ᾽, ὁ δ᾽ οὐκ ἔχει·
κοινοῖσι δ᾽ αὐτοῖς χρώμεθ᾽· ᾧ δ᾽ ἂν ἐν δόμοις
5 χρόνον συνοικῇ πλεῖστον, οὗτος εὐγενής.

Stobaeus 4.31.24

5 εὐγενής Grotius: εὐτυχής Stob.

23

ἀλλ᾽ ἢ τὸ γῆρας τὴν Κύπριν χαίρειν ἐᾷ,
ἤ τ᾽ Ἀφροδίτη τοῖς γέρουσιν ἄχθεται . . .

21
⟨AEOLUS⟩

Do you think you could live in a country where the entire
population of its poor governed the city without the rich?
Good and bad would not be separate; yet there is a mixture
of them where things can be well. What the poor man does
not have, the rich one gives; and what we rich do not pos-   5
sess, we get through our dealings with the poor: honour.[1]

[1] 'honour' is suspect: 'we pursue through our dealings with the
poor', Bergler.

22
⟨MACAREUS⟩

Don't speak to me of nobility, in heaven's name! This de-
pends upon money—don't take pride in it, father! Money
goes around in a circle: one man has it, another doesn't; but
we use it as common to all; and whoever has it dwelling
with him in his house the longest time is noble.[1]

[1] Nobility identified with wealth: cf. *Alcmene* F 95, *Erech-
theus* F 362.14–15, *Cretan Women* F 462.5 etc. Grotius corrected
Stobaeus' 'is fortunate'.

23
But either old age really does bid sex farewell, and Aphro-
dite is displeased with the old . . .

Stobaeus 4.50.71; Plutarch, *Moralia* 285b; v. 2: *Moralia* 786a
and 1094f.

1 ἀλλ' ἦ (Nauck) and ἀλλ' ἦ (interrogative: Stob., Plut.) are
both doubted

EURIPIDES

24

⟨ΑΙΟΛΟΣ⟩

κακὸν γυναῖκα πρὸς νέαν ζεῦξαι νέον·
μακρὰ γὰρ ἰσχὺς μᾶλλον ἀρσένων μένει,
θήλεια δ᾽ ἥβη θᾶσσον ἐκλείπει δέμας.

Stobaeus 4.22.111; v. 1: Clement of Alexandria, *Miscellanies* 6.2.8.4

24a (= 39 N)

Κλῆρος Ἑρμοῦ· συνήθεια ἀρχαία· ἔβαλλον οἱ κληροῦντες εἰς ὑδρίαν ἐλαίας φύλλον, ὃ προσηγόρευον Ἑρμῆν· καὶ πρῶτον ἐξῆρουν τοῦτο, τιμὴν τῷ θεῷ ταύτην ἀπονέμοντες· ἐλάγχανεν δὲ ὁ μετὰ τὸν θεόν. Εὐριπίδης ἐν Αἰόλῳ μνημονεύει τοῦ ἔθους τούτου.

Photius, *Lexicon* κ 774 Theodoridis = *Suda* κ 1785; Eustathius on Homer, *Iliad* 7.191; references in other lexica

24b (= 27 N)

ΧΟΡΟΣ

ἦ βραχύ τοι σθένος ἀνέρος· ἀλλὰ
    ποικιλίᾳ πραπίδων
δεινὰ μὲν πόντου χθονίων τ᾽ ὀρέων
δάμναται παιδεύματα.

Plutarch, *Moralia* 98e and 959d; vv. 1–2: Stobaeus 4.13.4

3–4 τ᾽ ὀρέων Wilamowitz: δὲ ὀρέων or τ᾽ ἀερίων τε Plut. 98e (959d is corrupt and disordered)

24

⟨AEOLUS⟩

It is bad to join a young man with a young wife; for males'
vigour is longer lasting, while a woman's youth abandons
her body more quickly.

24a (= 39 N)

'Hermes' lottery': an ancient custom. Those drawing lots
threw into an urn an olive leaf, which they called 'Hermes';
they drew this first, apportioning this honour to the gods; and
the winner was the one who drew after the god. Euripides in
Aeolus mentions this custom.[1]

[1] Cf. test. ii (Hypothesis), 29–33. Hermes was god of luck.

24b (= 27 N)

CHORUS

A man's strength is indeed slight; but his ingenuity of mind
overcomes the terrible offspring of the sea and of earth's
mountains.[1]

[1] Cf. Sophocles, *Antigone* 342–50, in the 'hymn' to man's
extraordinary abilities.

25

⟨ΑΙΟΛΟΣ⟩

φεῦ φεῦ, παλαιὸς αἶνος ὡς καλῶς ἔχει·
γέροντες οὐδέν ἐσμεν ἄλλο πλὴν ψόφος
καὶ σχῆμ᾽, ὀνείρων δ᾽ ἕρπομεν μιμήματα·
νοῦς δ᾽ οὐκ ἔνεστιν, οἰόμεσθα δ᾽ εὖ φρονεῖν.

Stobaeus 4.50.38; v. 1 = *Dictys* F 333.1

26

τῇ δ᾽ Ἀφροδίτῃ πόλλ᾽ ἔνεστι ποικίλα·
τέρπει τε γὰρ μάλιστα καὶ λυπεῖ βροτούς·
τύχοιμι δ᾽ αὐτῆς ἡνίκ᾽ ἐστὶν εὐμενής.

Stobaeus 4.20.1

(27 N = 24b above)

28

παῖδες, σοφοῦ πρὸς ἀνδρός, ὅστις ἐν βραχεῖ
πολλοὺς καλῶς οἷός τε συντέμνειν λόγους.

Stobaeus 3.35.3; σοφοῦ . . . λόγους = Aristophanes, *Women at the Thesmophoria* 177–8

29

σιγᾶν †φρονοῦντα κρεῖσσον ἢ εἰς ὁμιλίαν†
πεσόντα· τούτῳ δ᾽ ἀνδρὶ μήτ᾽ εἴην φίλος
μήτε ξυνείην, ὅστις αὐτάρκη φρονεῖν
πέποιθε δούλους τοὺς φίλους ἡγούμενος.

Stobaeus 3.22.14

25

⟨AEOLUS⟩

Oh, alas, how true the ancient saying is: we old men are nothing but noise and mere shapes,[1] and we move as imitations of dreams; there is no intelligence in us, yet we think we have good sense.

[1] Similarly *Melanippe* F 509, *Andromache* 745–6, *Heracles* 111–2.

26

Aphrodite is very fickle; she brings men the greatest delights and the greatest pains. I wish I may meet with her when she is kind!

(27 N = 24b above)

28

My children, it's a clever man who has the ability to condense many words well in a brief space.

29

†A thinking man(?) is better† silent †than when fallen into company†.[1] I wish I may be neither friend nor companion to the man who believes his thoughts are self-sufficient while deeming his friends slaves.

[1] Textual corruption in v. 1 obscures the progression of ideas into vv. 2–4. 'Silence is better when one has fallen into the company of thinking men', Bothe ('a thinking man', Wilamowitz). 'A thinking man is better silent ⟨ . . . ⟩ (than/or) when fallen into the company ⟨ . . . ⟩', Collard.

---

1 φρονούντων (-ος Wilamowitz) κρεῖσσον εἰς Bothe: lacuna after κρεῖσσον (and ἤ corrupt)? Collard

30
ἀλλ᾽ ὅμως
οἰκτρός τις αἰὼν πατρίδος ἐκλιπεῖν ὅρους.

Stobaeus 3.39.5

31
ὀργῇ γὰρ ὅστις εὐθέως χαρίζεται,
κακῶς τελευτᾷ· πλεῖστα γὰρ σφάλλει βροτούς.

Stobaeus 3.20.7

32
κακῆς ⟨ἀπ᾽⟩ ἀρχῆς γίγνεται τέλος κακόν.

Stobaeus 3.4.11

33
οἴμοι, τίς ἀλγεῖν οὐκ ἐπίσταται κακοῖς;
τίς ἂν κλύων τῶνδ᾽ οὐκ ἂν ἐκβάλοι δάκρυ;

Stobaeus 4.49.9

34
γλυκεῖα γάρ μοι φροντὶς οὐδαμῇ βίου.

Stobaeus 4.34.31

35
ἀεὶ τὸ μὲν ζῇ, τὸ δὲ μεθίσταται κακόν,
τὸ δ᾽ ἐκπέφηνεν αὖθις ἐξ ἀρχῆς νέον.

Stobaeus 4.40.10

30

. . . but still it is a pretty miserable life to leave behind the borders of one's fatherland.

31

The man who immediately gratifies anger, meets a bad end; for it very often trips men up.

32

A bad end comes from a bad beginning.

33

Oh me! Who does not know how to feel pain for others' troubles? Who could hear these things and not shed a tear?

34

Nowhere in my life do I have a pleasant thought.

35

There is always one trouble alive and well, with another giving way, while another appears in turn fresh from the beginning.

36

γυναῖκα δ᾽ ὅστις παύσεται λέγων κακῶς,
δύστηνος ἆρα κοὐ σοφὸς κεκλήσεται.

Stobaeus 4.22.155

37

μοχθεῖν ἀνάγκη· τὰς δὲ δαιμόνων τύχας
ὅστις φέρει κάλλιστ᾽ ἀνήρ, οὗτος σοφός.

Stobaeus 4.44.49

38

τὰ πόλλ᾽ ἀνάγκη διαφέρει τολμήματα.

Stobaeus 4.9.6

**38a (= 112 N)

ὁ χρόνος ἅπαντα τοῖσιν ὕστερον φράσει.

Stobaeus 1.8.20, with attribution uncertainly read as *Aeolus,
Alope* (= F 112 N) or some other play; the lemma may be mis-
placed. Stobaeus attaches a second, corrupt verse, ἄλλος ἐστὶν
οὗτος, οὐκ ἐρωτῶσιν λέγει ('he is another(?), he speaks to those
who do not ask'), probably a comic fragment whose lemma has
been lost (see *PCG* VII.317).

(39 N = 24a above)

36

The man who will stop speaking ill of a woman will in fact be called a wretch and short of understanding.

37

Suffering is inevitable. The man who bears most nobly what fortune the gods give, is wise.

38

Fate defers most bold ventures.[1]

[1] Or (e.g.) 'Fate diverts . . .'; any translation is insecure without the context.

**38a (= 112 N)

Time will tell future men everything.[1]

[1] Cf. *Alexander* F 60, *Antiope* F 222, 223.107, *Bellerophon* F 303, *Hippolytus Veiled* F 441.

(39 N = 24a above)

ALEXANDER

B. Snell, *Euripides Alexandros etc.* (Berlin, 1937), 1–68; R. A. Coles, *A New Oxyrhynchus Papyrus: the Hypothesis of Euripides' Alexandros* (London, 1974); Diggle, *TrGFS* 80–4 (Hypothesis and F 46, 61d, 62a, 62d); F. Jouan in ed. Budé VIII.1.39–76; M. Cropp in *SFP* II.35–91. See also under test. iii and F 46 below.

G. Murray, *Greek Studies* (Oxford, 1946), 127–44 (orig. 1932); J. Davreux, *La légende de la prophétesse Cassandre* (Liège, 1942), 37–41, 108–17 with Figs. 7–21; D. Lanza, *SIFC* 34 (1963), 230–45; J. Hanson, *Hermes* 92 (1964), 171–81; T. C. W. Stinton, *Euripides and the Judgement of Paris* (London, 1965: repr. in *Collected Papers,* Oxford, 1990), 64–71; Jouan (1966), 113–42; Webster 165–74; G. Koniaris, *HSCP* 77 (1973), 85–124; R. Scodel, *The Trojan Trilogy of Euripides* (Göttingen, 1980), 20–42, 68–121, 138–42; *LIMC* I.i.494–7, 500–5, 523, 526–8 'Alexandros'; D. Kovacs, *HSCP* 88 (1984), 47–70; M. Huys, *ZPE* 62 (1986), 9–36 and *The Tale,* relevant sections; M. Hose, *Drama und Gesellschaft* (Stuttgart, 1995), 36–45; S. Timpanaro, *RFIC* 124 (1996), 5–70; Matthiessen 251–3.

Alexander is the alternative name of Paris, prince of Troy. Before he was born his mother Hecuba dreamed she would give birth to a firebrand; her daughter Cassandra inter-

preted this, correctly, as meaning he would cause the destruction of Troy. Hecuba and Priam therefore had the baby exposed to die, but he was spared and reared by peasants on Mount Ida. After reaching maturity Paris returned unknown to Troy and competed as an outsider in the athletic games instituted by the king and queen to commemorate their supposedly dead son. He was so successful that the jealous queen and her sons tried to kill him, but his identity was discovered in the nick of time; he was accepted into the family, and as foretold went on to bring about Troy's ruin through the abduction of Helen.

The story of Paris as a 'curse-child' may have been an old one, but the dream is first known to us in a papyrus fragment of Pindar's Paeans (fr. 52i(A).14–25 Snell–Maehler), and the story of Paris's exposure, return and recognition appears first in tragedy. Sophocles seems to have told a similar story in his Alexander, probably before Euripides; its few fragments (F 91a–100a) include mention of town and country people, midwifery and suckling, and a herdsman defeating townsmen. Sophocles' plot may be more or less closely reflected in Hyginus, Fab. 91 (= test. ivb(2)), in which Paris competes in the games in order to win back a favourite bull commandeered as a prize. Euripides elsewhere mentions Hecuba's failure to kill the baby Paris (Andromache 293–300, Trojan Women 597–8, 919–21) and the exposure and rustic upbringing (IA 1283–99); perhaps also the torch-dream (Trojan Women 922, but this may be an interpolation). In his Alexander the drama was built around a conflict between Paris and his fellow-herdsmen, Priam's decision to admit him to the games, and the characters of Hecuba and Paris—a grieving mother turn-

*ing to murder, and a young man who by proving his nobil-
ity and talents achieves his destiny as destroyer of Troy.*

   *Much of the play's outline can be inferred from the pa-
pyrus hypothesis (test. iii) and the numerous fragments,
especially those in the Strasbourg papyrus (published in
1922 and partly re-organized by Coles when he published
the Oxyrhynchus hypothesis in 1974). The play was set be-
fore the royal palace, with the temple of Apollo probably
close by. The Chorus probably comprised Trojan women
(friends of the dramatically central Hecuba). A prologue
speech giving the story of Paris's early life and the context
of the impending games (test. iii.4–14, F 41a–42d) was de-
livered either by a god such as Aphrodite or Hermes, or
possibly by Paris's foster-father, a herdsman. F 43–46 are
plausibly assigned to a parodos and following dialogue in
which the chorus consoled Hecuba's grief over her long-
lost son. If Wilamowitz's supplements at the end of F 46 are
correct (see note there), Cassandra then entered, presum-
ably to converse with Hecuba, although the Hypothesis
overlooks this scene and the purpose of Cassandra's ap-
pearance is unclear; if she delivered prophecies about Paris
at this point as Snell suggested, these would have antici-
pated those at the end of the play. F 46a seems to represent
a further scene in which Priam discusses the preparations
for the games, perhaps with Hecuba. Then came the en-
trance of a secondary chorus of herdsmen arraigning Paris
before Priam because of his 'arrogant behaviour' towards
them (test. iii.15–17, test. v). The shape of the ensuing epi-
sode is unclear, but the accusations of the herdsmen seem to
have given way to a rhetorical debate in which an oppo-
nent attacked Paris's slave background and resisted his ad-*

mission to the games (F 48–51; and F 59?), Paris defended himself successfully (test. iii.17–19, F 55; also F 56–57, 61?), and Priam was led to allow Paris to compete (test. iii.19–21, F 60); the choral reflections on true nobility (F 61b–c) probably come from a stasimon following this debate. The identity of the opponent is something of a mystery: Deiphobus seems a likely candidate in view of his later hostility to Paris (test. iii.22–5, F 62a–d), but a son of Priam can hardly have addressed to him the condescending F 48 (this might however be attributed to the chorus leader). Hecuba herself seems a plausible choice, giving a drama built consistently, and in Euripidean style, around a conflicted female character.

The games and Paris's successes in them were reported, probably to Hecuba, in a messenger's speech (F 61d; also F 61a, 54?). Then Hector and Deiphobus returned, and a scene in which Deiphobus and Hecuba plotted to murder Paris despite Hector's objections is well represented by the papyrus fragments F 62a–d (perhaps from five consecutive papyrus columns and spanning around 170 lines of text: cf. Coles 35–58, Huys [1986]). In F 62d col. iii their plot is complete and the chorus excitedly anticipates its fulfilment, then greets a newly arriving person who may well be Alexander himself, lured into the trap (cf. F 62d.27–9) like other tragic victims such as Lycus in both Heracles *and* Antiope. *Although the Hypothesis identifies Hecuba as his prospective killer (test. iii.24–5, 29), it seems likely (as Huys argues) that she was to be aided by Deiphobus and/or some subordinates; but the paucity of the remaining fragments leaves the ensuing action very unclear. The Hypothesis (test. iii.25–32) has Alexander arriving, Cassandra*

*recognizing him in a mantic fit (cf. most or all of F 62e–h),
Hecuba prevented from killing him, and his foster-father
arriving to confirm his identity; this presumably led to a re-
union celebration (F 62?). Later iconography (see below)
suggests that Paris had taken refuge at the altar of Zeus (F
62i?), as in Hyginus. Such a sequence seems to require the
almost continuous presence of Hecuba and Paris, in which
case the actor playing Cassandra must have exited after
her prophecies so as to reappear as the foster-father, and
Deiphobus (let alone Priam) can hardly have had a speak-
ing role at this point; perhaps he waited in the palace while
Hecuba persuaded Paris to go inside, and he could have
reappeared as a mute as Paris emerged fleeing to the altar.
For suggested reconstructions more or less close to the
Hypothesis see especially Scodel 35–8, Jouan in ed. Budé
53–7, Timpanaro 47–9. A divine speech at the end is un-
likely since the future had to remain unknown to everyone
except Cassandra (cf. Lanza 232–5, Scodel 39–40, Timpa-
naro 66–8).*

*Brief fragments: F 62k (further scraps of P. Strasbourg
with a few words), F 63 'the unnamed maiden' (i.e.
Persephone). Other ascriptions: F 867, 937–8 (see note
there), 958, 960, 976, 1050, 1068, 1082 (see note); adesp. F
71 'I call to witness the (majesty?) of Zeus Herkeios', adesp.
F 286 'How like Priam's sons this herdsman is!', adesp. F
289 'Out came the Hectors and the Sarpedons'; adesp. F
721b–c perhaps includes a few damaged lines from Cas-
sandra's prophetic speech.*

*Alexander was the first play of Euripides' 'Trojan tril-
ogy' of 415 B.C., with* Palamedes *and the extant* Trojan
Women; *the satyr play was* Sisyphus. *Our source for this*

information (Aelian, Historical Miscellanies *2.8.) complains that Xenocles with his* Oedipus, Lycaon, Bacchae *and* Athamas *was awarded first prize ahead of Euripides. There must have been a broad thematic coherence between* Alexander *and* Trojan Women *(and possibly* Palamedes) *insofar as the fate of Troy was concerned, but the earlier play's events are surprisingly unprominent in the later one, despite the strong presences of Hecuba and Cassandra in both; the survival of Paris is mentioned only at Tro. 597–8 and 919–21. Still, the ironies implicit in* Alexander's *particular working out of the recognition-and-reunion plot, by contrast with its normal culmination in joy and release, must have been strongly felt, as they are in Sophocles'* Oedipus. *And we can sense from the fragments how the characters of Hecuba, Priam and Paris will have been portrayed as elements in the fulfilment of Troy's fate.*

Sophocles' Alexander *has been mentioned above, and a third* Alexander *is recorded, by the Hellenistic tragedian Nicomachus of Alexandria Troas (TrGF 127 F 1). Ennius' Latin* Alexander *is said by Varro to have been modelled on Euripides' play; its fragments (included in ed. Budé 77–80, SFP II.88–91) provide useful supplementation for the prologue speech, the report of the games, and Cassandra's mantic scene (also possibly the earlier dialogue between Cassandra and Hecuba), although they do not certainly replicate Euripides. Nothing in Greek art can be confidently connected with the play, but many Etruscan mirrors and ash-urns show Paris taking sanctuary on the altar and attacked by a male and/or a female figure (Deiphobus and Hecuba?), sometimes with supporting figures (see Davreux 108–17, LIMC nos. 19–43); these may reflect loosely the Euripidean plot and a Greek icono-*

graphic tradition lost to us. Beyond that the story of Paris's exposure and return appears infrequently in extant classical literature and art, but see Ovid, Heroides *16.43ff., 89ff., 359ff., 17.237ff., 'Dictys of Crete' 3.26, Dracontius 8.78–212, and for more recent works OGCMA II.818–20.*

ΑΛΕΞΑΝΔΡΟΣ

test. iii (Hypothesis)

Ἀλέξαν]δρ[ος οὗ ἀρχή·

      ] καὶ τὸ κλεινὸν [Ἴ]λιον,

ἡ δὲ ὑ]πόθεσις·

      ] Ἑκάβης καθ᾽ ὕπνον ὄψεις

5   ἔ]δωκεν ἐκθεῖναι βρέφος

      ]ν ἐξέθρεψεν υἱὸν Ἀλέ-

ξανδρ[ον Π]άριν προσαγορεύσας. Ἑκά-

βη δὲ τὴ[ν ἡ]μέραν ἐκείνην πενθοῦ-

σα ἅμα κ[αὶ] τιμῆς ἀξιοῦσα κατωδύ-

10   ρατο μὲν [τὸ]ν ἐκτεθέντα, Πρίαμον [δ᾽ ἔ-

πε[ι]σε πο[λυτ]ελεῖς ἀγῶνας ἐπ᾽ α[ὐ]τῷ κα-

ταστήσ[ασ]θα[ι]· διελθόντ[ων δὲ ἐτῶ]ν εἴ-

κοσι ὁ μὲν παῖς ἔδοξε [κρείττων τ]ὴν

φύσιν εἶναι βουκόλο[υ τοῦ θρέψα]ντος,

15   οἱ δ᾽ ἄλλοι νομεῖς διὰ [τ]ὴν ὑπερήφανον

συμβίωσιν [δ]ήσαντες ἐπ[ὶ] Πρίαμον ἀνήγα-

γον αὐτόν·......ηθεὶς [δ]ὲ ἐπὶ τοῦ δυνά-

στου...ω[.].....[.(.)]ρειτο καὶ τοὺς δι-

P. Oxy. 3650 col. i, ed. R. A. Coles (1984, previously in Coles 1974: see bibl. above); see also van Rossum-Steenbeek 186–7, Diggle *TrGFS* 80–1.

ALEXANDER

test. iii (Hypothesis)

Alexander, which begins, ' . . . and famous Ilium'; the plot is as
follows: (because) Hecuba (had seen) visions in her sleep,
(Priam) gave her infant son to be exposed. (The herdsman
who took him) reared him as his son, calling Alexander Paris.[1]   5
But Hecuba, grieving because of that day but also thinking it
should be honoured, lamented the exposed child and per-
suaded Priam to establish lavish games for him. When twenty   10
years had passed, the boy seemed to have a nature (superior)
to that of the herdsman (who had reared him), and the other
shepherds, because of his arrogant behaviour towards them,   15
bound him and brought him before Priam. When he (was ar-
raigned?) before the ruler, he (readily defended himself?) and

---

[1] Or possibly 'calling him Alexander Paris'; the double name
appears in some mythographic sources. But see the note on F 42d.

---

13 [κρείττων Luppe: ἔδοξε[ν ἀμείνων Coles
17 ἐπερωτηθεὶς Coles (ἀν- Bremer): ἀπολογηθεὶς Luppe
18 ῥᾳδίω[ς συνη[γο]ρεῖτο Kannicht, after Coles

αβάλλοντας ἑκάστ[ο]υς ἔλαβε καὶ τῶν
20 ἐπ' αὐτῷ τελ[ο]υμέν[ων] ἀγώνων εἰάθη
μετασχεῖν. δρόμον δὲ καὶ πένταθλον,
ἔτι †δαπαξητηνττεφ†...ἀπεθηρίωσε
τοὺς περὶ Δηΐφοβον, οἵτινες ἡττᾶσθαι δια-
λαβ[ό]ντες ὑπὸ δούλου κατηξίωσαν τὴν
25 Ἑκάβην ὅπως ἂν αὐτὸν ἀποκτείνῃ· πα-
ραγενηθέντα δὲ τὸν Ἀλέξανδρον
Κασ[σάν]δρ[α μ]ὲν ἐμμανὴς ἐπέγνω
καὶ π[ερὶ τῶ]ν μελλόντων ἐθέσπισεν,
Ἑκάβη [δὲ ἀπο]κτεῖναι θέλουσα διεκω-
30 λύθη. π[α]ρα[γενό]μενος δ' ὁ θρέψας αὐτὸν
διὰ τὸν κίνδυνον ἠναγκάσθη λέγειν τὴν
ἀλήθειαν. Ἑκάβη μὲν οὖν υἱὸν ἀνεῦρε . . .

22 ἔτι δὲ πὺξ Coles: ἔτι δὲ πυγμὴν Huys   στεφθεὶς Bremer

test. v

(Hippolytus' entrance at *Hipp.* 58 ff. seems to have been accompanied by a secondary chorus of huntsmen.) ἕτεροί εἰσι τοῦ χοροῦ, καθάπερ ἐν τῷ Ἀλεξάνδρῳ οἱ ποιμένες. ἐνταῦθα μὲν οὖν δύναται προαποχρήσασθαι τοῖς ἀπὸ τοῦ χοροῦ, ἐκεῖ δὲ συνεστῶτος τοῦ χοροῦ ἐπεισάγει τοῦτο τὸ ἄθροισμα, ὡς καὶ ἐν τῇ Ἀντιόπῃ δύο χοροὺς εἰσάγει, τόν τε τῶν Ἀθηναίων γερόντων διόλου καὶ τὸν μετὰ Δίρκης.

Schol. on Euripides, *Hippolytus* 58

caught out each of those slandering him, and was allowed to take part in the games which were being celebrated in his honour. By (winning the crown?) in running and the pentathlon, and also (in boxing?), he enraged Deiphobus and his companions who, realising that they had been worsted by a slave, called on Hecuba to kill him. When Alexander arrived, Cassandra became possessed and recognized him, and prophesied about what was going to happen; and Hecuba tried to kill him and was prevented. The man who had raised him arrived, and because of the danger (to Paris) was compelled to tell the truth. Thus Hecuba rediscovered her son . . . 20 25 30

test. v

(The huntsmen who enter with Hippolytus at *Hipp*. 58ff.) are different from the chorus, like the herdsmen in *Alexander*. Notice that here (in *Hippolytus*) Euripides can use some of the chorus-members in advance (i.e. before the entrance of the full chorus), whereas in *Alexander* he brings on this group with the (main) chorus already present, as he also introduces two choruses in *Antiope*, the one comprising the old Athenians generally and the one with Dirce.

EURIPIDES

41a

] καὶ τὸ κλεινὸν ['Ἴ]λιον

See test. iii.2 above

42

... καὶ χρόνου προύβαινε πούς.

Schol. on Aristophanes, *Frogs* 100 (cf. 311); Suda π 356.

(42a–c N–Sn = 62f–h below)

42d

γενόμενος δὲ νεανίσκος καὶ πολλῶν διαφέρων κάλλει τε
καὶ ῥώμῃ αὖθις Ἀλέξανδρος προσωνομάσθη, λῃστὰς
ἀμυνόμενος καὶ τοῖς ποιμνίοις ἀλεξήσας.

Apollodorus 3.12.5

43 (= 46 N)

ΧΟΡΟΣ

πάντων τὸ θανεῖν· τὸ δὲ κοινὸν ἄχος
μετρίως ἀλγεῖν σοφία μελετᾷ.

Stobaeus 4.44.47

44 (= 45 N)

⟨ΧΟΡΟΣ⟩

ὥστ' οὔτις ἀνδρῶν εἰς ἅπαντ' εὐδαιμονεῖ.

Stobaeus 4.41.33

44

41a

From the play's first line:
. . . and famous Ilium . . .

42

. . . and time's foot moved on.

(42a–c N–Sn = 62f–h below)

42d

When he (Paris) became a young man and excelled many in beauty and strength, he was given a second name, Alexander, because he drove off brigands and protected the flocks.[1]

[1] Alexander's name is explained by reference to the verb ἀλέγω, 'protect'. Varro, *On the Latin Language* 7.82 cites a line from Ennius' *Alexander* (fr. 20 Jocelyn: *quapropter Parim pastores nunc Alexandrum uocant*, 'And so the herdsmen now call Paris Alexander'), noting that this etymology was clear in Euripides' Greek but not in Ennius' Latin. This suggests the re-naming was mentioned in the prologues of both plays. For similar etymologies see *Antiope* F 181–2, *Melanippe Captive* F *489 etc.

43 (= 46 N)

CHORUS

All of us must die; but wisdom practises feeling the pain of this common woe in moderation.

44 (= 45 N)

⟨CHORUS⟩

And so no man is fortunate in everything.

45 (= 44 N)

⟨ΧΟΡΟΣ⟩

οἶδ'· ἀλλὰ κάμπτειν τῷ χρόνῳ λύπας χρεών.

⟨ΕΚΑΒΗ⟩

χρή· τοῦτο δ' εἰπεῖν ῥᾷον ἢ φέρειν κακά.

Stobaeus 4.49.8

46 (46 N = 43 above)

⟨ΧΟΡΟΣ⟩

ἔστιν τέκνων σοι πλ[

⟨ΕΚΑΒΗ⟩

ἐ[γὼ δὲ θ]ρηνῶ γ' ὅτι βρ[έφ-

⟨ΧΟΡΟΣ⟩

τλήμων γε Πρίαμος κ[

⟨ΕΚΑΒΗ⟩

ὡς ἴσμεν οἱ παθόντες ο[

⟨ΧΟΡΟΣ⟩

5 παλαιὰ καινοῖς δακρύοις οὐ χρὴ στένειν.

F 46, 46a, 61d, 62a–e, 62k: P. Strasbourg 2342–4, ed. W. Crönert, *Nachrichten* . . . *Göttingen* (1922), 1–17; re-ed. Snell, Coles and others (see bibl. above).

F 46: P. Strasbourg 2344.1; v. 5: Stobaeus 4.56.20

1 πλ[ήρες ἀρσένων στέγος Crönert: πλ[ῆθος ἀρσένων ἔτι Diggle   2 βρ[έφος Crönert: then κατέκταμεν Snell (διώλεσα Diggle, κτανεῖν ἔτλην Lee, προυθήκαμεν Collard) 3 κ[αὶ ἡ (= χἠ) τεκοῦσα Crönert: then δύσμορος Snell 4 ο[ἱ τλάντες θ' ἅμα Collard

45 (= 44 N)

⟨CHORUS⟩

I know, but one should bring grieving to an end in time.

⟨HECUBA⟩

One should, but it is easier to say this than to bear the affliction.

46 (46 N = 43 above)

⟨CHORUS⟩

You have . . . of children . . . [1]

⟨HECUBA⟩

And yet I grieve because (I/we killed/exposed our) child.

⟨CHORUS⟩

Unhappy Priam, and . . . [2]

⟨HECUBA⟩

As we know well, who suffered . . . [3]

⟨CHORUS⟩

One should not lament old troubles with fresh tears.   5

[1] 'a home filled with male children', Crönert; 'still an abundance of male children', Diggle.   [2] 'and ill-fated she who bore the child', Crönert, Snell.   [3] 'who both suffered and dared the deed', Collard.

⟨EKABH⟩

.]εν.ων τις ἡ τεκοῦσ[α

⟨ΧΟΡΟΣ?⟩

..]‗. μέν, ὥς φασ᾽, ὤλετ[

⟨EKABH⟩

.. μα]κάριον τἄρ᾽ οὐκ[

]εστι τοῖ᾽ ἐμο[

10]πνας πρὸς κακ[

⟨ΧΟΡΟΣ?⟩

δέ]δορκα παῖδα κ[

]ν ἀδύτων ω[

traces of two more lines

7 perhaps ὁ πα]ῖς μέν Crönert   10]πνας or]μνας
Kannicht   11–12 καὶ μὴν δέ]δορκα παῖδα Κ[ασσάνδραν
σέθεν | ἤκουσα]ν ἀδύτων ὦ[δε Φοιβείων πάρος (e.g.) Wilamo-
witz (στείχουσα]ν Diggle; end ἄπο Webster)

46a

col. i   *remains of three line-ends, then:*

]μν[..]ος[..]λλοις ἔριν

5].τ[..]ω..[.]δης λάτρις

]νδε πω[λι]κοῖς ὄχοις

]ντατη[...]ους θανεῖν

] ὃν τετίμη[κ]ας τέκνων

].ελ.[...]υ[..]αι γένος

10]ρ οἵπερ ἵσταν[τ]αι πον[

] τήνδ᾽ ἀφαγνίζεις χθόνα

κα]ὶ ἐπικηδείους πόνους

48

ALEXANDER

‹HECUBA›

A . . . , his mother . . .

‹CHORUS?›

(The child) perished, so they say . . .

‹HECUBA›

. . . not, then, blessed . . . such . . . there are for me(?) . . . because of (*or* added to) my afflictions(?) . . .   10

‹CHORUS?›

. . . I see your(?) daughter . . . (from?) the shrine . . . [4]

(traces of two more lines)

[4] Wilamowitz's bold supplement makes vv. 11–12 an entrance announcement, 'But now I see your daughter Cassandra coming out here from Apollo's sacred precinct.' On this possibility see the Introduction above.

46a

(remains of three lines) . . . strife . . . servant . . . horse-   5
drawn carriage . . . to die . . . the child you have honoured(?) . . . family . . . (the trials) which are being put on   10
. . . you are cleansing this land . . . and funeral trials . . . the

]ων ἤδη πόλιν
]ονῳ σπουδῇ λάβῃ
15   ]υδενω νέμων πόλιν
]τασιν τε γῆς
π]ορσ[ύν]οις κακῶν
τ]ῷ τεθ[ν]ηκότι
] καλὸν τόδε

ends of two more lines

col. ii   *beginnings of seventeen lines*

      P. Strasbourg 2342.1

     16 ἀνάσ]τασίν Crönert   17 beg. ἀποστροφὴν δ᾽ ἂν
τῶνδε (e.g.) Snell   18 παιδὶ τ]ῷ Crönert

(47 N = 61a below)

48

σοφὸς μὲν οὖν εἶ, Πρίαμ᾽, ὅμως δέ σοι λέγω·
δούλου φρονοῦντος μεῖζον ἢ φρονεῖν χρεὼν
οὐκ ἔστιν ἄχθος μεῖζον οὐδὲ δώμασι
κτῆσις κακίων οὐδ᾽ ἀνωφελεστέρα.

   Stobaeus 4.19.14; vv. 2–4 partly preserved in an inscription on
a herm (of Euripides?) now in Copenhagen (Ny-Carlsberg Glypt.
414b).

   2 μεῖζον inscr.: μᾶλλον Stob.

49

ἤλεγχον· οὕτω γὰρ κακὸν δοῦλον γένος·
γαστὴρ ἅπαντα, τοὐπίσω δ᾽ οὐδὲν σκοπεῖ.

50

city already . . . eagerness grips (you?) . . . ruling the city . . .   15
(ruination?) of the land . . . you could provide (relief from
her?) afflictions . . . for the dead (child?) . . . (if?) this is
good . . . *(ends of two more lines)*

(47 N = 61a below)

48

You are certainly wise, Priam, but still I tell you: there is no
greater burden than a slave who has bigger ideas than he
should, nor a possession more vile nor more worthless in a
household.

49

I've tested it (*or* them): so vile is the race of slaves, all belly
and looking to nothing beyond that.

Stobaeus 4.19.15

50

δούλων ὅσοι φιλοῦσι δεσποτῶν γένος
πρὸς τῶν ὁμοίων πόλεμον αἴρονται μέγαν.

Stobaeus 4.19.16

2 αἴρονται Elmsley: αἱροῦνται Stob.

51

δούλους γὰρ οὐ
καλὸν πεπᾶσθαι κρείσσονας τῶν δεσποτῶν.

Stobaeus 4.19.20

(52, 53 N = 61b, 61c below)

54

κακόν τι παίδευμ᾽ ἦν ἄρ᾽ εἰς εὐανδρίαν
ὁ πλοῦτος ἀνθρώποισιν αἵ τ᾽ ἄγαν τρυφαί·
πενία δὲ δύστηνον μέν, ἀλλ᾽ ὅμως τρέφει
μοχθεῖν τ᾽ ἀμείνω τέκνα καὶ δραστήρια.

Stobaeus 4.33.3; vv. 1–2: Clement of Alexandria, *Miscellanies* 4.5.24.3

1 παίδευμ᾽ Clem.: βούλευμ᾽ Stob.   4 μοχθεῖν τ᾽ Conington: μοχθοῦντ᾽ Stob.

55

⟨ΑΛΕΞΑΝΔΡΟΣ?⟩
ἄδικον ὁ πλοῦτος, πολλὰ δ᾽ οὐκ ὀρθῶς ποιεῖ.

Stobaeus 4.31.71

50

Slaves who become attached to their masters' kind earn serious enmity from their own sort.

51

It is not good to own slaves who are better than their masters.

(52, 53 N = 61b, 61c below)

54

Wealth and excessive luxury, it turns out, are a bad sort of training for manliness. Poverty is a misfortune, but all the same it rears children who are better at working hard and get things done.[1]

[1] If these lines belong in the debate scene the speaker will be Paris (cf. the next fragment). But they may well be a comment on Paris's successes in the games made by the Messenger at the end of his report.

55

⟨ALEXANDER?⟩

Wealth is unjust and does many things wrongly.

EURIPIDES

56

〈ΑΛΕΞΑΝΔΡΟΣ〉

ἄναξ, διαβολαὶ δεινὸν ἀνθρώποις κακόν·
ἀγλωσσίᾳ δὲ πολλάκις ληφθεὶς ἀνὴρ
δίκαια λέξας ἧσσον εὐγλώσσου φέρει.

Stobaeus 3.42.3; vv. 2–3: Clement of Alexandria, *Miscellanies* 1.8.41.1

57

〈ΑΛΕΞΑΝΔΡΟΣ?〉

ὦ παγκάκιστοι καὶ τὸ δοῦλον οὐ λόγῳ
ἔχοντες, ἀλλὰ τῇ τύχῃ κεκτημένοι.

Stobaeus 4.19.18

2 τύχῃ Stob.: φύσει Jacobs (then οὐ τύχῃ . . . ἀλλ' ἐν τῇ φύσει Cobet)

(58 N = 62i below)

59

ἐκ τῶν ὁμοίων οἱ κακοὶ γαμοῦσ' ἀεί.

Stobaeus 4.22.87

60

〈ΠΡΙΑΜΟΣ〉

χρόνος δὲ δείξει σ'· ᾧ τεκμηρίῳ μαθὼν
ἢ χρηστὸν ὄντα γνωσόμεσθά σ' ἢ κακόν.

Clement of Alexandria, *Miscellanies* 6.2.10.8

56
⟨ALEXANDER⟩

My lord, slander is a terrible thing for men. Often a man disadvantaged by ineloquence loses out to an eloquent one even though his case is just.[1]

[1] Such complaints are frequent amongst Euripidean speakers, e.g. *Antiope* F 206.1–3, F 928b, *Hecuba* 1187–91.

57
⟨ALEXANDER?⟩

O vilest creatures—not slaves in name but slaves in reality.[1]

[1] Or 'slaves by nature', Jacobs; 'not slaves by chance but in your/their nature', Cobet.

(58 N = 62i below)

59

Low people always marry from their own kind.

60
⟨PRIAM⟩

Time will show what you are; by that evidence I shall learn whether you are a man of worth or not.[1]

[1] Cf. *Aeolus* F **38a with note.

61

†μισῶ σοφὸν ἐν λόγοισιν†, ἐς δ᾽ ὄνησιν οὐ σοφόν.

Orion 1.3 Haffner

μισῶ σοφὸν | ⟨ὄντ᾽⟩ ἐν λόγοισιν Meineke

61a (= 47 N)

ὅθεν δὲ νικᾶν χρῆν σε, δυστυχεῖς, ἄναξ·
ὅθεν δέ σ᾽ οὐ χρῆν, εὐτυχεῖς. δούλοισι γὰρ
τοῖς σοῖσι νικᾷς, τοῖς δ᾽ ἐλευθέροισιν οὔ.

Stobaeus 3.4.31

61b (= 52 N)

ΧΟΡΟΣ

περισσόμυθος ὁ λόγος εὐγένειαν εἰ
    βρότειον εὐλογήσομεν.
τὸ γὰρ πάλαι καὶ πρῶτον ὅτ᾽ ἐγενόμεθα, διὰ
    δ᾽ ἔκρινεν ἁ τεκοῦσα γᾶ
5   βροτούς, ὁμοίαν χθὼν ἅπασιν ἐξεπαί-
    δευσεν ὄψιν· ἴδιον οὐδὲν ἔσχομεν.
μία δὲ γονὰ τό τ᾽ εὐγενὲς καὶ δυσγενές,
νόμῳ δὲ γαῦρον αὐτὸ κραίνει χρόνος.
τὸ φρόνιμον εὐγένεια καὶ τὸ συνετόν, ὁ δὲ
10   θεὸς δίδωσιν, οὐχ ὁ πλοῦτος . . .

Stobaeus 4.29.2

---

[1] The Chorus uses a 'scientific' account of the origins of human life to show that the distinction between 'good' and 'bad' birth is merely conventional. 'Good' birth is no guarantee

61

I detest a man who is clever in words but not clever at do-
ing good service.[1]

[1] The slightly unmetrical Greek text is best mended by
Meineke.

61a (= 47 N)

You fail with those you should be winning with, my lord,
and succeed with those you should not be. You win with
your slaves, and not with your free men.[1]

[1] If from the debate scene, a comment on Priam's decision to
admit Paris to the games. But the present-tense verbs suggest that
this may be the Messenger quoting someone's complaint to Priam
during the games.

61b (= 52 N)
CHORUS

Our talk will be idle if we sing the praises of human good
birth. For long ago at the beginning, when we came into
existence and mother earth produced distinct human be-
ings, she made us all grow up with a similar appearance; we   5
got no special feature. Well-born and low-born are a single
breed, but time through convention has made the well-
born proud. Intelligence and understanding make nobility,
and god bestows it, not wealth . . . [1]

of true (moral) nobility, even though the same word (*eugeneia*)
is commonly applied to both. For similar observations about the
artificiality of human social conventions see Herodotus 3.38, Anti-
phon B 44(b) DK, Hippias C 1.17–20 DK (= Plato, *Protagoras*
337c–d). The equation of wealth with nobility (or poverty with the
lack of it) was proverbial: see on *Aeolus* F 22.

61c (= 53 N)

ΧΟΡΟΣ

οὐκ ἔστιν ἐν κακοῖσιν εὐγένεια, παρ' ἀ-
γαθοῖσι δ' ἀνδρῶν.

Stobaeus 4.29.7

61d

remains of three lines, then:

⟨ΧΟΡΟΣ⟩

τύχῃ δ[...].ι πα[

⟨ΑΓΓΕΛΟΣ⟩

5   κρείσσω⟨ν⟩ πεφυκὼς [

⟨ΧΟΡΟΣ⟩

ἦ καὶ στέφουσιν αὐτὸ[ν

⟨ΑΓΓΕΛΟΣ⟩

καί φασιν εἶναί γ' ἄξιον [

⟨ΧΟΡΟΣ⟩

ὁ δ' ὧδε μορφῇ διαφερ[

⟨ΑΓΓΕΛΟΣ⟩

ἄπανθ' ὅσ' ἄνδρα χρη[

⟨ΧΟΡΟΣ⟩

10   ]γαν βουκ[ολ-

61c (= 53 N)

CHORUS

Nobility is found not in men who are bad but in those who
are good.[1]

[1] Possibly the beginning of an antistrophe following F 61b.

61d

remains of three lines, then:

⟨CHORUS⟩

(I credit everything?) to fortune . . .

⟨MESSENGER⟩

Being naturally superior . . .   5

⟨CHORUS⟩

And are they actually crowning him . . . ?

⟨MESSENGER⟩

Yes, and declaring him worthy . . .

⟨CHORUS⟩

And (is) he so outstanding in beauty . . . ?

⟨MESSENGER⟩

Everything that . . . a man . . .[1]

⟨CHORUS⟩

. . . herdsman . . .   10

[1] 'Everything that it befits a well-born man to achieve',
Crönert, Page; 'Everything that a man of worth . . . ', Coles,
Kannicht.

⟨ΑΓΓΕΛΟΣ⟩

traces of one line

⟨ΧΟΡΟΣ⟩

ἀγῶνα ποῦ κ[

⟨ΑΓΓΕΛΟΣ⟩

Πρίαμος τίθησιν [

⟨ΧΟΡΟΣ⟩

εἰς τόνδε νικη.[

⟨ΑΓΓΕΛΟΣ⟩

15 *remains of one line*

P. Strasbourg 2344.2

4 δ[ίδω]μι Crönert, Kannicht   πά[ντα Lefke
8 διαφέρ[ων or διαφέρ[ει Crönert   9 χρὴ (Crönert) [τὸν
εὐγενῆ τελεῖν (e.g.) Page: perhaps χρή[σιμον Coles: χρη[στὸν
ὄντα Kannicht   12 κ[ρίνουσι Crönert
14 νικητ[ήρι(α) Crönert

62

Ἑκάβη, τὸ θεῖον ὡς ἄελπτον ἔρχεται
θνητοῖσιν, ἕλκει δ᾽ οὔποτ᾽ ἐκ ταὐτοῦ τύχας.

Stobaeus 4.47.10

ALEXANDER

⟨MESSENGER⟩

traces of one line

⟨CHORUS⟩
Where (are they deciding?) the contest . . .

⟨MESSENGER⟩
Priam is arranging . . .

⟨CHORUS⟩
To this (man?) . . . victory(-prizes?) . . .

⟨MESSENGER⟩
remains of one line

62
Hecuba, how unexpectedly divine action comes upon men, never drawing events from the same source![1]

[1] If from the Messenger scene these lines refer to Paris's victories. But they may well be a comment on the discovery of his identity near the end of the play.

62a

trace of one line, then:

⟨ΧΟΡΟΣ⟩

καὶ μὴν ὁρῶ τόν]δ᾽ Ἕκτορ᾽ ἐξ ἀγωνίω[ν
περῶντα μό]χθων σύγγονόν τε, παῖδε σώ,
........] εἰς δ᾽ ἄμιλλαν ἥκουσιν λόγων.

⟨ΔΗΙΦΟΒΟΣ⟩

5 αἰνῶ μὲν οὐ]δέν᾽ ὅστις ἐστὶ δυσχερής
........]. κακοῖσι μαλθάσσει φρένας.

⟨ΕΚΤΩΡ⟩

ἐγὼ δέ γ᾽ ὅσ]τις σμίκρ᾽ ἔχων ἐγκλήματα
μεγάλα νο]μίζει καὶ συνέστηκεν †φόβῳ†.

⟨ΔΗΙΦΟΒΟΣ⟩

καὶ πῶς, κα]σίγνηθ᾽ Ἕκτορ, οὐκ ἀλγεῖς φρένα[ς
10 δούλου πρὸς] ἀνδρὸς ἆθλ᾽ ἀπεστερημέν[ος;

⟨ΕΚΤΩΡ⟩

........]. εις, Δηΐφοβε· τί γάρ με δεῖ
.... οὐ] καιρὸς ὠδίνειν φ[ρέ]νας.

P. Strasbourg 2342.2

4 Δηΐφοβον] Diggle: πρὸς οἶκον] Kannicht   6 ἁλοὺς
δὲ τοῖ]ς Crönert (δ]ἡ Kannicht): αὖθις δὲ τοῖ]ς Diggle
8 †φόβῳ†: perhaps φθόνῳ Collard, Cropp   11 μάτην
ἀθυ]μεῖς Kannicht following Wilamowitz   12 ὀργὴν ἔχειν;
οὐ] or δυσθυμίας; οὐ] Collard

62a

trace of one line, then:

<CHORUS>

(And now I see) Hector (here), (coming) from the exertions of the games, with his brother—your two sons— . . . ;[1] and they have fallen into a dispute.

<DEIPHOBUS>

(I do not approve of) anyone who feels aggrieved . . . (by/ 5 to) troubles, softens his attitude.[2]

<HECTOR>

   (Nor I) of anyone who has small complaints but reckons them (great) and is overwrought †with fear†.[3]

<DEIPHOBUS>

(And how,) brother Hector, can you not feel anguish, when you have been robbed of prizes (by a slave)?   10

<HECTOR>

You (are needlessly distressed?), Deiphobus. Why do I need (to feel angry/dispirited)? This is not an occasion for tormenting our spirits.

---

[1] 'Deiphobus', Diggle; 'to the house', Kannicht.   [2] 'yet even though vexed by troubles, softens his attitude', Crönert; 'yet in turn softens his attitude to his troubles', Diggle.   [3] Perhaps 'with envy' (Collard–Cropp).

⟨ΔΗΙΦΟΒΟΣ⟩

............]. ῥᾳδίως φέρεις τάδε

.... Φρ]υξὶν ἐμφανὴς ἔσῃ.

15   ⟨ΕΚΤΩΡ?⟩

.............]ς νέον φῦσαι με[

.... βο]ύλεται δ᾽ οὐ σωφρ[ον-

remains of five more lines

    13–14 σὺ δειλίᾳ μὲ]ν . . . | ἥσσων δὲ δούλου Φρ]υξὶν . . .
Lefke   16 σωφρ[ονεῖν Crönert

62b

col. i   *extreme ends of thirteen lines with a few letters visible,*
perhaps from below F 62a

col. ii   ⟨ΔΗΙΦΟΒΟΣ?⟩

traces of one line

ἐλε]ύθεροι μὲν πα.[

δο]ῦλοι δ᾽ ἂν ἤσκουν [

25 πα]ντοῖ ἐκείνων ατ[

  ...]ν δ᾽ ἀπῆσαν μν[

remains of three lines, then:

            ⟨ΕΚΤΩΡ⟩

30 οὔ[τ᾽ οἶκο]ν αὔξων οὔτ[ε

  πρόθυμ᾽ ἔπρασσε δοῦλος ὢν απ..[

    P. Strasbourg 2343.2 (lower part)

    23 παῖ[δες Crönert: πάν[τες Snell   30 οὔτ[ε πρὸς
κέρδος βλέπων Reitzenstein (κερδαίνειν θέλων Collard)

⟨DEIPHOBUS⟩

... you bear these things lightly ... you will be plainly ... in the eyes of the Trojans.[4]

⟨HECTOR?⟩

... to produce (a?) new (*or* young) ... and wants (to act?) 15
intemperate(ly) ...

remains of five more lines

4 'You bear these things lightly through lack of spirit; but you will be plainly inferior to a slave in the eyes of the Trojans', Lefke.

62b
(col. ii)

⟨DEIPHOBUS?⟩

... free (men?)[1] ..., while slaves would be practising ... of all kinds ... of(?) them ... and ... would be absent ... 25
remains of three lines, then:

⟨HECTOR⟩

... neither building up (his estate) nor (looking to profit?), 30
he acted resolutely, though being a slave ... not ... my own

1 'free sons', Crönert; 'all free men', Snell.

ψυχῆς [ἐ]μαυτοῦ μὴ κατα[
εἰ δ᾽ ἐστὶ κρείσσω⟨ν⟩, σοῦ κόλαζε τὴν φ[ύσιν,
ὑφ᾽ ἧς ἐνίκω· κυριώτερος γὰρ εἶ.
35 ἐγὼ †δενε[ ]ρω† κεῖνον· εἰ γὰρ .[
κράτιστος [

<ΧΟΡΟΣ?>

ἀε[ὶ γὰρ] Ἕκτωρ [..]...[
τα.[..].ι αὐτοῦ καὶ δομ[

<ΕΚΑΒΗ>

οὗτος μὲν ἀεὶ τέκν[ο]ν[
40 Δηΐφοβε, καὶ τἆλλ᾽ ουθ[
ῥέξεις δ᾽ ἃ λυπούμεσθα [
κτανόντες ἄνδρα δοῦ[λον

35 δ᾽ ἐνε[ί]ρω Snell: δ᾽ ἐπαινῶ Körte   εἰ γάρ ἐ[στ᾽ ἀνὴρ
Reitzenstein

62c
(perhaps from below F 62d col. i)

<ΕΚΑΒΗ?>

beginning of one line, then:
πάρεργον [
νῦν οὖν ἐμοισο[
καὶ τοὺς λαθραι..[
5 δούλης γυναικὸς [
μή νυν ἔτ᾽ εἰσιν τ[
ἀλλ[᾽ ο]ὺκ, ἰώ μοι, δ[

P. Strasbourg 2342.3

spirit . . . And if he is superior, punish your own nature
which is what defeated you; for you have more authority[2].
(But?) I . . . him[3]; for if (he is?) the strongest . . .   35

<CHORUS?>
Hector always . . . his . . . and . . . house . . .

<HECUBA>
This man always . . . child . . . , Deiphobus, and (in?) other
matters . . . But you will do . . . which we feel distress at,   40
killing a man who is a slave . . .

2 Implication a little unclear: either 'you are more responsible
for your failure than he is', or 'you have more right to punish your-
self than to punish him'.   3 The papyrus seems to have 'But I
weave him', which Snell implausibly interpreted as 'I garland him'
(recognizing his victory). Körte's conjecture 'I congratulate him'
gives better sense.

62c
(perhaps from below F 62d col. i)

<HECUBA?>
. . . an incidental matter . . . so now for me (*or* for my) . . .
and those secret(ly?) . . . of a slave woman . . .[1] Surely they   5
are not . . . ? But . . . not—woe is me!— . . .[2]

[1] 'and those secretly saying that a slave-woman's child de-
feated free-born sons', Snell, Page.   [2] 'But it is not—woe is
me!—possible to behold this', Körte.

---

4 λέ[γοντας Snell, then καὶ τοὺς λάθρᾳ λέ[γοντας ὡς
ἐλεύθερα | δούλης γυναικὸς [παῖς ἐνίκησεν τέκνα (e.g.) Page
7 δ[υνατόν ἐστ᾽ ἰδεῖν τόδε Körte

EURIPIDES

62d

ten line-ends, perhaps from above F 62c

<ΕΚΑΒΗ>

22 κεῖνον μὲν ὄνθ' ὅς ἐστι θαυμάζειν Φρύγας,
    Πριάμου δὲ νικ…. γεραίρεσθαι δόμους.

<ΔΗΙΦΟΒΟΣ>

πῶς οὖν.[…(.)]……… ὥστ' ἔχειν καλῶς;

<ΕΚΑΒΗ>

25 …………ιδε χειρὶ δεῖ θανεῖν.

<ΔΗΙΦΟΒΟΣ>

οὐ μὴν ἄτρωτός γ' εἶσιν εἰς "Αιδου δόμους.

<ΕΚΑΒΗ>

ποῦ νυν [ἂ]ν εἴη καλλίνικ' ἔχων στέφη;

<ΔΗΙΦΟΒΟΣ>

πᾶν ἄστυ πληροῖ Τρωϊκὸν γαυρούμενος.

<ΕΚΑΒΗ>

…… δ]εῦρ', εἰς βόλον γὰρ ἂν πέσοι.

<ΔΗΙΦΟΒΟΣ>

30 ………]ιδῃς γ' ὅτ[ι κρ]ατεῖ τῶν σῶν τέκνων.

23 νίκη μὴ Page   24]λει ταῦτά γ' read doubtfully by
Crönert, Snell, Coles   25 τῇδε Crönert: σῇ δὲ Murray
30 μηπώποτ' ἐπ]ίδῃς γ' ὅτ[ι Snell (οὐ μή ποτ' Lee, ε]ἰδῇς Page)

62d
(col. ii, perhaps immediately after F 62c)

(HECUBA)

. . . that he, being who he is, should be admired by the Tro-
jans, and Priam's house (not) be honoured (by) victory!

(DEIPHOBUS)

How then (can we arrange these matters?) so that they
turn out well?

(HECUBA)

. . . he must die by (my *or* your) hand.   25

(DEIPHOBUS)

He will surely not go unwounded to Hades' halls!

(HECUBA)

Where might he be then, wearing his victor's garlands?

(DEIPHOBUS)

He is filling the whole town of Troy with his exultation.

(HECUBA)

(Let him just come) here; that way he would fall into the
net.

(DEIPHOBUS)

(You shall never come to see?) that he proves superior to
your sons.   30

⟨ΕΚΑΒΗ?⟩

ἁ]μμάτων ἔσω
]ειν σε βούλομαι
ἐσ]τὶ δοῦλος, ἀλλ' ὅμως
] ..λ[.].δ' ἐμοῖς
35   ]... φόνον
]ην ἅπαξ
]αύσεται

traces of five more line-ends, then c. 15–20 lines missing,
then:

col. iii δούλου ρ[

⟨ΗΜΙΧΟΡΙΟΝ Α′?⟩

μεταβολ[
45 νικω...[
σιν παραεθ[
οἶκον εξ.[

⟨ΗΜΙΧΟΡΙΟΝ Β′?⟩

δέσποινα[ἐ-
πὶ δεσποτ[
50 φύλλοις ν[

⟨ΑΛΕΞΑΝΔΡΟΣ?⟩

ποῦ μοι π[
Ἑκάβη, φρά[σον μοι
τὴν καλλ[ίνικον

P. Strasbourg 2343.1–2 (upper parts)

44 μεταβολ[ὰ κακῶν Crönert (but perhaps μεταβολ[αί)

70

ALEXANDER

(HECUBA?)

. . . inside the net . . . I wish to . . . you . . . he is a slave, but
still . . . my . . . murder . . . once . . . shall cease (*or* shall   35
regret) . . .

*traces of five more line-ends, then c. 15–20 lines missing,
then:*
. . . of (*or* from) a slave . . .

⟨SEMICHORUS 1?⟩

Change(s?) (from misfortunes?) . . . . the house . . .   44–47

⟨SEMICHORUS 2?⟩

The (*or* O) mistress . . . to the master . . . with (victor's)
leaves . . .   48–50

⟨ALEXANDER?⟩

Where . . . Hecuba, tell (me) . . . the victory-song . . .

<ΧΟΡΟΣ?>

πρέσβυς πε[
55 Ἑκάβην δὲ β[
beginnings of eight more lines (speaker changes at 56, 63)

62e
]ης ἤκουσ᾽ ἔπος
β]ακχεύει φρένα[
remains of two more line-ends

P. Strasbourg 2344.4

*62f (= 935 N, 42a N–Sn)
ΚΑΣΣΑΝΔΡΑ
ἀλλ᾽ ὦ φίλιπποι Τρῶες

[Longinus], *On the Sublime* 15.4

**62g (= 42b N–Sn)
ΚΑΣΣΑΝΔΡΑ
ἄκραντα γάρ μ᾽ ἔθηκε θεσπίζειν θεός,
καὶ πρὸς παθόντων κἂν κακοῖσι κειμένων
σοφὴ κέκλημαι, πρὶν παθεῖν δὲ μαίνομαι.

Plutarch, *Moralia* 821b–c; cf. Cicero, *Letters to Atticus* 8.11.3.

*62h (= 968 N, 42c N–Sn)
<ΚΑΣΣΑΝΔΡΑ>
Ἑκάτης ἄγαλμα φωσφόρου κύων ἔσῃ.

Plutarch, *Moralia* 379d; imitated by Aristophanes F 608 *PCG*
(καὶ κύων ἀκράχολος, | Ἑκάτης ἄγαλμα φωσφόρου, γενή-
σομαι)

<CHORUS?>

The old man . . . , but Hecuba . . .   55
beginnings of eight more lines (speaker changes at 56, 63)

62e

I (*or* she) heard . . . pronouncement . . . she is raving . . .
remains of two more line-ends

*62f (= 935 N, 42a N-Sn)

CASSANDRA

Come now, horse-loving Trojans . . .

**62g (= 42b N-Sn)

CASSANDRA

The god caused me to make ineffectual prophecies; by
those who have suffered and are beset by troubles I am
called wise, but until they suffer I am mad.

*62h (= 968 N, 42c N-Sn)

<CASSANDRA>

You will be a dog, a favourite of torch-bearing Hecate.[1]

---

[1] Hecuba was supposed to have turned into a dog and leapt
into the Hellespont as the Greeks departed with their captives af-
ter the sack of Troy. She was associated with the promontory of
Cynossema ('Dog's Monument'). See especially *Hecuba* 1259–73.

62i

⟨ΑΛΕΞΑΝΔΡΟΣ⟩

οἴμοι, θανοῦμαι διὰ τὸ χρήσιμον φρενῶν,
ὃ τοῖσιν ἄλλοις γίγνεται σωτηρία.

Stobaeus 3.38.20

(64 N = 42d above)

62i
⟨ALEXANDER⟩

Ah! I am going to die because of my virtue, which for others is a source of protection.

(64 N = 42d above)

ALCMEON IN PSOPHIS

and

ALCMEON IN CORINTH

Pairs of plays with identical name-characters were almost certainly not distinguished in the earliest records at Athens, and seldom in later references or citations, although Alexandrian scholars around 200 B.C. had given some of them supplementary titles. Few quotations are therefore firmly ascribed to one or other Alcmeon *(as with the two* Autolycus, Melanippe *and* Phrixus *plays).*

ALCMEON IN PSOPHIS

Van Looy (1964), 78–102 and in ed. Budé VIII.1.81–116.
   M. Delcourt, *Oreste et Alcméon* (Liège–Paris, 1939),
31–54; Webster 39–43; *LIMC* I.i.546–52 'Alkmaion'; F.
Jouan in F. Jouan (ed.), *Mythe et Politique* (Liège, 1990),
155–66; Gantz 522–8, esp. 526–7, cf. 507–8; M. Telò, *Ma-
teriali e Discussioni* 51 (2003), 163–78 (chiefly on F 74).

Alcmeon's story was told in the lost epic Alcmeonis, *proba-
bly of c. 500* B.C., *and in passing in the similarly lost but
earlier* Thebais *and the possibly later* Epigoni *('The De-
scendants'). His father Amphiaraus of Argos took part in
the disastrous expedition of the Seven against Thebes to
recover the city for Oedipus' son Polynices (see Aeschylus'
play and Euripides'* Phoenician Women*), although as a
seer he predicted his own death there. Polynices fomented
the expedition from Argos; he gave a famous necklace once
owned by Harmonia, wife of Thebes' founder Cadmus, to
Amphiaraus' wife Eriphyle, and in return she persuaded
her husband to participate (cf. F *70). Knowing that this
would cause his death, however, Amphiaraus ordered his
sons to kill their mother and to attack Thebes for a second
time (cf. F *69); an oracle foretold Alcmeon's victory in
command of the Epigoni. These details are in Apollodorus*

3.6.2, 3.7.2 and 3.7.5 (= test. *ii (a) and (b)), where the matricide follows the victory.

For killing his mother Alcmeon was persecuted by the Furies with madness (like Orestes: see Delcourt). He fled for purification to Phegeus king of Psophis in the northern Peloponnese (cf. F 71; such recourse to a foreign king was normal, as with Bellerophon in Stheneboea*). He married Phegeus' daughter Arsinoe (or Alphesiboea), and gave her the fateful necklace (cf. F 72?); but Psophis was blighted still by his presence as a matricide (Apollodorus 3.7.5 and Pausanias 8.24.8 = test. *ii (c)). He fled and sought guidance at Apollo's Delphi (also like Orestes), which directed him for absolute purification to the river god Achelous, whose daughter Callirhoe he then married; she desired the necklace, however, and sent Alcmeon unwillingly back to Psophis to recover it. Alcmeon deceived Phegeus by telling of Apollo's prediction that his madness would end only if the necklace were dedicated to the god at Delphi; as he left Psophis his true purpose was betrayed, and he was ambushed and killed by Phegeus' sons (Apollodorus 3.7.5 and Pausanias 8.24.10 = test. *ii (d)).*

A few of the certain fragments (F 69–72 above) relate to these past events. The play traced Alcmeon's adventures between the matricide and his death; it was set at Phegeus' palace in Psophis and began with excitement amongst the Chorus of young women (F 65–6) at Alcmeon's second arrival to recover the necklace. This is the view of most critics, influenced especially by Schadewaldt (who hazardously used the unassigned F 86 in reconstruction); others however begin the play with his first arrival seeking purification, so that a very long interval of dramatic time would elapse before his death. The play probably ended with a

*messenger's narrative of it, and Apollo's repeated order (if
he rather than another god pronounced the divine settle-
ment) that the necklace should indeed be dedicated to him.
There is one particular temptation for reconstructors: to
introduce elements from the Latin* Alcmeons *of Ennius and
Accius, and from the latter's* Alphesiboea, *especially a de-
scription of his madness by Alcmeon himself from Ennius
frs. 14–16 Jocelyn; the idea gains support from an appar-
ent reference to Euripides' mad Alcmeon in the 2nd cen-
tury* A.D. *Tatian,* Oration to the Greeks *24 (= test. iii, but
the text is uncertain: see Webster 40–1, Van Looy in ed.
Budé 95–7).*

Brief fragment: F 73, 'to whiten'. Other ascriptions:
Alcmene *F 88a (=* Alcmeon *F 67 N),* Bellerophon *F 304a
(=* Alcmeon *F 68 N), F 1022; see also F 953e.*

The play was produced in 438 B.C., *together with*
Cretan Women, Telephus *and the surviving* Alcestis *(see
its hypothesis =* Alcm. Psoph. *test. i). The story was ex-
tremely popular with dramatists (cf. Aristotle,* Poetics
*1453a20 on 'family stories', and Antiphanes F 189.1–16
PCG). Sophocles handled it in his* Alcmeon *and* Epigoni;
*at least six tragedies are known in title from the 4th cen-
tury, and a satyr-play and two comedies. For Ennius and
Accius see above; they were probably dependent on Eurip-
ides. Yet no certain representation of* Alcmeon in Psophis
*in ancient art is known (see LIMC 'Amphiaraos' no. 74,
Todisco Ap 174), and none is established for* Alcmeon in
Corinth *(see below).*

ΑΛΚΜΕΩΝ Ο ΔΙΑ ΨΩΦΙΔΟΣ

65
⟨ΧΟΡΟΣ⟩
ἥκω δ' ἀτενὴς ἀπ' οἴκων.

Hesychius α 8048 Latte

66
οὐδὲ πυνθάνεσθε ταῦτ', ὦ παρθένοι, τὰν τῇ πόλει;

Aristophanes, *Knights* 1302 and Schol.

(67 N = *Alcmene* F 88a)

(68 N = *Bellerophon* F 304a)

*69
⟨ΑΛΚΜΕΩΝ⟩
μάλιστα μέν μ' ἐπῆρ' ἐπισκήψας πατήρ,
ὅθ' ἅρματ' εἰσέβαινεν εἰς Θήβας ἰών.

Aristotle, *Nicomachean Ethics* 1110a26

ALCMEON IN PSOPHIS

65
‹CHORUS›
I come in haste from my house.

66
And do you not enquire, young women, about these happenings in the city?[1]

[1] In Aristophanes' comedy (422 B.C.) the Greek words make a trochaic tetrameter. Since tetrameters are (so far) unattested so early in Euripides, and the precise metrical shape is unparalleled anywhere in his work, Aristophanes may be parodying Euripides' original line.

(67 N = *Alcmene* F 88a)

(68 N = *Bellerophon* F 304a)

*69
‹ALCMEON›
I was especially moved by my father's injunction when he mounted his chariot to go to Thebes.

*70

⟨ΑΛΚΜΕΩΝ⟩

ὃς Οἰδίπουν ἀπώλεσ᾽, Οἰδίπους δ᾽ ἐμέ,
χρυσοῦν ἐνεγκὼν ὅρμον εἰς Ἄργους πόλιν.

Schol. on Pindar, *Nemeans* 4.32, and one late grammarian

71

αἷμα μητρὸς ἀπενίψατο.

Michael Italicus, in *Anecdota Oxoniensia* III.194.1 Cramer

72

ΑΛΚΜΕΩΝ

χαῖρ᾽, ὦ γεραιέ· τήν τε παῖδ᾽ ἐκδοὺς ἐμοὶ
γαμβρὸς νομίζῃ καὶ πατὴρ σωτήρ τ᾽ ἐμός.

Photius, *Lexicon*, ʻπενθεράʼ (II.74 Naber) = Suda π 963 (=
Aelius Dionysius, *Attic Vocabulary* π 34 Erbse), with ascription
to Alcmeon addressing Phegeus

1 χαῖρ᾽ Meineke: καὶ σ(ὲ) Phot., Suda, retained by some edi-
tors with loss of a line after γεραιέ   παῖδ᾽ ἐκδοὺς Nauck: παῖδα
μὴ δοὺς Suda (μὴ δῷς Phot.)   2 νομίζῃ Phot., Suda: -ου
Valckenaer

*70

⟨ALCMEON⟩

. . . who destroyed Oedipus, as Oedipus destroyed me, by bringing the golden necklace to the city of Argos.[1]

[1] Apollo is meant, whose oracle to Oedipus' father Laius began the family's destruction. Oedipus' curse on his sons caused Polynices to be exiled from Thebes and bring the necklace of Harmonia to Argos (see Introduction above).

71

He had his mother's blood washed from his hands.[1]

[1] Alcmeon purified of Eriphyle's death by Phegeus of Phocis (cf. next fragment). The Greek (unmetrical) is a paraphrase.

72

⟨ALCMEON⟩

Greetings, old sir! In giving your daughter to me as wife you are deemed my father-in-law, and also my father and my saviour.[1]

[1] For the rhetorical phrasing cf. F 866 with note.

ALCMEON IN CORINTH

Van Looy (1964), 103–31 and in ed. Budé VIII.1.81–116.
T. Zielinski, *Mnemosyne* 50 (1922), 305–27; Webster 265–8; *LIMC*, Jouan and Gantz under *Alcmeon in Psophis* above.

This play dealt with earlier adventures of Alcmeon than those of Alcmeon in Psophis. *Apollodorus 3.7.7 (= test. ii), the only account of them, attributes them to Euripides, who perhaps developed them from the now lost* Alcmeonis *or another epic, or even invented them (see below). Alcmeon had two children by the unmarried Manto ('Prophetess'), daughter of the Theban seer Tiresias (F 73a), a son Amphilochus and a daughter Tisiphone; this must have been soon after his victory at Thebes. He gave them to Creon king of Corinth to bring up; Creon's wife Merope became jealous of Tisiphone's beauty and sold her into slavery. Alcmeon bought her in ignorance; when he returned to Corinth to recover his children, she accompanied him. A typical Euripidean recognition and reunion would have followed; the son Amphilochus was foretold as founder of Amphilochian Argos in S.W. mainland Greece.*

The plot's course can nevertheless only be guessed (cf. Van Looy in ed. Budé 100): probably Alcmeon's leaving his children with Creon and the later selling-away of

Tisiphone were narrated by Apollo in his prologue (F 73a); the action, set in Corinth, began with Alcmeon's return to reclaim his children, accompanied by Tisiphone, still unknown to him just as he is unrecognised by the Corinthian chorus (F 74). Merope must have had a speaking part so as to identify the girl, who probably had a role herself; her brother Amphilochus certainly did. He is addressed in F 75 in the belief that he is Creon's son (the speaker may be Tisiphone; hardly Alcmeon?). When Amphilochus' true birth comes out, Creon flees, his high hopes of a proud succession destroyed (F *76, cf. perhaps the unassigned F 80). Apollo perhaps spoke the epilogue too, rewarding the children of a mortal woman whom he had himself raped, if unsuccessfully (cf. F 73a again; compare his 'rewarding' Creusa in Ion *with the boy's great future at Athens). As in* Alcmeon in Psophis, *however, the unassigned F 78–86 (and inferences from the fragments of Ennius and Accius) are too indefinite to aid reconstruction. Alcmeon's madness, which seems to fit better in* Alcmeon in Psophis, *is located with difficulty by some in* Alcmeon in Corinth *(Webster 266, following Zielinski).*

Brief fragment: F 77, 'who knows no paean' (i.e. Hades). Other ascriptions: F 1084, adesp. F 641 (papyrus, 28 badly damaged lines of dialogue about a matricide); cf. also F 953e, F 1068.

The play was composed shortly before 406 B.C. *and produced posthumously in 405 together with* Bacchae *and* Iphigenia in Aulis *(Schol. on Aristophanes, Frogs 66–7 = Alcm. Cor. test. i). Jouan (1990) strongly favours Zielinski's contention that even while the Peloponnesian War made Athens' inevitable defeat imminent, Euripides devised the plot as polemic against his city's old enemy Corinth:*

Alcmeon's son Amphilochus, an Argive by lineage wrongly appropriated by Creon of Corinth, is revealed as the true founder of a city and of the influence in western Greece which the Corinthians had long claimed as theirs. Both Creon and Merope are portrayed unfavourably. The play was nevertheless a 'romantic' melodrama typical of Euripides' last phase, with the separation, danger and reunion of blood relatives (cf. Alexander, Hypsipyle *and* Antiope, *but also e.g. the earlier* Cresphontes*).* No reflection of Alcmeon in Corinth *in ancient art is certainly known (see* LIMC *no. 19, Van Looy in ed. Budé 98–9, Todisco Ap 69 for rejection of a vase-painting used in reconstruction by Zielinski).*

ΑΛΚΜΕΩΝ Ο ΔΙΑ ΚΟΡΙΝΘΟΥ

73a

〈ΑΠΟΛΛΩΝ〉

κἀγὼ μὲν ἄτεκνος ἐγενόμην κείνης ἄπο,
Ἀλκμέωνι δ' ἔτεκε δίδυμα τέκνα παρθένος.

P. Oxy. 1611 fr. 1 col. iv.90–3 (a literary commentary)

74

ΧΟΡΟΣ

φίλαι φίλαι,
πρόβατε, μόλε〈τε〉· τίς ὅδε, ποδαπὸς ὁ ξένος
Κορινθίοις ἔμολεν ἀγχιάλοις;

Tzetzes, *On Tragedy*, in *Anecdota Parisiana* I.19–20 Cramer

2 πρόβατ', ἔμολε τις ὧδε Τelò

75

ὦ παῖ Κρέοντος, ὡς ἀληθὲς ἦν ἄρα,
ἐσθλῶν ἀπ' ἀνδρῶν ἐσθλὰ γίγνεσθαι τέκνα,
κακῶν δ' ὅμοια τῇ φύσει τῇ τοῦ πατρός.

Stobaeus 4.30.2

ALCMEON IN CORINTH

73a

⟨APOLLO⟩

And I myself was childless by her; but the unmarried girl
bore Alcmeon two children.[1]

[1] Manto and Amphilochus (see Introduction). In Euripides
Apollo fails to have a child by her, but Apollodorus 3.7.4 names a
son Mopsus.

74

CHORUS

Friends, friends, come forward, do come! Who is this
stranger here, from what country has he come to Corinth
by the sea?[1]

[1] Alcmeon arrives in Corinth. The Greek metre is not estab-
lished, and some editors favour a text like Telò's 'come forward;
some stranger has come here . . . '

75

Son of Creon, how true then it has proved, that from noble
fathers noble children are born, and from base ones chil-
dren resembling their father's nature.[1]

[1] Amphilochus is addressed in the belief that he is Creon's son
rather than Alcmeon's: see Introduction. Moral character inher-
ited: *Antigone* F 166, *Archelaus* F 231–2, etc.; Theognis 183–90.

*76

ὁρᾶτε τὸν τύραννον ὡς ἄπαις γέρων
φεύγει· φρονεῖν δὲ θνητὸν ὄντ᾽ οὐ χρὴ μέγα.

Stobaeus 3.22.13

*76

See how the king is fleeing into exile, childless in old age;
one who is mortal should not think proudly.[1]

---

[1] The fragment is attributed only to 'Euripides' *Alcmeon*', but
'the king' must be Creon of Corinth, for Phegeus in *Alcm. Psoph.*
is neither childless (F 72) nor in exile.

ΑΛΚΜΕΩΝ Ο ΔΙΑ ΨΩΦΙΔΟΣ
or Ο ΔΙΑ ΚΟΡΙΝΘΟΥ

78
⟨ΧΟΡΟΣ⟩

γυναῖκα καὶ ὠφελίαν
καὶ νόσον ἀνδρὶ φέρειν
μεγίσταν †ἐδίδαξα τ᾽ ἐμῷ λόγῳ†

Stobaeus 4.22.74

3 So Stob. ms. M (ἐδιδάξατ᾽ ἐμῷ editors): ἐδίδαξα τῷ ἐμῶ
ms. A (τῷμῷ Valckenaer)

78a
⟨—⟩

ὡς ἄπεπλον, ὦ δύστηνε, σῶμ᾽ ἔχεις σέθεν.

⟨ΑΛΚΜΕΩΝ⟩

ἐν τοῖσδ᾽ ἄησιν καὶ θέρος διέρχομαι.

Photius, *Lexicon* α 448 Theodoridis

79
βροτοῖς τὰ μείζω τῶν μέσων τίκτει νόσους·
θεῶν δὲ θνητοὺς κόσμον οὐ πρέπει φέρειν.

Stobaeus 3.22.8

ALCMEON IN PSOPHIS
or IN CORINTH

78
<CHORUS>

That a wife brings a husband both the greatest help and the greatest harm, †I have (both?) taught through my words† . . . [1]

[1] Text, sense and metre uncertain.

78a
< — >

How poorly dressed your body is, you poor man!

<ALCMEON>

I go through winter and summer in these things.

79

Anything beyond the middling creates trouble for men; mortals should not wear the trappings of gods.[1]

[1] If 'trappings of gods' means Harmonia's necklace, the fragment refers to the story of *Alcmeon in Psophis*, and may come from that play.

80

φεῦ ‹φεῦ›, τὰ μεγάλα μεγάλα καὶ πάσχει κακά.

Stobaeus 4.8.6

81

ταπεινὰ γὰρ χρὴ τοὺς κακῶς πεπραγότας
λέγειν, ἐς ὄγκον δ᾽ οὐκ ἄνω βλέπειν τύχης.

Stobaeus 3.22.24

82

τὰ τῶν τεκόντων ὡς μετέρχεται θεὸς
μιάσματ(α).

Stobaeus 4.25.15

83

εἰ τοῦ τεκόντος οὐδὲν ἐντρέπῃ πατρός

Priscian, *Grammar* 3.311.14 Keil–Hertz

84

ἢ τί πλέον εἶναι παῖδας ἀνθρώποις, πάτερ,
εἰ μὴ ᾽πὶ τοῖς δεινοῖσιν ὠφελήσομεν;

Stobaeus 4.25.23

85

μέτεστι τοῖς δούλοισι δεσποτῶν νόσου.

Stobaeus 4.19.23

80

Alas, greatness also suffers great disaster!

81

Those who have fared badly should speak humbly, and not
look back to their fortune in its pomp.[1]

[1] Translation insecure, but the thought resembles *Hippolytus
Veiled* F 437; also F 957.

82

. . . that god pursues for punishment foul sins committed
against fathers.[1]

[1] This sense partly paraphrases Stobaeus' chapter heading;
also possible is ' . . . sins committed by fathers' (when god punishes
their children: F 980).

83

. . . if you pay no heed to the father who got you.

84

. . . or what advantage are children for men, father, if we are
not going to help in their predicaments?

85

Slaves have a share in their masters' affliction.

EURIPIDES

86

col. i   *a few letters from glosses on col. ii.1–3*

col. ii   ἀλλ' ἕρπ' ἐς οἴκ[ους

       μητου[̣]εμη[

       ὑμῖν τ' ἀπαυδ[ῶ

       εἴ τις λακοῦσα τ[

5   μή μ' αἰτιᾶσθ[αι

       ὅστις δὲ δούλῳ φωτὶ πιστεύει βροτῶν,

       πολλὴν παρ' ἡμῖν μωρίαν ὀφλισκάνει.

       ⟨ΧΟΡΟΣ⟩

       beginnings of 13 more lines, with some part-words pre-
       served:

       8 γλυκεια[, 9 μαινομ[, 10 ὑπὸ γαία[, 11 τέκνοισ ̣[,
       16 κυλινδ[, 20 λατρ ̣ ̣αλλαβιου[

PSI 1302, ed. G. Vitelli (1953), earlier W. Schadewaldt, *Hermes*
80 (1952), 46–66 = *Hellas und Hesperien* I.516–34; re-ed. Austin,
NFE 83 (fr. 150). Assigned to *Alcm. Psoph.* by Schadewaldt, fol-
lowed by Webster 41; strongly doubted by Van Looy in ed. Budé
95–6.   Vv. 6–7 (= F 86 N): Stobaeus 4.19.25.

87

γυναῖκες, ὁρμήθητε μηδ' ἀθυμία
σχέθη τις ὑμᾶς· ταῦτα γὰρ σκεθρῶς ὁρᾶν
ἡμᾶς ἀνάγκη τοὺς νομίζοντας τέχνην.

Erotian σ 46

98

86

But go into the house . . . (*one line*) . . . and I forbid you . . . if
any (woman) crying out . . . to blame me . . . . Whoever   5
among men puts trust in a slave, incurs great folly in my
eyes.

⟨CHORUS⟩

. . . sweet . . . madly(?) . . . under the earth . . . (to?) children   10
. . . roll[1] . . . (be a?) lackey but(?) live . . .   20

[1] Possibly of a succession of woes: *Phrixus* F 822.7, Sophocles,
Antigone 590.

87

Women, go quickly and let no despondency hold you back;
for we who practise this skill[1] must look accurately at these
things.[1]

[1] Divination (suggested by 'look accurately').

ALCMENE

H. Van Looy in ed. Budé VIII.1.117–35.

Webster 92–4, 298; Trendall–Webster III.3.6–8; *LIMC* I.i.552–6 'Alkmene'; R. Aélion, *Revue de Philologie* 55 (1981), 225–36; E. Stärk, *RhM* 125 (1982), 275–303; E. Lefèvre, *Maccus Vortit Barbare* (Wiesbaden, 1982); S. West, *CQ* 34 (1984), 294–5; D. M. Christenson, *Plautus: Amphitruo* (Cambridge, 2000), 45–55; E. A. Schmidt, *Museum Helveticum* 60 (2003), 80–104; Sourvinou-Inwood 471–2; Evamaria Schmidt, *Antike Kunst* 46 (2003), 56–71 with Taf. 13–14; Taplin 170–4, 263.

Alcmene granddaughter of Perseus was married to her cousin Amphitryon and went with him into exile at Thebes after he had unintentionally killed her father Electryon. Her brothers had also been killed in a feud with the Taphians or Teleboans who held the Echinades islands off the west coast of Greece, and Alcmene refused to allow Amphitryon to consummate their marriage until he had avenged their deaths. He did this, but as he returned from the campaign Zeus visited and seduced Alcmene, in some accounts taking her husband's form and reporting his achievements, and tripling the night's length so as to increase his pleasure. Alcmene became pregnant by Zeus with the demigod Heracles, and by Amphitryon with Heracles' inferior twin brother Iphicles.

Zeus's affair with Alcmene was well known in early Greek epic (cf. Homer, Iliad 14.323–4, 19.95ff., Odyssey 11.266–8, Hesiod, Theogony 943–4), and the episode was told in full in the Hesiodic Catalogue of Women (Hes. F 195.8–63 = Shield of Heracles 1–56). The likelihood that it was the subject of Euripides' Alcmene is now strongly supported by the papyrus prologue fragment F *87b, which almost certainly belongs to this play. Neither this nor the book fragments give much guidance as to the dramatic action, but later sources—especially Apollodorus 2.4.8, Hyginus Fab. 29, the vase-paintings mentioned below, and in part Plautus' Amphitruo—seem to reflect the essentials of a plot that may well go back to Euripides and was set on the day after Zeus's visit to Alcmene (rather than the day of Heracles' birth as Webster for example prefers). Amphitryon on his return discovers that Alcmene has slept with someone else, refuses to accept her explanation that she has been deceived, and determines to kill her; Alcmene takes refuge at an altar, and Amphitryon has logs piled about the altar so as to burn her out; Zeus then saves her by causing a storm to quench the fire. Amphitryon probably learned and accepted the truth from a divine speech at the end (or perhaps from Tiresias as in Apollodorus; he appears in the most recently published vase paintings). The inclusion of the altar episode has been doubted (see Aélion), but Plautus, Rudens 86 associates a destructive wind with 'Euripides' Alcumena', and eight 4th c. South Italian vases (or fragments) portray, with varying details, Alcmene trapped on the altar-pyre and the divine inter-

vention; the earliest is dated about 400 B.C., not much later than Euripides' play (all are discussed by Evamaria Schmidt). Some scholars think the scene must have been reported since staging the flames and the storm would have been impracticable, but they could have been simulated or imagined (like for example the earthquake in Erechtheus, *F 370.45–54), and scenes of refuge at the altar were very popular in tragedy.*

Within such an outline F 88 may belong with F *87b in the prologue, F 92 and 95–6 in an early scene where Amphitryon accused Alcmene of succumbing to a wealthy mortal (a gold cup and necklace given to Alcmene by Zeus may have been featured here: cf. Pausanias 5.18.3), F 88a (if from this play) in a speech of Alcmene defending herself, F 90 in the altar scene, F 89 in the god's speech at the end, and F 103 in a final choral comment welcoming the reconciliation of husband and wife. F 97–99 and F 102 suggest that at some point Amphitryon rejected an attempt to console him for being cuckolded, and F 104 perhaps refers to Zeus's 'long night' with Alcmene. Hermes, who appears with Zeus on the two earliest vases and speaks the prologue of Plautus' Amphitruo, may have spoken either the prologue or the god's speech at the end. Most scholars think it unlikely that Zeus himself appeared in the play or as deus ex machina *as in Plautus' Amphitruo (but West and Sourvinou-Inwood argue for his appearance as* deus). *A man named Antenor who assists Amphitryon on one of the vases (LIMC no. 5, Trendall–Webster III.3.8, Todisco P 15) could have accompanied or preceded the victorious Amphitryon in the play.*

Brief fragment: F 104 'gloomy night'. Other ascriptions: F 87 (see Alcmeon); *F 1002.*

The play probably resembled Ion *in combining humour with high emotions and exploring the tragic potential of human misapprehensions manipulated by uncaring gods. The metrical resolutions in F *87b.15 and (if from* Alcmene) *F 88a.1 hint at a date not earlier than about 420 (so* Alcmene *might possibly have been produced with the more 'tragic'* Heracles *which concerns the hero's later life and features the aged Amphitryon). Other* Alcmene *tragedies are recorded, with little or no detail, for Aeschylus and Ion of Chios in the 5th century, Astydamas and Dionysius of Syracuse in the 4th; Sophocles'* Amphitryon *and Accius'* Amphitruo *appear to have had different subject matter. Plautus' extant 'tragicomedy'* Amphitruo *has some strongly Euripidean features, but it is hard to prove a direct dependence or to use* Amphitruo *as a basis for reconstructing* Alcmene. *The comic* Long Night *by Aristophanes' contemporary Plato, the burlesque* Amphitryon *by Rhinthon of Syracuse (around 300* B.C.), *and a hypothetical Latin tragedy based on Euripides have all been thought of as possible intermediaries. For recent discussions of* Amphitruo *and* Alcmene *see Stärk, Lefèvre, Christenson (a balanced survey), and E. A. Schmidt. The impact of* Amphitruo *on European literature has been immense: see* OGCMA I.99–102; L. Shero, TAPA 87 (1956), 192–240; M. Kunze et al., Amphitryon: ein griechisches Motif in der europäischen Literatur *(Münster, 1993).*

ΑΛΚΜΗΝΗ

*87b

remains of six lines

Θήβας επι‿‿μοις τοισ[
ληισταὶ γὰρ [‿]νι‿‿‿‿[
Τάφιοι μολόντες τασα[
10   νήσους ἁλιτενεῖς, ἃς καλ[οῦσ᾽ Ἐχινάδας.
ἡ δ᾽ ἐξομεῖται μηδενὸ[ς
ὃς μὴ μετέλθοι συγγόν[ων
Ταφίους· λιγὺς δὲ χρησ[μὸς
Ἀμφιτρύων γὰρ ἐπὶ γά[μοις
20   *remains of one more line*

P. Hamburg 119 col. iii, ed. E. Siegmann (1954); re-ed. Austin, *NFE* 84–5 (fr. 151)

11 μηδενὸ[ς ψαύσειν γάμων (e.g.) Kassel, Snell
12 συγγόν[ων ὑπὲρ φόνου (e.g.) Siegmann

88
πολὺς δ᾽ ἀνεῖρπε κισσός, εὐφυὴς κλάδος,
ἀηδόνων μουσεῖον

Schol. on Aristophanes, *Frogs* 93 (similarly Suda χ 187)

2 ἀηδόνων Meineke: χελιδόνων Schol. Ar., Sud.

ALCMENE

*87b

(remains of six lines) . . . Thebes . . . for Taphian brigands coming . . . sea-bound islands which are called (Echinades). But she will vow not (to accept marriage with) any man who does not go after the Taphians (for the killing of her) brothers. But a clear-voiced oracle . . . For Amphitryon . . . for marriage . . . *(remains of one more line)*

88

Ivy crept up abundantly, a vigorous branch, a nightingales' place of song . . .[1]

[1] Zeus may have caused ivy to enclose Alcmene's chamber while he visited her.

88a (= *Alcmeon* F 67 N)

ὁ φόβος, ὅταν τι‹ς› σώματος μέλλῃ πέρι
λέγειν καταστὰς εἰς ἀγῶν᾽ ἐναντίον,
τό τε στόμ᾽ εἰς ἔκπληξιν ἀνθρώπων ἄγει
τὸν νοῦν τ᾽ ἀπείργει μὴ λέγειν ἃ βούλεται.
5 {τῷ μὲν γὰρ ἔνι κίνδυνος, ὁ δ᾽ ἀθῷος μένει.}
ὅμως δ᾽ ἀγῶνα τόνδε δεῖ μ᾽ ὑπεκδραμεῖν·
ψυχὴν γὰρ ἆθλα τιθεμένην ἐμὴν ὁρῶ.

Stobaeus 3.8.12 ms. S (with play title abbreviated as ἀκμί, i.e. either *Alcmene* or *Alcmeon*)

5 Verse deleted by Wilamowitz   6 ὑπεκδραμεῖν is suspect, corrected to ὑπερδραμεῖν in Stob. ms. Paris. 1985: ἤδη δραμεῖν Bergk

89

οὐ γάρ ποτ᾽ εἴων Σθένελον εἰς τὸν εὐτυχῆ
χωροῦντα τοῖχον τῆς δίκης ‹σ᾽› ἀποστερεῖν.

Schol. on Aristophanes, *Frogs* 536

2 ‹σ᾽› Grotius

90

πόθεν δὲ πεύκης πανὸν ἐξηῦρες λαβεῖν;

Pollux 10.117

106

88a (= *Alcmeon* F 67 N)

When someone is about to speak in defence of his life and
has entered into a trial face to face, fear makes him tongue-
tied before his audience and hinders his mind from saying
what it wants to.[1] {For he is at risk, while his opponent re-
mains unaffected.} Nevertheless I must get safely through
this trial, for I see that in it my own life is at stake.

[1] The speaker may have been Alcmene even though the argu-
ment is put in masculine terms, as such generalizations usually are
(e.g. *Andromeda* F 119).

89

For I never allowed Sthenelus to get on the fortunate side[1]
and deprive you of your right.

[1] The source explains that moving to the 'fortunate' (i.e. more
sheltered) side of a ship in a storm was proverbial for looking-
after yourself. 'You' (restored to the text by Grotius) will be
Amphitryon, addressed by the god who appeared at the end of the
play. Sthenelus was Amphitryon's brother and dynastic rival, and
father of Eurystheus who through Hera's contrivance inherited
the power that Zeus had intended for Heracles (Homer, *Iliad*
19.95ff; cf. our Introduction to *Eurystheus*). According to Apol-
lodorus 2.4.6, Sthenelus used the killing of Electryon as a pretext
for banishing Amphitryon.

90

Where did you contrive to get a pine torch?

91

⟨ΧΟΡΟΣ⟩

ἀτρέκεια δ᾽ ἄριστον ἀνδρὸς ἐν πόλει δικαίου.

Stobaeus 4.1.24, supplying a verb πέλει at end

92

ἴστω τ᾽ ἄφρων ὢν ὅστις ἄνθρωπος γεγὼς
δῆμον κολούει χρήμασιν γαυρούμενος.

Stobaeus 4.4.9

93

ἀεὶ δ᾽ ἀρέσκειν τοῖς κρατοῦσι· ταῦτα γὰρ
δούλοις ἄριστα· κἀφ᾽ ὅτῳ τεταγμένος
εἴη τις, ἁνδάνοντα δεσπόταις ποιεῖν.

Stobaeus 4.19.27

94

τῶν γὰρ δυναστῶν πλεῖστος ἐν πόλει λόγος.

Stobaeus 4.4.7

95

ἀλλ᾽ οὐδὲν ηὐγένεια πρὸς τὰ χρήματα·
τὸν γὰρ κάκιστον πλοῦτος εἰς πρώτους ἄγει.

Stobaeus 4.31.35

96

σκαιόν τι χρῆμα πλοῦτος ἥ τ᾽ ἀπειρία.

Stobaeus 4.31.72

91

<CHORUS>

A just man's honesty is a city's best asset.

92

A man who is merely human yet disdains the people and prides himself on his wealth should understand that he is a fool.

93

. . . and always to please those in power—that is the best thing for slaves—and whatever job one is given, to do what gratifies one's masters.

94

What the powerful say carries the most weight in a city.

95

Good birth is nothing in comparison with money. Wealth brings the lowest of men into the highest rank.[1]

[1] For the thought cf. *Danae* F 326.1–5 with note.

96

Wealth joined with ignorance[1] is a boorish thing.

[1] The word ἀπειρία suggests ἀπειροκαλία, 'unfamiliarity with the finer things of life', 'poor taste'; cf. *Auge* F 269.3.

97

ἀλλ' οὐ γὰρ ὀρθῶς ταῦτα, γενναίως ⟨δ'⟩ ἴσως
ἔπραξας· αἰνεῖσθαι δὲ δυστυχῶν ἐγὼ
μισῶ· λόγος γὰρ τοὖργον οὐ νικᾷ ποτε.

Stobaeus 4.35.32

3 λόγος Porson: λογισμὸς Stob. ms. S (-οὺς mss. MA)

98

ἀλλ' εὖ φέρειν χρὴ συμφορὰς τὸν εὐγενῆ.

Stobaeus 4.44.48; [Menander], *Monostichs* 721 Jaekel

99

τὸν εὐτυχοῦντα χρῆν σοφὸν πεφυκέναι.

Stobaeus 4.4.12

χρῆν Meineke: χρὴ Stob.

100

θάρσει, τάχ' ἂν γένοιτο· πολλά τοι θεὸς
κἀκ τῶν ἀέλπτων εὔπορ' ἀνθρώποις τελεῖ.

Stobaeus 4.47.9

101

ἀλλ' ἡμέρα τοι πολλὰ καὶ μέλαινα νὺξ
τίκτει βροτοῖσιν.

Stobaeus 4.34.21

97

You did this improperly, though perhaps honestly. I dislike being praised when I am suffering misfortune, for what is said never overcomes the reality.

98

The well-born man should bear misfortunes well.

99

A man enjoying good fortune had best be wise.

100

Cheer up, it might happen. God brings men many good outcomes even from desperate situations.

101

Day and dark night produce many things for mortals.

102

σοφώτεροι γὰρ συμφορὰς τὰς τῶν πέλας
πάντες διαθρεῖν ἢ τύχας τὰς οἴκοθεν.

Stobaeus 4.49.4

2 διαθρεῖν Valckenaer: διαιρεῖν Stob.

103

⟨ΧΟΡΟΣ⟩

δεινόν τι τέκνων φίλτρον ἔθηκεν
θεὸς ἀνθρώποις.

Stobaeus 4.26.6

102

Everyone is cleverer at analysing their neighbours' misfortunes than their own.

103

⟨CHORUS⟩

God has made children a formidable love charm for men.[1]

---

[1] Similarly *Protesilaus* F 652, *Danae* F 323; cf. *Danae* F 316, *Dictys* F 345–6 etc.

ALOPE

H. Van Looy in ed. Budé VIII.1.137–46.

B. Borecký in *Studia antiqua A. Salač . . . oblata* (Prague, 1955), 82–9; Webster 94; *LIMC* I.i.572–3 'Alope'; Huys, *The Tale*, relevant sections; I. Karamanou, *AC* 72 (2003), 25–40.

Alope was the daughter of the great wrestler Cercyon, who challenged and killed travellers on the road between Megara and Eleusis until Theseus outwrestled and killed him. Raped by Poseidon, she became the mother of Hippothoon, one of the ten tribal heroes of democratic Athens. Alope's story is known largely from Hyginus, Fab. 187 (test. *ii b below): she had her illicit child exposed to die, but he was fed by a mare and rescued by a herdsman who gave him to another herdsman to rear as his own; but the herdsmen quarrelled over the ownership of the identifying tokens left with the baby, and when they brought their quarrel before Cercyon the true origin of the child was revealed. Cercyon imprisoned Alope and ordered the child exposed again, but again he was fed by the mare and rescued. His subsequent upbringing is not described, and Hyginus' narrative ends with Theseus later killing Cercyon and restoring Hippothoon to his birthright, and with Poseidon transforming Alope into a spring.

*Earlier reconstructions attempted to fit all of Hyginus'
narrative, including the later events, within Euripides'
plot (and Karamanou revives the idea that the killing of
Cercyon by Theseus was reported in a messenger-speech).
Since Borecky's study, however, it has been widely ac-
cepted that the play's action will have proceeded only
as far as the imprisonment of Alope and re-exposure of
Hippothoon, with the later events—or some of them—
being foretold in a speech from a god (perhaps Poseidon
himself) at the end; such a speech must at least have pro-
claimed Cercyon's error and Hippothoon's heroic future.
The fate of Alope remains uncertain: others in her situation
survived to encounter their sons in later life (Auge in*
Telephus, *Melanippe in* Wise Melanippe *or at least its se-
quel, Tyro in Sophocles'* Tyro). *Huys suggests it is unlikely
that Poseidon failed to protect her, but no sequel for her is
known and it seems possible that in this case Cercyon's will
was fulfilled (like Theseus' in* Hippolytus) *and the transfor-
mation of Alope into a spring introduced as a consolation
for her sad fate. The spring at Eleusis is mentioned by
Hesychius α 3239, and Pausanias 1.39.3 describes a memo-
rial of Alope on the Eleusis–Megara road, with the sup-
posed palaestra of Cercyon nearby.*

*The usually accepted outline implies speaking roles at
least for Alope, her Nurse, Cercyon, the two Herdsmen
whose dispute leads to Cercyon's discovery of his daugh-
ter's child, and Poseidon or another god at the end. A cho-
rus of local men associated with Cercyon and his exercise
ground is introduced in F 105. Alope's predicament is the
subject of F 106 (probably from a prologue narrative by
Alope or the Nurse) and F 107 (perhaps likewise, but possi-
bly a later jibe by Cercyon), while F 108 presumably refers*

to the Nurse's assistance. F 109–111 probably belong to Cercyon's condemnation of Alope. The extant arbitration scene (vv. 218–375) of Menander's Epitrepontes ('Men at Arbitration'), involving a similar dispute between two countrymen over the valuables found with an exposed child, was very probably modelled on the Euripidean scene; but the degree of similarity cannot be determined (for discussion of Menander's inventive adaptation see C. Cusset, Ménandre ou la comédie tragique [Paris, 2003], 168–87).

Brief fragments: F **105a 'Don't be sullen'; F 112a (= 845 N) 'unwarmed by the sun'; F 113 'to sell'. Other ascription: F 1061.

The play's date is unknown, and no reliable guidance can be had from the content or metrical style of its few fragments. Pausanias 1.14.3 ascribes an Alope to Choerilus, one of the earliest Athenian tragedians, and Aeschylus produced a satyr play Cercyon, presumably about his wrestling bout with Theseus, from which a few words are preserved. We know from Aristotle, Nicomachean Ethics 1150b.6–10 of an Alope by Carcinus (early 4th c.) in which Cercyon's grief over his daughter's violation was sympathetically treated: see TrGF 70 F 1b.

ΑΛΟΠΗ

test. iia

Ἀλόπη· Λυκοῦργος ἐν τῷ περὶ τῆς ἱερείας (fr. 33 Blass,
fr. VI.6 Conomis)· Κερκυόνος θυγάτηρ, ἐξ ἧς καὶ Ποσει-
δῶνος Ἱπποθόων ὁ τῆς Ἱπποθοωντίδος φυλῆς ἐπώνυμος,
ὡς Ἑλλάνικός τε ἐν β΄ Ἀτθίδος (FGrH 4 F 43) καὶ
Εὐριπίδης ἐν τῷ ὁμωνύμῳ δράματι . . .

Harpocration, *Lexicon to the Ten Attic Orators*, A 81 Keaney

test. *iib

ALOPE. Alope Cercyonis filia formosissima cum esset, Nep-
tunus eam compressit, qua ex compressione peperit infantem,
quem inscio patre nutrici dedit exponendum. Qui cum exposi-
tus esset, equa uenit et ei lac praestabat. (2) Quidam pas-
tor equam persecutus uidit infantem atque eum sustulit, qui
ueste regia indutum cum in casam tulisset, alter compastor ro-
gauit ut sibi eum infantem donaret. (3) Ille ei donauit sine
ueste; cum autem inter eos iurgium esset, quod qui puerum
acceperat insignia ingenuitatis reposceret, ille autem non da-
ret, contendentes ad regem Cercyonem uenerunt et conten-
dere coeperunt. (4) Ille autem qui infantem donatum accepe-

Hyginus, *Fab*. 187

118

ALOPE

Alope: Lycurgus in (his speech) *On the Priestess*: daughter of
Cercyon, and mother by Poseidon of Hippothoon the epony-
mous hero of the Hippothoontid tribe, as Hellanicus (relates)
in Book 2 of his *Atthis*, and Euripides in his play named after
her . . .

test. *iib

ALOPE. Alope daughter of Cercyon was very beautiful, and
so Neptune raped her; consequently she bore a child, and
without her father's knowledge gave it to her nurse to be ex-
posed. When he had been exposed, a mare came and supplied
him with milk. (2) A herdsman who had followed the mare saw
the child and took him up, and when he had taken him into his
hut, dressed in royal clothing, another fellow-herdsman asked
him to give him the child. (3) He gave him to him without the
clothing; and when a quarrel broke out between them as the
one who had received the child demanded the marks of his
free birth,[1] and the other would not give them, they took their
dispute to Cercyon and began to argue. (4) The one who had
received the child began to demand the marks, and when

---

[1] Presumably a family symbol woven into the cloth.
[2] The name means 'Swift-horse'.

rat, repetere insignia coepit; quae cum allata essent, et ag-
nosceret Cercyon ea esse ex ueste scissa filiae suae, Alopes
nutrix timens regi indicium fecit infantem eum Alopes esse,
qui filiam iussit ad necem includi, infantem autem proici.
(5) Quem iterum equa nutriebat, pastores iterum inuentum
sustulerunt, sentientes eum deorum numine educari, atque
nutrierunt, nomenque ei imposuerunt Hippothoum. (6) The-
seus cum ea iter faceret a Troezene Cercyonem interfecit.
Hippothous autem ad Theseum uenit regnaque auita rogauit;
cui Theseus libens dedit, cum sciret eum Neptuni filium esse,
unde ipse genus ducebat. (7) Alopes autem corpus Neptunus
in fontem commutauit, qui ex nomine Alopes est cognomina-
tus.

105

ὁρῶ μὲν ἀνδρῶν τόνδε γυμνάδα στόλον
στείχονθ᾽ ἑῷον ἐκ τρόχων πεπαυμένον.

Ammonius, *On Similar and Different Words* 478 (= Tryphon,
On Attic Prosody fr. 11 von Velsen)

2 στείχονθ᾽ ἑῷον Dindorf: στείχοντα θεωρὸν Ammon.

106

. . . γέμουσαν κύματος θεοσπόρου . . .

Eustathius on Homer, *Iliad* 6.474 (and again on *Iliad* 21.306,
Odyssey 9.486 and 11.253), citing 'Euripides in *Cercyon*'

107

πλήσας δὲ νηδὺν οὐδ᾽ ὄναρ κατ᾽ εὐφρόνην
φίλοις ἔδειξεν αὐτόν.

Eustathius on Homer, *Odyssey* 21.79 (cf. on *Od.* 8.495), citing
'Euripides in *Cercyon*'

these had been brought, and Cercyon recognized that they had been cut from his daughter's dress, Alope's nurse in fear informed the king that the child was Alope's. Cercyon ordered his daughter to be shut away to die, and the child to be cast forth. (5) Again the mare fed him, and again the herdsmen took him up, sensing that he was being reared by divine power; they fed him, and gave him the name Hippothous.[2] (6) When Theseus passed that way from Troezen, he killed Cercyon, and Hippothous came to Theseus and requested his grandfather's kingdom. Theseus gladly gave it to him since he knew he was a son of Neptune, from whom he himself traced his birth. (7) Neptune transformed Alope's body into a spring which gets its name from hers.

105

I see coming here in the early morning a group of men, stripped for exercise after finishing at the track.

106

. . . heavy with god-sown child . . .

107

Having filled her womb he (Poseidon) did not show himself to his loved one even as a dream in the night.

108

γυνὴ γυναικὶ σύμμαχος πέφυκέ πως.

Stobaeus 4.22.150

109

⟨ΚΕΡΚΤΩΝ⟩

οὐ μὴν σύ γ᾽ ἡμᾶς τοὺς τεκόντας ᾐδέσω.

Etymologicum Genuinum AB 'ᾐδέσθην,' cf. *Etym. Magnum*
p. 420.16 Gaisford (= Orus, *Attic Lexicon* fr. B 76 Alpers)

110

⟨ΚΕΡΚΤΩΝ?⟩

ἐγὼ δ᾽, ὃ μὲν μέγιστον, ἄρξομαι λέγειν
ἐκ τοῦδε πρῶτον· πατρὶ πείθεσθαι χρεὼν
παῖδας νομίζειν τ᾽ αὐτὸ τοῦτ᾽ εἶναι δίκην.

Stobaeus 4.25.29; Orion, Euripidean Appendix 12 Haffner

111

⟨ΚΕΡΚΤΩΝ?⟩

τί δῆτα μοχθεῖν δεῖ γυναικεῖον γάμον
φρουροῦντας; αἱ γὰρ εὖ τεθραμμέναι πλέον
σφάλλουσιν οἴκους τῶν παρημελημένων.

Stobaeus 4.23.17

(112 N = *Aeolus* F **38a)

108
A woman is a woman's natural ally.

109
<CERCYON?>
Yet you showed no respect for us, your own parents.[1]

[1] The Greek plurals may suggest singular 'me, your own father' (cf. F 110).

110
<CERCYON?>
I shall start my argument first of all with this, the main point: children should obey their father and consider this in itself to be right conduct.

111
<CERCYON?>
Why should we exert ourselves safeguarding a woman's marriage, when the well-raised ones do their families more damage than those who have been neglected?

(112 N = *Aeolus* F **38a)

ANDROMEDA

F. Bubel, *Euripides, Andromeda* (Stuttgart, 1991); R. Klimek-Winter, *Andromedatragödien* (Stuttgart, 1993: with Sophocles, Livius Andronicus, Ennius, Accius); H. Van Looy in ed. Budé VIII.1 (1998), 147–90; J. Gibert in *SFP* II.133–68.

Webster 192–9, 304–5; Rau, *Paratragodia* 65–89; Trendall–Webster III.3.10–13; *LIMC* I.i.774–90 'Andromeda I' (also VI.i.6–10 'Kepheus I', VII.i.342–5 'Perseus and Andromeda'); Aélion (1986) 171–7, 180–3; Gantz 211–2, 307–9; J. Gibert, *ICS* 24–25 (1999–2000), 75–91; M. Wright, *Euripides' Escape Tragedies* (Oxford, 2005: on *Helen, Andromeda, Iphigenia in Tauris*); Taplin 174–84.

Perseus' birth and his return to the island of Seriphos with the head of the Gorgon Medusa were the subjects of Euripides' Danae *and* Dictys *(see later in this volume). In* Andromeda, *produced much later in 412 B.C., Perseus while returning to Seriphos reached Ethiopia (here probably located on the western borders of the inhabited earth: F 145) and found the princess Andromeda exposed as a sacrifice to a sea monster sent by Poseidon to afflict her father Cepheus' kingdom (his wife Cassiepeia had insulted Poseidon's daughters the Nereids by claiming to be more beauti-*

ful than them). Perseus fell in love with Andromeda, killed the monster and released the princess, who then defied her parents' opposition and departed with him to be his bride and mother of the future kings of Mycenae. Perseus' marriage with Andromeda is attested in the Hesiodic Catalogue of Women *(Hes. F 135.6), and a mid-6th c. Corinthian vase painting shows him battling against the sea monster with her help (LIMC no. 1); but very little is known about pre-Euripidean versions of the story, which included a play by Sophocles (see below). For complete accounts we rely on later sources, especially Apollodorus 2.4.3 (probably drawing on the 5th c. Athenian mythographer Pherecydes) and Ovid,* Metamorphoses *4.668–5.238 which has Euripidean features but is also eclectic and inventive. Excerpts from astronomical handbooks concerning the constellations Andromeda, Cassiepeia and Cepheus (= test. iiia–b, reproduced in part below) refer to Euripides' account and include a few helpful details. The play's novelties and impact are vividly attested in the parody of its opening scenes in Aristophanes'* Women at the Thesmophoria *(1008–1134), produced in the following year; here a kinsman of Euripides has joined a women's ritual gathering in order to defend the poet against the women's charges of misogyny; he is exposed in a scene parodying Euripides'* Telephus *(see our Introduction there), and Euripides in his attempts to rescue him appears first as Menelaus rescuing Helen, then as Perseus rescuing Andromeda.*

Aristophanes' parody and the ancient scholia provide glimpses of the tragedy's opening scenes. Its setting was the seashore, with the heroine bound to a rock in front of a cave (the stage building). It opened, uniquely, with an anapaestic monody of Andromeda awaiting the monster's approach (F 114–6), her laments being echoed from the cave by the offstage voice of Echo (an easy target for Aristophanes' comic parody); scholia identify F 114 as the play's first lines and indicate that Echo's responses began as early as v. 6. The monody must have been long enough to convey the information usually given in a prologue speech, but our next fragments (F 117–8) have Andromeda dismissing Echo as she greets the arriving Chorus of sympathetic friends, and F 119–20 and 122 come from a lyric dialogue between her and the Chorus (monody and lyric dialogue are similarly deployed in Electra, Ion and Hypsipyle). The next known event, Perseus' arrival, probably followed soon after; his spectacular appearance on the theatrical crane was also made much of by Aristophanes (F 124). After first mistaking her for a sculpture (F 125) and overcoming her modest reluctance to converse with him (F 126), Perseus ascertained her plight (F 127–8?) and, struck with love, undertook to save her in return for her hand (F 129, 129a, probably also F 130–1 and 135; his account of the Gorgon adventure, F 133–134a, could come here or later). His famous demand for Eros' help (F 136) came in a scene-ending speech as he departed on his mission, and his triumphant return was heralded, naturally, by a messenger's report of the slaying of the monster (F 145–6), surely delivered to the still captive Andromeda, now to be released by the returning hero.

Beyond this the play's action is very unclear, except that it involved resistance to the marriage of Perseus and Andromeda and thus had a general structural similarity with plays such as Archelaus (where the king double-crossed the hero after promising him his daughter in re-

turn for his aid), or Alexander *(where the hero's athletic successes provoked hostility from Hecuba and Deiphobus). In Ovid, Cepheus and Cassiepeia promise Andromeda to Perseus as the monster approaches, and resistance comes later from Cepheus' brother Phineus who has expected to marry Andromeda himself and is turned to stone by the Gorgon's head when he attacks Perseus. Apollodorus' summary is essentially similar (Hyginus, Fab. 64 has Cepheus plotting with a fiancé named Agenor against Perseus), but the astronomical sources suggest that in Euripides Andromeda made the promise (cf. F 129, 129a, 131) and her parents tried to undo it; there is little sign in the 4th c. vases of a substantial role for Phineus (or, for that matter, Cassiepeia). If the astronomical sources are accurate, the second half of the play would seem to have consisted largely of debates amongst parents and lovers about Andromeda's duty to her parents, her attachment to Perseus, and his suitability as a husband (cf. F 138, 138a, F 141). But a more eventful plot remains possible and not unlikely—for example, Cepheus revoking an agreement to give Perseus his daughter under pressure from his haughty wife, or Phineus intervening violently (F 147–8 might suggest Ovid's celebratory feast at which the fighting broke out). Whatever conflict there was will have been resolved by Athena's appearance at the end, validating Andromeda's departure with Perseus and her dynastic future.*

Brief fragments: F 148 'final' (designating the third bowl of wine mixed at symposia and dedicated to Zeus the Preserver), F 155 'spoils of the hunt', F 155a (= 1096 N) 'dim vision', F 156 'gets in return' (= 'saves by interceding', if the text of this lexicon entry is correct). Other ascriptions: F 881, **889 (= Women at the Thesmophoria *1122*),

127

897, **955h, 985, 1013; adesp. F 537 'It is better to give succour; I would rather die gloriously than live ingloriously . . .' Further tragic-sounding bits from the scene in Women at the Thesmophoria *have been attributed to* Andromeda *by various scholars, especially vv. 1047–55, 1056, 1058, 1059 (= F 114a N–Sn), 1105–6 (= F 125a N–Sn), 1113, 1116–8, 1122, 1128–9 (= F 139 N), 1134; but these are at least as likely to be Aristophanes' own inventions.*

The scholia on Aristophanes (= test. iia–c) attest that Andromeda *was produced with* Helen *at the Dionysia of 412, and* Women at the Thesmophoria *in the following year (Wright suggests that* Iphigenia in Tauris *and* Cyclops *were the companion pieces of 412). The astronomical sources say that Sophocles'* Andromeda *treated the same story, but this play is represented only by a dozen uninformative fragments; a date near 450 is usually inferred from a group of mid-5th century Attic vases showing Andromeda being tied to stakes by Ethiopians under Cepheus' direction, or found by Perseus in that posture (see* LIMC *nos. 2–6 with Schauenburg's commentary, Trendall–Webster III.2.1–3; J. R. Green,* Theatre in Ancient Greek Society *[London, 1994], 20–2). The continuing impact of Euripides' play can be seen in* Frogs *52–4, where Dionysus admits a longing for the now dead playwright stirred by a reading of this play, and it must have contributed to the immense popularity of the subject in the art of the 4th century and later—but here as in Ovid there is a constant difficulty in disentangling the Euripidean details. Nothing is known of later Greek tragedies by Lycophron and Phrynichus II (TrGF I nos. 100 and 212) or of a comedy by Antiphanes, and only a little more of*

ANDROMEDA

Latin tragedies by Livius Andronicus, Ennius and Accius (on these see Klimek-Winter: Ennius may have used Euripides' plot, Accius Sophocles'). The story's ancient popularity is undiminished in the art, literature and music of more recent times (OGCMA II.875–83).

ΑΝΔΡΟΜΕΔΑ

test. iiia (a)

(15) Κηφέως· . . . ἦν δέ, ὡς Εὐριπίδης φησίν, Αἰθιόπων βασιλεύς, Ἀνδρομέδας δὲ πατήρ· τὴν δ' αὑτοῦ θυγατέρα δοκεῖ παραθεῖναι τῷ κήτει βοράν, ἣν Περσεὺς ὁ Διὸς διέσωσε· δι' ἣν καὶ αὐτὸς ἐν τοῖς ἄστροις ἐτέθη Ἀθηνᾶς γνώμῃ.

(17) Ἀνδρομέδας· αὕτη κεῖται ἐν τοῖς ἄστροις διὰ τὴν Ἀθηνᾶν, τῶν Περσέως ἄθλων ὑπόμνημα, διατεταμένη τὰς χεῖρας, ὡς καὶ προετέθη τῷ κήτει· ἀνθ' ὧν σωθεῖσα ὑπὸ τοῦ Περσέως οὐχ εἵλετο τῷ πατρὶ συμμένειν οὐδὲ τῇ μητρί, ἀλλ' αὐθαίρετος εἰς τὸ Ἄργος ἀπῆλθε μετ' ἐκείνου, εὐγενές τι φρονήσασα. λέγει δὲ καὶ Εὐριπίδης σαφῶς ἐν τῷ περὶ αὐτῆς γεγραμμένῳ δράματι.

[Eratosthenes], *Catasterisms* 15 and 17; similarly in Latin Hyginus, *Astronomy* 2.9 and 2.11, Schol. on Germanicus Caesar's translation of Aratus' *Phaenomena*, 184ff., 201ff. (pp. 77, 78 Breysig), and other derivative sources.

test. iiib

Cassiepia: De hac Euripides et Sophocles et alii complures dixerunt ut gloriata sit se forma Nereidas praestare. Pro quo facto inter sidera sedens in siliquastro constituta est . . .

ANDROMEDA

(15) (Constellation) of Cepheus: ... He was, as Euripides says, king of the Ethiopians and father of Andromeda. He is supposed to have offered his own daughter as food to the sea monster, and Zeus's son Perseus rescued her. Because of her he too was placed amongst the stars by the decision of Athena.

(17) (Constellation) of Andromeda: She was placed amongst the stars through Athena's agency, to commemorate Perseus' labours, with her arms stretched out just as when she was exposed to the sea monster. Because of this, when she was rescued by Perseus she refused to stay with her father and her mother and chose to go away with Perseus to Argos, making a noble decision. Euripides gives an accurate account in the play he wrote about her.

test. iiib

Cassiepeia: Euripides, Sophocles and many others have told how she boasted that she excelled the Nereids in beauty. For this reason she is placed on a throne as she sits amongst the stars ...

Hyginus, *Astronomy* 2.10

131

EURIPIDES

114

ΑΝΔΡΟΜΕΔΑ

Ὦ Νὺξ ἱερά,
　ὡς μακρὸν ἵππευμα διώκεις
ἀστεροειδέα νῶτα διφρεύουσ'
αἰθέρος ἱερᾶς
5　　τοῦ σεμνοτάτου δι' Ὀλύμπου.

ΗΧΩ
　　—δι' Ὀλύμπου.

Aristophanes, *Women at the Thesmophoria* 1065–9 with
Schol.; vv. 1–3: Schol. on Theocritus 2.165/166b; vv. 1–2: Schol.
on Oribasius, *Medical Collections*, lib. incert. 42.1; v. 1: Schol. on
Homer, *Iliad* 24.12–13

115

ΑΝΔΡΟΜΕΔΑ

τί ποτ' Ἀνδρομέδα
περίαλλα κακῶν μέρος ἐξέλαχον,
θανάτου τλήμων μέλλουσα τυχεῖν;

Aristophanes, *Women at the Thesmophoria* 1070–2 with
Schol.

115a (= 121 N)

⟨ΑΝΔΡΟΜΕΔΑ⟩

ἐκθεῖναι κήτει φορβάν

Schol. on Aristophanes, *Birds* 348

ANDROMEDA

114
(Opening of the play)

ANDROMEDA

O sacred Night, how long is your chariot-drive across the
sacred heaven's starry expanse, through holiest Olympus![1] 5

ECHO

'Olympus!'[2]

[1] 'Olympus', originally the mountain, came to be used of the
heaven as home of the gods.   [2] The echo is sung by Euripi-
des in Aristophanes' play and ascribed by the scholiast to Echo.
Some editors doubt that her interventions began so early in Eu-
ripides' play.

115
ANDROMEDA

Why have I, Andromeda, been given a share of suffering
above all others—I, who in my misery here am facing
death?

115a (= 121 N)
‹ANDROMEDA›

. . . to set (me) out as food for the sea monster . . .

116
⟨ΑΝΔΡΟΜΕΔΑ?⟩
ποῖαι λιβάδες, ποία σειρήν . . .

Schol. on Aristophanes, *Lysistrata* 963

117
⟨ΑΝΔΡΟΜΕΔΑ⟩
φίλαι παρθένοι, φίλαι μοι . . .

Aristophanes, *Women at the Thesmophoria* 1016 with Schol.

118
ΑΝΔΡΟΜΕΔΑ
κλύεις ὤ;
προσαυδῶ σε τὰν ἐν ἄντροις,
ἀπόπαυσον, ἔασον, Ἀχοῖ, με σὺν
φίλαις γόου πόθον λαβεῖν

Aristophanes, *Women at the Thesmophoria* 1018–9 with Schol.

2 προσαυδῶ σε τὰν Bothe, Hermann (προσαυδῶσα Brunck): προσαιδοῦσσαι τὰς Aristoph. and (-ουσσαι) Schol.: προσᾴδουσ᾽ αὖτὰς Mitsdörffer (προσᾴδουσ᾽ Elmsley, αὖτὰς Burges)

116
<ANDROMEDA?>

What tear-drops, what siren[1] . . . ?

[1] Sirens are depicted as divine mourners on Attic gravestones from the late 5th century. Helen asks them to assist her lament, *Helen* 167–73. Here the words are more likely Andromeda's than the Chorus's as in Aristophanes.

117
<ANDROMEDA>
(*to the chorus*)

Dear maidens, my friends . . .

118
ANDROMEDA

Hallo, do you hear? I appeal to you in the cave[1]—leave off, Echo, and let me mourn as I long to with my friends.

[1] Or perhaps 'Do you hear, you who sing cries in the cave accompanying mine' (Mitsdörffer).

119 + 120

⟨ΑΝΔΡΟΜΕΔΑ⟩

(119) συνάλγησον, ὡς ὁ κάμνων
       δακρύων μεταδοὺς ἔχει
       κουφότητα μόχθων.

ΧΟΡΟΣ

(120) ἄνοικτος ὃς τεκών σε τὰν
5   πολυπονωτάταν βροτῶν
       μεθῆκεν Ἅιδα πάτρας ὑπερθανεῖν.

*remains of five more lines in the papyrus fr. 1, and five lines
in fr. 2 (= F 120a)*

P. Oxy. 2628 fr. 1 (line-ends only); vv. 1–3: Stobaeus 4.48.17;
vv. 4–6: Schol. on Aristophanes, *Women at the Thesmophoria*
1022

(121 N = 115a above)

122

⟨ΑΝΔΡΟΜΕΔΑ⟩

óρᾷς; οὐ χοροῖσιν οὐδ᾽
    ὑφ᾽ ἡλίκων νεανίδων   (1030)

κημὸν ἕστηκ᾽ ἔχουσ᾽,

ἀλλ᾽ ἐν πυκνοῖς δεσμοῖσιν ἐμπεπλεγμένη

Aristophanes, *Women at the Thesmophoria* 1029–41. The scholia
suggest that the words printed in larger type are taken from
Andromeda's monody, but the indications are imprecise. Most of
the rest is in tragic style and may reflect the monody more or less
closely, except for the comic adaptations printed with underline
(italics in the translation).

119 + 120

‹ANDROMEDA›

Feel my pain with me, for the sufferer who shares his tears
has some relief from his burden.[1]

CHORUS

Pitiless the man who fathered you but now has dispatched
you, most tormented of mortals, to Hades to die for your   5
homeland... *(further remnants)* ...

[1] Such commonplaces are usually expressed in masculine
form even by a female character. For the pleasure of lamentation
and shared grief see especially Homer, *Iliad* 24.507–14; cf.
Archelaus F 263, *Oeneus* F 563, *Oenomaus* F 573, etc.

(121 = 115a above)

122[1]

‹ANDROMEDA›

Do you see? Not in dancing choruses nor amongst the girls
of my age *do I stand holding my voter's funnel,*[2] but entangled in close
bonds I am presented as food for the monster *Glaucetes,*[3] with a paean   5

[1] The fragment is a pastiche including direct quotation
and parody: see note beneath the text opposite. In Aristophanes'
play the monody is sung by Euripides' kinsman, who has been
arrested and pilloried by a Scythian policeman ('the man' in v. 12).
[2] The funnel through which an Athenian juror would drop his vot-
ing-pebble into an urn to be counted. The Greek word has usually
been so understood here, but a juror would not in fact 'hold' the
funnel, and in their recent commentary on Aristophanes' play
(2004) C. Austin and S. D. Olson take it to be a piece of female or-
namentation (a sense attested in ancient lexica).   [3] A glutton
particularly fond of fish, cf. Aristophanes' *Peace* 1008, Plato Com.
F 114 *PCG.*

5   κήτει βορὰ <u>Γλαυκέτῃ</u> πρόκειμαι,

γαμηλίῳ μὲν οὐ ξὺν

παιῶνι, δεσμίῳ δὲ.   (1035)

γοᾶσθε μ᾽, ὦ γυναῖκες, ὡς

μέλεα μὲν πέπονθα μέλεος

10   – ὦ τάλας ἐγώ, τάλας –

ἀπὸ δὲ συγγόνων ἄλλ᾽ ἄνομα πάθεα,

φῶτα λιτομέναν,   (1040)

πολυδάκρυτον Ἀΐδα γόον φλέγουσαν.

11 ἄλλ᾽ ἄνομα Scaliger: ἄλλαν ἄνομα Aristoph. ms.
13 φλέγουσαν Musgrave (-α Enger): φεύγουσαν Aristoph. ms.:
χέουσαν Casaubon (-α Rau)

(123 N = 124.5–6 below)

124 (= 124 + adesp. 157 + 123 N)

ΠΕΡΣΕΤΣ

ὦ θεοί, τίν᾽ ἐς γῆν βαρβάρων ἀφίγμεθα

ταχεῖ πεδίλῳ; διὰ μέσου γὰρ αἰθέρος

τέμνων κέλευθον πόδα τίθημ᾽ ὑπόπτερον

ὑπέρ τε πόντου χεῦμ᾽ ὑπέρ τε Πλειάδα,

5   Περσεύς, πρὸς Ἄργος ναυστολῶν, τὸ Γοργόνος

κάρα κομίζων.

vv. 1–3, 5–6: Aristophanes, *Women at the Thesmophoria*
1098–1102 with Schol. (ascription of vv. 5–6 is unclear and de-
bated); v. 4 (inserted here by Meineke): Eusebius, *Preparation for
the Gospel* 15.62.8

not for my wedding *but for my binding*. Bewail me, women, for I
have suffered pitiful things in my pitiful plight—*O suffering,
suffering man that I am!*—and other lawless afflictions from my 10
kin, though I implored *the man*, as I light[4] a lament filled with tears
for my death.

[4] Musgrave corrected the impossible ms. 'flee' (but some edi-
tors prefer Casaubon's 'pour out'). Song is often imaged as fire or
flame in Greek poetry (cf. J. Diggle, *Euripidea* [Oxford, 1994],
11–12).

(123 N = 124.5–6 below)

124 (= 124 + adesp. 157 + 123 N)

PERSEUS

(flying in above the stage)

O gods, to what barbarians' land has my swift sandal
brought me? Through middle heaven I cut my path, set-
ting winged foot over flowing sea and Pleiad[1]—I, Perseus,
as I voyage for Argos bearing the Gorgon's head.[2]   5

[1] The Pleiades represent stars in general: cf. *Phaethon* 65–6.
Perseus flies amongst the stars in Ovid, *Met*. 4.623–4, 789.
[2] Vv. 5–6 are uncertainly included in the fragment: see apparatus
opposite.

125

⟨ΠΕΡΣΕΥΣ⟩

ἔα· τίν' ὄχθον τόνδ' ὁρῶ περίρρυτον
ἀφρῷ θαλάσσης, παρθένου δ' εἰκὼ τίνα,
ἐξ αὐτομόρφων λαΐνων τυκισμάτων
σοφῆς ἄγαλμα χειρός;

vv. 1–2: Schol. on Aristophanes, *Women at the Thesmophoria*
1105; vv. 2–4 (παρθένου . . . χειρός): Maximus Confessor, *Scholia
on Works of Dionysius the Areopagite* 234 (*PG* 4.424a)

126

⟨ΠΕΡΣΕΥΣ?⟩

σιγᾷς; σιωπὴ δ' ἄπορος ἑρμηνεὺς λόγων.

Stobaeus 3.34.12

127

⟨ΠΕΡΣΕΥΣ⟩

ὦ παρθέν', οἰκτίρω σε κρεμαμένην ὁρῶν.

Aristophanes, *Women at the Thesmophoria* 1110, attributed
to *Andromeda* by Barnes but perhaps only paratragic (see Rau,
Paratragodia 86–7).

128

⟨ΑΝΔΡΟΜΕΔΑ⟩

ὦ ξένε, κατοίκτιρόν με, τὴν παναθλίαν.

Aristophanes, *Women at the Thesmophoria* 1107–8, attri-
buted to *Andromeda* by Canter (questionably: cf. on F 127
above); some editors add the next three words, λῦσόν με δεσμῶν
('free me from my bonds!').

125
⟨PERSEUS⟩

Hold—what promontory do I see here, lapped by sea-foam, and what maiden's likeness, a statue carved by an expert hand to her very form in stone?[1]

[1] Ovid, *Met.* 4.673–5: 'Had a light breeze not stirred her locks and warm tears welled in her eyes, he would have thought her a work of marble.'

126
⟨PERSEUS?⟩

You do not speak? But silence is a poor interpreter of words.[1]

[1] Ovid, *Met.* 4.682–4: 'At first the maid is mute, nor dares to address a man; she would have hidden her face with her hands for modesty, had she not been bound.'

127[1]
⟨PERSEUS⟩

Maiden, I pity you seeing you hanging there.

[1] Doubtful fragment: see opposite.

128[1]
⟨ANDROMEDA⟩

Stranger, take pity on me, all wretched as I am.

[1] Doubtful fragment: see opposite.

129

ΠΕΡΣΕΤΣ

ὦ παρθέν', εἰ σώσαιμί σ', εἴσῃ μοι χάριν;

Diogenes Laertius 4.29 (cf. Suda ει 258); Schol. on Homer, *Iliad* 14.235c; Eubulus F 26 *PCG*

129a (= 132 N)

ΑΝΔΡΟΜΕΔΑ

ἄγου δέ μ', ὦ ξεῖν', εἴτε πρόσπολον θέλεις
εἴτ' ἄλοχον εἴτε δμωΐδ'...

Herodian, *On Figures* 45; Diogenes Laertius 4.29 (following F 129)

130

ΠΕΡΣΕΤΣ

τὰς συμφορὰς γὰρ τῶν κακῶς πεπραγότων
οὐ πώποθ' ὕβρισ', αὐτὸς ὀρρωδῶν παθεῖν.

Stobaeus 4.48.2 and 3.3.39; Ammonius, *On Similar and Different Words* 80

131

⟨ΑΝΔΡΟΜΕΔΑ⟩

μή μοι προτείνων ἐλπίδ' ἐξάγου δάκρυ·
γένοιτό τἂν πόλλ' ὧν δόκησις οὐκ ἔνι.

Stobaeus 4.47.2; vv. 1 and 2 assigned to different speakers by Grotius (to Andromeda and Perseus by Matthiae).

129

PERSEUS

Maiden, if I should rescue you, will you show me gratitude?[1]

---

[1] In the Greek, 'gratitude' may suggest a sexual response (e.g. *Hecuba* 830; LSJ χάρις III.2).

129a (= 132 N)

ANDROMEDA

Take me with you, stranger, whether you want me as a servant, a wife, or a slave.

130

PERSEUS

I have never abused the unfortunate in their adversity, for I fear I may suffer adversity myself.

131

⟨ANDROMEDA⟩

Do not bring me to tears by offering me hope; many things may happen that are unanticipated.[1]

---

[1] If Andromeda speaks both lines, she is rejecting a hope that may prove to be unfounded (similar wording in [Aeschylus], *Prometheus Bound* 777). If v. 2 is someone else's reply (see opposite), it is a reassurance against despair.

(132 N = 129a above)

133

⟨ΠΕΡΣΕΤΣ?⟩

ἀλλ' ἡδύ τοι σωθέντα μεμνῆσθαι πόνων.

Stobaeus 3.29.57; Aristotle, *Rhetoric* 1370b4 with Schol. (*CAG* XXI.ii.65.17); Plutarch, *Moralia* 630e; Macrobius, *Saturnalia* 7.2.9; repeated, translated or paraphrased elsewhere as a commonplace.

134

⟨ΠΕΡΣΕΤΣ?⟩

εὔκλειαν ἔλαβον οὐκ ἄνευ πολλῶν πόνων.

Stobaeus 3.29.20

134a (= 149 N)

⟨ΠΕΡΣΕΤΣ?⟩

νεότης μ' ἐπῆρε καὶ θράσος τοῦ νοῦ πλέον.

Stobaeus 4.11.4; Lucian 38.1

135

ἦ που τὸ μέλλον ἐκφοβεῖ καθ' ἡμέραν·
ὡς τοῦ γε πάσχειν τοὐπιὸν μεῖζον κακόν.

Stobaeus 4.35.22

ANDROMEDA

(132 N = 129a above)

133
⟨PERSEUS?⟩

But it's pleasant to remember one's trials once one has been saved.[1]

[1] For the thought cf. Homer, *Odyssey* 15.400–1 (quoted by Aristotle together with this fragment). Euripides' verse was much re-used (see opposite).

134
⟨PERSEUS?⟩

I gained glory, not without many trials.

134a (= 149 N)
⟨PERSEUS?⟩

Youth and rashness incited me more than my good sense.

135

For sure, the future puts one in daily fear; for an evil seems greater in anticipation than in the experience.

136

ΠΕΡΣΕΤΣ

σὺ δ᾽ ὦ θεῶν τύραννε κἀνθρώπων Ἔρως,
ἢ μὴ δίδασκε τὰ καλὰ φαίνεσθαι καλά,
ἢ τοῖς ἐρῶσιν ὧν σὺ δημιουργὸς εἶ
μοχθοῦσι μόχθους εὐτυχῶς συνεκπόνει.
5 καὶ ταῦτα μὲν δρῶν τίμιος θνητοῖς ἔσῃ,
μὴ δρῶν δ᾽ ὑπ᾽ αὐτοῦ τοῦ διδάσκεσθαι φιλεῖν
ἀφαιρεθήσῃ χάριτας αἷς τιμῶσί σε.

Athenaeus 13.561b; vv. 1–4: Stobaeus 4.20.42; v. 1: Lucian 59.1

3–4 as a single verse, ἢ τοῖς ἐρῶσιν εὐμενὴς παρίστασο Stob.   5 θνητοῖς (or βροτοῖς) Dobree: θεοῖς Ath.

137

⟨ΧΟΡΟΣ⟩

τῶν γὰρ πλούτων ὅδ᾽ ἄριστος
γενναῖον λέχος εὑρεῖν.

Stobaeus 4.22.11

138

ὅσοι γὰρ εἰς ἔρωτα πίπτουσιν βροτῶν,
ἐσθλῶν ὅταν τύχωσι τῶν ἐρωμένων,
οὐκ ἔσθ᾽ ὁποίας λείπεται τόδ᾽ ἡδονῆς.

Stobaeus 4.20.22

136

PERSEUS

And you, Eros, tyrant over gods and men—either don't
teach us to see beauty in what is beautiful, or help those
who are in love to succeed in their efforts as they suffer the
toils that you yourself have crafted.[1] If you do this, you will
be honoured by mortals,[2] but if you do not, their learning   5
to love will itself deprive you of the thanks with which they
honour you.

[1] In other words, 'either stop making people fall in love, or
help those who do fall in love to achieve fulfilment'. Stobaeus
simplifies vv. 3–4 as 'or stand benevolently by those who are in
love'.   [2] Athenaeus has 'by the gods'; Dobree's 'by mortals',
or something similar, is clearly needed.

137

⟨CHORUS⟩

This is the best kind of wealth, to find a noble spouse.

138

Whenever mortals who have fallen in love find their loved
one is virtuous, no joy exceeds the joy of it.

EURIPIDES

138a (= 1054 N)

ἔρωτα δεινὸν ἔχομεν, ἐκ δὲ τῶν λόγων
ἑλοῦ τὰ βέλτισθ᾽· ὡς ἄπιστόν ἐστ᾽ ἔρως,
κἂν τῷ κακίστῳ τῶν φρενῶν οἰκεῖν φιλεῖ.

Stobaeus 4.20.44 (with attribution to Eur. *Andromeda*, questioned by Fritzsche)

(139N: see Introduction)
140

ὦ τλῆμον, ὥς σοι τὰς τύχας μὲν ἀσθενεῖς
ἔδωχ᾽ ὁ δαίμων, μέγα φρονοῦσι δ᾽ οἱ λόγοι.

Stobaeus 2.4.7; PSI 1476 (a gnomology) has parts of each verse.

141

ἐγὼ δὲ παῖδας οὐκ ἐῶ νόθους λαβεῖν·
τῶν γνησίων γὰρ οὐδὲν ὄντες ἐνδεεῖς
νόμῳ νοσοῦσιν· ὅ σε φυλάξασθαι χρεών.

Stobaeus 4.24.45

1 παῖδας <σ᾽> Mekler

138a (= 1054 N)

We have a terrible love;[1] but you must choose the best course from rational consideration; for love is unreliable and tends to occupy the poorest part of the mind.

[1] Sense and speaker are unclear without a context. Possibly Perseus to Andromeda ('We are terribly in love'), possibly Cepheus counselling Andromeda ('Love is a terrible influence on us humans'). The rest is clear enough: 'Don't be guided by love, for it makes us think irrationally and act against our own best interests'.

(139N: see Introduction)

140

Daring (*or* foolhardy?) man! Your fortune has put you in a weak situation, but your words are high-spirited.

141

I forbid the acquiring of illegitimate sons. Though in no way inferior to legitimate ones, they are handicapped by convention, and this is something you must beware of.[1]

[1] 'I forbid ⟨you⟩ to acquire . . .', Mekler: but a general prohibition has more force. For the 'natural' equality of illegitimate sons cf. *Antigone* F 168, *Eurystheus* F 377, Sophocles F 84 (all cited together with this fragment by Stobaeus). Here Cepheus or Cassiepeia might be warning Andromeda against bearing non-Ethiopian sons through marrying Perseus, but 'acquire' is an unlikely term for this (so various alternatives for λαβεῖν, such as τεκεῖν 'bear' or 'beget', have been proposed; cf. φυτεύειν in F 377.2). In some accounts Cepheus had no sons of his own, so one might think of Cassiepeia discouraging him from adopting a son, as Praxithea warns Erechtheus in *Erechtheus* F 359.

149

142

χρυσὸν μάλιστα βούλομαι δόμοις ἔχειν·
καὶ δοῦλος ὢν γὰρ τίμιος πλουτῶν ἀνήρ,
ἐλεύθερος δὲ χρεῖος ὢν οὐδὲν σθένει.
χρυσοῦ νόμιζε σαυτὸν οὕνεκ' εὐτυχεῖν.

Stobaeus 4.31.21 and 22; Hense following Musgrave printed
v. 4 (= his no. 22) as a separate extract from an unidentified work.

143

χρήμασιν γὰρ εὐτυχῶ·
ταῖς συμφοραῖσι δ', ὡς ὁρᾷς, οὐκ εὐτυχῶ.

Stobaeus 4.34.30

*144

μὴ τὸν ἐμὸν οἴκει νοῦν· ἐγὼ γὰρ ἀρκέσω.

Aristophanes, *Frogs* 105 with Schol. (whence Suda μ 1000),
attributing the verse to *Andromache* (*Andromeda*: Matthiae)

145

⟨ΑΓΓΕΛΟΣ⟩
ὁρῶ δὲ πρὸς τὰ παρθένου θοινάματα
κῆτος θοάζον ἐξ Ἀτλαντικῆς ἁλός.

v. 1: Tiberius, *On Demosthenic Figures* 47 (= Caecilius of
Calacte F 75 Ofenloch); v. 2: Plutarch, *Moralia* 22e; v. 2 (κῆτος
θοάζων [*sic*]): Schol. on *Orestes* 335

142

Gold is what I most desire to have in my house. A man who is rich gets respect even if he is a slave, while a free man who is needy has no power. You'd better believe that gold is what makes you successful.[1]

[1] The last sentence may be a separate fragment (see opposite).

143

I am well off for money but not, as you can see, in my fortunes.

*144

Don't try to govern my mind: I can handle that myself.

145

⟨MESSENGER⟩

I saw the monster hurrying from the Atlantic water towards its maiden-feast.[1]

[1] Mention of the Atlantic suggests that Euripides' play was set in the far west, where the Gorgons also lived. Homer, *Odyssey* 1.23–4 locates Ethiopians in the land of the setting sun as well as the rising sun.

EURIPIDES

146

<αΓΓΕΛΟΣ>

. . . πᾶς δὲ ποιμένων ἔρρει λεώς,
ὁ μὲν γάλακτος κίσσινον φέρων σκύφος
πόνων ἀναψυκτῆρ᾽, ὁ δ᾽ ἀμπέλων γάνος.

Athenaeus 11.477a; Macrobius, *Saturnalia* 5.21.13

147

ἄγορος· καὶ ἄγοροι Εὐριπίδης Ἀνδρομέδα· οἱ κατ᾽ οἶκον
ἀμφὶ δαῖτα καὶ τράπεζαν †Αἰθίοπες σημαίνει†.

Anecdota Graeca I.339.5 Bekker

(149N = 134a above)

150

οὐκ ἔστιν ὅστις εὐτυχὴς ἔφυ βροτῶν,
†ὃν μὴ τὸ θεῖον ὡς τὰ πολλὰ συνθέλει†.

Stobaeus 4.41.32

2 ὃν Stob.: ᾧ Porson: ἂν . . . συνθέλῃ Blaydes, Klimek-
Winter: ὃν . . . συστελεῖ Hense

151

τήν τοι Δίκην λέγουσι παῖδ᾽ εἶναι Διὸς
ἐγγύς τε ναίειν τῆς βροτῶν ἁμαρτίας.

Stobaeus 1.3.23 with attribution to Euripides' *Andromachus*
(*Andromeda*: Musgrave); Orion, Euripidean Appendix 17 Haffner

1 Διὸς Stob.: χρόνου Orion (the verse is then identical with
Antiope F 222)   2 ἁμαρτίας Orion: τιμωρίας Stob.

146
<MESSENGER>

. . . and all the herding folk came, one bearing an ivywood cup of milk to refresh him from his labours, and another lustrous grape-juice.

147

'Gathering', and 'gatherings': Euripides in *Andromeda*: those in the house around feast and table †denotes Ethiopians(?)†.[1]

[1] A corrupt lexicon entry (grammatically incoherent at the end) perhaps showing that Euripides used the word 'gathering(s)' in a description of Ethiopians gathered for a feast. In the Greek, 'those in the house around feast and table' makes the greater part of a trochaic tetrameter.

(149N = 134a above)

150

No mortal is successful †whom divine power does not for the most part consent.†[1]

[1] Perhaps 'consent <should be well off>' can be understood, but the syntax is difficult: 'to whom the divine power does not . . . consent', Porson; 'if the divine power . . . ', Blaydes; 'whom the divine power will not . . . bring low' Hense.

151

They say that Justice is the daughter of Zeus and dwells close to mortal wrongdoing.[1]

[1] Cf. especially Hesiod, *Works and Days* 222–4, 256; contrast *Melanippe* F 506.7–8 with our note. Orion's 'wrongdoing' is better than Stobaeus' 'punishment', but his 'daughter of Time' is probably due to confusion with *Antiope* F 222.

152

⟨ΧΟΡΟΣ⟩

τὸ δαιμόνιον οὐχ ὁρᾷς
ὅπῃ μοίρα⟨ς⟩ διεξέρχεται;
στρέφει δ᾽ ἄλλους ἄλλως εἰς ἀμέραν.

Stobaeus 1.5.2

2 μοίρα⟨ς⟩ Grotius: μοῖρα or μοῖρα Stob.: μοίρα⟨ν⟩
Meineke   3 ἄλλους ἄλλως Stob.: ἄλλον ἄλλοσ᾽ Fritzsche:
ἄλλοσ᾽ ἄλλους Ellis

153

⟨ΧΟΡΟΣ⟩

ὁ μὲν ὄλβιος ἦν, τὸ δ᾽ ἀπέκρυψεν
θεὸς ἐ⟨κ⟩ κείνων τῶν ποτε λαμπρῶν·
νεύει βίοτος, νεύει δὲ τύχη
κατὰ πνεῦμ᾽ ἀνέμων.

Stobaeus 4.41.17

1 τὸ Stob.: τὸν Valckenaer

154

τὸ ζῆν ἀφέντες τὸ κατὰ γῆς τιμῶσί †σου† –
κενόν γ᾽· ὅταν γὰρ ζῇ τις εὐτυχεῖν χρεών.

Stobaeus 4.55.4

1 τὸ ζῆν Stob.: τὸ ζῶν Tucker   σου Stob.: που Collard
2 εὐτυχεῖν χρεών Musgrave (perhaps εὐσεβεῖν Cropp): εὐτυχεῖ
κρέων Stob. (κρεῶν ms. M)

---

[1] Text slightly confused, but the point is probably that giving
expensive honours to the dead is futile (cf. *Polyidus* F 640, cited

152
⟨CHORUS⟩

Do you not see in what destined way[1] the divine power reaches completion? Each day it turns different men in different ways.

[1] Literally, 'in what way of destiny'. The transmitted text is slightly incoherent: 'Do you not see the divine power, in what way destiny reaches completion'. Meineke suggested 'Do you not see in what way the divine power brings destiny to completion'. In v. 3 Fritzsche and Ellis adjusted 'in different ways' to 'in different directions'.

153
⟨CHORUS⟩

He was blessed with good fortune, but god hid it away[1] after that erstwhile splendour. Life sways, and fortune sways, as the wind blows.

[1] Valckenaer's widely accepted conjecture gives 'One man was blessed with good fortune, another (*or* the other) god hid away etc.'; but what follows seems to be a reflection on a single man's fall.

154

Dismissing life, they give honour to what is †of you† beneath the earth—vainly, for it is when a man lives that he should prosper.[1]

with this fragment in Stobaeus' chapter 'On Burial'; also *Trojan Women* 1248–50). If so, 'he should prosper' (Musgrave's adjustment of Stobaeus' meaningless final phrase) makes a contrast between wealth in life and wealth in the form of funeral offerings etc. Tucker suggested 'Dismissing what is alive . . .', and Collard ' . . . to what is beneath the earth, I suppose' (with ironic tone). At the end Cropp suggests ' . . . that one should show him respect' (cf. *Suppliant Women* 559).

ANTIGONE

H. Van Looy in ed. Budé VIII.1.191–212.

J. M. Paton, *HSCP* 12 (1901), 267–76; J. Mesk, *Wiener Studien* 49 (1931), 1–11; Webster 181–4; *LIMC* I.i.818–28 'Antigone'; Aélion (1986) 71–5; L. Inglese, *Rivista di Cultura Classica e Medioevale* 34 (1992), 175–90; Gantz 519–21; C. Zimmermann, *Der Antigone-Mythos in der antiken Literatur und Kunst* (Mainz, 1993), esp. 161–88, 217–22; Taplin 185–6.

Sophocles' surviving Antigone is the earliest evidence we have for its heroine's famous story, for the ending of Aeschylus' Seven Against Thebes (467 B.C.) is spurious. In fact we have only one previous record even of Antigone's name as daughter of Oedipus (Pherecydes FGrH 3 F 95: see Gantz 519–20). Sophocles' play canonized Antigone: after her brothers Eteocles and Polynices had killed each other disputing the throne of Thebes, the new king Creon forbade burial for Polynices as a traitor (for he had led the Seven against Thebes to attack his native city: see under Alcmeon in Psophis*). Antigone defied the interdict, was detected giving Polynices symbolic burial, and was sentenced to death. She was however the expected bride of Creon's son Haemon, who killed himself upon her body after she had hanged herself. Creon was left broken.*

The Aristophanic hypothesis to Sophocles' play states

that Euripides' Antigone *told the same story except that Antigone was detected at the burial together with Haemon; she was given in marriage to him, and bore a son Maeon (see test. iia below, paraphrased by the derivative sources in test. iib but without the detail of Maeon). Most recent scholars agree on the implication of this, that not just Haemon's love for Antigone, but his sharing or at least awareness of her action, led to their marriage. The play must therefore have developed something at least of the moral and paternal tensions found in Sophocles, while resolving them happily rather than concluding with the tragic Sophoclean ending. The only other hard evidence for Euripides' play consists in the fragments themselves, which are almost all sententious, and come without context.*

Amid many speculative reconstructions, a few things are clear and agreed. F 157–8 begins the play, but the speaker is unknown. F 159 is from choral lyric recounting the deaths of the Seven; it names Capaneus. F 177 is addressed to Dionysus, possibly as the deus ex machina *who has saved Antigone and Haemon from death ('you are in no way to be resisted by mortal men'), and who forecasts the birth of Maeon (but some think that this fragment is an ordinary apostrophe of the god). Of the other fragments, some may relate to an argument about Creon's edict (F 173 and 176 look certain, 171 and 172 probable), some to Haemon's love for Antigone and its difficulty for Creon (F 161, 162, 162a; cf. on* Antiope *F 212–215 in the next paragraph).*

A special difficulty is the seeming coincidence of the book-fragment F 175, two gnomic verses attributed to Antigone, with the end of P. Oxy. 3317, an unattributed and damaged scene of hostility apparently in a Dionysiac *setting. While F 177 and *178 offer some Dionysiac reference in* Antigone, *no explanation of how F 175 and the papyrus might have fitted in the play convinces, and it is safer to assign them to* Antiope *(see there before F 221, with note 1 to the translation). Ancient scribes regularly confuse the titles* Antigone *and* Antiope, *so that the attributions to one or other play of* Antigone *F 162a, 166, 175 itself, 177, *178 and* Antiope *F 212–5 (four fragments apparently from a debate about marriage) are disputed.*

F 164 and 174 are lost except for their headings in Stobaeus 4.22.13 (see Hippothous, TrGF 210 F 3a) and 4.44.4. Other ascriptions: Andromeda *F 154; adesp. F 553 'I do have (a response), for the action being good in itself will furnish me good arguments'; for F **164a N–Sn (= adesp. F 84 N), 'the spear carried by the earth-born' (i.e. the birthmark on descendants of the legendary Theban Sown Men), see under Carcinus II, TrGF 70 F 1.*

Hyginus, Fab. *72 recounts Antigone's story so very differently from Sophocles that it cannot be considered for reconstructing Euripides (cf. Jebb in his* Antigone *p. xxxvii and Paton [1901], followed by most editors). It is now widely agreed that Hyginus and one or two 4th c. vases reflect the* Antigone *of Astydamas the Younger (TrGF 1 60 T 5), although Taplin keeps open their possible relation to Euripides' play.*[1]

[1] M. Huys, *APF* 43 (1997), 18–19 observes that Hyginus repeats the typical Euripidean motif of happy love, but this may well be due to Euripidean influence upon Astydamas. For bibliography on this whole issue see *TrGF* 5, 262–3, esp. Inglese; for the vases also *LIMC* nos. 14–15 = Todisco Ap 89, Ap 136 (no. 14 = Taplin no. 63).

Metrical criteria point to composition in the years 420–406 (Cropp–Fick 74), the period also of Euripides' Oedipus *and* Phoenician Women; *both show yet further Euripidean innovations in the myth, and in* Phoenician Women *Antigone has a minor part but rejects marriage to Haemon, resolving instead to accompany Oedipus into exile (1679ff., if the text is genuinely Euripidean; cf. Sophocles'* Oedipus at Colonus). *There is no other evidence of date; Zimmermann 189–90 links the theme of Polynices as traitor denied burial with similar measures against Archeptolemus and Antiphon in the events at Athens in 411.*

Sophocles' play rather than Euripides' was probably a source for Accius' Latin tragedy; on Astydamas see above. For Antigone in classical literature and art see Zimmermann, and in post-classical art and thought OGCMA I.105–9 and G. Steiner, Antigones *(Oxford, 1984[2]).*

ΑΝΤΙΓΟΝΗ

test. iia

Ἀντιγόνη παρὰ τὴν πρόσταξιν τῆς πόλεως θάψασα τὸν
Πολυνείκην ἐφωράθη καὶ εἰς μνημεῖον κατάγειον ἐντε-
θεῖσα παρὰ τοῦ Κρέοντος ἀνῄρηται. ἐφ' ᾗ καὶ Αἵμων
δυσπαθήσας διὰ τὸν εἰς αὐτὴν ἔρωτα ξίφει ἑαυτὸν διεχει-
ρίσατο . . . κεῖται ἡ μυθοποία καὶ παρὰ Εὐριπίδῃ ἐν
Ἀντιγόνῃ· πλὴν ἐκεῖ φωραθεῖσα μετὰ τοῦ Αἵμονος δίδο-
ται πρὸς γάμου κοινωνίαν· καὶ τέκνον τίκτει τὸν Μαίονα.

Aristophanes of Byzantium, hypothesis to Sophocles' *Anti-
gone*. Nearly the same details, except for the birth of Maeon, in
Sallustius' hypothesis to *Antigone* with Schol. *Ant*. 1351 (= test.
iib).

Μαίονα Nauck: Αἵμονα or Μαίμονα mss.

157 + 158

Ἦν Οἰδίπους τὸ πρῶτον εὐτυχὴς ἀνήρ,
εἶτ' ἐγένετ' αὖθις ἀθλιώτατος βροτῶν.

Aristophanes, *Frogs* 1182 (= v. 1) and 1187 (= v. 2), both attri-
buted by the scholia to *Antigone*; joined by D. Canter, and later
found linked in Favorinus, *On Exile* col. ii.39 Barigazzi. Both lines
are attested separately elsewhere.

160

ANTIGONE

test. iia
Antigone buried Polynices against the city's injunction. She
was detected, put into an underground tomb by Creon, and
her life taken. Haemon too, distraught because of his love
for her, slew himself over her body with a sword . . . The
plot is found also in Euripides in *Antigone*, except that there
Antigone is detected in company with Haemon and is joined
with him in marriage; and she gives birth to a child, Maeon.[1]

[1] The name Maeon and his birth were thought by Mesk to be a
commentator's addition on the basis of Homer, *Iliad* 4.394.

157 + 158
Oedipus was at first a man of happy fortune; then he be-
came in turn the most wretched of mortal men.[1]

[1] The play's opening lines, as Aristophanes indicates.

---

1 εὐτυχὴς *Frogs* 1182, other witnesses: εὐδαίμων some mss.
of Aristophanes, one other witness

159

⟨ΧΟΡΟΣ⟩

ἐπὶ χρυσεόνωτον ἀσπίδα τὰν Καπανέως

Schol. on *Phoenician Women* 1130

160

νέοι νέοισι συννοσοῦσι τἀφανῆ . . .

Stobaeus 2.33.5 (sentence probably incomplete)

τἀφανῆ Stob.: τάφρονα Usener

161

ἤρων· τὸ μαίνεσθαι δ᾽ ἄρ᾽ ἦν ἔρως βροτοῖς.

Stobaeus 4.20.38; Plutarch fr. 136 Sandbach (from Stobaeus 4.20.68)

162

ἀνδρὸς δ᾽ ὁρῶντος εἰς Κύπριν νεανίου
ἀφύλακτος ἡ τήρησις, ὡς κἂν φαῦλος ᾖ
τἄλλ᾽, εἰς ἔρωτα πᾶς ἀνὴρ σοφώτατος.
†ἢν δ᾽ ἂν προσῆται Κύπρις, ἥδιστον λαβεῖν†

Stobaeus 4.20.4

2 ὡς κἂν Nauck: κἂν γὰρ Stobaeus   3 σοφώτατος Herwerden, Meineke: σοφώτερος Stob.

159

⟨CHORUS⟩

. . . on to the golden-backed shield of Capaneus . . .[1]

[1] The Chorus evokes the attack of the Seven against Thebes; Capaneus' gold-lettered shield appears first at Aeschylus, *Seven against Thebes* 430–4.

160

Young share their faults with young . . . in their uncertainties(?).[1]

[1] The sentence appears incomplete; but Usener read 'with young in their follies'.

161

I was (*or* they were?) in love; and that showed love is madness for mortals.[1]

[1] Haemon is the probable speaker, as also of F 162a, and F 162 is spoken about him; but the translation is insecure, and 'they were in love' might refer to the mutual love of Antigone and Haemon.

162

When a young man looks to Aphrodite, there's no watch can be kept on him; for even if he's bad at other things, every man is very clever in the pursuit of love. †If Aphrodite approves (love? *or* allows love to come), it is very sweet to seize it.†[1]

[1] The Greek is corrupt and the sense not certain.

162a (= 1058 N)

ἐγὼ γὰρ ἔξω λέκτρ' ἅ τοι καλῶς ἔχειν
δίκαιόν ἐστιν οἷσι συγγηράσομαι.

P. Oxy. 3214.2–4 (very damaged); Stobaeus 4.22.113

1 ἅ τοι P. Oxy.: αὐτοῖς Stob.

163

ἀνδρὸς †φίλου† δὲ χρυσὸς ἀμαθίας μέτα
ἄχρηστος, εἰ μὴ κἀρετὴν ἔχων τύχοι.

Stobaeus 4.31.70

(**164a N–Sn: see Introduction)

165

ἄκουσον· οὐ γὰρ οἱ κακῶς πεπραγότες
σὺν ταῖς τύχαισι τοὺς λόγους ἀπώλεσαν.

Stobaeus 3.13.7

166

τὸ μῶρον αὐτῷ τοῦ πατρὸς νόσημ' ἔνι·
φιλεῖ γὰρ οὕτως ἐκ κακῶν εἶναι κακούς.

Stobaeus 4.30.1

1 αὐτῷ Stob.: αὐτῇ Süvern

167

ἡ γὰρ δόκησις πατράσι παῖδας εἰκέναι·
τὰ πολλὰ ταύτῃ γίγνεται τέκνων πέρι.

Stobaeus 4.29.7

1 πατράσι Gesner: ἅπασι Stob.

162a (= 1058 N)

For I shall have a marriage which it is right should do well,
I tell you, with a wife with whom I shall grow old.[1]

[1] The translation slightly expands the Greek, for clarity.
Stobaeus' chapter is headed 'The need to consider similar ages in
those who marry'.

163

Gold coupled with ignorance in a †friendly† man is use-
less, unless he should happen to possess virtue too.[1]

[1] No plausible context in the play for a rich but ignorant
'friend' has been suggested.

(**164a N–Sn: see Introduction)

165

Listen: for those who have come off badly do not lose their
power of argument together with their luck.

166

His father's folly is a weakness in him; bad men usually
come from bad this way.[1]

[1] Spoken of Haemon, perhaps, but by whom? Süvern's alter-
ation gives 'Her father's folly in her', i.e. Antigone as daughter of
Oedipus (cf. Sophocles, *Antigone* 469–72). For moral character
inherited see on *Alcmeon in Corinth* F 75.

167

Opinion is, sons resemble fathers; this is generally the way
with children.[1]

[1] Text suspect; without a context, both meaning and point are
uncertain.

168

ὀνόματι μεμπτὸν τὸ νόθον, ἡ φύσις δ᾽ ἴση.

Stobaeus 4.24.43; Clement of Alexandria, *Miscellanies* 6.2.10.4

169

. . . ἐπ᾽ ἄκραν ἥκομεν γραμμὴν κακῶν.

Stobaeus 4.40.8

170

οὐκ ἔστι Πειθοῦς ἱερὸν ἄλλο πλὴν λόγος,
καὶ βωμὸς αὐτῆς ἔστ᾽ ἐν ἀνθρώπου φύσει.

Orion 1.1 Haffner; v. 1: Aristophanes, *Frogs* 1391; other citations and allusions

171

δεῖ τοῖσι πολλοῖς τὸν τύραννον ἁνδάνειν.

Stobaeus 4.7.6

172

οὔτ᾽ εἰκὸς ἄρχειν οὔτ᾽ ἐχρῆν ἄνευ νόμων
τύραννον εἶναι· μωρία δὲ καὶ θέλειν
⟨   ⟩
ὃς τῶν ὁμοίων βούλεται κρατεῖν μόνος.

Stobaeus 4.8.5

1 ἄνευ νόμων Bothe: εἶναι νόμον Stob.   2 lacuna between 2 and 3, Dindorf

168

Bastardy is open to censure in name, but has equality in nature.[1]

[1] Possibly a reference to Polynices, deemed 'illegitimate' because the child of incest. For the thought see on *Andromeda* F 141.

169

We have reached the furthest limit[1] of our troubles.

[1] In the Greek, a metaphor from the finishing line of a foot-race.

170

Persuasion has no other temple than speech, and her altar is in human nature.

171

The king must please the many.

172

It is neither reasonable to rule, nor ought there to be a king, without laws. It is folly (for a man) even to want < . . . > who wishes to hold sole power over his peers.[1]

[1] Cf. *Suppliant Women* 429–32, 'nothing is more inimical to a city than an absolute ruler, where in the first place there are no laws in common, and one man has power after taking the law into his own hands.'

173

οἰκεῖος ἀνθρώποισι γίγνεσθαι φιλεῖ
πόλεμος ἐν ἀστοῖς, ἢν διχοστατῇ πόλις.

Stobaeus 4.1.22

(175 with P. Oxy. 3317: see *Antiope*, before F 221)

176

θάνατος γὰρ ἀνθρώποισι νεικέων τέλος
ἔχει· μαθεῖν δὲ πᾶσίν ἐστιν εὐμαρές.
τίς γὰρ πετραῖον σκόπελον οὐτάζων δορὶ
ὀδύναισι δώσει, τίς δ᾽ ἀτιμάζων νέκυν,
5 εἰ μηδὲν αἰσθάνοιντο τῶν παθημάτων;

Stobaeus 4.57.5 and (vv. 1–2) 4.52.23

2 so Stob. 4.52: ἔχει· τί γὰρ τῶνδ᾽ ἐστὶ μεῖζον ἐν βροτοῖς;
Stob. 4.57: verse deleted by Weil

177

ὦ παῖ Διώνης, ὡς ἔφυς μέγας θεός,
Διόνυσε, θνητοῖς τ᾽ οὐδαμῶς ὑποστατός.

Schol. on Pindar, *Pythians* 3.99

*178

τὴν Σφίγγα ὁ Διόνυσος ἔπεμψε τοῖς Θηβαίοις, ὡς ἐν
Ἀντιγόνῃ λέγει.

Schol. on *Phoenician Women* 1031

173

Men usually have internal feudings occur among citizens,
if their city is divided.

(175 with P. Oxy. 3317: see *Antiope*, before F 221)

176

Death is the end of their quarrels for men; and this is easy
for everyone to understand.[1] For who will inflict pain on a
lofty crag by wounding it with a spear, and who on a corpse
by dishonouring it, if these felt nothing of what they under-
went?[2]

[1] V. 2 in Stobaeus 4.52 is judged by many to be a facile interpo-
lation; in 4.57 it is senseless ('For what is greater than this among
mortal men?'). Weil's deletion is attractive.   [2] A protest at
the folly of punishing Polynices by refusing to bury his corpse; cf.
Sophocles, *Antigone* 1029–30.

177

O son of Dione, Dionysus, how great a god you are, and in
no way to be resisted by mortal men.[1]

[1] Dione is the mother of Dionysus elsewhere only at adesp. F
204, otherwise of Aphrodite. Euripides may associate the two
names (so Kannicht); there is another such play at *Archelaus* F
228a.21–2. On the fragment itself see Introduction.

*178

Dionysus sent the Sphinx to the Thebans, as (Euripides) says
in *Antigone*.[1]

[1] Euripides may have been alone in naming Dionysus (cf.
Schol. on *Phoenician Women* 934, where Euripides speaks also of
Ares' ancient anger against Thebes): the Sphinx is usually one fur-
ther affliction from Apollo (cf. *Oedipus* F 539a), and its riddle (F
540a) a reflex of the god's enigmatic oracular voice.

ANTIOPE

H. Schaal, *De Euripidis Antiopa* (Berlin, 1914); J. Kambitsis, *L'Antiope d'Euripide* (Athens, 1972); Diggle, *TrGFS* 85–93 (F 187–8, 206, 175, 223); Van Looy in ed. Budé VIII.1.213–74; C. Collard in *SFP* II.259–329. V. di Benedetto in Bastianini–Casanova, *Euripide e i papiri*, 97–122 discusses many fragments, esp. F 185, 196, 202, and the uncertain F 910. See also under F 175 (after F 220) and F 223 below.

N. Wecklein, *Philologus* 79 (1923), 51–69; F. Solmsen, *Hermes* 69 (1934), 410–5; U. Haussman, *MDAI(A)* 73 (1958 [1962]), 50–72 with Plates 53–7; Webster 205–11, 305; B. Snell, *Szenen aus griechischen Dramen* (Berlin, 1971), 76–103; Trendall–Webster III.3.14–15; P. A. de Nicola, *RAAN* 48 (1973), 195–236; *LIMC* I.i.718–22 'Amphion', I.i.854–7 'Antiope', III.i.635–44 'Dirke'; A. D. Trendall in H. Brijder et al., *Enthousiasmos . . . Essays . . . Hemelrijk* (Amsterdam, 1986), 157–66; Gantz 483–8; Huys, *The Tale*, relevant sections; A. J. Podlecki, *Ancient World* 27 (1996), 131–46; O. Taplin, *Antike Kunst* 41 (1998), 33–9, and *Pots and Plays* 187–91; B. S. Ridgeon, *Journal of Roman Archaeology* 12 (1999), 512–20; P. Wilson, *ICS* 24–25 (1999–2000), 440–9; L. B. Joyce, *Classical Antiquity* 20 (2001), 221–39; Matthiessen 253–6.

The beautiful Antiope, daughter of Nycteus king of Boeotia, attracted Zeus's eye, and he impregnated her. To escape her father's anger when she gave birth, she fled, encountered Epopeus of nearby Sicyon, and became his wife. Nycteus, broken and dying, ordered his brother and successor as king, Lycus, to attack Epopeus and recover Antiope, and to punish her; and this he did. On her way back to Boeotia as a captive, Antiope gave birth to twin sons by Zeus, Zethus and Amphion, at Eleutherae on the Attic–Boeotian border, near the god Dionysus' shrine (cf. F 207). She had to abandon the twins, but a herdsman found them and brought them up to young manhood (cf. F 179–182); Zethus was physically strong and active, while Amphion devoted himself to quiet pursuits, especially music. All this time, Antiope was kept in servitude to Lycus' wife Dirce.

This story is the background to Euripides' play; it is told, and the plot itself largely summarized, in three accounts all dependent upon a lost narrative hypothesis: Hyginus, Fab. 8, Apollodorus 3.5.5, and Scholia on Apollonius of Rhodes 4.1090 (= test. iii (a)–(c), of which test. iii (a) is printed below; see especially Luppe noted there, Gantz 232, 483–6, Huys, The Tale 104–7 and APF 42 [1996], 171–2). Incidental details, some corroborative, others discrepant, are found or inferred from many other sources, in particular some certain or probable fragments of Pacuvius' Latin adaptation Antiopa (= test. viib, printed in TrGF, ed. Budé 272–4, SFP II.326–9), which give some help in reconstruction.

The play's outline is fairly secure therefore, but its overall structure and centre are not at all clear. It is set at

171

Eleutherae, outside a cave which seems to double as the Herdsman's home and Dionysus' shrine (F 203, 223.19, 29–33). In his prologue speech the Herdsman appears anxious, for he prays to Dionysus (F 179); he may have had a dream (Pacuvius fr. 12 d'Anna), for Antiope, it later emerges, has escaped from captivity and fled to Eleutherae—and will be pursued, bringing danger for all there. The Herdsman relates how he long ago found and named the abandoned twins (F 181–2). This is all we have of the prologue, for the fragments plunge us almost at once into a debate between Zethus and Amphion which contrasts activity and quietude as social or political philosophies; this was famous in antiquity after Plato cited it in his Gorgias 485e–6d (cf. F 182b.1a). Amphion has entered singing (F 182a; F 195?), possibly even before the Chorus (perhaps of elderly Athenian countrymen: Schol. Eur. Hippolytus 58 = test. v, cf. F 223.17–18); he explains to the Chorus the history of the lyre (F 190, 192 and perhaps 191 probably belong here, cf. Pacuvius fr. 1 d'Anna). Zethus interrupts Amphion to upbraid his idleness (F 183). The debate formed the first episode and encompassed F 183–9, 193–202, and perhaps 191, 219–20; cf. Pacuvius frs. 2, 4, 5 d'Anna). Amphion's later prominence in the action (F 210, 223) suggests that his quietude 'won' the argument, for his calm and steely intelligence directs the punishments of Dirce and Lycus (F 223.1–16, 60–6, cf. F 175.1–8, printed before F 221); these, together with the god Hermes' intervention to save Lycus and ordain the future (F 223.67–end), conclude the play. The first choral ode, following Amphion's 'victory', is thought by many editors to have been introduced by the chanted anapaestic system F 910

(Uncertain Fragment, below at end). It celebrates meta-physical speculation by a thinking man who avoids political or moral wrongdoing; but some locate it later in the play.

The central scenes dramatized (1) Antiope's arrival: in some accounts, e.g. Apollodorus 3.5.5 (test. iii (b)), she has escaped miraculously when Dionysus loosed her bonds. She meets the Chorus and narrates her torment under Dirce (F 204–5, cf. Pacuvius frs. 7, 16–18 d'Anna); she seeks sanctuary. If the twins are present, Zethus may have rejected her, while Amphion was more sympathetic (cf. Hyginus 8.4, Propertius 3.15.29ff.). In such a scene, rather than later, Amphion may have scorned her assertion that she gave birth to Zeus's sons (F 206–8, 210) and gone off with Zethus, leaving Antiope to herself, with no 'recognition and reunion' (for the Herdsman seems never to have told the twins the story of their finding). The Chorus comments sadly on her extreme misfortune (F 211).

(2) Dirce enters, accompanied by a secondary chorus (test. v: see also Alexander *test. v), comprised almost certainly of her women; they come possessed by Dionysus, to worship him (Hyginus 8.4, cf. Pacuvius fr. 10 d'Anna), and the women probably sang in his praise on entering (compare the secondary choruses at* Hipp. *61–71 and* Phaethon *227–44). It looks as if Dionysus answers the Herdsman's prayer (F 179) for a second time. Dirce and Antiope perhaps argue (F 216–8 on slavery may belong here); the Herdsman probably returns to the cave, told by the twins of the woman seeking sanctuary; he may try to drive Dirce's noisy band away (cf. Pacuvius fr. 13 d'Anna). Presumably he identifies Antiope, and goes to fetch the twins,*

*to save their mother, while Dirce and her women prepare
to drag Antiope away to be killed (Hyginus 8.4).*

(3) *Either the twins come quickly and halt Dirce at once
or, in a new episode or scene, return with her as captive.
They are now reunited with their mother and intend to
avenge her by killing Dirce (from this point onward Zethus
will have been played by a mute). F 175 (= P. Oxy. 3317), if
from this play, belongs here, with Amphion(?) accusing
Dirce of presuming upon the god (1–8) and Dirce defiantly
anticipating death (9–15; Kannicht argues that P. Oxy. can
belong only if Dirce is brought back in a second entry, and
unaccompanied).*[1] *She is taken away, to be tied to a bull,
like Mazeppa to a horse, and torn or trampled to death
(Hyginus 8.5).*

(4) *A messenger reports Dirce's terrible end (F 221, cf.
the Chorus(?) in F 222).*

*This last scene perhaps ran quickly into the exodos if
the messenger also reported the approach of Lycus with
armed men, aiming to recover Antiope and perhaps also
the absent Dirce. Almost the whole exodos survives as F
223: Amphion proclaims 'triumph over Lycus or our own
deaths' (1–16), before he, Zethus and Antiope enter the
cave. Lycus arrives, and the Herdsman lures him inside,
without guards, where he is seized and brought out again
for execution (17–65); Hermes the god prevents it and or-
ders Lycus to hand over his kingdom to the twins, for them
to build the new Thebes (66–103); Lycus submits (104–16).*

F 209 and F 212–5 (on marriage) cannot be located

---

[1] F 175 is here ascribed to *Antiope* rather than *Antigone*, and
printed below after F 220. See note 1 there on the question of
attribution.

in this action; they are sometimes ascribed to Antigone
*(see Introduction there).   Brief fragments: F 180 'Hysiae'
(a place near Eleutherae, Antiope's birthplace), F 226 'to
have a weakness (of character)'?, F 227 'a straightforward
citizen'.   Other ascriptions:* Andromeda *F 144,* Antigone
*F 177, F 853, 911, 941, 1028, adesp. F 88a 'There's no city-
leader in you'. (On F 175 and 910 see above.)*

The Scholia on Aristophanes, Frogs *53 (= test. ii) seem
to date* Antiope, Hypsipyle *and* Phoenician Women *all
later than 412, although metrical criteria suggest a date
for* Antiope *before 418 (Cropp–Fick 74–6). Dramatic ele-
ments like reunion and a luring plot leading to revenge are
familiar in earlier plays, and there are marked similarities
between* Antiope *and* Ion *(c. 414–410?) in their heroines'
fortunes. 'Antiope' in the* Frogs *scholion could be another
error for* Antigone *as Cropp–Fick suggest, but a date near
410 still seems most likely.*

*Euripides' tragedy seems to have been unique. Perfor-
mances of it may have inspired three 4th c. South Italian
vases depicting the killing of Dirce and in one case the at-
tack on Lycus (LIMC 'Antiope' nos. 4–6, Todisco L 11, S 5,
Ap 214: see Haussmann, Taplin, Ridgeon, Joyce). Eubulus
in the mid-4th c. may have popularized it through his bur-
lesque* Antiope *(F 9 PCG). Pacuvius' Latin adaptation has
been mentioned above. Two later famous works of sculp-
ture are the late Roman 'Farnese Bull', recovered in the
1540's (see Taplin [1998], 33), and Canova's 'Dirce' of
1819; see also OGCMA I.109–12.*

ANTIOΠH

test. iii (a)

EADEM (i.e. ANTIOPA) EURIPIDIS. Nyctei regis in Boeo-
tia fuit filia Antiopa; eius formae bonitate Iuppiter adductus
grauidam fecit. (2) Quam pater cum punire uellet propter stu-
prum, minitans periculum Antiopa effugit. Casu in eodem
loco quo illa peruenerat Epopeus Sicyonius stabat; is mulie-
rem aduectam domo matrimonio suo iunxit. (3) Id Nycteus
aegre ferens cum moreretur Lyco fratri suo per obtestationem
mandat, cui tum regnum relinquebat, ne impune Antiopa fer-
ret. Huius post mortem Lycus Sicyonem uenit; interfecto
Epopeo Antiopam uinctam adduxit. In Cithaerone parit gemi-
nos et reliquit, quos pastor educauit, Zetum et Amphionem
nominauit. (4) Antiopa Dirce uxori Lyci data erat in crucia-
tum; ea occasione nacta fugae se mandauit; deuenit ad filios
suos, ex quibus Zetus existimans fugitiuam non recepit. In

Hyginus, *Fab*. 8 (the title is transmitted as *Eadem Euripidis
quam scribit Ennius*); largely similar accounts, also derived from
a narrative hypothesis, in Apollodorus 3.5.5 and Schol. on
Apollonius of Rhodes 4.1090 (= test. iii (b) and (c)): see especially
W. Luppe, *Philologus* 128 (1984), 41–57, and note on the transla-
tion.

ANTIOPE

test. iii (a)

THE SAME (i.e. ANTIOPE) BY EURIPIDES.[1] Antiope was
the daughter of Nycteus king of Boeotia. Jupiter was attracted
by her shapely beauty and made her pregnant. (2) When her
father was meaning to punish her because of this shaming vio-
lation, Antiope fled from the threatening danger. By chance
Epaphus of Sicyon was staying in the same place that she had
reached; he took the woman home and married her as his
wife. (3) Nycteus was angry; when he was dying, before wit-
nesses he charged his brother Lycus, to whom he was leaving
his kingdom, that Antiope should not go unscathed. After
Nycteus' death Lycus came to Sicyon; he killed Epaphus and
took Antiope back in bonds. On Mt. Cithaeron she gave birth
to twins and abandoned them; they were brought up by a
herdsman who named them Zethus and Amphion. (4) Antiope
was given to Dirce the wife of Lycus to torture; she got an op-
portunity to escape and committed herself to it. She reached
her sons, but Zethus thought her a fugitive and would not re-

---

[1] Hyginus has a more concise summary in *Fab*. 7 headed sim-
ply 'Antiope', then *Fab*. 8 headed 'The same by Euripides, which
Ennius wrote' (the reference to Ennius is probably due to a confu-
sion). Cf. *Fab*. 4 (= *Ino* test. iii) headed 'Euripides' Ino'. The aeti-
ology of Dirce's spring given in F 223.76–7 is omitted in *Fab*. 8 but
appears in the more concise *Fab*. 7: cf. M. Huys, *APF* 42 (1996),
171–2 and the apparatus opposite.

177

eundem locum Dirce per bacchationem Liberi ilico delata est; ibi Antiopam repertam ad mortem extrahebat. (5) Sed ab educatore pastore adulescentes certiores facti eam esse matrem suam, celeriter consecuti matrem eripuerunt, Dircen ad taurum crinibus religatam necant. (6) Lycum cum occidere uellent, uetuit eos Mercurius, et simul iussit Lycum concedere regnum Amphioni.

(4) *ilico* Kannicht: *illuc* Hyginus

179

⟨ΒΟΤΚΟΛΟΣ⟩

. . . ἔχεις,

εὖ μοι διδοίης δεσπότῃ θ’ ὃς Οἰνόης
σύγχορτα ναίει πεδία ταῖσδ’ Ἐλευθεραῖς.

Strabo 8.6.16; v. 3: Schol. on Homer, *Iliad* 11.774; lexicographers

3 ναίει Strabo ms. P (-ειν other mss.): ναίω other sources

181–182

⟨ΒΟΤΚΟΛΟΣ⟩

181 τὸν μὲν κικλήσκω Ζῆθον· ἐζήτησε γὰρ
τόκοισιν εὐμάρειαν ἡ τεκοῦσά νιν . . .

182 (τὸν δὲ . . . Ἀμφίονα) . . . παρὰ τὸ ἀμφ’ ὁδὸν . . .
γεννηθῆναι.

F 181: *Etymologicum Gudianum* in *Etym. Magnum* p. 411.12 Gaisford; v. 1 (end)–2: *Etym. Gudianum* p. 230.57 Sturz. F 182 is drawn from a paraphrase in *Etym. Gudianum* α 746 Lasserre–Livadaras (= *Etym. Magnum* p. 92.24 Gaisford). Both fragments are reflected in Hyginus, *Fab.* 7.3–4.

1 κικλήσκω Bothe: κίκλησκε (imperative, probably a mere copying error) *Et. Gud*.

178

ceive her. There and then[2] Dirce was brought to the same spot through her ecstatic possession by Dionysus; she found Antiope there and began to drag her away to death. (5) The young men however were informed by the herdsman who had brought them up that she was their mother; they quickly pursued Dirce and tore their mother free; they killed Dirce by tying her bodily by her hair to a bull. (6) When they were meaning to kill Lycus, Hermes forbade them, and at the same time ordered Lycus to cede his kingom to Amphion.

[2] Kannicht's 'there and then' replaces a redundant 'to that place' in Hyginus.

179
⟨HERDSMAN⟩

. . . you (who?) hold . . . , may you grant me good fortune, and my master who lives on the plain of Oenoe with its pastures bordering Eleutherae here![1]

[1] Lines very near the play's beginning, addressed to Dionysus whose famous shrine lay at Eleutherae on the Attic–Boeotian border. For 'you hold . . .' in an opening address to a god cf. *Sciron* F 674a. 'My master . . . Oenoe' plays on his name, Oeneus.

181–182
⟨HERDSMAN⟩

I call the one Zethus; for his mother sought a place of comfort for his birthing . . . (and the other Amphion) . . . from his being born by the roadside.[1]

[1] The Herdsman named the twins after Antiope abandoned them (cf. F 207, 208). English cannot reproduce the etymological plays here, which derive Zethus' name from the Greek verb 'sought' (*zēt-*) and Amphion's from Greek 'by the roadside' (*amphi hodon*). For such etymologies see on *Alexander* F 42d.

EURIPIDES

182a (= 225 + 1023 N)

ΑΜΦΙΩΝ

Αἰθέρα καὶ Γαῖαν πάντων γενέτειραν ἀείδω . . .

Sextus Empiricus, *Against the Experts* 10.314–5 (= F 1023 N); also reflected in Probus on Virgil, *Eclogues* 6.31 (Servius III.2, p. 343.24 Thilo-Hagen) (= F 225 N); two other late citations.

(182b–189: see below after F 192)

190

⟨ΑΜΦΙΩΝ⟩

λύρα βοῶν ⟨γὰρ⟩ ῥύσι᾽ ἐξερρύσατο.

Anon., *On Lyric Poets*, in Appendix to *Lexicon Vindobonense* p. 322.18 Nauck

λυρᾷ . . . ⟨γὰρ⟩ . . . ἐξελύσατο Schneidewin

191

⟨ΑΜΦΙΩΝ⟩

(μελετὴ) . . . κρεῖσσον ὄλβου κτῆμα . . .

Philostratus, *Lives of the Sophists* 2.27.4

192

ΑΜΦΙΩΝ

χρόνος θεῶν ⟨τε⟩ πνεῦμ᾽ ἔρως θ᾽ ὑμνῳδίας

Julian, *Letters* 30; Suda α 1751

(182b: see opposite)

180

182a (= 225 + 1023 N)

AMPHION

I sing of Heaven, and Earth the mother of all . . . [1]

[1] Amphion enters singing to his lyre (F 190, cf. F 223.91 and Pacuvius, *Antiopa* fr. 1 d'Anna). For 'Heaven and Earth' cf. *Chrysippus* F 839 and note, and for 'Earth the mother of all', F 195 below.

(182b–189: see below after F 192)

190

⟨AMPHION⟩

(For) the lyre discharged the penalty for the cattle.[1]

[1] The trickster god Hermes as a miraculous baby stole Apollo's cattle, and in recompense gave Apollo the lyre he had invented by stringing a tortoiseshell. There is a hidden etymological play between Greek *lura* 'lyre' and *lutron* 'recompense', which induced Schneidewin's conjecture 'For with the lyre (Hermes) paid off (*exelusato*) the recompense for the cattle'.

191

⟨AMPHION⟩

(practice) . . . a possession better than wealth . . .

192

AMPHION

. . . time and the gods' inspiration and a love of singing praise . . .

(F 182b in *TrGF* gathers evidence for the debate between Zethus and Amphion to which F 183–9 and 193–202 are assigned.)

183

ΖΗΘΟΣ

κακῶν κατάρχεις τήνδε μοῦσαν εἰσάγων
ἀργόν, φίλοινον, χρημάτων ἀτημελῆ.

Dio Chrysostom, *Orations* 73.10 (paraphrase); v. 1 was altered
for parody by Plutarch, *Moralia* 634e = Athenaeus 14.616c; v. 2 is
differently worded in Sextus Empiricus, *Against the Experts* 6.27;
fragment reconstructed by Porson, Wilamowitz

1 end: ἄτοπον, ἀσύμφορόν τι inserted by Hartung as an
incomplete verse, from Dio and Sextus

184

ΖΗΘΟΣ

ἐν τούτῳ ⟨γέ τοι⟩
λαμπρός θ' ἕκαστος κἀπὶ τοῦτ' ἐπείγεται,
νέμων τὸ πλεῖστον ἡμέρας τούτῳ μέρος,
ἵν' αὐτὸς αὑτοῦ τυγχάνει βέλτιστος ὤν.

Plato, *Gorgias* 484d–e (vv. 1–2 in paraphrase) and Schol.; v. 2
(κἀπὶ)–4: Aristotle, *Rhetoric* 1371b31, [Aristotle], *Problems*
917a13; vv. 3–4: Plato, *Alcibiades II* 146a (τούτῳ . . . μέρος), Plu-
tarch, *Moralia* 514a; v. 4 alone: Plut. *Mor.* 622a, 630b and 43b

4 βέλτιστος Pl. *Gorg.*, Aristotle: κράτιστος others

183
ZETHUS

You start the trouble by introducing music here: it's idle, it loves wine, it neglects affairs.[1]

[1] Before 'it's idle' Hartung's insertion adds 'it's out of place, it's disadvantageous . . .'

184
ZETHUS

It's in this (I tell you) that each man is distinguished, and for this that he is eager, giving the most part of his day to this—where he himself is actually at his best.

EURIPIDES

185

ΖΗΘΟΣ

(ἀμελεῖς ὧν δεῖ σε ἐπιμελεῖσθαι·)
ψυχῆς φύσιν ⟨γὰρ⟩ ὧδε γενναίαν ⟨λαχὼν⟩
γυναικομίμῳ διαπρέπεις μορφώματι·
κοὔτ' ἂν δίκης βουλαῖσι προσθεῖ' ἂν λόγον
5 οὔτ' εἰκὸς ἂν καὶ πιθανὸν ⟨οὐδὲν⟩ ἂν λάκοις
.... κοὔτ' ἂν ἀσπίδος κύτει
⟨καλῶς⟩ ὁμιλήσει⟨α⟩ς οὔτ' ἄλλων ὕπερ
νεανικὸν βούλευμα βουλεύσαιό ⟨τι⟩.

Vv. 1–5, 7–8 partly paraphrased, partly cited by Plato, *Gorgias* 485e–6a (cf. Schol. on 485e, p. 150 Greene); v. 3 (without διαπρέπεις): Philostratus, *Life of Apollonius* 4.21; vv. 4–7 in part: Olympiodorus, *On Plato's Gorgias* 26.22 (on 486a1). Di Benedetto (2004) constructs from Plato and Olympiodorus a very different text of this fragment.

4–5 so Dodds: as one verse, κοὔτ' ἂν δίκης βουλαῖσι πιθανὸν ἂν λάκοις Merkelbach   λάκοις Bonitz: λάβοις Plato
7 ⟨καλῶς⟩ Nauck

186

ΖΗΘΟΣ

καὶ πῶς σοφὸν τοῦτ' ἐστίν, ἥτις εὐφυᾶ
λαβοῦσα τέχνη φῶτ' ἔθηκε χείρονα;

Plato, *Gorgias* 486b4–5

185

ZETHUS

(You neglect things which should be your concern.) (For) though naturally (endowed) with a noble spirit you stand out with an appearance imitating a woman's! You'd neither contribute a word to deliberations about justice nor voice anything likely or persuasive[1] . . . neither would you keep   5 (bravely) close to a shield's hollow nor offer (any) forceful counsel on others' behalf.

[1] 'Likely' is a catch-word of contemporary rhetoric (e.g. *Cretans* F 472e.11, 19). For 'persuasive' cf. *Antigone* F 170. Dodds's reconstruction of vv. 4–5 takes fuller account of Plato's paraphrase than Merkelbach's 'nor have a persuasive voice in deliberations about justice'.

186

ZETHUS

And how is this wise—an art that takes a naturally robust man and makes him inferior?

EURIPIDES

187

<ΖΗΘΟΣ>

ἀνὴρ γὰρ ὅστις εὖ βίον κεκτημένος
τὰ μὲν κατ᾽ οἴκους ἀμελίᾳ παρεὶς ἐᾷ,
μολπαῖσι δ᾽ ἡσθεὶς τοῦτ᾽ ἀεὶ θηρεύεται,
ἀργὸς μὲν οἴκοι κἂν πόλει γενήσεται,
5 φίλοισι δ᾽ οὐδείς· ἡ φύσις γὰρ οἴχεται,
ὅταν γλυκείας ἡδονῆς ἥσσων τις ᾖ.

Stobaeus 3.30.1; v. 1 = Diphilus F 74.4 *PCG*; vv. 3–6: Sextus
Empiricus, *Against the Experts* 6.35

4 οἴκοι κἂν πόλει Walker, Diggle: οἴκοις καὶ πόλει Stob.,
Sext.   5 end ἀλλ᾽ ἄφαντος οἴχεται (= *Orestes* 1557) Sext.

*187a

<ΖΗΘΟΣ>

(i) ῥῖψον τὴν λύραν, κέχρησο δὲ ὅπλοις.

(ii) μάτην κιθαρίζεις μηδὲν ὠφελῶν, ἀλλὰ ἔξελθε· στρα-
τιωτικὸν βίον ζῆσον καὶ <εὐ>πόρησον καὶ τυράννησον.

Paraphrases in (i) Schol. on Plato, *Gorgias* 485e and (ii)
Olympiodorus, *On Plato's Gorgias* 34.4, both attributing these
sentiments to 'Zethus abusing Amphion's music'; clarified by
Borthwick.

187
⟨ZETHUS⟩

A man who possesses a good livelihood but neglects matters in his own house and lets them slip, and from his pleasure in singing pursues this all the time, will become idle at home and in his city, and a nobody for those close to him: a man's nature is lost and gone when he is overcome by pleasure's sweetness.

*187a
⟨ZETHUS⟩

(i) Throw away the lyre, and use weapons!

(ii) Your singing to the lyre is useless, you do no good! Rather, go out of doors: live a soldier's life, and be well provided, and be a ruler!

188

ΖΗΘΟΣ

ἀλλ' ἐμοὶ πιθοῦ·
παῦσαι ματάζων καὶ πόνων εὐμουσίαν
ἄσκει· τοιαῦτ' ἄειδε καὶ δόξεις φρονεῖν,
σκάπτων, ἀρῶν γῆν, ποιμνίοις ἐπιστατῶν,
5 ἄλλοις τὰ κομψὰ ταῦτ' ἀφεὶς σοφίσματα,
ἐξ ὧν κενοῖσιν ἐγκατοικήσεις δόμοις.

Plato, *Gorgias* 486c, partly paraphrased; vv. 2–3 and 6: Olym-
piodorus, *On Plato's Gorgias* 26.24–5; vv. 3 (τοιαῦτα)–5: Stobaeus
4.15.13; v. 6: Dio Chrysostom, *Orations* 73.10

2 ματάζων Plato some mss.: δ' ἐλέγχων others   καὶ πόνων
Borthwick: πραγμάτων δ' Plato: πολέμων δ' Olympiod.

189

< ΧΟΡΟΣ? >

ἐκ παντὸς ἄν τις πράγματος δισσῶν λόγων
ἀγῶνα θεῖτ' ἄν, εἰ λέγειν εἴη σοφός.

Stobaeus 2.2.9, Athenaeus 15.677b

(190–2: see above after F 182a)

193

< ΑΜΦΙΩΝ >

ὅστις δὲ πράσσει πολλὰ μὴ πράσσειν παρόν,
μῶρος, παρὸν ζῆν ἡδέως ἀπράγμονα.

Stobaeus 4.16.2

2 the second πάρον is suspect

188
ZETHUS

No, let me persuade you! Cease this idle folly, and practise the fine music of hard work! Make this your song, and you will seem sensible, digging, ploughing the land, watching over flocks, leaving to others these pretty arts of yours which will have you keeping house in a bare home.

189
⟨CHORUS?⟩

A man could make a contest between two arguments from any matter, if he were a clever speaker.[1]

[1] An axiom originating with the Sophist Protagoras (Diogenes Laertius 9.51), with many echoes in Euripides.

(190–2: see above after F 182a)

193
⟨AMPHION⟩

Whoever is very active when he may be inactive, is a fool, when he may live pleasurably without activity.[1]

[1] Amphion taking the offensive, rather than maintaining his defence (cf. F 196)? For the general idea cf. *Philoctetes* F 787.

EURIPIDES

194

⟨ΑΜΦΙΩΝ⟩

ὁ δ' ἥσυχος φίλοισί τ' ἀσφαλὴς φίλος
πόλει τ' ἄριστος. μὴ τὰ κινδυνεύματα
αἰνεῖτ'· ἐγὼ γὰρ οὔτε ναυτίλον φιλῶ
τολμῶντα λίαν οὔτε προστάτην χθονός.

Stobaeus 4.7.10

195

⟨ΑΜΦΙΩΝ?⟩

ἅπαντα τίκτει χθὼν πάλιν τε λαμβάνει.

Orion 2.1 Haffner

196

⟨ΑΜΦΙΩΝ?⟩

τοιόσδε θνητῶν τῶν ταλαιπώρων βίος·
οὔτ' εὐτυχεῖ τὸ πάμπαν οὔτε δυστυχεῖ.
{εὐδαιμονεῖ τε καὖθις οὐκ εὐδαιμονεῖ.}
τί δῆτ' ἐν ὄλβῳ μὴ σαφεῖ βεβηκότες
5 οὐ ζῶμεν ὡς ἥδιστα μὴ λυπούμενοι;

Stobaeus 4.41.11; v. 2: *Comparison of Menander and Philistion* 1.29 Jaekel; vv. 4–5: Clement of Alexandria, *Miscellanies* 6.2.13.4

3 deleted by Nauck

190

194
⟨AMPHION⟩

The quiet man is a sure friend for friends, and best for a city. Don't praise risky undertakings:[1] I love neither a sailor nor a city leader who is too venturesome.[2]

[1] A response to Zethus' F 187a (ii).　[2] Cf. *Suppliant Women* 508–9.

195
⟨AMPHION?⟩

The earth gives birth to all things, and takes them back again.[1]

[1] The fragment could belong with F 190; its inclusion in the debate is disputed.

196
⟨AMPHION?⟩

Such is the life of wretched mortals: a man is neither completely fortunate nor unfortunate. {He prospers under god's blessing, and then again does not prosper}. Why then, when we have entered upon an insecure prosperity, do we not live as pleasurably as possible, causing ourselves no distress?[1]

[1] Cf. *Telephus* F 714, *Heracles* 503–5.

EURIPIDES

197

⟨ΑΜΦΙΩΝ?⟩

. . . βροτοῖσιν εὐκρὰς οὐ γένοιτ᾽ ἂν ἡδέως . . .

Photius, *Lexicon* ε 2231 Theodoridis; other lexica cite the whole line or the single word εὐκράς or εὔκρας (some offer the form εὔκρατος)

ἡδέως Phot.: ἡδονή Lobeck

198

⟨ΑΜΦΙΩΝ⟩

εἰ δ᾽ εὐτυχῶν τις καὶ βίον κεκτημένος
μηδὲν δόμοισι τῶν καλῶν θηράσεται,
ἐγὼ μὲν αὐτὸν οὔποτ᾽ ὄλβιον καλῶ,
φύλακα δὲ μᾶλλον χρημάτων εὐδαίμονα.

Stobaeus 3.16.4; P. Petrie 3 (= P. Lit. Lond. 57 and 71) 6–9 has the lines with defective beginnings and ends, but assigned to Epicharmus (F 272 *PCG*).

2 θηρασετ[P. Petrie: πειράσεται Stob.

199

⟨ΑΜΦΙΩΝ⟩

τὸ δ᾽ ἀσθενές μου καὶ τὸ θῆλυ σώματος
κακῶς ἐμέμφθης· εἰ γὰρ εὖ φρονεῖν ἔχω,
κρεῖσσον τόδ᾽ ἐστὶ καρτεροῦ βραχίονος.

Stobaeus 3.3.2

197

⟨AMPHION?⟩

... men's (life?) would not be well-mixed, pleasurably ... [1]

[1] The fragment seems to cohere with F 196, cf. F 198. Lobeck's conjecture would separate it, 'pleasure would not be well-mixed for men'.

198

⟨AMPHION⟩

If someone who has good fortune and possesses a livelihood is going to pursue none of the finer things[1] in his house, I shall myself never call him blessed with prosperity but rather a fortunate guardian of wealth.

[1] The arts, especially Amphion's own music.

199

⟨AMPHION⟩

You were wrong to blame my body's weakness and femininity: for if I have sound thinking, this is superior to a strong arm.

200

⟨ΑΜΦΙΩΝ⟩

γνώμαις γὰρ ἀνδρὸς εὖ μὲν οἰκοῦνται πόλεις,
εὖ δ' οἶκος, εἴς τ' αὖ πόλεμον ἰσχύει μέγα·
σοφὸν γὰρ ἓν βούλευμα τὰς πολλὰς χέρας
νικᾷ, σὺν ὄχλῳ δ' ἀμαθία πλεῖστον κακόν.

Stobaeus 4.13.3; Orion, Euripidean Appendix 18a–b Haffner
(with punctuation suggesting vv. 3–4 may be a separate fragment);
[Plutarch,] *On Homer* 156.2; vv. 1–2 (οἶκος) or v. 1 alone are
cited, sometimes in adaptation, in three further sources; vv. 3–4
are cited in whole or part in many sources.

1 γνώμαις Orion, others: γνώμῃ Stob.: βουλαῖς Clement of
Alexandria, *Miscellanies* 2.19.102.7   ἀνδρὸς Stob., [Plut.]: -ῶν
others

201

⟨ΑΜΦΙΩΝ⟩

καὶ μὴν ὅσοι μὲν σαρκὸς εἰς εὐεξίαν
ἀσκοῦσι βίοτον, ἢν σφαλῶσι χρημάτων,
κακοὶ πολῖται· δεῖ γὰρ ἄνδρ' εἰθισμένον
ἀκόλαστον ἦθος γαστρὸς ἐν ταὐτῷ μένειν.

Stobaeus 3.6.1

202

⟨ΑΜΦΙΩΝ⟩

ἐγὼ μὲν οὖν ᾄδοιμι καὶ λέγοιμί τι
σοφόν, ταράσσων μηδὲν ὧν πόλις νοσεῖ.

Stobaeus 3.1.63

200

‹AMPHION›

Cities are well managed by a man's judgements, and his
house well, and he is a great resource in war;[1] for one wise
counsel defeats many hands,[2] and crassness partnered
with a mob is the greatest evil.

[1] Some editors prefer Stobaeus' singular 'judgement', then 'it
(judgement) is a great resource'.   [2] Alluding to a mass vote
in a political gathering.

201

‹AMPHION›

Look! All those whose regimen of life is to acquire a fine
physique are bad citizens if ever their money fails; for once
a man is accustomed to undisciplined habits of appetite, he
inevitably stays in that condition.[1]

[1] A similar but even stronger attack on athletes in *Autolycus* F
282, esp. 1–9.

202

‹AMPHION›

No, rather may I myself sing and say something wise, with-
out stirring up any of the city's ills.

203

ἔνδον δὲ θαλάμοις βουκόλου . . . *(text lost)* . . .
κομῶντα κισσῷ στῦλον εὐίου θεοῦ . . .

Clement of Alexandria, *Miscellanies* 1.24.163.5

1 ἔνδον Clem.: εἶδον Bothe; other editors also supplement
the defective text with a verb of seeing   βουκόλου Toup: -ον
Clem.

204

⟨ΑΝΤΙΟΠΗ?⟩

πόλλ᾽ ἐστὶν ἀνθρώποισιν, ὦ ξένοι, κακά.

Stobaeus 4.34.35

205

⟨ΑΝΤΙΟΠΗ⟩

φρονῶ δ᾽ ἃ πάσχω, καὶ τόδ᾽ οὐ σμικρὸν κακόν·
τὸ μὴ εἰδέναι γὰρ ἡδονὴν ἔχει τινὰ
νοσοῦντα, κέρδος δ᾽ ἐν κακοῖς ἀγνωσία.

Stobaeus 4.35.24; v. 1: Erotian κ 22

206

⟨ΑΝΤΙΟΠΗ?⟩

ὦ παῖ, γένοιντ᾽ ἂν εὖ λελεγμένοι λόγοι
ψευδεῖς, ἐπῶν δὲ κάλλεσιν νικῷεν ἂν
τἀληθές· ἀλλ᾽ οὐ τοῦτο τἀκριβέστατον,
ἀλλ᾽ ἡ φύσις καὶ τοὐρθόν· ὃς δ᾽ εὐγλωσσίᾳ
5 νικᾷ, σοφὸς μέν, ἀλλ᾽ ἐγὼ τὰ πράγματα
κρείσσω νομίζω τῶν λόγων ἀεί ποτε.

203

. . . and inside in the herdsman's dwelling (I saw) a pillar
festooned with ivy for the god of celebration . . . [1]

[1] Dionysus, inspiring ecstasy and cries of *Euoi* in his cele-
brants. Ivy, an evergreen, symbolizes the vitality of nature in the
god's gift; it was worn or carried by his worshippers. For the dwell-
ing, see Introduction above.

204

⟨ANTIOPE?⟩

Mankind has many troubles, strangers.

205

⟨ANTIOPE⟩

I realise what I suffer, and this is no small misery; for not
knowing that one is in trouble has a certain pleasure, and
ignorance amid misery is a gain.

206

⟨ANTIOPE?⟩

My son,[1] speeches well phrased might be false, and over-
come the truth through the beauties of words; but this is
not the surest criterion: nature and right are that. The man
who overcomes through eloquence is clever, but I consider
the facts to be stronger than speeches every time.　　5

[1] Addressed to Amphion by Antiope, most probably; 'my son'
then need not be dramatic irony before his identity is made
known, but means just 'listen: you are younger'. But some editors
infer that the speaker is the Herdsman, Amphion's surrogate fa-
ther. For the complaint in the first sentence cf. *Alexander* F 56
with note.

Clement of Alexandria, *Miscellanies* 1.8.41.5; vv. 4–6:
Stobaeus 2.15.12

207

ΑΝΤΙΟΠΗ

ἡνίκ᾽ ἠγόμην πάλιν,
κύουσα τίκτω.

Ammonius, *On Similar and Different Words* 288; v. 2: Eustathius on Homer, *Odyssey* 16.190

208

ΑΝΤΙΟΠΗ

εἰ δ᾽ ἠμελήθην ἐκ θεῶν καὶ παῖδ᾽ ἐμώ,
ἔχει λόγον καὶ τοῦτο· τῶν πολλῶν βροτῶν
δεῖ τοὺς μὲν εἶναι δυστυχεῖς, τοὺς δ᾽ εὐτυχεῖς.

Stobaeus 4.34.37; vv. 1–2: Marcus Aurelius, *Meditations* 7.41 and 11.6; v. 3 = [Menander], *Monostichs* 187 Jaekel

209

οὐ σωφρονίζειν ἔμαθον· αἰδεῖσθαι δὲ χρή,
γύναι, τὸ λίαν καὶ φυλάσσεσθαι φθόνον.

Stobaeus 4.23.18

210

ΑΜΦΙΩΝ

οὐδὲ γὰρ λάθρᾳ δοκῶ
θηρὸς κακούργου σχήματ᾽ ἐκμιμούμενον
σοὶ Ζῆν᾽ ἐς εὐνὴν ὥσπερ ἄνθρωπον μολεῖν.

Clement of Alexandria, *Miscellanies* 5.14.111.2, whence Eusebius, *Preparation for the Gospel* 13.13.28; v. 2: John of Damascus, *PG* XCVI.825c

207
ANTIOPE

. . . when I was being brought back again, I was pregnant and gave birth.

208
ANTIOPE

If I and my two sons were neglected by the gods,[1] this too has reason: out of the great number of mortal men, some must be unfortunate, others fortunate.

[1] Antiope is thinking of Zeus himself as their father, but Zethus and Amphion have yet to learn of this (F 210, cf. F 223.2, 11–13).

209

I did not learn to teach moderation; but one must fight shy of excess, woman, and guard oneself against envy.

210
AMPHION

Nor do I think that Zeus secretly imitated the form of an evil beast and came into your bed just like a man.[1]

[1] See on F 208. The Scholia on Apollonius of Rhodes (test. iii (c) [1]) and John Malalas, *Chronicles* 2.16 Thurn = 2.35 Jeffreys-Scott (test. ivc) record a story that Zeus disguised himself as a satyr when making love to Antiope.

---

2 θηρὸς John: φωτὸς Clem.   3 Ζῆν᾽ Valckenaer: τήνδ᾽ Clem.

211

⟨ΧΟΡΟΣ⟩

φεῦ φεῦ, βροτείων πημάτων ὅσαι τύχαι
ὅσαι τε μορφαί· τέρμα δ' οὐκ εἴποι τις ἄν.

Stobaeus 4.34.33, Clement of Alexandria, *Miscellanies* 3.3.23.2

(F 212–6: see below after F 223)

217

. . . τὸ δοῦλον οὐχ ὁρᾷς ὅσον κακόν;

Stobaeus 4.19.12

218

⟨ΧΟΡΟΣ?⟩

φεῦ, φεῦ, τὸ δοῦλον ὡς ἁπανταχῇ γένος
πρὸς τὴν ἐλάσσω μοῖραν ὥρισεν θεός.

Stobaeus 4.19.41

219

κόσμος δὲ σιγή, στέφανος ἀνδρὸς οὐ κακοῦ·
τὸ δ' ἐκλαλοῦν τοῦθ' ἡδονῆς μὲν ἅπτεται,
κακὸν δ' ὁμίλημ', ἀσθενὲς δὲ καὶ πόλει.

Stobaeus 3.36.10

1 σιγή, στέφανος Ellis: σιγῆς στέφανος Stob.

211
<CHORUS>

Oh, alas! How many are the accidents, and how many the forms, of mankind's sufferings! One could not speak of an end to them.

(F 212–6: see below after F 223)

217

. . . do you not see how great an evil the condition of slavery is?

218
<CHORUS?>

Oh, alas! How completely god has marked out slaves as a class for the inferior estate!

219

Silence is an ornament, a crown for a man without vice; while chattering of this kind fastens upon pleasure, and makes bad company, and is a weakness too for a city.[1]

[1] Either the Herdsman defends his not having told the twins of their descent, or Zethus in the debate faults Amphion's 'political' uselessness: see Introduction. Stobaeus is slightly less good: 'Decorous silence is a crown, etc.'

220

‹ΑΜΦΙΩΝ?›

πολλοὶ δὲ θνητῶν τοῦτο πάσχουσιν κακόν·
γνώμῃ φρονοῦντες οὐ θέλουσ᾽ ὑπηρετεῖν
ψυχῇ τὰ πολλὰ πρὸς φίλων νικώμενοι.

Stobaeus 3.30.9

175
(assigned to *Antigone* in *TrGF*)

220

⟨AMPHION?⟩

Many men experience this trouble: despite good sense they are generally unwilling to obey their judgement, their heart being overcome by friends.[1]

[1] This straightforward translation gives good sense, but both text and meaning are disputed. The fragment is often assigned to the debate (after F 202).

175

(assigned to *Antigone* in *TrGF*)[1]

Dirce has come to Eleutherae to honour Dionysus, attended by fellow-worshippers who form a second chorus (see Introduction). She is costumed as a bacchant, a free-ranging celebrant of the god (5–7); she is threatened with forcible removal from the shrine, for as a tormentor of Antiope her presence there is impure (8: for this reason Amphion is a more likely speaker than Antiope herself). She strikes an attitude of noble acceptance of imminent death, however (9–15).

[1] The ascription of this fragment to *Antiope* is disputed. Vv. 14–15 of the papyrus are cited in Stobaeus as coming from *Antigone*. Ascription of the whole to *Antiope* was suggested by Luppe in 1981, and is supported by Diggle (most recently in *TrGFS* 87), Taplin (1998) 37–9 and *Pots and Plays* 285 n.70, and Collard (*SFP* II.311), because the 'Dionysiac' content suits Antiope much more easily: in Hyginus, *Fab.* 8.4 (= test. iii (a) above), Dirce is brought to Eleutherae 'through possession by Bacchus'. The fragment is retained for *Antigone* by R. Scodel, *ZPE* 46 (1982), 37–42, Inglese 180–4, Zimmermann 165–8, Van Looy in ed. Budé, and Kannicht in *TrGF* (for Inglese and Zimmermann see our bibliography for *Antigone*).

EURIPIDES

<AMΦIΩN?>

οὔκουν] ἑκοῦσα τήνδ᾽ ἐρημώσ[εις ἕδραν,
μὴ χειρία]ν ἕλκωσί σ᾽ οἵδε προσπ[
6–7 letters ἐ]θείρας· οὐ γὰρ ἐν τρυφαῖ[ς ἔτι
μέλαθρα] ναίεις Ἡράκλει· οὐδεστ[
5 7–8 letters]δ᾽ ἥκεις ἢ δι᾽ οἰωνῶν πλ[άκας
7–8 letters] πεδία δι[ε]φόρου χωρὶς μ[
6–7 letters ν]εβρίδος ἐξανημμένη[
7–8 letters]ν· ἱερὰ γὰρ τάδ᾽ οὐ σαυτῆς ἔ[χεις.

<ΔIΡKH?>

7–8 letters]μέλλον συνθανεῖν πρε[
10 μηδεὶς θί]γῃ μου δοῦλος ὢν ἐλε[υθέρας
7–8 letters].. χρῶτ᾽· ἀλλ᾽ ἑκοῦσα πε[ίσομαι.
ἐν τοῖς κακοῖς γὰρ ηὐγένει᾽ ὅτῳ παρῇ
τραχεῖα κὠξύθυμος ἀμαθίαν ἔχει·
ὅστις δὲ πρὸς τὸ πῖπτον εὐόργως φέρει
15 τὸν δαίμον᾽, οὗτος ῥᾷον ἀθλιωτ[

P. Oxy. 3317, ed. D. Hughes (1980); re-ed. W. Luppe, ZPE 42
(1981), 27–30; Diggle, TrGFS 87 (previously APF 42 (1996), 164–
7); vv. 12–13: Stobaeus 3.20.39, unattributed (= adesp. F 524 N);
vv. 14–15: Stobaeus 4.44.14, attributed to Antigone. On the dis-
puted attribution see note 1 to the translation, and introductions
to Antiope and Antigone.

1 or <ANTIOΠH> Luppe   2 πρόσπ[ολοι ed. pr.
4–5 οὐδὲ στ[έγος | φίλον τό]δ᾽ ἥκεις (e.g.) Diggle   5 ἢ
Mette· ἦ editors   6 δι[ε]φόρου is uncertain   8 οὐχ
ὅσιο]ν Collard   9 σαφὲς τὸ] μέλλον· συνθανεῖν πρέ[πει
φίλοις (e.g.) Luppe   12 ὅτῳ P. Oxy.: ὅταν Stob.

ANTIOPE

⟨AMPHION?⟩

Leave your (place) here willingly (then, so) these (atten-
dants? won't) drag you (forcibly) . . . by your . . . hair. You
are no (longer) living in luxury in Heracles' (palace),[2] nor
. . . have you come . . . [3] you who ranged(?) the (open fields)
of birds . . . plains without . . . with . . . of a fawnskin   5
(draped?) from you . . . [4] These sacred emblems are not
yours (to have).

⟨DIRCE?⟩

. . . (the?) future . . . to die with[5] . . . Let (no one) who is a
slave touch me: I am (free)! . . . (my) body; but I (shall suf-   10
fer) willingly: for amid disaster for any woman of high birth
to become harsh and quick to temper, is crass folly; but
whoever bears their fate with equanimity in the face of
what befalls, more easily . . . the most wretched . . . [6]   15

[2] In Thebes; the detail is allusive rather than accurate, for
Heracles became king of Thebes after Dirce's husband Lycus.
[3] 'nor have you come to a (friendly roof) here', Diggle.   [4] '(It
is irreligious)', Collard.   [5] The phrase is a major problem in
accepting this fragment for *Antiope*, with or without Luppe's
'(The) future (is clear: it is fitting) to die with (friends)'. Who is
present to share Dirce's death, except her women?   [6] 'more
easily (endures) the most wretched (sufferings)', Kannicht.

---

14 εὐόργως P. Oxy.: εὐλόγως Stob.   15 τὸν δαίμονα δ'
οὗτος ἧσσόν ἐστιν ὄλβιος (corrupt) Stob.; ἀθλιω[τάτους |
πόνους διαντλεῖ (e.g.) Kannicht

221

⟨ΑΓΓΕΛΟΣ⟩

εἰ δέ που τύχοι

πέριξ ἑλίξας ⟨   ⟩ εἶλχ᾽ ὁμοῦ λαβὼν

γυναῖκα πέτραν δρῦν μεταλλάσσων ἀεί.

[Longinus] *On the Sublime* 40.4

2 ⟨ταῦρος⟩ Valckenaer: ⟨εἶλκεν⟩ Adam: ἑλίξας εἶλκε
⟨πάνθ᾽⟩ Bergk

222

τήν τοι Δίκην λέγουσι παῖδ᾽ εἶναι Χρόνου,
δείκνυσι δ᾽ ἡμῶν ὅστις ἐστὶ μὴ κακός.

Stobaeus 1.3.33; see note opposite

223

⟨ΑΜΦΙΩΝ⟩

fr. a col. i   7 *letters* το]ύσδε μηδ᾽ ὅπως φευξούμεθα.
εἴπερ γὰρ ἡ]μᾶς Ζεὺς ἐγέννησεν πατήρ,

P. Petrie 1 and 2 (= P. Lit. Lond. 70), ed. J. Mahaffy (with J. B.
Bury, H. Weil), *Hermathena* 8 (1891), 38–51 and *Flinders Petrie
Papyri* I (1891); re-ed. A. W. Pickard-Cambridge in J. U. Powell,
New Chapters in the History of Greek Literature: Third Series
(Oxford, 1933) 105–13; C. Roberts, *CQ* 29 (1935), 164–6;
Kambitsis (1972); Diggle, *TrGFS* 88–93 (previously *PCPS* 42
(1996), 106–26); vv. 57–8: Stobaeus 1.3.25 (= F 223 N).   The text
here is almost wholly as edited by Diggle in *TrGFS* (Kannicht in
TrGF hardly differs). The numbering of vv. 28–116 is that most
commonly adopted now, but some editors (including Kannicht in
TrGF) number vv. 28–116 as 57–145, allowing for the twenty-nine
lines missing after v. 27.

221

〈MESSENGER〉

If (the bull) happened to twist round anywhere (it) . . .
dragged woman, rock, oak-tree along with it as it kept
shifting about.[1]

[1] Dirce dragged to her death by the bull (F 223.59). The miss-
ing word is a free guess: '〈the bull〉 dragged' Valckenaer; 'dragged,
〈dragged〉' (emphatic) Adam; 'dragged 〈everything,〉 woman
etc.' Bergk.

222

They say, indeed, that Justice is the child of Time, and
shows which of us is not bad.[1]

[1] Compare F 223.57–8, Justice's eventual revelation of the *im-
pious* man (some editors alter to that sense here); also F 223.107–
8, *Aeolus* F **38a with note. Wilamowitz suggested a connection
with F 216–8, on the condition of slaves.

223

*From the play's final scene: Amphion (68) is with Antiope
(10) and Zethus (87 etc.); the three are menaced by the ar-
rival of Lycus with armed men (17). Antiope and Zethus
seem to be played now by mutes, unless they have spoken
before the fragment begins and leave before Lycus enters
(thus freeing an actor to play Lycus); certainly Zethus re-
turns at 59 with Amphion, and Antiope may do so too.*

〈AMPHION〉

. . . these men, nor how we shall escape them. (If) Zeus is
(really) our father and sired us, he will (save) us, and with

σώσ]ει μεθ' ἡμῶν τ' ἐχθρὸν ἄνδρα τείσεται.
ἱ]κται δὲ πάντως εἰς τοσόνδε συμφορᾶς
5 ὥσ]τ' οὐδ' ἂν ἐκφύγοιμεν εἰ βουλοίμεθα
Δίρκης νεωρὲς αἷμα μὴ δοῦναι δίκην.
μένου]σι δ' ἡμῖν εἰς τόδ' ἔρχεται τύχη
ὥστ' ἢ] θανεῖν δεῖ τῷδ' ἐν ἡμέρας φάει
ἢ καὶ] τροπαῖα πολεμίων στῆσαι χερί.
10 .....(.) μ]ὲν οὕτω, μῆτερ, ἐξαυδῶ τάδε·
σοὶ δ' ὃς τ]ὸ λαμπρὸν αἰθέρος ναίεις πέδον,
λέγω τ]οσοῦτον, μὴ γαμεῖν μὲν ἡδέως,
γήμαν]τα δ' εἶναι σοῖς τέκνοις ἀνωφελῆ·
οὐ γὰρ κ]αλὸν τόδ', ἀλλὰ συμμαχεῖν φίλοις.
15 .....] πρὸς ἄγραν τ' εὐτυχῶς εἴη μολεῖν,
ὅπως ἕ]λωμεν ἄνδρα δυσσεβέστατον.

⟨ΧΟΡΟΣ⟩

ὅδ'] αὐ[τ]ός, εἰ χρὴ δοξάσαι τυραννικῷ
σκήπτρῳ, Λύκος πάρεστι· σιγῶμεν, φίλοι.

⟨ΛΥΚΟΣ⟩

ποῦ σ[traces of 22–23 letters   ]αι πέτραν
20 δρασμοῖς ε[traces of 22–23 letters
τίνες δὲ καὶ ... δρῶντες; ἐκ ποίας χθο[νός;
σημήνατ', εἴπατ' ε[traces of at least 16–17 letters
δεινὸν νομίζων αὐτὸς οὐκ ἀτιμάσας

---

4 beg. Bury; πάντως Weil, others: πάντων P. Petrie
10 πᾶσιν μ]ὲν Diggle: ἡμῖν μ]ὲν Cropp   15 πιθοῦ] Schaal
21 Such obvious supplements as [πῶς] and [τί] seem not to fit
the traces.

us punish the man who is our enemy. Things have (come)
to so great a pass that even if we wanted we could not es-
cape penalty for Dirce's newly shed blood. (If we stay,) our 5
fortunes come to this: (either) we must die within this day's
light (or in fact) triumph over our foes by action. I state this
. . . ,[1] mother; (but to you who) dwell in heaven's bright 10
expanse,[2] (I say) this much: do not lie with a woman for
pleasure and after doing so fail to help your children. That
is (not) honourable, while aiding one's family is . . .[3] and
may we go after our quarry successfully, (to trap) a most 15
impious man!

(The twins and Antiope withdraw into the cave.)

<CHORUS>
(Here) is Lycus himself, to judge by his ruler's sceptre! Let
us keep silent, my friends.

<LYCUS>
(entering with his men)
Where . . . cave(?) . . . runnings . . . ? Who and . . . acting 20
. . . ?[4] From what country? *(to his men)* Show me! Tell me
. . . In my anger I have myself not disdained . . . 23

---

[1] Perhaps 'to all' (i.e. those within hearing), Diggle; or 'to us'
(himself, Antiope, Zethus), Cropp.   [2] I.e. Zeus, their father.
[3] To fill the gap Schaal suggested 'Accept my words' (addressed to
Zeus).   [4] Obvious supplements such as '(how) acting' or 'do-
ing (what)' seem not to match the traces. Lycus seems to know of
suspicious activity near Eleutherae, by the strangers of 34 or 38;
these are apparently the persons whom the Herdsman refers to
as 'those men' in 30, where he begins his false reassurance of
Lycus; alternatively, Lycus is pursuing Dirce's ecstatic 'runnings'
(20, cf. F 175.5–6 before F 221 above).

fragments of four lines, then about twenty-nine lines missing at the foot of this column and top of the next, then:

⟨ΒΟΤΚΟΛΟΣ⟩

fr. b col. i   *about 13 letters*]σας ἥδομαι κακὸν ‥α.[

⟨ΛΤΚΟΣ⟩

οὐκ ἀσφαλὲς τόδ᾽ εἶπας, ἄνθρωπε, στέγ[ος.

⟨ΒΟΤΚΟΛΟΣ⟩

30   δρᾶν δεῖ τι· κείνους δ᾽ οἶδ᾽ ἐγὼ τεθνηκό[τας.

⟨ΛΤΚΟΣ⟩

καλῶς ἄρ᾽, εἴπερ οἶσθα, ταξόμεσθα νῦν.

⟨ΒΟΤΚΟΛΟΣ⟩

τάξιν] τίν᾽ ἄλλην ἢ δόμων στείχει[ν] ἔσω;
about 14 letters] καὶ πρὶν οἰκοῦμεν [
about 14 letters] τοὺς ξένους ἐὼν μ.[‥].[
35   *about 14 letters*] δορυφόρους ἔξω πέτ[ρας
     remains of one line
c. 11–12 letters ἡμ]εῖς καὶ σὺ θήσομεν καλῶς.

⟨ΛΤΚΟΣ⟩

πόσοι δὲ δὴ τὸ πλ]ῆθός εἰσιν οἱ ξένοι;

⟨ΒΟΤΚΟΛΟΣ⟩

εἷς ἢ δύ᾽· ἔγχη] δ᾽ οὐκ ἔχουσιν ἐν χεροῖν.

30 τι P. Petrie: τί; West   31 ταξόμεσθα Diggle: ταξώ-
μεσθα P. Petrie   32–7 stichomythia may continue through-
out, perhaps irregularly

(The Herdsman may have heard Lycus' words from within the cave. During the next very fragmentary or missing thirty or more lines he has come out of the cave and been roughly addressed [cf. 29] by Lycus; but he sets about luring him into the cave unguarded.)

⟨HERDSMAN⟩

... I am glad ... trouble ...   28

⟨LYCUS⟩

You mean this house is not safe, fellow!

⟨HERDSMAN⟩

Something must be done;[5] I know those men are dead.   30

⟨LYCUS⟩

Then since you know it, we shall now make[6] good arrangements.

⟨HERDSMAN⟩[7]

What (arrangements), other than to go inside the house?
... and we have been living here before(?) ... allowing the
strangers ... armed men outside (the cave) ... (*one line*) ...   35
we and you will arrange ... well.

⟨LYCUS⟩

(And how many in fact) in number are the strangers?

⟨HERDSMAN⟩

(One or two;) and they don't have (weapons) in their
hands.

---

[5] 'What must be done', West.   [6] Some editors retain 'let
us make' from P. Petrie.   [7] Vv. 32–7 may continue the
stichomythic exchange, or the Herdsman may speak all of them.

⟨ΛΥΚΟΣ⟩

40 ὅπλοισί νυν φ]ρουρεῖτε περίβολον πέτρας
    about 11 letters]ντες, κἄν τι[ς ἐ]κπίπτῃ δόμων,
    λάζυσθ᾽· ἐγ]ὼ δὲ παῖδα Νυκτέως ἐμῇ
    about 10 letters]σαι χειρὶ καὶ τάχ᾽ εἴσεται

fr. c col. i *about 14 letters*]ντας ὡς μάτην λόγων
45 *about 12 letters* σ]υμμάχους ἀνωφελεῖς.

⟨ΒΟΥΚΟΛΟΣ⟩

    about 13 letters] .ος ἦν θεὸς θέλῃ
    about 14 letters] τήνδ᾽ ἀνὰ στέγην τάχα.

⟨ΧΟΡΟΣ⟩

    about 14 letters]ριων σθένος βρόχοισι κατα-
    10–11 letters] βροτῶν δ᾽ αὖ τέχναις
50a *remains of one half-line*

⟨ΛΥΚΟΣ⟩

50b   ἰώ μοί μοι.

⟨ΧΟΡΟΣ⟩

ἔ]α ἔα·
καὶ δὴ [πρὸς ἔργῳ] τῶν νεανιῶν χέρες.

⟨ΛΥΚΟΣ⟩

ὦ πρόσπ[ολοι ....]ντες οὐκ ἀρήξετε;

⟨ΧΟΡΟΣ⟩

ἀλαλάζετα[ι ἁ στ]έγα· βοᾷ
θανάσιμον μέλος.

46 ⟨ΒΟΥΚΟΛΟΣ⟩ von Arnim: ⟨ΧΟΡΟΣ⟩ Blass   ἦν Diggle: αν
P. Petrie   52 κλυό]ντες Snell

⟨LYCUS⟩
(to his men)

Keep (armed) watch on the cave's surroundings (now) . . .   40
and if anyone bursts from the house, (seize him; I) . . .
Nycteus' daughter with my hand, and she'll soon know . . .
that . . . in vain . . . of words . . . useless allies.   45

(Lycus' men disperse and he enters the cave alone.)

⟨HERDSMAN⟩
. . . if god be willing . . . up into this house soon!

(The Herdsman too enters the cave.)

⟨CHORUS⟩
. . . strength . . . with nooses . . . and through the arts of men,
moreover . . . [8]   50

⟨LYCUS⟩
(shouting from inside)

Oh me, no!

⟨CHORUS⟩
Listen, there it is! The young men's hands are indeed (at work)!

⟨LYCUS⟩
Attendants, there! Will you not . . . and help?[9]

⟨CHORUS⟩
(The house) is loud with shouting; it cries a song of death!

---

[8] Some editors take 'strength' and 'nooses' to evoke the means by which gods ensnare men no less than 'the arts of men' which ensnare Lycus here.   [9] 'Did you not hear and will you not help', Snell.

⟨ΛΥΚΟΣ⟩

55 ὦ] γαῖα Κάδ[μου κ]αὶ πόλισμ᾽ Ἀσωπικόν.

⟨ΧΟΡΟΣ⟩

κλύεις ὁρᾷ⟨ς⟩;
πα[ρα]καλεῖ πόλιν φοβερὸς αἵματος·
Δίκα τοι Δίκα χρόνιος ἀλλ᾽ ὅμως
ἐπιπεσοῦσ᾽ ἔλαθεν ἔλαβεν ὅταν ἴ[δ]ῃ
τιν᾽ ἀσεβῆ βροτῶν.

⟨ΛΥΚΟΣ⟩

οἴμοι θανοῦμαι πρὸς δυοῖν ἀσύμμαχος.

⟨ΑΜΦΙΩΝ⟩

60 τὴν δ᾽ ἐν νεκροῖσιν οὐ στένεις δάμαρτα σήν;

⟨ΛΥΚΟΣ⟩

ἦ γὰρ τέθνηκε; καινὸν αὖ λέγεις κακόν.

⟨ΑΜΦΙΩΝ⟩

ὁλκοῖς γε ταυρείοισι διαφορουμένη.

⟨ΛΥΚΟΣ⟩

πρὸς τοῦ; πρὸς ὑμῶν; τοῦτο γὰρ θέλω μαθεῖν.

⟨ΑΜΦΙΩΝ⟩

ἐκμανθάνοις ἂν ὡς ὄλωλ᾽ ἡμῶν ὕπο.

⟨ΛΥΚΟΣ⟩

65 ἀλλ᾽ ἦ τινω[ν] πεφύκαθ᾽ ὧν οὐκ οἶδ᾽ ἐγώ;

56–8 text most uncertain   58 ἐπιπεσοῦσ᾽ Heeren (ὑπο-
Stob.): ἔπεσεν (at line end) P. Petrie   ἔλαθεν ἔλαβεν Wecklein:
ἔλαθεν alone Stob.: ἔλαβεν alone P. Petrie

⟨LYCUS⟩

(O) Cadmus' land and Asopus' city![10]   55

⟨CHORUS⟩

Do you hear, do you see? He calls on the city for aid, in fear of bloodshed! Justice, I tell you, Justice delays but still falls on any impious mortal unawares when she sees him, and seizes him.

(*Lycus is brought out of the cave by Amphion and Zethus.*)

⟨LYCUS⟩

Oh me! I shall be killed by two men, without my allies!

⟨AMPHION⟩

But do you not lament your wife, who is among the dead?   60

⟨LYCUS⟩

Why, is she dead? Unexpected and further disaster there, in your words!

⟨AMPHION⟩

Yes, dragged about and torn apart by a bull.

⟨LYCUS⟩

At whose hands? At yours, the two of you? I want to know this!

⟨AMPHION⟩

You're welcome to learn, if you wish, that we caused her death.

⟨LYCUS⟩

Then you are the sons of parents unknown to me—yes?[11]   65

---

[10] Cadmus founded Thebes (cf. 86, 110), with its rivers Asopus and (cf. 87) Ismenus.   [11] The needs of stichomythia create an awkwardly compressed allusion, i.e. 'You are not the mere slaves I took you for'.

EURIPIDES

‹ΑΜΦΙΩΝ›

τί τοῦτ' ἐρευν[ᾷ]ς; ἐν νεκροῖς π[ε]ύσῃ θανών.

‹ΕΡΜΗΣ›

fr. b col. ii   c. 13–14 letters   ]ιον ἐξορμωμένους
5–6 letters ἄνα]ξ Ἀμφίον· ἐντολὰς δὲ σοὶ
Ἑρμῆς ὁ] Μαίας τ[c. 11–12 letters] ̦ενος
70   .....] Διὸς κήρυγ[μ c. 8 letters]ν φέρων.
     καὶ πρῶτα μέν σφ[ῶν μητ]ρὸ[ς] ἐξερῶ πέρι,
ὡς Ζεὺς ἐμίχθη κ[οὐκ ἀ]παρνεῖται τάδε.
τί δη̣τανε[a few letters legible at line-end
Ζηνὸς μολοῦσα λέ[κτρα   a few letters legible
75 ἐπεὶ δ' ὁρίζει καί δι[c. 8 letters] κακά,
αὐτή τε δεινῆς [συμφορᾶς ἀπη]λλάγη
παῖδάς τε τούσδ' [ἀνηῦρε]ν ὄντας ἐκ Διός.
     ὧν χρή σ' ἀκούειν [καὶ χ]θονὸς μοναρχίαν
ἑκόντα δοῦνα[ι τοῖσδε Κ]αδμείας, ἄναξ.
fr. c col. ii   ὅταν δὲ θάπτῃς ἄλοχον εἰς πυρὰν τιθείς,
81 σαρκῶν ἀθροίσας τῆς ταλαιπώρου φύσιν
ὀστᾶ πυρώσας Ἄρεος εἰς κρήνην βαλεῖν,
ὡς ἂν τὸ Δίρκης ὄνομ' ἐπώνυμον λάβῃ
κρήνης ἀπόρρους ὃς δίεισιν ἄστεως
85 πεδία τ[ὰ Θή]βης ὕδασιν ἐξάρδων ἀεί.

    70 φέρων is uncertainly read   79 τοῖσδε Κ]αδμείας
Schaal, Page: Κ]αδμείοις P. Petrie

⟨AMPHION⟩

Why ask this question? You will find out among the dead,
after you are killed.

*(The god Hermes suddenly intervenes, probably from the
theatrical 'crane'.)*

⟨HERMES⟩

... in your hasty purpose ... (lord) Amphion: I am (Her-
mes the son) of Maia ... instructions for you ... bringing
Zeus's proclamation.   70

First I shall speak openly to (both of) you about your
(mother): Zeus lay with her and does (not) deny it. Why
indeed(?) ... when she had come to Zeus's (bed) ... ? Since
he limits and ... misery, she was herself released from   75
dreadful (misfortune), and (discovered) that these are in-
deed her sons from Zeus.

(To Lycus) You must obey them (and) willingly give
(them) sovereignty over Cadmus' land, my lord. Also,
when you bury your wife and place her on a pyre, you are to   80
gather the substance of the wretched woman's body, and
from the fire throw her bones into Ares' spring, so that its
outflow may be called Dirce to mark her name, the spring
which goes through the city and continually soaks Thebe's
plain with its waters.[12]   85

[12] The spring is called Ares' spring at *Suppliant Women* 660,
but is renamed here for a typical Euripidean cult aetiology (re-
peated in 112–5): cf. the Hyacinthides at *Erechtheus* F 370.73–80.
For Dirce and Thebes see D. W. Berman, *Greece and Rome* 54
(2007), 18–39, esp. 28–39 for Euripides. 'Thebe' is the archaic
name, a nymph's: she is to marry Zethus (100, cf. Apollodorus
3.5.6).

ὑμεῖς δ᾽, [ἐπ]ειδὰν ὅσιος ᾖ Κάδμου πόλις,
χωρεῖτε, [παῖδ]ες, ἄστυ δ᾽ Ἰσμηνὸν πάρα
ἑπτάσ[το]μον πύλαισιν ἐξαρτύετε.
σὺ μὲν .[.]..το. ἔρυμα πολεμίων λαβὼν
(one or more lines missing)

90   Ζήθῳ τάδ᾽ εἶπον· δεύτερον δ᾽ Ἀμφίονα
λύραν ἄνωγα διὰ χερῶν ὡπλισμένον
μέλπειν θεοὺς ᾠδαῖσιν· ἕψονται δέ σοι
πέτραι τ᾽ ἐρυμναὶ μουσικῇ κηλούμεναι
δένδρη τε μητρὸς ἐκλιπόνθ᾽ ἑδώλια,

95   ὥστ᾽ εὐμ[ά]ρειαν τεκτόνων θήσῃ χερί.
Ζεὺς τήνδε τιμὴν σὺν δ᾽ ἐγὼ δίδωμί σοι,
οὗπερ τόδ᾽ εὕρημ᾽ ἔσχες, Ἀμφίων ἄναξ.
λευκὼ δὲ πώλω τὼ Διὸς κεκλημένοι
τιμὰς μεγίστας ἕξετ᾽ ἐν Κάδμου πόλει.

100   καὶ λέκτρ᾽ ὁ μὲν Θηβαῖα λή[ψ]εται γάμων,
ὁ] δ᾽ ἐκ Φρυγῶν κάλλιστον εὐνατήριον,
τὴν Ταντάλου παῖδ᾽· ἀλλ᾽ ὅσον τάχιστα χρὴ
σπεύδειν θεοῦ πέμψαντος οἷα βούλεται.

<ΛΥΚΟΣ>

ὦ πόλλ᾽ ἄελπτα Ζεῦ τιθεὶς καθ᾽ ἡμέραν,
105   ἔδειξας [5–6 letters] τάσδ᾽ ἀβουλίας ἐμὰς

89 ἔρυμα uncertain in P. Petrie (previously conjectured by
Ellis)

You (sons of Antiope), when you may enter Cadmus'
city without pollution, are to go and build by the Ismenus a
complete city with seven gated openings. (*To Zethus*) You
. . . taking (as?) a stout defence against foes[13] . . . (*one or
more lines missing*). . . To Zethus I say that; and secondly I
bid Amphion, hands armed with his lyre, to sing the gods'   90
praise; solid rocks charmed by the music will follow you,
and trees leaving their seats in mother earth, so that you
will make light work for builders' hands.[14] Zeus gives you   95
this honour, and I with him, from whom you had this in-
vention, lord Amphion.[15] You shall be called the two white
colts[16] of Zeus, and have the greatest honours in Cadmus'
city. Marriages too: Zethus will have a Theban bride, and   100
Amphion a most beautiful partner for his bed from among
the Phrygians, the daughter of Tantalus[17]—but you must
hasten with all speed, now the god has sent to tell you the
nature of his wishes.
(*Hermes leaves as abruptly as he came.*)

⟨LYCUS⟩

O Zeus, you who daily bring about much that is unex-
pected, you have shown . . . these follies of mine . . . who   105

---

[13] As Zethus the soldier, F *187a. Text and translation are in-
secure.   [14] Or perhaps 'they (rocks and trees) will make . . .'.
[15] Hermes invented the lyre as a miraculous child: F 190 with
note.   [16] A hieratic name for twin sons; cf. *Heracles* 29. The
better known 'white colts of Zeus' were Castor and Pollux (*Helen*
639 etc.).   [17] I.e. Niobe: Hermes leaves unsaid the future
disasters to her children when she boasted of them and Apollo, or
Apollo and Artemis together, killed them (cf. *Cresphontes* F 455).

ἐσσφ[7 letters] δοκοῦντας οὐκ εἶναι Διός.
πάρεστε καὶ ζῆθ'· ηὗρε μηνυτὴς χρόνος
ψευδεῖς μὲν ἡμᾶς, σφῷν δὲ μητέρ' εὐτυχῆ.
ἴτε νυν, κρατύνετ' ἀντ' ἐμοῦ τῆσδε χθονὸς

110 λαβόντε Κάδμου σκῆπτρα· τὴν γὰρ ἀξίαν
σφῷν προστίθησι Ζεὺς ἐγώ τε σὺν Διί.
Ἑρμῇ [δὲ πίσυνος] Ἄρεος εἰς κρήνην [β]αλῶ
γυναῖκα θάψας, τῆσδ' ὅπ[ως] ξυνοῦσα γῆς
νασμοῖσι τέγγῃ πεδία Θηβαίας χθονός,

115 Δίρκη πρὸς ἀνδρῶν ὑστέρων κεκλημένη.
λύω δὲ νείκη καὶ τὰ πρὶν πεπραγμένα . . .

106 ἐσσφ[ραγίσας] suggested in ed. pr., discerned in P.
Petrie by Roberts. Lacuna after 106 suggested by Milne.
108 εὐτυχῆ Nauck: -εῖν P. Petrie   112 [δὲ πίσυνος] Page,
perhaps fitting the traces

(224 N = Eubulus F 9.1–2, 4–5 PCG)

(225 N: see F 182a above)

seemed not to be Zeus's sons.[18] (*To Amphion and Zethus*)
You are here and living: time the revealer[19] has discovered
me to be deceived, but your mother happy in her fortune.
Go now, rule this land instead of me, the two of you taking
Cadmus' sceptre; Zeus accords you this your due, and I
with him.[20] (Obedient) to Hermes I shall throw my wife   110
into Ares' spring after her funeral, so she may unite with
this land's streams and water the plains of Theban terri-
tory, and be called Dirce by men of later times. I end my   115
feuds and . . . what was done before . . . [21]

[18] Mahaffy and Roberts thought they read 'setting your seal
upon (i.e. authenticating) those who seemed etc.', Lycus echoing
Hermes' words at 77. It is quite possible that text has been lost af-
ter 106 (Milne).   [19] Cf. F 222, *Aeolus* F **38a with note.
[20] Lycus echoes Hermes' words at 96, here with solemnity.
[21] Perhaps a complete sentence, 'I am done with feuds and (my)
former actions'; and just possibly the last spoken words of the play,
before the Chorus' formal ending.

(224 N = Eubulus F 9.1–2, 4–5 *PCG*)

(225 N: see F 182a above)

ANTIOPE or ANTIGONE

212

εἰ νοῦς ἔνεστιν· εἰ δὲ μή, τί δεῖ καλῆς
γυναικός, εἰ μὴ τὰς φρένας χρηστὰς ἔχοι;

Stobaeus 4.22.127

213

κόρος δὲ πάντων· καὶ γὰρ ἐκ καλλιόνων
λέκτροις ἐπ' αἰσχροῖς εἶδον ἐκπεπληγμένους,
δαιτὸς δὲ πληρωθείς τις ἄσμενος πάλιν
φαύλῃ διαίτῃ προσβαλὼν ἤσθη στόμα.

Stobaeus 4.20.2; v. 4: Athenaeus 10.421f (adapted)

214

κῆδος καθ' αὑτὸν τὸν σοφὸν κτᾶσθαι χρεών.

P. Oxy. 3214.5–6 (damaged); Stobaeus 4.22.93

ANTIOPE or ANTIGONE

212
. . . if there is sense in her—if not, what need of a beautiful wife, unless she had good sense?

213
There is satiety in all things—truly, for I have seen men driven beside themselves for an ill-looking wife after having a more beautiful one, and a man filled with a banquet in turn happily taking pleasure in putting his mouth to simple fare.

214
The wise man should get himself a marriage at his own level.[1]

[1] Cf. *Melanippe* F 502 with note.

215

πᾶσι δ᾽ ἀγγέλλω βροτοῖς
ἐσθλῶν ἀπ᾽ ἀνδρῶν εὐγενῆ σπείρειν τέκνα
(one or more lines lost?)
οὐ γάρ ποτ᾽ ἄν πράξειαν ἐς τέλος κακῶς.

Stobaeus 4.22.100; v. 3 = *Andromache* 1283 (see note opposite)

216

οὐ χρή ποτ᾽ ἄνδρα δοῦλον ὄντ᾽ ἐλευθέρας
γνώμας διώκειν οὐδ᾽ ἐς ἀργίαν βλέπειν.

P. Berlin 21144.8–9 (badly damaged); Stobaeus 4.19.4

215

I proclaim to all mankind: father well-born children from
(wives of) noble stock . . . They would never do well to the
end.[1]

[1] V. 3 follows vv. 1–2 unsatisfactorily; an almost identical verse
occurs as *Andromache* 1283, where it follows 1282 unsatisfacto-
rily. Here, either text is lost or the three lines have been errone-
ously combined in Stobaeus.

216

No man who is a slave should ever pursue free thought, nor
look to laziness.[1]

[1] Perhaps from the confrontation between Dirce and Antiope:
see Introduction above.

ANTIOPE, UNCERTAIN
FRAGMENT

910

ὄλβιος ὅστις τῆς ἱστορίας
ἔσχε μάθησιν,
μήτε πολιτῶν ἐπὶ πημοσύνην
μήτ᾽ εἰς ἀδίκους πράξεις ὁρμῶν,
5 ἀλλ᾽ ἀθανάτου καθορῶν φύσεως
κόσμον ἀγήρων, πῇ τε συνέστη
καὶ ὅθεν καὶ ὅπως.
τοῖς δὲ τοιούτοις οὐδέποτ᾽ αἰσχρῶν
ἔργων μελέτημα προσίζει.

Clement of Alexandria, *Miscellanies* 4.25.155.1; vv. 3–6
adapted in Themistius, *Oration* 24, 307d. First assigned to
Antiope by Wecklein.

7 ὅθεν Wilamowitz: ὅπῃ Clement

ANTIOPE, UNCERTAIN
FRAGMENT

910

Happy the man who has gained knowledge through in-
quiry, not aiming to trouble his fellow citizens, nor to act
unjustly, but observing eternal nature's ageless order, the   5
way it was formed, and whence and how. Such men are
never inclined to practise shameful deeds.[1]

[1] On the attribution of this fragment see Introduction above
and especially Di Benedetto 102–6. It may have preceded a full
choral ode, as perhaps did *Chrysippus* F 839, which has a similar
philosophical and cosmogonical content, and like this fragment
can be linked with contemporary Greek speculation. On these
topics in F 910 see now R. Hannah, *Ramus* 31 (2002), 19–32.

ARCHELAUS

Austin, *NFE* 11–21; A. Harder, *Euripides' Kresphontes and Archelaos* (Leiden, 1985), 125–290; H. Van Looy in ed. Budé VIII.1.275–307; Diggle, *TrGFS* 94–5 (F 228, 228a); J. Gibert in *SFP* II.330–62.

Webster 255–7; L. di Gregorio, *CCC* 8 (1987), 279–318 and *Aevum* 62 (1988), 16–49; J. M. Bremer in H. Hofmann and A. Harder, *Fragmenta Dramatica* (Göttingen, 1991), 39–60, esp. 42–4; G. Xanthakis-Karamanos, *Parnassos* 35 (1993), 510–33, reprinted in her *Dramatica* (Athens, 2002), 21–46 ; M. Huys, *APF* 43 (1997), 28–9; Matthiessen 256–8; Sourvinou-Inwood 41–5; S. Scullion, *CQ* 53 (2003), 389–400 and in D. Cairns and V. Liapis (eds.) *Dionysalexandros: Essays . . . in honour of A. F. Garvie* (Swansea, 2006), 185–200; A. Katsouris in Bastianini–Casanova, *Euripide e i papiri* 205–26.

The Archelaus of this story was a son of Temenus, one of the great-great-grandsons of Heracles (but in this play, grandsons: F 228a.17) who were said to have reconquered the Peloponnese, divided it amongst them, and established the Dorian kingdoms of Argos under Temenus, Messenia under his brother Cresphontes (see Introduction to Cresphontes*), and Sparta under the sons of a third brother Aristodemus. Euripides treated the story of Temenus and*

229

his sons in Temenus *and* Temenidae, *and seems to have gone out of his way to give Archelaus an important role in the story of the reconquest: in* Temenidae/Temenus *test. vi he is said to have 'reassigned the exploits of Temenus to Archelaus', and in test. iv there it is Archelaus who distinguishes himself in the crucial battle and earns the right to inherit Temenus' kingdom (his name also appears in the very fragmentary test. i). It is very probable, in fact, that Euripides invented this Archelaus in order to provide the late 5th c. Macedonian ruler Archelaus with a mythical ancestor, and that the stories of the three plays were at least loosely interconnected (see below on the circumstances of the play's production and on the question of a trilogy).*

The plot of Archelaus *is probably reflected in Hyginus, Fab. 219 (= test. *iiia below; this is questioned by Huys, but there is no obvious alternative to Euripides as Hyginus' ultimate source). Archelaus, exiled by his brothers (and so perhaps cheated of the rightful inheritance mentioned above), arrived at the palace of the Thracian King Cisseus. The king was in need of an ally against his hostile neighbours and promised Archelaus his kingdom and his daughter in return for his aid; Archelaus agreed and won a great victory; Cisseus, persuaded by 'friends' to double-cross him, tried to kill him by luring him into a fiery pit, but Archelaus, warned by a royal servant, threw Cisseus into the pit instead; afterwards, instructed by Apollo, he followed a goat into Macedonia and founded the city of Aegeae ('Goat-town'). The main features of the drama, then, will have been Archelaus' initial encounter with Cisseus leading to his agreement to lead the army, a report of his great victory, Cisseus' change of mind and preparation of the trap (whether before or after Archelaus' return*

*from the battle), the servant's warning and the reversal
of Cisseus' plot, and an appearance of Apollo justifying
Archelaus' action and directing his destiny.*

Few of the fragments can be placed with certainty, but
many can be distributed tentatively within this outline. F
228 and 228a come from a prologue speech spoken by the
arriving Archelaus (but there is doubt whether F 228 was
the original beginning: see notes there and on F 846). F 229
and 230 are from the choral parodos (the chorus being
probably Thracian elders) in which the threat to Cisseus
and his people was described. A series of gnomic fragments
could well come from the negotiations between Cisseus and
Archelaus, in which the latter's inherited nobility and de-
votion to toil and glory were emphasized (F 231–4, 236–40,
242–4). In F 241 Cisseus presumably addresses Archelaus,
probably after his victory but possibly earlier on his ap-
pointment as general. F 246–251 would fit well enough in a
scene in which a plot against Archelaus was proposed and
debated. The largely papyrus fragment F 245, with the end
of a scene in trochaic tetrameters and the beginning of a
presumably choral lyric, probably represents a moment of
crisis as the servant(?) urges Archelaus to retaliate against
Cisseus. F 252–5 (and F 235?) could represent a scene of
recrimination between Archelaus and Cisseus before the
latter went to his death, and F 262 a chorus-leader's com-
ment on that outcome. The lyric fragment F 263 may well
be the chorus regretting Cisseus' death, and the anapaestic
F 264 is surely from its play-closing comments. The re-
maining fragments are harder to locate even speculatively:
F 256 on respect for god, F 257–9 on controlling anger
(someone tries to restrain Archelaus' vengeance?), F 260
and 261 (see notes below on these). It has been suggested

that Cisseus' daughter had a role in the play, but Hyginus'
summary offers no support for this and the only fragments
that might hint at it (F 232, 234) are easily accounted for in
other ways.

    Brief fragments: none.   Other ascriptions: F 846 (see
above), 850, 911, 956, 969, 1038, 1045, 1052, 1053; adesp.
F *108 'be gone; do not put a wreath on my head' (cf. F
241); adesp. F *193 'to honour the Macedonians for their
valour'; adesp. F *638 (damaged papyrus lines: someone
consoled after a betrayal by false friends?); adesp. F 646
(damaged papyrus lines of uncertain content, including
'sons of the Macedonians'); Diogenes of Sinope TrGF 88 F
6 (= adesp. F 522 N).

    According to the ancient biographical tradition (test.
iia) Euripides composed Archelaus *after leaving Athens in*
408/7 to live at the court of Archelaus, who had seized the
Macedonian throne violently in 413 and was in turn assas-
sinated in 399; the tradition adds that Euripides died (in
406) in Macedonia. The essential point here, that the play
was composed for Archelaus and first performed in Mace-
donia, seems reliable; Euripides will have adapted existing
traditions which linked the Argead dynasty of Macedo-
nia with descendants of Temenus of Argos (e.g. Herodotus
8.137–8) in order to give the founder's role to a heroic and
'Heraclean' son of Temenus named Archelaus (note the
emphasis on ancestry and on the achievement of glory
through toil in F 228a, 231–3, 236–40). Scullion (2003)
however provides strong reasons for doubting the tradi-
tion of Euripides' 'exile' and death in Macedonia, and ar-
gues that the parody in Aristophanes, Frogs *1206–8 (= F*
846) points to a subsequent production before an Athenian
audience. Scullion argues further (2006) that Temenus,

Temenidae *and* Archelaus *may well have formed a connected trilogy (an idea proposed by Zielinski in 1925, rejected by recent editors; but see also Webster 252–3, Di Gregorio, Katsouris 206–8).*

The first performance has been linked with Archelaus' foundation of a dramatic festival at Dion beneath Mount Olympus (Diodorus 17.16.3), or with Aegeae (modern Vergina), the old Macedonian capital, in view of the mention of its foundation at the end of the play (test. *iiia(5)); for discussion see Sourvinou-Inwood, who favours Aegeae. We happen to have inscriptional evidence of 3rd c. performances at Argos and Dodona (test. iib), but the play seems to have had no literary influence. The historical Archelaus became a byword for tyrannical cruelty and excess (see especially Plato, Gorgias 471a–c, 525b–c).

ΑΡΧΕΛΑΟΣ

test. *iiia

ARCHELAUS. Archelaus Temeni filius exsul a fratribus eiectus in Thraciam ad regem Cisseum uenit, qui cum a finitimis oppugnaretur Archelao regnum et filiam in coniugium dare pollicetur si se ab hoste tutatus esset Archelaus, quia ab Hercule esset oriundus; nam Temenus Herculis filius fuit. (2) Qui hostes uno proelio fugauit et ab rege pollicita petit. Ille ab amicis dissuasus fidem fraudauit eumque per dolum interficere uoluit. (3) Itaque foueam iussit fieri et multos carbones eo ingeri et incendi et super uirgulta tenuia poni, quo cum Archelaus uenisset ut decideret. (4) Hoc regis seruus Archelao patefecit; qui re cognita dicit se cum rege colloqui uelle secreto; arbitris semotis Archelaus regem arreptum in foueam coniecit atque ita eum perdidit. (5) Inde profugit ex responso Apollinis in Macedoniam capra duce, oppidumque ex nomine caprae Aegeas constituit.

Hyginus, *Fab.* 219

(1) *Thraciam* Robert: *Macedoniam* Hyginus

F 228 below was the beginning of the play in the text known to Alexandrian and later scholars, but F 846 (= Aristophanes, Frogs 1206–8) may have been its original beginning: see further on F 846.

ARCHELAUS

test. *iiia

ARCHELAUS. Archelaus, son of Temenus, was cast into exile by his brothers and came to king Cisseus in Thrace. Since Cisseus was being attacked by his neighbours, he promised to give Archelaus his kingdom and his daughter in marriage if Archelaus rescued him from his enemy, as Archelaus could claim descent from Hercules; for Temenus was a son of Hercules. (2) Archelaus routed the enemy in a single battle and sought from the king what he had promised. But the king, persuaded otherwise by his friends, betrayed his pledge and decided to kill Archelaus by deceit. (3) So he ordered a pit to be made and many coals to be piled in it and lit, and light branches to be laid over it, so that when Archelaus came to it he would fall in. (4) A servant of the king revealed this to Archelaus, and he on learning of it said that he wished to speak with the king in secret. After removing all witnesses he seized the king and threw him into the pit, and thus killed him. (5) Then, instructed by an oracle of Apollo, he fled from that place into Macedonia, led by a goat, and founded the city of Aegeae which he named after the goat.

228

ΑΡΧΕΛΑΟΣ

Δαναὸς ὁ πεντήκοντα θυγατέρων πατὴρ
Νείλου λιπὼν κάλλιστον †ἐκ γαίας† ὕδωρ,
{ὃς ἐκ μελαμβρότοιο πληροῦται ῥοὰς
Αἰθιοπίδος γῆς, ἡνίκ' ἂν τακῇ χιὼν
5 †τεθριππεύοντος† ἡλίου κατ' αἰθέρα,}
ἐλθὼν ἐς Ἄργος ᾤκισ' Ἰνάχου πόλιν·
Πελασγιώτας δ' ὠνομασμένους τὸ πρὶν
Δαναοὺς καλεῖσθαι νόμον ἔθηκ' ἀν' Ἑλλάδα.

(F 228a follows almost immediately)

Vv. 1–6: Tiberius, *On Figures* 48; vv. 1–5: Anon., *On the
Flooding of the Nile* (= *FGrH* 647 F 1) 2; Tzetzes on *Iliad* 1.426;
vv. 1, 6–8: Strabo 5.2.4 (7–8 again in 8.6.9); vv. 2–4: Diodorus
Siculus 1.38.4 and derivatives; vv. 1 and 4 cited variously else-
where ([Plutarch], *Moralia* 837e identifies v. 1 as the play's first
line).

2 ἐκ γαίας most sources: ἐν γαίας West   3–5 Deleted
by Diggle (previously suspected by others) as an interpolation
5 τεθριππεύοντος sources: τέθριππ' ἄγοντος F. W. Schmidt

---

1 See however the note preceding F 228, on p. 234.
2 Danaus was a descendant of Zeus and Io, daughter of the Argive
river-god Inachus. He fled from Egypt to Argos with his fifty
daughters (the Danaids) in an attempt to save them from mar-
riages with the fifty sons of his brother Aegyptus. Forced into
these marriages, all but one of the Danaids killed their husbands
on their wedding night. The fiftieth couple, Hypermestra and

228
(Beginning of the play)[1]

ARCHELAUS

Danaus, who fathered fifty daughters,[2] left the most lovely
water †in the world†[3] of the Nile {which fills its streams
from the dark-peopled land of Ethiopia when the snow
melts as the sun †drives his chariot† through the sky}[4] and   5
reaching Argos founded Inachus' city,[5] laying down the
rule that those once named Pelasgians should now be
known as Danaans all over Hellas.[6]

*(F 228a follows almost immediately, continuing Archelaus'
prologue speech)*

Lynceus, were the great-grandparents of Danae (see F 228a). A
lost archaic epic, the *Danais*, told this story at length. Aeschylus'
Suppliant Women is (probably) the first play of a tetralogy which
also told the story extensively.   [3] 'The world's single most
lovely water', West.   [4] Interruption of the main sentence
and some linguistic peculiarities make it likely that vv. 3–5 are an
interpolation (but Scullion [2006] notes that they could be part
of the revised version of the play's opening that he envisages). In
v. 5 Schmidt's conjecture offers the same sense as the sources'
unmetrical and otherwise unattested word.   [5] The city is
identified with its local god (see note 1). In Aeschylus' play the
city of Argos already exists when the refugees arrive, and its
king Pelasgus persuades his people to protect them. According to
other sources Danaus succeeded Pelasgus as king. Strabo 8.6.9
makes him the builder of the Argive acropolis.   [6] The
Pelasgians usually appear in Greek legend as a pre-Greek popula-
tion. 'Danaans' is a Homeric term, equivalent to 'Argives' or more
generally 'Achaeans'.

228a

three lines almost entirely lost, then:

.... οὐκ ἔψαυσε· Λυγκέως ......
5 Ἄ[β]ας ἐγένετο· τοῦ δὲ δίπτυχον γένο[ς·
Προῖτος μανε[ι]σῶν θυγατέρων τρισσῶν πατήρ,
ὅς τ' ἐγκατῆγεν χαλκέῳ νυμφεύματ[ι
Δανάην ...θεις ...... Ἀκρίσιός ποτε.
Δανάης δὲ Περσεὺς ἐγένετ' ἐκ χρυσορρύτων
10 σταγόνων, ὃς ἐλθὼν Γοργόνος καρατόμος
Αἰθίοπ' ἔγημεν Ἀνδρομέδαν τὴν Κηφέως,
ἣ τριπτύχους ἐγείνατ' ἐκ Περσέως κόρους,
Ἀλκαῖον ἠδὲ Σθένελον ὅς τ' Ἄργους πόλιν
ε[ἶ]χεν Μυκήνας, πατέρα δ' Ἀλκμήνης τρίτον
15 Ἠλεκτρύωνα· Ζ[ε]ὺς δ' ἐς Ἀλκμήνης λέχος
πε[σ]ὼν τὸ κλειν[ὸ]ν Ἡρακλέους σπείρει δέμας.
Ὕλλος δὲ τοῦδ[ε], Τήμενος δ' Ὕλλου πατρός,
ὃς Ἄργος ᾤκησ' Ἡρακλέους γεγὼς ἄπο.
ἀπαιδίᾳ δὲ χρώμενος πατὴρ ἐμὸς
20 Τήμενος ἐς ἁγνῆς ἦλθε Δωδώνης πτύχας
τέκνων ἔρωτι· τῆς δ' ὁμωνύμου Διὸς
πρόπολ[ο]ς Διώνης εἶπε Τημένῳ τάδε·
ᵌΩ παῖ πεφυκὼς ἐκ γονῶν Ἡρακλέους,
Ζεύς σ[οι] δίδωσι παῖδ', ἐγὼ μαντεύομαι,
25 ὃν Ἀρχ[έλ]αον χρὴ καλεῖν ...α[.].[.].[

A further column has fourteen line-beginnings perhaps continuing this speech.

P. Hamburg. 118a col. ii, ed. E. Siegmann (1954)
14 ε[ἶ]χεν or ἔ[σ]χεν P. Hamb.

228a

. . . *(three lines almost entirely lost)* . . . did not touch (her):
from Lynceus . . . Abas was born, and his offspring was two-
fold: Proetus, the father of three maddened daughters, 5
and Acrisius, who once led Danae . . . down into a bronze
bridal chamber.[1] Danae's son, conceived from the shower
of gold, was Perseus, who after cutting off the Gorgon's
head came to Ethiopia and married Cepheus' daughter 10
Andromeda.[2] She had three sons by Perseus: Alcaeus,
Sthenelus, and thirdly Alcmene's father Electryon, who
held the city of Mycenae in the Argolid.[3] Zeus entered
Alcmene's bed and sired glorious Heracles. Heracles fa-
thered Hyllus, and Hyllus fathered Temenus, who reset- 15
tled Argos being from Heracles' stock.[4]

Temenus, my father, was without offspring, so he went
to holy Dodona's vales in his desire for children; and the 20
priestess of Dione, Zeus's namesake,[5] said to him: 'You son
of Heracles' stock, Zeus will give you a son, I prophesy,
whom you must call Archelaus . . .'
25

[1] For Lynceus and Hypermestra see on F 228. The daughters
of Proetus were driven mad by Hera or Dionysus because of their
disrespect, and were later cured by the seer Melampus. Danae's
story was the subject of Euripides' *Danae* (later in this volume).
[2] The story of Perseus and Andromeda was the subject of Euripi-
des' *Andromeda* (above).   [3] For Electryon, Alcmene and
the siring of Heracles see *Alcmene*, Introduction.   [4] For
Temenus see further on *Temenidae* and *Temenus*. He was usually
said to be not Hyllus' son but his great-grandson, invading the
Peloponnese 100 years after Hyllus' failed attempt (see Intro-
duction above).   [5] 'Dione' is the feminine equivalent of the
name Zeus (root 'Di-'). She was worshipped as his wife at the orac-
ular sanctuary of Dodona in Epirus. See also on *Antigone* F 177.

229 + 230

ΧΟΡΟΣ

229 βασιλεῦ χώρας τῆς πολυβώλου,
Κισσεῦ, πεδίον πυρὶ μαρμαίρει.

* * *

230 οὐ γὰρ ὑπερθεῖν κύματος ἄκραν
δυνάμεσθ᾽· ἔτι γὰρ θάλλει πενία
κακὸν ἔχθιστον, φεύγει δ᾽ ὄλβος.

F 229: Dionysius of Halicarnassus, *On Arrangement of Words*
25.203   F 230: Stobaeus 4.32.39

231

⟨ΑΡΧΕΛΑΟΣ?⟩

ἡμῶν τί δῆτα τυγχάνεις χρείαν ἔχων;

⟨ΚΙΣΣΕΤΣ?⟩

πατέρων γὰρ ἐσθλῶν ἐλπίδας δίδως γεγώς.

Stobaeus 4.29.42; divided between two speakers by Musgrave

232

ἐν τοῖς τέκνοις γὰρ ἀρετὴ τῶν εὐγενῶν
ἔλαμψε κρείσσων τ᾽ ἐστὶ πλουσίου γάμου·
πένης ⟨ἀνὴρ⟩ γὰρ οὐκ ἐκεῖν᾽ ἀπώλεσεν,
τὸ τοῦ πατρὸς γενναῖον.

Stobaeus 4.29.44

2 ἔλαμψε Nauck (ἐνέλαμψε Valckenaer): ἐν ἔλαβε Stob. mss.
SM (ἔλαβε ms. A)   3 ⟨ἀνὴρ⟩ Harder

229 + 230
CHORUS

King of this fertile land, Cisseus, the plain is glinting with
fire[1] ... *(some lines lost)* ... We cannot surmount the wave-
crest; poverty still thrives—that most hateful evil—and
prosperity is banished.

[1] I.e. full of men armed with glinting shields and weapons: cf.
Homer, *Iliad* 20.156, Eur. *Phoenician Women* 110–1, *Hypsipyle* F
752f.30–1. These may be the chorus's opening words.

231
⟨ARCHELAUS?⟩

Well then, what need do you have of me?

⟨CISSEUS?⟩

You give me hopes since you have distinguished forebears.

232

The excellence of noble men shines in their children, and
is superior to a wealthy marriage. A man may be poor, but
his father's nobility is something he does not lose.[1]

[1] Cf. *Temenidae* F 739; F 1066.

233

σοὶ δ᾽ εἶπον, ὦ παῖ, τὰς τύχας ἐκ τῶν πόνων
θηρᾶν· ὁρᾷς γὰρ σὸν πατέρα τιμώμενον . . .

Stobaeus 3.29.13

234

πατρὸς δ᾽ ἀνάγκη παισὶ πείθεσθαι λόγῳ.

Stobaeus 4.25.19

235

πλουτεῖς· ὁ πλοῦτος δ᾽ ἀμαθία δειλόν θ᾽ ἅμα.

Stobaeus 4.31.69

236

σὺν μυρίοισι τὰ καλὰ γίγνεται πόνοις.

Stobaeus 3.29.44; [Menander], *Monostichs* 252 Jaekel

237

νεανίαν γὰρ ἄνδρα χρὴ τολμᾶν ἀεί·
οὐδεὶς γὰρ ὢν ῥᾴθυμος εὐκλεὴς ἀνήρ,
ἀλλ᾽ οἱ πόνοι τίκτουσι τὴν εὐανδρίαν.

Stobaeus 4.10.4; Orion, Euripidean Appendix 22b Haffner;
vv. 2–3: Stobaeus 3.29.32

3 εὐανδρίαν Stob. 3.29.32, Orion: εὐδοξίαν Stob. 4.10.4: cf.
Eur. F 1052.7

(238 N = Stobaeus 3.29.14, falsely ascribed
to Eur. *Archelaus*)

233

I tell you, boy: seek your fortunes from hard work. You can
see your father is honoured . . . [1]

[1] Perhaps Temenus quoted by his son Archelaus in conversa-
tion with Cisseus.

234

Children must obey their father's word.[1]

[1] Archelaus referring to his father's advice (F 233)?

235

You are rich: but wealth is both ignorant and mean-
spirited.

236

Fine things are achieved through countless toils.

237

A young man should constantly act boldly. No man gets
glory by being idle; it's toil that brings about manly
achievement.

(238 N = Stobaeus 3.29.14, falsely ascribed
to Euripides' *Archelaus*)

239

ὁ δ᾽ ἡδὺς αἰὼν ἡ κακή τ᾽ ἀνανδρία
οὔτ᾽ οἶκον οὔτε πόλιν ἀνορθώσειεν ἄν.

Stobaeus 3.8.13; appended (with variations) to *Erechtheus*
F 364 in Stobaeus 3.29.22 and Orion 7.2 Haffner

240

⟨ΑΡΧΕΛΑΟΣ?⟩
ἐμὲ δ᾽ ἄρ᾽ οὐ
μοχθεῖν δίκαιον; τίς δ᾽ ἄμοχθος εὐκλεής;
τίς τῶν μεγίστων δειλὸς ὢν ὠρέξατο;

Stobaeus 4.10.8; v. 3 may be a separate fragment (Badham)

241

ἐγὼ δὲ τὸν σὸν κρᾶτ᾽ ἀναστέψαι θέλω.

Schol. on *Phoenician Women* 1149

242

φέρει δὲ καὶ τοῦτ᾽ οὐχὶ μικρόν, εὐγενὴς
ἀνὴρ στρατηγῶν εὐκλεᾶ τ᾽ ἔχων φάτιν.

Stobaeus 4.13.11 and 4.29.43

1 φέρει Stob. 4.29.43: ἔχει Stob. 4.13.11

243

ὀλίγον ἄλκιμον δόρυ
κρεῖσσον στρατηγῷ μυρίου στρατεύματος.

Stobaeus 4.13.10

244

239

A pleasant life and base unmanliness cannot restore a family or a city.

240

⟨ARCHELAUS?⟩

Shall I not rightly strive then? Who can get glory without striving for it? What shirker ever reached for the greatest prizes?

241

I want to place a wreath upon your head.

242

This too brings no small benefit—a well-born man of fine repute in command.

243

A small but valiant force is worth more to a general than a vast army.

244

ὀλίγοι γὰρ ἐσθλοὶ κρείσσονες πολλῶν κακῶν.

Stobaeus 4.10.11; Orion 7.3 Haffner

245

remains of five lines, then:
– ∪ Φοῖ]β᾽ ἄναξ, κάθιζε π[
– ∪ –]τ᾽, ὦ παῖ, προβαλλ[
ἐν δέ σοι μόνον προφωνῶ· μὴ ᾽πὶ δουλείαν ποτὲ
ζῶν ἑκὼν ἔλθῃς παρόν σοι κατθανεῖν ἐλευθέρως
10 – ∪]των ἔσωθε κα[
– ∪ –]ν· εἰ δ᾽ εὐτυχήσουσ[᾽
– ∪ –]εστω τὸ λοιπὸν [

⟨ΧΟΡΟΣ?⟩
ἄ]νδρα χρὴ διατων[
]ν ἁμέραν·
15]εἶ γὰρ αἱ τύχα[ι
remains of one more line

P. Oxy. 419, ed. B. P. Grenfell and A. S. Hunt (1903); vv. 8–9:
Stobaeus 3.7.4

246

νεανίας τε καὶ πένης σοφός θ᾽ ἅμα·
ταῦτ᾽ εἰς ἓν ἐλθόντ᾽ ἄξι᾽ ἐνθυμήσεως.

Stobaeus 4.11.9

244

A few good men are worth more than many cowards.

245

... *(remains of five lines)* ..., lord Phoebus, set ... (O) son
... just one thing I urge upon you: never consent to live and
go into slavery when you can choose to die as befits a free
man ... inside ... but if they succeed ... in the future ...   10

(CHORUS?)

... a man must ... day ... for fortunes ...   15

246

He is young and poor, and clever as well: when these things
are united, they are worth taking seriously.

247

247

τί δ᾽ οὐκ ἂν εἴη χρηστὸς ὄλβιος γεγώς;

Stobaeus 4.31.17

248

οὐκ ἔστι Πενίας ἱερὸν αἰσχίστης θεοῦ.
μισῶ γὰρ ὄντως οἵτινες φρονοῦσι μέν,
φρονοῦσι δ᾽ †οὐδενός τε† χρημάτων ὕπερ.

Stobaeus 4.32.41; vv. 1 and 2–3 are probably separate fragments (Musgrave)

3 οὐδὲν τῶν γε Düntzer

249

μὴ πλούσιον θῇς· ἐνδεέστερος γὰρ ὢν
ταπεινὸς ἔσται· κεῖνο δ᾽ ἰσχύει μέγα,
πλοῦτος λαβών <τε> τοῦτον εὐγενὴς ἀνήρ.

Stobaeus 4.31.19

250

. . .

τυραννίδ᾽ ἢ θεῶν δευτέρα νομίζεται·
τὸ μὴ θανεῖν γὰρ οὐκ ἔχει, τὰ δ᾽ ἄλλ᾽ ἔχει.

Stobaeus 4.6.5

251

κρείσσω γὰρ οὔτε δοῦλον οὔτ᾽ ἐλεύθερον
τρέφειν ἐν οἴκοις ἀσφαλὲς τοῖς σώφροσιν.

Stobaeus 4.19.11

247

Why would he not give good service once he is wealthy?

248

There is no shrine of Poverty, that vilest of deities. I truly detest those who are capable of thought, but think . . . over money.[1]

---

[1] The Greek in v. 3 does not make sense. Vv. 2–3 may well be a separate fragment, but in any case the sense should fit the topic of Stobaeus' chapter, 'Condemnation of Poverty'; so something like Düntzer's 'but have no thought at all for material possessions' seems needed.

249

Don't make him rich; if he's poor, he'll be submissive—but wealth with a well-born man in possession of it is a very powerful thing.

250

. . . tyranny, which is rated second only to the gods. It does not have immortality, but it has the rest.[1]

---

[1] For tyranny rhetorically deified see *Phoenician Women* 506.

251

Sensible people find it safe not to keep anyone superior in their house, whether slave or free.

252

ἐκ τῶν δικαίων γὰρ νόμοι ταὐξήματα
μεγάλα φέρουσι, πάντα δ' ἀνθρώποις ‹καλά›.
τάδ' ἐστὶ χρήματ', ἤν τις εὐσεβῇ θεόν.

Orion 3.1 Haffner; v. 3 could be a separate fragment
(Meineke)

2 ‹καλά› Blaydes

253

ἁπλοῦς ὁ μῦθος· μὴ λέγ' εὖ. τὸ γὰρ λέγειν
εὖ δεινόν ἐστιν, εἰ φέρει τινὰ βλάβην.

Stobaeus 3.34.2 and (unattributed) 3.13.9

254

‹—›

πόλλ', ὦ τέκνον, σφάλλουσιν ἀνθρώπους θεοί.

‹—›

τὸ ῥᾷστον εἶπας, αἰτιάσασθαι θεούς.

Plutarch, *Moralia* 20d; v. 1: [Justin], *On Monarchy* 5.6; v. 2:
Plutarch, *Moralia* 1049e and 1049f.; vv. 1 and 2 assigned to differ-
ent speakers by Grotius.

252

Laws bring about great increase as a result of just actions, and thus make everything (good?) for mortals. This is genuine wealth: respect for god.[1]

[1] 'God' simply means 'divine power', as in F 256 and often elsewhere. V. 3 is perhaps a separate fragment (Meineke).

253

It can be simply said: do not speak well. Eloquence is a terrible thing if it brings any harm.[1]

[1] A common warning about rhetoric misused, e.g. *Alexander* F 56.

254

⟨—⟩

Child, the gods often cause men to slip.

⟨—⟩

You've used the easiest excuse—blaming the gods.

255

δοκεῖς τὰ τῶν θεῶν ξυνετὰ νικήσειν ποτὲ
καὶ τὴν Δίκην που μακρ᾿ ἀπῳκίσθαι βροτῶν;
ἥδ᾿ ἐγγύς ἐστιν, οὐχ ὁρωμένη δ᾿ ὁρᾷ,
ὃν χρὴ κολάζειν τ᾿ οἶδεν· ἀλλ᾿ οὐκ οἶσθα σύ,
5 ὁπόταν ἄφνω μολοῦσα διολέσῃ κακούς.

Stobaeus 1.3.47; vv. 1–3: Orion 5.1 Haffner

2 μακρ᾿ Grotius (questioned by Harder): μακρὰν Stob.,
Orion: {που} μακράν ⟨γ᾿⟩ Schneidewin   3 ἥδ᾿ Orion: ἡ δ᾿
Stob.   5 ὁπόταν is suspect: ἕως Wecklein

256

μακάριος ὅστις νοῦν ἔχων τιμᾷ θεὸν
καὶ κέρδος αὑτῷ τοῦτο ποιεῖται μέγα.

Orion 3.2 Haffner

257

πολλοὺς δ᾿ ὁ θυμὸς ὁ μέγας ὤλεσεν βροτῶν
ἥ τ᾿ ἀξυνεσία, δύο κακὼ τοῖς χρωμένοις.

Stobaeus 3.20.11

258

τῷ γὰρ βιαίῳ κἀγρίῳ τὸ μαλθακὸν
εἰς ταὐτὸν ἐλθὸν τοῦ λίαν παρείλετο.

Stobaeus 3.20.25

259

ὀργῇ δὲ φαύλῃ πόλλ᾿ ἔνεστ᾿ ἀσχήμονα.

Stobaeus 3.20.12

255

Do you think you will ever get the better of the wisdom of the gods, and that Justice is settled somewhere far from mortals? She is here nearby, and though unseen she sees, and knows whom she should punish, while you remain unaware each time she suddenly arrives and destroys the wicked.[1]

[1] The thought here is traditional: cf. Hesiod, *Works and Days* 220–4, *Antiope* F 223.57–8. *Melanippe* F 506 puts a more sophisticated view in similar language. In v. 5 Wecklein's 'until' improves the sense but supposes an unlikely corruption.

256

Happy the man who has the good sense to honour god and to turn this to great advantage for himself.

257

Many men have been ruined by great anger and lack of insight—a pair of evils for those who suffer them.

258

When gentleness meets violence and savagery, it restrains them from going too far.

259

Petty anger gives rise to much unseemly behaviour.

260

ἔπαυσ᾿ ὁδουροὺς λυμεῶνας . . .

Schol. on Pindar, *Pythians* 2.57

261

ἔσωσα δούλην οὖσαν· οἱ γὰρ ἥσσονες
τοῖς κρείσσοσιν φιλοῦσι δουλεύειν βροτῶν.

Stobaeus 4.19.13 (assigned improbably to the Chorus in ms. S)

262

πάλαι σκοποῦμαι τὰς †τύχας τῶν βροτῶν†
ὡς εὖ μεταλλάσσουσιν· ὃς γὰρ ἂν σφαλῇ,
εἰς ὀρθὸν ἔστη, χὠ πρὶν εὐτυχῶν πίτνει.

Stobaeus 4.41.31; Orion 8.2 Haffner

1 τύχας ⟨τὰς⟩ τῶν βροτῶν conjectured in Stob. ms. Paris. 1985: τὰς βροτησίας τύχας Busche (τύχ- βροτ- Collard)

263

⟨ΧΟΡΟΣ⟩

ἔστι ⟨τι⟩ καὶ παρὰ δάκρυσι κείμενον
ἡδὺ βροτοῖς, ὅταν ἄνδρα φίλον στενά-
χῃ τις ἐν οἴκτῳ.

Stobaeus 4.54.7

1 ⟨τι⟩ Meineke: ⟨δὲ⟩ Herwerden, Wilamowitz   2 οἴκτῳ Stob. ms. S: οἴκῳ mss. MA

260

I (*or* he) checked wayside molesters . . . [1]

[1] 'I' might be Archelaus stating his record of achievement before reaching Cisseus' court. 'He' might be Theseus or Heracles mentioned as exemplars of heroic achievement (cf. *Busiris, Sciron, Syleus*).

261

I rescued her when she was enslaved.[1] The weaker amongst us tend to be enslaved by the stronger.

[1] Reference obscure: possibly 'she' is Cisseus' land, and the speaker Cisseus or Archelaus.

262

I have long observed how easily mortals' fortunes change. The one who has slipped gets up, and the one who was prospering falls.

263
<CHORUS>

There's a pleasure that accompanies tears, when we mourn a friend with lamentation.[1]

[1] Cf. *Andromeda* F 119 with note. Metre (dactylic) and phrasing suggest these lines belong to the Chorus, perhaps expressing some regret at Cisseus' death. Mss. MA of Stobaeus have 'in one's house' rather than 'with lamentation', probably through a simple corruption (so the topic need not be a family member's death).

264

⟨ΧΟΡΟΣ⟩

τὰ γὰρ οὐκ ὀρθῶς πρασσόμεν' ὀρθῶς
τοῖς πράσσουσιν κακὸν ἦλθε.

Stobaeus 1.3.35

264
⟨CHORUS⟩

Deeds done not rightly have rightly come out badly for those that did them.[1]

---

[1] Almost certainly from the Chorus's play-closing reflections.

AUGE

H. Van Looy in ed. Budé VIII.1.309–28.

Wilamowitz, *Analecta* 186–93; T. Zielinski, *Eos* 30 (1927), 33–53, 416; Webster 238–41; L. Koenen, *ZPE* 4 (1969), 7–18; W. S. Anderson, *GRBS* 23 (1982), 165–77; *LIMC* III.i.45–51 'Auge'; M. Huys, *Sacris Eruditi* 31 (1989–90), 169–85, and *The Tale*, relevant sections; Gantz 429–32; P. Brulé in C. Jourdain-Annequin and C. Bonnet (eds.), *Héraclès, les femmes et le féminin* (Brussels, 1996), 35–49.

Auge, daughter of Aleus and virgin priestess of Athena Alea at Tegea in Arcadia, was raped by her father's guest Heracles and gave birth to Telephus (his later story was the subject of Euripides' Telephus: see our Introduction there). In some accounts of Telephus' birth Aleus discovers Auge's pregnancy and commissions Nauplius to drown her (as Catreus seems to have ordered Aerope drowned in Cretan Women*), and she gives birth to Telephus on Mount Parthenion between Tegea and Nauplion; in others Auge bears Telephus secretly in the temple at Tegea, and Aleus discovering this tries to kill them both. Aleus' hostility is sometimes attributed to his fear that a son of Auge will kill him (cf.* Danae*), sometimes simply to his daughter's disgrace and the pollution caused by the birth in the temple. Accounts of Telephus' and Auge's survival also vary: in* some, the child is raised by herdsmen in Arcadia while the mother escapes death but is shipped to Mysia (sometimes in a chest like Danae) where Telephus finds her years later; in others, mother and child are both cast adrift and so reach Mysia together. Nearly always Auge becomes the wife of the Mysian king Teuthras, and Telephus sooner or later becomes his adopted son; thus through Telephus the historical rulers of Mysia—notably the Attalids of Pergamum in the Hellenistic period—could claim descent from Heracles.

In Euripides' play Auge has given birth in the temple (see test. iii and F 266 below). Most scholars accept Wilamowitz's view that the essentials of the plot can be found in a narrative summary by the Armenian rhetorician Moses of Chorene (8th c. A.D.?) based on late Greek sources (= test. iib below), with the addition of a detail from Apollodorus 2.7.4 (cf. 3.9.1) where pollution and famine caused by the birth in the temple are said to have led to the child's discovery. The very fragmentary papyrus hypothesis (test. iia below) appears to add the important detail that Auge was raped during a festival of Athena, perhaps as she washed the goddess's robe at a spring near the temple (see test. ii, note 2). If this is a reliable basis, we can surmise that the play began (like Alope and Melanippe Wise) with a prologue speech explaining the rape, the birth and concealment of the baby, the resulting pollution, and Aleus' search for its cause. In F 266 Auge complains to Athena about the goddess's unfair attitude to pollution, and F 267 might refer to the city's need to find the pollution's cause. In F 271, 271a and 271b Auge, advised perhaps by her nurse, seems to be looking for a means of keeping her child concealed; but her efforts were probably forestalled by the discovery of the baby and Auge's ar-

raignment (for a comparable sequence see Hypsipyle *F 754 b–c). Aleus will then have dispatched the baby to be exposed and condemned Auge to death, but Auge may have been still at hand when Heracles later appeared with the baby after finding it being suckled by a doe in the countryside (cf. Moses' summary: the suckling was a very popular subject in later classical art); this will have led to the recognition of Telephus as Heracles' son with the aid of a ring (cf. Moses again) lost by Heracles during the rape and attached by Auge to the baby as a mark of his identity. F 272 and *272a have Heracles playing with the baby before or after the recognition. F 265a and 272b probably come from his apology in a subsequent scene, and F 269 might do so but could be someone else's comment. F 268 may come from Heracles' plea to his guest-friend Aleus for understanding, and F 272c and 274 may be Aleus responding, first censoriously then with more consideration. The sentiments in F 273 and 275 cannot be placed. Probably Aleus was persuaded by Heracles to relent, so that a divine intervention to save Auge was not needed; but a god may have directed Auge and Telephus to Mysia at the end. Strabo (= test. iv below) says that according to Euripides Auge and Telephus were cast adrift in a chest and floated to Mysia, whereas Moses says only that Teuthras took Auge as his wife and Telephus as his son in obedience to an oracle of Apollo. The voyage might perhaps have been decreed so as to satisfy the continuing resentment of Aleus (Webster) or of Athena (Huys), but it seems more likely that Strabo is inaccurate and the pair were simply told by a god that they would find their destiny with Teuthras in Mysia.*

Brief fragments: F 278 'an upright horn' (perhaps a euphemism for Heracles' erect penis); F 279 'you cast aside

*(sorrows?)'; F 280 'he spent/wasted time'?; F 281 'fond
of nurturing' (the doe that suckled Telephus?). A verse
identical with Eur.* Electra *379, 'It's best to dismiss these
things (i.e. uncertainties in assessing virtue) and leave
them in confusion', seems to be ascribed to* Auge *in Dioge-
nes Laertius 2.33, and Wilamowitz therefore ascribed all of*
Electra *373–9 to* Auge; *but the case for denying these lines
to* Electra *is much debated. Other proposed ascriptions:
adesp. F 399 'to nurture this child in a way that is worthy
of Heracles and of myself'; adesp. F 402 'Did you (i.e.
Heracles) get your pleasure by force or by persuading the
girl?'; adesp. F 570 'Wine, the highest of gods, persuaded
me (i.e. Heracles?)'.*

*The metrical character of the fragments makes it almost
certain that this was a very late play, probably from the last
few years of Euripides' life. It no doubt shared the senti-
mental and melodramatic features of such plays as* Ion *and*
Hypsipyle, *including the threat to the heroine's life, a baby
on stage, the recognition, and a 'human' Heracles mending
the consequences of his drunken crime.*

Another tragic Auge *was produced by Isocrates' adop-
tive son Aphareus at the Dionysia of 341 (TrGF 73 F 1),
and comic ones, perhaps burlesquing Euripides, by
Philyllius (5th–4th c.: three fragments) and Eubulus (4th
c.: one fragment). A Sicilian vase-painting of the 330s
(LIMC no. 6) shows a comic play with Heracles accosting
Auge in the sanctuary. Four murals from Pompeii (LIMC
nos. 12–15) showing Heracles assaulting her as she washes
the robe at the spring seem to reflect Euripides' account
(test. ii a with note 2). The influence of* Auge *is also evident
in Menander's* Epitrepontes *('Men at Arbitration', which
also drew on Euripides'* Alope*), where a child born after a*

rape at a nocturnal festival is recognized by means of a ring and its parents (married in the meantime but estranged) are reunited; F 265a is quoted explicitly at a critical moment in Menander's play (vv. 1123–4). For discussions of Menander's adaptation see J. R. Porter, ICS *24–25 (1999–2000), 157–73; C. Cusset,* Ménandre ou la comédie tragique *(Paris, 2003), 158–62.*

ΑΥΓΗ

test. iia (Hypothesis)

Αὔγη,] ἧς ἡ ἀρχή·
Ἀλέας Ἀθά]νας ὅδε πολ[ύχρυσος δόμος·
ἡ δ᾽ ὑπό]θεσις·
Ἄλεος ὁ τῆ]ς Ἀρκαδίας δ[υνάστης ἔχων θυγατέ-
5 ρα Αὔγην π]άσας κάλλει[τε καὶ σωφροσύνῃ ὑ-
περέχουσ]αν τῆς Ἀλέα[ς Ἀθηνᾶς ἱέρειαν αὐτὴν
ἐποίησεν.] ἡ δὲ τῆς πα[ννυχίδος
                                ]στάσης χορ[
                                ]ς ὤλισθεν [
10   ἐσθ]ῆτα πλύν[ουσ-
πλ]ησίον κρή[νη

P. Köln 1, ed. B. Krämer (1976) after L. Koenen, *ZPE* 4 (1969), 7–18; cf. W. Luppe, *APF* 29 (1983), 19–23, van Rossum-Steenbeek 188, W. S. Barrett, *Greek Lyric, Tragedy, and Textual Criticism* (Oxford, 2007), 454–65.

2 See on F 264a below   4–7 Luppe (e.g.), adapting Koenen 7–11 See note on the translation opposite. For plausible supplements see Luppe (adapting Koenen), Kannicht *ad loc.*, and Barrett.

AUGE

test. iia (Hypothesis)
(*Auge*), which begins, 'This (is the house of Athena Alea, rich
in gold' [F 264a]; the) plot is as follows: (Aleus, ruler) of Arca-
dia, (had a daughter Auge who excelled) all women in beauty
(and virtue; and he made her priestess of Athena) Alea. But
she, when the (all-night festival) ... chorus(es?) ... fell (into
disgrace?)[1] ... wash(ing ... clothing) ... (the) nearby spring
(*or* near the spring)[2] ... by (*or* according to) the ... (he) being

[1] The same Greek verb is used in the narrative hypothesis
to *Hippolytus*, where Phaedra 'fell into desire' for Hippolytus.
Barrett however supplements here so that Auge simply slipped
and fell on muddy ground while dancing, and so hurried to the
spring to wash her own dress, not the goddess's (see note 2).
[2] The damaged text suggests that Auge was raped by a drunken
Heracles at a spring near the temple as she washed some cloth-
ing during a festival which included maidens' dances and an all-
night revel. Pausanias 8.47.4 mentions the spring, and the wall-
paintings at Pompeii (see Introduction above) depict the rape
in these terms. Koenen connected the festival with the widely
known 'Plynteria' type in which maidens purified the goddess's
sanctuary, image and robe. Barrett's supplement (see note 1) pro-
vides a different interpretation. The revel involved a degree of
licensed sexual freedom which is reflected in the ultimately 'justi-
fied' rapes in both *Auge* and Menander's *Men at Arbitration*. On
the ritual see also Brulé, and on the location of the rape in Euripi-
des, O. Musso in Bastianini–Casanova, *Euripide e i papiri* 123–6.

]δε κατὰ τὴ[ν

] οἰνωμένο[ς

remains of one more line

13] οἰνωμένο[ς West, Barrett: θ]οινωμενο[Koenen, Luppe

test. iib

Dum in Arcadiae quadam urbe festum Mineruae celebrare-
tur, cum eiusdem sacerdote Augea Alei filia choreas in noctur-
nis sacris agitante rem Hercules habuit, qui et huius furti tes-
tem relinquens ei anulum porro migrauit. Illa ex eo grauida
Telephum peperit, quod nomen ex euentu adhaesit. Iam
Augeae pater stupro cognito excandescens Telephum quidem
deserto loco abici, ubi is cerua nutritus est, Augeam autem
abysso submergi mandauit. Interim Hercules ad eam regio-
nem delatus deque re gesta sua ex anulo admonitus et puerum
ex se genitum sibi imposuit et parentem ipsam ab instante
mortis discrimine expediuit. Tum rursus pronuntiant Teu-
thrantem ex oraculo Apollinis Augeam deinde uxorem duxisse
Telephumque in filii loco habuisse.

Moses of Chorene, *Progymnasmata* 3.3 (in Armenian: Latin
translation by A. Mai and J. Zohrab, 1818), followed by a sum-
mary of *Peliades* (*Pel*. test. iiib) explicitly ascribed to Euripides.

test. iii

Αὔγη, ἡ Ἀλέου θυγατήρ, ἱέρεια δ᾽ Ἀθηνᾶς, ἐν τῷ ἱερῷ
γεννᾷ Τήλεφον.

Tzetzes on Aristophanes, *Frogs* 1080 ('and did he (Euripides)
not show women giving birth in sanctuaries?')

drunk with wine[3] . . . *(remains of one more line)* . . .

[3] Or possibly 'banqueting' (Koenen, Luppe).

test. iib

While a festival of Athena was being celebrated in a certain city in Arcadia, Heracles had his way with Athena's priestess Auge, daughter of Aleus, as she conducted the dances during the nocturnal rites. He left her a ring as evidence of his offence, and then travelled far away. Auge became pregnant by him and gave birth to Telephus—this name became attached to him because of what happened.[1] Auge's father now learned of her violation and in his anger ordered Telephus to be cast out in a deserted place, where he was suckled by a doe, and Auge to be drowned in the ocean. Meanwhile Heracles had returned to that region and was informed by means of the ring[2] of what he had done. He acknowledged that he had fathered the child, and rescued the mother from the imminent danger of death. They also say that Teuthras, instructed by an oracle of Apollo, then took Auge as his wife and adopted Telephus as his son.

[1] The name Telephus was sometimes explained by reference to his suckling at the teat (*thêlê*) of a doe (*elaphos*), as narrated in the next sentence. For an alternative etymology see *Telephus* F 696.11–13.   [2] Probably Heracles' ring, torn by Auge from his finger during the rape and left by her with the exposed baby as a proof of his paternity (like Charisius' ring in Menander's *Men at Arbitration*).

test. iii

Auge, daughter of Aleus and priestess of Athena, gives birth to Telephus in the sanctuary.

test. iv

Εὐριπίδης δ᾽ ὑπὸ Ἀλέου φησὶ τοῦ τῆς Αὔγης πατρὸς εἰς
λάρνακα τὴν Αὔγην κατατεθεῖσαν ἅμα τῷ παιδὶ Τηλέφῳ
καταποντωθῆναι, φωράσαντος τὴν ἐξ Ἡρακλέους φθο-
ράν· Ἀθηνᾶς δὲ προνοίᾳ τὴν λάρνακα περαιωθεῖσαν
ἐκπεσεῖν εἰς τὸ στόμα τοῦ Καΐκου, τὸν δὲ Τεύθραντα
ἀναλαβόντα τὰ σώματα τῇ μὲν ὡς γαμετῇ χρήσασθαι,
τῷ δ᾽ ὡς ἑαυτοῦ παιδί.

Strabo 13.1.69

264a

Ἀλέας Ἀθά]νας ὅδε πολ[ύχρυσος δόμος

The play's opening line (= test. iia.2 above), reconstructed by
Merkelbach with ref. to Menander, *Hero* 84 (Ἀλέας Ἀθάνας)
and Favorinus, *On Exile* col. 2.43, p. 378 Barigazzi (πολύχρυσος
δόμος).

(265 N = 272b below)

265a (= 920 N)

ἡ φύσις ἐβούλεθ᾽, ᾗ νόμων οὐδὲν μέλει·
γυνὴ δ᾽ ἐπ᾽ αὐτῷ τῷδ᾽ ἔφυ . . .

Menander, *Men at Arbitration* 1123–4; v. 1 is quoted or
adapted several times elsewhere, and parodied in Anaxandrides F
66 *PCG*.

test. iv

Euripides says that Auge was put in a chest with her son Telephus and cast into the sea by her father Aleus, after he detected her rape by Heracles; but by Athena's providence the chest was carried across the sea and landed at the mouth of the Caicus river. Teuthras then rescued them and made Auge his wife and Telephus his own son.[1]

[1] Strabo's attribution of this story to Euripides seems questionable: see Introduction above.

264a

This (is the house of Athena Alea, rich in gold) . . .

(265 N = 272b below)

265a (= 920 N)

Nature willed it, which cares nothing for convention. A woman was created by nature for this very purpose . . . [1]

[1] That is, for sexual submission to a man. In Menander's *Men at Arbitration* a slave quotes these words in order to persuade Smicrines to accept the fact that his daughter Pamphile was raped and made pregnant at a nocturnal festival.

EURIPIDES

266

σκῦλα μὲν βροτοφθόρα
χαίρεις ὁρῶσα καὶ νεκρῶν ἐρείπια,
κοὺ μιαρά σοι ταῦτ' ἐστίν· εἰ δ' ἐγὼ 'τεκον,
δεινὸν τόδ' ἡγῇ;

Clement of Alexandria, *Miscellanies* 7.3.23.4, with ascription to 'Auge justifying herself to Athena over Athena's displeasure at her having given birth in the sanctuary'.

267

δεινὴ πόλις νοσοῦσ' ἀνευρίσκειν κακά.

Stobaeus 4.1.12

268

καὶ βουθυτεῖν γὰρ ἠξίους ἐμὴν χάριν.

Apollonius Dyscolus, *On Conjunctions*, in *Gramm. Gr.* II.i.247.3 (= Tryphon fr. 56 von Velsen)

269

Ἔρωτα δ' ὅστις μὴ θεὸν κρίνει μέγαν
{καὶ τῶν ἁπάντων δαιμόνων ὑπέρτατον}
ἢ σκαιός ἐστιν ἢ καλῶν ἄπειρος ὢν
οὐκ οἶδε τὸν μέγιστον ἀνθρώποις θεόν.

Stobaeus 4.20.11; vv. 1, 3–4: Athenaeus 13.600d; vv. 1, 3 are imitated in Latin by Caecilius Statius fr. incert. fab. 15 Ribbeck (= Cicero, *Tusculan Disputations* 4.32.68).

1 μὴ θεὸν κρίνει μέγαν Stob.: μὴ μόνον κρίνει θεὸν Ath.
2 omitted by Athenaeus, deleted by Wilamowitz

266

You enjoy looking on spoils stripped from the dead and the wreckage of corpses; these do not pollute you. Yet you think it a dreadful thing if I have given birth?

267

A city that is sick is clever at seeking out wrongs.[1]

[1] Possibly referring to the search for the cause of pollution and famine in Tegea (see Introduction above).

268

In fact you thought it proper to sacrifice oxen for my sake.[1]

[1] Probably Heracles reminding Aleus of his earlier hospitality towards him.

269

Anyone who does not count Love a great god {and highest of all the divine powers} is either obtuse or, lacking experience in his delights, is unacquainted with men's greatest god.

(270 N = 272c below)

271

⟨ΤΡΟΦΟΣ?⟩

πτηνὰς διώκεις, ὦ τέκνον, τὰς ἐλπίδας.

⟨ΑΥΓΗ?⟩

†οὐχ ἡ τύχη γε·† τῆς τύχης δ' οὐχ εἷς τρόπος.

Stobaeus 4.47.1 (attributed to *Auge* in ms. S, to *Aegeus* in ms. A)

1, 2 assigned to different speakers by Herwerden   2 οὐκ ηὐτύχησα Herwerden: οὐκ ἦν τύχω γε Zielinski

271a (= 276 N)

⟨ΑΥΓΗ?⟩

γυναῖκές ἐσμεν· τὰ μὲν ὄκνῳ νικώμεθα,
τὰ δ' οὐκ ἂν ἡμῶν θράσος ὑπερβάλοιτό τις.

Stobaeus 4.22.153

271b (= 277 N)

⟨ΤΡΟΦΟΣ ἢ ΑΥΓΗ?⟩

ποῖ; πῶς δὲ λήσει; τίς δὲ νῷν πιστὸς φίλος;

Stobaeus 3.22.7. Identified as dialogue by Enger, assigning vv. 1 and 3 to Auge: *vice versa* Zielinski

1 λήσω or λήσεις Meineke

AUGE

(270 N = 272c below)

271

\<NURSE?\>

These hopes you chase are flighty, my child.

\<AUGE?\>

†Not fortune at least†,[1] but fortune is not unchanging.

[1] The transmitted text makes no sense. Herwerden suggested 'I have been unfortunate', Zielinski 'Not if I succeed'.

271a (= 276 N)

\<AUGE?\>

We are women. In some things timidity overcomes us, but in others no one could exceed our courage.[1]

[1] Cf. *Medea* 263–6: 'In other matters a woman is full of fear, and bad at facing up to boldness and steel; but when she finds herself wronged with regard to her marriage-bed, there is no other mind more murderous.'

271b (= 277 N)

\<NURSE *or* AUGE?\>

Where? How will he[1] escape notice? What loyal friend do we have?

[1] The new-born Telephus, if the Greek text is correct. Meineke suggested 'I escape' (if Auge speaks vv. 1 and 3), or 'you escape' (if the Nurse does). F 271 (and 272?) suggests that Auge is for action and the Nurse for caution: cf. Hypsipyle and the Chorus-leader in *Hypsipyle* F 754b. In Sophocles, *Women of Trachis* 590–3 the Chorus-leader urges action on Deianeira in similar terms, but there the point is that Deianeira is persuaded, with disastrous results.

⟨ΑΥΓΗ ἢ ΤΡΟΦΟΣ?⟩
ζητῶμεν· ἡ δόκησις ἀνθρώποις κακόν.
⟨ΤΡΟΦΟΣ ἢ ΑΥΓΗ?⟩
καὶ τοὐπιχειρεῖν γ' ἐξαμαρτάνειν φιλεῖ.

272
⟨ΗΡΑΚΛΗΣ?⟩
τίς δ' οὐχὶ χαίρει νηπίοις ἀθύρμασιν;

Stobaeus 4.24.49

*272a (= 864 N)
ΗΡΑΚΛΗΣ
παίζω· μεταβολὰς γὰρ πόνων ἀεὶ φιλῶ.

Aelian, *Miscellany* 12.15, with attribution to Heracles 'while holding a baby'

272b (= 265 N)
⟨ΗΡΑΚΛΗΣ⟩
νῦν δ' οἶνος ἐξέστησέ μ'· ὁμολογῶ δέ σε
ἀδικεῖν, τὸ δ' ἀδίκημ' ἐγένετ' οὐχ ἑκούσιον.

Stobaeus 3.18.19

272c (= 270 N)
οὐ τῶν κακούργων οἶκτος ἀλλὰ τῆς δίκης.

Stobaeus 4.5.5

⟨AUGE *or* NURSE?⟩
Let's try to find one one. Mere supposition does people no good.

⟨NURSE *or* AUGE?⟩
And action attempted also tends to go wrong.

272
⟨HERACLES?⟩
Who does not take pleasure in childish toys?

*272a (= 864 N)
⟨HERACLES⟩
(holding the baby)
I'm playing; I always like a change from my labours.

272b (= 265 N)
⟨HERACLES⟩
As it is, wine made me lose control. I admit I wronged you, but the wrong was not intentional.

272c (= 270 N)
Pity is not for criminals but for those in the right.

273

πᾶσιν γὰρ ἀνθρώποισιν, οὐχ ἡμῖν μόνον,
ἢ καὶ παραυτίκ᾽ ἢ χρόνῳ δαίμων βίον
ἔσφηλε, κοὐδεὶς διὰ τέλους εὐδαιμονεῖ.

Stobaeus 4.41.15

274

. . . τὸ δ᾽ ἐπιεικὲς ὠφελεῖ τὰς ξυμφοράς.

Stobaeus 3.37.19

275

κακῶς δ᾽ ὄλοιντο πάντες οἳ μοναρχίᾳ
χαίρουσιν ὀλίγων τ᾽ ἐν πόλει τυραννίδι.
τοὐλεύθερον γὰρ ὄνομα παντὸς ἄξιον·
κἂν σμίκρ᾽ ἔχῃ τις, μεγάλ᾽ ἔχειν νομίζεται.

Stobaeus 4.8.3; vv. 3–4: Philo, *That Every Good Man is Free*
141

1–2 μοναρχίᾳ . . . τυραννίδι Hense: τυραννίδι . . .
μοναρχίᾳ Stob.   4 νομίζεται Stob.: νομιζέτω Philo

(276, 277 N = 271a, 271b above)

273

It happens to everyone, not just to us: sooner or later fortune spoils our life, and no one has good fortune right through to the end.

274

. . . decency helps us in our misfortunes.

275

A miserable death to all those who are happy with monarchy, or with the tyranny of a few in their city! The title 'free' is worth everything; (with this) even a man who has little is reckoned to have much.

(276, 277 N = 271a, 271b above)

AUTOLYCUS A *and* B

Pechstein 39–122; Krumeich 403–12; H. Van Looy in ed.
Budé VIII.1.329–40; I. Mangidis, *Euripides' Satyrspiel
Autolyokos* (Bern, 2003).

LIMC III.i.55–6 'Autolykos I'; V. Masciadri, *Museum
Helveticum* 44 (1987), 1–7; R. Kannicht, *Dioniso* 61.2
(1991), 91–9; F. Angiò, *Dioniso* 62.2 (1992), 83–94; Gantz
109–10, 176; Voelke 71, 264–7 (F 282), 364–5.

For pairs of plays named for the same main character see
Alcmeon *(introductory note).*

*Autolycus was a son of Hermes the patron god of
thieves, from whom he learned trickery and perjury
(Homer,* Odyssey *19.395); his special ability was to make
substitutes for what he stole and thus deceive owners that
they had lost nothing (Ovid,* Metamorphoses *11.313–5;
Hyginus,* Fab. *201.1), or to make it disappear altogether
(Hesiod fr. 67: see test. iv below, and for the entire mythical
background Gantz and Mangidis 71–107). Autolycus was
ideal for the sly world of satyr drama.*

A 2nd c. A.D. *papyrus first published in 1939 (P. Vindob.
19766 = P. Rain. 3.32 = test. iiib) preserves just enough of a
'narrative' hypothesis to confirm a long-doubted ancient
testimony that Euripides wrote a 'first', and so presumably
also a second, play of this name (Athenaeus 10.413c = test.*

iiia; a similar doubt long existed about Phrixus A *and* B); Mangidis 110–8, *cf.* 205, *argues however, following a suggestion of Reichenbach in 1889, that the papyrus confirms that Athenaeus meant two performances, or a reperformance, rather than two versions of the play. The plot of one play had been conjectured from Hyginus,* Fab. 201 (= test. *va), supported by a now lost 2nd c.* B.C. *Boeotian jug* (LIMC *'Antikleia' no. 2 = test. *vb): Autolycus stole cattle from* Sisyphus, *himself a trickster (see* Sisyphus, *Introduction; Voelke 358–64); Sisyphus suspected the theft and marked the hooves of his other cattle, enabling him to challenge Autolycus and recover them when they too were stolen; but he also raped Autolycus' daughter Anticlea (and so 'shared' with Laertes the fathering of the wily Odysseus). The jug has Autolycus arguing with Sisyphus about cattle, Sisyphus managing two yoked cattle near Autolycus and Laertes (who is exclaiming), and Sisyphus about to rape Anticlea, all being named (O. Touchefeu in* LIMC *however doubts the association with such a plot, as does Pechstein in Krumeich 409). A very different and broad content for the second play has been conjectured by Masciadri from* Tzetzes, Chiliades *8.435–53 (= test.* iv *below), a view shared by Pechstein and by Kannicht (1991): Tzetzes tells how Autolycus in two other thefts or abductions substituted for them a creature or person inferior but not recognized by his victims, an ass for a horse, an ugly male satyr for a young daughter; this would provide material for at least two play-scenes or episodes, and the ugly/young contrast would suit a light play. Mangidis's reconstruction of his single play (summary on 201–2, cf. 206–8) accommodates everything from Hyginus, Tzetzes and the two vases (170–82, augmented by a recently found cup from Pella,*

which Kannicht, TrGF 5.344 allows may relate to
Autolycus *rather than* Sisyphus: *details at TrGF 5.658).*

*In content F 282a (see note), 283 and 284 could belong
to either play. We cannot know to which of the two sup-
posed plots we should refer F 282 in the light of Athenaeus'
attribution to the 'first' play. This is a long criticism of
selfish and socially unproductive athletes. Athletics as a
topic is not rare in satyr drama (see R. Seaford,* Euripides:
Cyclops *[Oxford, 1984], 39–40; Voelke 261–72); one of
Pratinas' satyr plays was titled* Wrestlers *and one of Aes-
chylus'* Contestants *(or* Visitors) *at the Isthmian Games.
Perhaps the regular over-eating and over-drinking of the
satyrs (e.g.* Cyclops *139–61, 545–65; Voelke 183–202)
drew the criticism in F 282; and perhaps it came from the
crafty Autolycus himself when he was persuading the fa-
ther of the young girl to trust his assertions against those
of the satyrs who witnessed his attempted deception (cf.
Pechstein 82–5). The length and rhetorical tone of F 282
are also not impossible for a satyr play (cf. the Cyclops'
speech defending his voracity, Cyc. 315–46). Neverthe-
less Angiò and others have thought the fragment tragic in
style, and one of the two plays therefore to have been a
tragedy; of this possibility Pechstein 39–40 and 114 asks
whether the play containing F 282 may have been 'pro-
satyric', like Alcestis in Euripides' production of 438. Con-
versely Voelke 71, 264, 364 holds that only one play was
certainly satyric, and that F 282 belonged to it.*

*No other satyr play about Autolycus is known (unless
he figured in the* Sisyphus *or in other dramatists' plays of
that name). The comedian Eupolis may have used the myth
to tease the victorious Athenian boy athlete Autolycus in
420 B.C., in the first version of his* Autolycus *(F 48–75*

PCG: *see* I. Storey, Eupolis *[Oxford, 2003] 84–6, who debates inconclusively the question whether Euripides' F 282 also 'reflects' the boy or Eupolis, and in what order of time; if this link can be established, Euripides' play is dated. Mangidis 134–54 concludes that Eupolis' play, or 422, provides the latest date for the first performance of his single play). Autolycus' most famous dramatic descendant is the thief in* The Winter's Tale *(see especially 4.3.24–7); Shakespeare would have known both Ovid and Hyginus.*

ΑΥΤΟΛΥΚΟΣ Α, Β

test. iv

435 Ἑρμοῦ παῖς ὁ Αὐτόλυκος . . .

         . . . πένης δὲ ὑπάρχων ἄγαν,

ἐκ τοῦ Ἑρμοῦ χαρίζεται τὴν κλεπτικὴν τὴν τέχνην,

438 ὡς . . .

442   . . . πάντα νικᾶν κλέπτην.

κλέπτων καὶ γὰρ μετήμειβεν ἄλλα διδοὺς ἀντ' ἄλλων.

ἐδόκουν δ' οἱ λαμβάνοντες τὰ σφῶν λαμβάνειν πάλιν,

445 οὐκ ἠπατῆσθαι τούτῳ δὲ καὶ ἕτερα λαμβάνειν.

ἵππον γὰρ κλέπτων ἄριστον ὄνον τῶν ψωριώντων

διδοὺς ἐποίει δόκησιν ἐκεῖνον δεδωκέναι·

καὶ κόρην νύμφην νεαρὰν κλέπτων ἐδίδου πάλιν

ἢ σειληνὸν ἢ σάτυρον, γερόντιον σαπρόν τι,

450 σιμόν, νωδόν, καὶ φαλακρόν, μυξῶδες, τῶν δυσμόρφων.

καὶ ὁ πατὴρ ἐνόμιζε τοῦτον ὡς θυγατέρα.

ἐν Αὐτολύκῳ δράματι σατυρικῷ τὰ πάντα

ὁ Εὐριπίδης ἀκριβῶς τὰ περὶ τούτου γράφει.

Tzetzes, *Chiliades* 8.435–53 Leone

AUTOLYCUS A *and* B

Autolycus was a son of Hermes . . . and being born extremely
poor, was favoured by Hermes with the art of stealing, so as . . .   437
to surpass every thief. Whenever he stole, he did an exchange   442
and returned one thing for another; the receivers thought they
were getting their own things back again, not that they had   445
been deceived by him and were getting different things. He
would steal a very good horse and give (back) an ass, one of the
mangy sort, and made it seem he had returned the former;[1]
and when he stole a marriageable young girl, he gave back
again either a silenus or a satyr, some decrepit little old man,
snub-nosed, toothless and bald, all snotty, one of the uglies[2] —   450
and her father thought of him as his daughter. In his satyr-play
Autolycus Euripides has written the whole story about him
accurately.

[1] Cf. F 283, 284.   [2] See F 282a below with note.

282

κακῶν γὰρ ὄντων μυρίων καθ᾽ Ἑλλάδα
οὐδὲν κάκιόν ἐστιν ἀθλητῶν γένους.
οἳ πρῶτον οἰκεῖν οὔτε μανθάνουσιν εὖ
οὔτ᾽ ἂν δύναιντο· πῶς γὰρ ὅστις ἔστ᾽ ἀνὴρ
5 γνάθου τε δοῦλος νηδύος θ᾽ ἡσσημένος
κτήσαιτ᾽ ἂν ὄλβον εἰς ὑπερβολὴν πατρός;
οὐδ᾽ αὖ πένεσθαι κἀξυπηρετεῖν τύχαις
οἷοί τ᾽· ἔθη γὰρ οὐκ ἐθισθέντες καλὰ
σκληρῶς μεταλλάσσουσιν εἰς τἀμήχανον.
10 λαμπροὶ δ᾽ ἐν ἥβῃ καὶ πόλεως ἀγάλματα
φοιτῶσ᾽· ὅταν δὲ προσπέσῃ γῆρας πικρόν,
τρίβωνες ἐκβαλόντες οἴχονται κρόκας.
ἐμεμψάμην δὲ καὶ τὸν Ἑλλήνων νόμον,
οἳ τῶνδ᾽ ἕκατι σύλλογον ποιούμενοι
15 τιμῶσ᾽ ἀχρείους ἡδονὰς δαιτὸς χάριν.
τίς γὰρ παλαίσας εὖ, τίς ὠκύπους ἀνὴρ
ἢ δίσκον ἄρας ἢ γνάθον παίσας καλῶς
πόλει πατρῴᾳ στέφανον ἤρκεσεν λαβών;
πότερα μαχοῦνται πολεμίοισιν ἐν χεροῖν

Athenaeus 10.413c; vv. 1–9: P. Oxy. 3699 (badly damaged); vv.
1–9 and 16–22: Galen, *Protrepticus* 10 and 13; v. 12: Diogenes
Laertius 1.56; v. 22: Plutarch, *Moralia* 581f

3 πρῶτον οἰκεῖν P. Oxy., Galen: πρῶτα μὲν ζῆν Ath.
6 εἰς ὑπερβολὴν πατρός Ath.: εἰς ὑπεκτροφὴν πάτρας Galen
(P. Oxy. defective)   7 κἀξυπηρετεῖν Galen: κἀξυπηρετμεῖν
Ath. (P. Oxy. defective)   12 ἐκβαλόντες Ath.: ἐκλείποντες
(or -λιπ-) Diog.

282

Of countless bad things existing throughout Greece none
is worse than athletes as a breed. First, they neither learn
well how to manage a household, nor would they be able to
learn—for how could a man who is a slave to eating and
dominated by his belly acquire wealth to exceed his fa-   5
ther's?[1] Moreover they cannot manage poverty or cope
with misfortunes: because they have not learned good hab-
its, a change towards difficulties is hard on them. They are
splendid in their prime and go proudly about as ornaments
to a city; but when old age in its harshness falls upon them,   10
they fade away like cloaks that have lost their threads. I
blame too the Greeks' custom of gathering because of
these men to value useless pleasures for the sake of a
feast.[2] Why—what man who has wrestled well, what man   15
fleet of foot or that has thrown a discus or boxed a jaw well,
has defended his ancestral city by winning a wreath? Are

---

[1] Perhaps 'to support his country's future generations'
(Galen).   [2] Victorious athletes sometimes threw a public feast,
or were themselves publicly feasted—both to no civic benefit
(similar phenomena are not unknown in modern times). For the
strictures on diet, regimen and civic obligation cf. *Antiope*
F 201.3–4.

20 δίσκους ἔχοντες ἢ δι' ἀσπίδων χερὶ
    θείνοντες ἐκβαλοῦσι πολεμίους πάτρας;
    οὐδεὶς σιδήρου ταῦτα μωραίνει πέλας
    †στάς†. ἄνδρας χρὴ σοφούς τε κἀγαθοὺς
    φύλλοις στέφεσθαι, χὤστις ἡγεῖται πόλει
25 κάλλιστα σώφρων καὶ δίκαιος ὢν ἀνήρ,
    ὅστις τε μύθοις ἔργ' ἀπαλλάσσει κακὰ
    μάχας τ' ἀφαιρῶν καὶ στάσεις· τοιαῦτα γὰρ
    πόλει τε πάσῃ πᾶσί θ' Ἕλλησιν καλά.

23 beg. ἱστάμενος Pechstein: στάς. ἄνδρας ⟨οὖν⟩ χρή⟨ν
τοὺς⟩ σοφούς Dobree (⟨οὖν⟩ Grotius)

282a
μηδὲν τῷ πατρὶ
μέμφεσθ' ἄωρον ἀποκαλοῦντες ἀνδρίον.

Photius, *Lexicon* a 1760 Theodoridis

283
. . . τοὺς ὄνους
τοὺς λαρκαγωγοὺς ἐξ ὄρους οἴσειν ξύλα . . .

Pollux 10.111 (printed here as iambic trimeters, but the words
also make a single trochaic tetrameter. F 284 presents a similar
difficulty: see note on translation.)

284
†σχοινίνας γὰρ ἵπποισι φλοΐνας ἡνίας πλέκει†

Pollux 10.178

286

they going to fight enemies with a discus in their hands, or   20
drive enemies from a fatherland by punching through
shields with a fist? No one is this stupid †when standing†[3]
near a sword! Wreathing with leaves[4] should be for men
who are wise and brave, and for the man who leads a city
best through being prudent and just, and whose words de-   25
liver it from evil acts by removing feuds and factions: such
are the things good for every city and all Greeks.[5]

[3] The Greek is unmetrical; Pechstein conjectured 'when tak-
ing his stand' (same sense).   [4] Victorious athletes wreathed:
Alexander F 61d.6, *Electra* 862; cf. *Hecuba* 574 (metaphor).
[5] The fragment is discussed at length by Mangidis 19–39, 190–
200, cf. 41–63 (with full bibliography for athletics).

282a

Don't criticize our father,[1] calling him an ugly little man.

[1] Silenus, 'father' of the satyrs ('old man' in *Eurystheus* F 372).

283

. . . that the asses which carry charcoal-baskets will bring
wood from the mountain . . .

284

† . . . weaves reins for horses made of rushes of bark . . . †[1]

[1] Text unmetrical and corrupt; probably either 'of rushes' or
'of bark' has intruded.

BELLEROPHON

C. Collard in *SFP* I.98–120, 285–6 (~ II.365–6); Diggle, *TrGFS* 98–100 (F 285, 286, 286b); F. Jouan in ed. Budé VIII.2.1–35; M. Curnis, *Il Bellerofonte di Euripide* (Torino, 2003).

A. Caputi, *Rendiconti dell'Accademia dei Lincei* 18 (1909), 509–26 (with older bibliography); Rau, *Paratragodia* 89–97; Webster 109–11; L. di Gregorio, *CCC* 4 (1983), 159–213, 365–82; Aélion (1986) 192–6; J. A. White, *AJP* 103 (1982), 119–27 (mythical and Biblical analogies); Gantz 313–6; *LIMC* VII.i.214–30 'Pegasus'; G. W. Dobrov, *Figures of Play* (Oxford, 2001), 89–104, esp. 91–7; D. Milo, *Vichiana* 6.2 (2004), 304–11. See also the notes to F 286, 286b, 289, 304a.

The handsome hero Bellerophon of Corinth is in some accounts a god's son; he mastered the winged horse Pegasus through the power of the goddess Athena (Pindar, Olympians 13.60–86). He had early dangerous adventures, escaping from the amorous Stheneboea and her vengeful husband Proetus at Tiryns; with the aid of Pegasus, he survived Proetus' plot, carried out in Lycia by Proetus' brother-in-law Iobates, to have him killed by monstrous opponents (Homer, Iliad 6.160–89); then he took vengeance by killing Stheneboea: this story forms the plot of

Stheneboea. *For a time Bellerophon enjoyed happiness (cf. F 285.19–20), for he had returned to Lycia and married Iobates' other daughter when that king realised that his feats meant he was a god's son; Bellerophon was expecting to inherit the kingdom, and his children were splendid (Iliad 6.196–9). Then he incurred the gods' hatred (6.200; the reason is not stated) and became embittered to the point of lonely wandering, 'eating out his heart' (6.201–2), and enduring 'melancholia' (Aristotle, Problems in Physics 953a21 = test. *iv); the Scholia on Iliad 6.200–5 prefer as the cause of his embitterment the death of two children (the name of one, Isander, is insecurely read in the narrative hypothesis, test. iiia.13 below). It is disappointing that this hypothesis and the even scrappier test. *iiib (P. Oxy. 4017, a few words only) describe mostly the play's background rather than its plot, and both include problematic details: see below on F 304a and 305, and the note to the translation of F 304a.*

Euripides' play is set in Lycia, perhaps on the plain where Bellerophon is wandering. It begins with his anger against the gods for his sufferings (two long fragments, F 285 and 286, the first at least from his prologue speech; cf. F 286a and 286b.7). Later he resolves to climb heaven on Pegasus (cf. F 306–309a; Pindar, Isthmians 7.43–8 and scholia), either to disprove the existence of gods so unjust, or perhaps to remonstrate with them. Zeus blocks his presumption, however, by having Pegasus throw him off (Pindar, Isthm. 7, cf. Olympians 13.91–3 and scholia); the disastrous flight is narrated either by a messenger or by Bellerophon himself (F 309, 309a). He falls to earth and is brought on stage mortally wounded (F 310–311; compare Phaethon's similar rashness and catastrophe, and

Hippolytus in the name play). A god ends the play, announcing that Pegasus now draws Zeus's 'chariot of lightning' (F 312, cf. Olympians 13.92–3). Aristophanes parodied Bellerophon's ragged dress and lameness in this play (Acharnians 426–9 = test. iic); sources such as Schol. on Aristophanes, Peace 136 say that these were consequences of his flight, but they may have registered Bellerophon's abject misery at the play's start, for they would be rather pointless if seen first in his death scene (Aristophanes also parodied the flight on Pegasus in Peace 135–48 = test. iia; on both parodies see Rau, Dobrov).

Beginning and end are thus clear in content, but the many intervening fragments (F 287–304) reveal little of the play's development and structure; they are sententious and their sources give no context. F 287–302 come from an early scene or episode, possibly more than one (Jouan 9–10, 14), in which a voice or voices try to comfort or dissuade Bellerophon; Iobates or Bellerophon's surviving son Glaucus are often suggested. F 303–4 are choral commonplaces on man's uncertain fortune, probably from two separate odes (the chorus were probably Lycians: cf. the Attic farmers in Antiope). Reconstructors have arranged these fragments as persuasively as possible (Caputi, Di Gregorio, Aélion and Jouan in particular), but invariably quite differently: the best policy is restraint (e.g. Curnis, Kannicht in TrGF), and many scholars have therefore concentrated on interpreting a few very difficult fragments (see Bibliography).

A special problem is whether F 304a and 305 belong at all. If authentic, they introduce a sequel to Stheneboea's killing by Bellerophon (F 304a): her son Megapenthes has pursued him to Lycia for vengeance after judicial prosecu-

291

tion in Argos (F 305: cf. the 'trial' in Orestes *844–956). The prose introduction to* Palatine Anthology *3.15, a poem describing a sculptured scene of this myth's figures, states Megapenthes' intention; early reconstructors related the passage to the play, and recent scholars use it more and more confidently (after Carlini [see under F 304a], e.g. Di Gregorio, Aélion, Jouan 10, 14–15 and Curnis 256–60); Webster, Collard and Kannicht have been more cautious. Such a scene—certainly before the Pegasus flight—would at least exacerbate Bellerophon's sense of persecution (cf. Jouan 15). Stheneboea's name occurs in a very scrappy narrative hypothesis, P. Oxy. 4017, and may indicate that it relates to her name-play; the mention of a 'ship' at test. iiia.21 (the other hypothesis) may relate to Megapenthes' journey from Argos to Lycia.*

Brief fragment: F 286a (damaged papyrus) 'the gods . . . lawful(?) . . . '   Some fragments of Stheneboea *are erroneously attributed in their sources to* Bellerophon: *F 661.4–5 (= 662 N), 666, 669; cf.* Danae *F 324.   Other ascriptions: F 911 (also ascribed to* Antiope), *adesp. F 60 'But what if (s)he falls into the sea's watery depth?' (also to* Cretans *and* Stheneboea), *adesp. F 129 (choral verses on the godlike powers of gold), adesp. F 181 (wealth and a bad reputation better than poverty and a good one), adesp. F 513 'Once I am dead let the earth be consumed by fire. It doesn't matter to me, for I'm all right.'*

In this play Euripides completed, or at least complemented, the hero's story in Stheneboea, *but his characterization is quite different and resembles such god-defiers as Heracles (compare* Heracles *1313–46 with F 286b.6–7) or Pentheus (*Bacchae). *The two plays must come from different years, and* Bellerophon *was certainly earlier than 425,*

the year of Aristophanes' parody in Acharnians *(above).*
Milo 307–8, following Curnis, relates F 286.10–12 *'small*
cities honouring the gods . . . subject to greater, more impi-
ous ones' to the siege and capture of Plataea in 429–7 B.C.
by the Thebans (whom he finds alluded to in F 295*), and*
dates the play to that period. Both Bellerophon *and*
Stheneboea *have elements common in other plays of the*
430s and 420s which examine the duties and failings of
hosts, guests, friends and allies (Alcestis, Medea, Children
of Heracles, Hecuba, Suppliants). *The two long fragments*
285 and 286 in their style of rhetorical analysis antici-
pate the later Suppliant Women 195–249 *(late 420's) and*
Electra 367–85.

The plot of Sophocles' Iobates *is not known. Astydamas*
the Younger wrote a Bellerophon *in the middle of the 4th*
century (a mere title for us); like Aristophanes, the come-
dian Eubulus exploited Euripides for parody in his own
Bellerophon *(*F 15 *PCG). For the modern era see OGCMA*
I.274–6.

ΒΕΛΛΕΡΟΦΟΝΤΗΣ

test. iia

ΠΑΙΔΙΟΝ

οὐκοῦν ἐχρῆν σε Πηγάσου ζεῦξαι πτερόν,
136 ὅπως ἐφαίνου τοῖς θεοῖς τραγικώτερος;

* * *

146 ἐκεῖνο τήρει, μὴ σφαλεὶς καταρρυῇς
ἐντεῦθεν, εἶτα χωλὸς ὢν Εὐριπίδῃ
λόγον παράσχῃς καὶ τραγῳδία γένῃ.

Aristophanes, *Peace* 135–6, 146–8

test. iiia (Hypothesis)
Beginnings of 22 lines from a narrative hypothesis:

1 διεγνωκότος   2 -σθαι προσελθὼ[ν   3 ἰδίου καὶ ἀδελφ[
4 Βελλεροφόντῃ[5 τὴν πρέπουσα[6 αὐ[τ]ὸς
[σ]υνέπε[ται   7 -θη· νεκρὸν .[8 -πειν τὸν ἐχθ[ρὸν

P. Oxy. 3651.1–22, ed. H. M. Cockle (1984); re-ed. W. Luppe,
Eikasmos 1 (1990), 171–7, van Rossum-Steenbeek 192–3

4–5 τιμωρίαν | τὴν πρέπουσα[ν (e.g.) Kannicht (δίκην
Luppe)

BELLEROPHON

TRYGAEUS' DAUGHTER
(*to Trygaeus*)

So shouldn't you have harnessed winged Pegasus, to make yourself seem more tragic to the gods?

* * *

Keep a look-out, so you don't slip and then fall off downwards, and then in your lameness provide Euripides with a plot, and become a tragedy!

test. iii a (Hypothesis)

. . . having decided . . . Having come to . . . his own(?) . . . and . . . brother[1] . . . Bellerophon . . . the appropriate . . .[2] himself follows(?) . . . corpse . . . the (his?) enemy . . . from the . . .   6

---

[1] Perhaps a reference to Bellerophon's fratricide before taking refuge with Proetus in Tiryns (*Stheneboea* test. iia.8, F 661.7 and 16–18).   [2] Perhaps 'the appropriate (penalty)' (Kannicht, Luppe), referring to Bellerophon's vengeful killing of Stheneboea (*Sthen.* test. Iiia.23–9).

9 ἀπὸ τῶν {σ}ταυ .[10 σαντα ὑπολ[
11 Βελ]λερο]φόντην[12 ...].. δρυ .[ποτα[μ
13 ...]νδρον εξε[14, 15 *a few letters each*   16] ..α τὴν
χώ[ραν   17 *a few letters*   18 τ]ὰς ποινὰς δ[19 .]αι τὸν
Βελλερ[οφόντην   20 ..].... Λυκία[ς   21 ...] τὴν ναῦν [
22 *a few letters*

12 ποτα[μ inserted above line by a later hand; possibly a gloss
(see note on translation)   13 ῎Ισα]νδρον or Μαία]νδρον
Cockle

285

ΒΕΛΛΕΡΟΦΟΝΤΗΣ

ἐγὼ τὸ μὲν δὴ πανταχοῦ θρυλούμενον
κράτιστον εἶναι φημὶ μὴ φῦναι βροτῷ·
τρισσῶν δὲ μοιρῶν ἐγκρινῶ νικᾶν μίαν,
πλούτου τε χὤτῳ σπέρμα γενναῖον προσῇ
5 πενίας τ'· ἀριθμὸν γὰρ τοσόνδε προυθέμην.
ὁ μὲν ζάπλουτος, εἰς γένος δ' οὐκ εὐτυχής,
ἀλγεῖ μὲν ἀλγεῖ, παγκαλῶς δ' ἀλγύνεται
ὄλβου διοίγων θάλαμον ἥδιστον χερί·
ἔξω δὲ βαίνων τοῦδε, τὸν πάρος χρόνον
10 πλουτῶν, ὑπ' ἄτης ζεύγλαν ἀσχάλλει πεσών.
ὅστις δὲ γαῦρον σπέρμα γενναῖόν τ' ἔχων
βίου σπανίζει, τῷ γένει μὲν εὐτυχεῖ,

Vv. 1–18: Stobaeus 4.33.16; vv. 1–2: Stob. 4.34.38; v. 8: Plu-
tarch, *Moralia* 1069b; vv. 11–14: Stob. 4.32b.23; vv. 15–20: Stob.
4.33.9a; v. 20: Stob. 3.32.3 without attribution

3 ἐγκρινῶ Matthiae (-ίνω Pierson): ἐν κρίνω Stob.
10 ζεύγλαν ἀ(ν)σχάλλει Salmasius: ζεύς τ' ἀνασχάλλει Stob.

Bellerophon . . . river[3] . . . the land . . . the penalty . . . 18
Bellerophon . . . Lycia(n?) . . . the ship . . . [4]

[3] In line 13 the names 'Isa]nder' (a son of Bellerophon:
Homer, *Iliad* 6.197) or 'Mea]nder' (the chief river of Lycia) have
been supplied: see Introduction.   [4] For 'Lycia' and 'the
ship', see Introduction on F 304a and 305.

285
BELLEROPHON

I myself affirm what is of course a common word every-
where, that it is best for a man not to be born;[1] but of (life's)
three estates I'll judge one superior—wealth, noble blood
in a man, and poverty: that is the total number I advance.   5
The man with great wealth, but unlucky in his birth, hurts
at this, he hurts, but it is a quite splendid pain[2] for him
when he opens his wealth's treasure-chamber to his hand's
great pleasure; when he leaves it, however, after his riches
before, he is distressed at falling under ruin's yoke. The   10
man of proud and noble descent who wants for a liveli-
hood, has the good fortune of birth but is diminished by

[1] An axiom found first in Theognis 425 (6th c.) and most
famously at Sophocles, *Oedipus at Colonus* 1224–5.   [2] An
oxymoron like *Trojan Women* 727 εὐγενῶς ἄλγει κακοῖς, 'feel
the hurt nobly!'

πενίᾳ δ' ἐλάσσων ἐστίν, ἐν δ' ἀλγύνεται
φρονῶν, ὑπ' αἰδοῦς δ' ἔργ' ἀπωθεῖται χερῶν.
15 ὁ δ' οὐδὲν οὐδείς, διὰ τέλους δὲ δυστυχῶν,
τοσῷδε νικᾷ· τοῦ γὰρ εὖ τητώμενος
οὐκ οἶδεν, αἰεὶ δυστυχῶν κακῶς τ' ἔχων.
οὕτως ἄριστον μὴ πεπειρᾶσθαι καλῶν.
ἐκεῖνο γὰρ μεμνήμεθ', οἷος ἦ ποτε
20 κἀγὼ μετ' ἀνδρῶν ἡνίκ' ηὐτύχουν βίῳ . . .

13–14 ἐν δ' ἀλγύνεται | φρονῶν Stob. 4.32b.23, obelized by
editors, defended by Kannicht (ἔνθ' Bothe): κεὶ βαρύνεται |
φρενῶν Stob. 4.33.16: ἦν ἀλγύνεται | φέρων F. W. Schmidt:
{ἐστίν} ἔνδοθεν δ' ἀλγύνεται | φρενῶν Curnis (. . . φέρων Milo)
14 ὑπ' αἰδοῦς δ' Stob. 4.33.16: δ' ὑπ' αἰδοῦς 4.32b.33
20 βίῳ Stob. 3.32.3: ποτε 4.33.9a

286

ΒΕΛΛΕΡΟΦΟΝΤΗΣ

φησίν τις εἶναι δῆτ' ἐν οὐρανῷ θεούς;
οὐκ εἰσίν, οὐκ εἴσ', εἴ τις ἀνθρώπων θέλει
μὴ τῷ παλαιῷ μῶρος ὢν χρῆσθαι λόγῳ.
σκέψασθε δ' αὐτοί, μὴ 'πὶ τοῖς ἐμοῖς λόγοις
5 γνώμην ἔχοντες. φήμ' ἐγὼ τυραννίδα
κτείνειν τε πλείστους κτημάτων τ' ἀποστερεῖν
ὅρκους τε παραβαίνοντας ἐκπορθεῖν πόλεις·
καὶ ταῦτα δρῶντες μᾶλλόν εἰσ' εὐδαίμονες
τῶν εὐσεβούντων ἡσυχῇ καθ' ἡμέραν.
10 πόλεις τε μικρὰς οἶδα τιμώσας θεούς,
αἳ μειζόνων κλύουσι δυσσεβεστέρων
λόγχης ἀριθμῷ πλείονος κρατούμεναι.

poverty, and is pained moreover by thinking of it;[3] but out
of shame he rejects manual work. The absolute nobody,
however, in continual misfortune, is superior inasmuch as   15
his deprivation of good keeps him unaware of it, being in
constant misfortune and evilly situated. Best therefore to
have no experience of good things! For this is what I re-
member—what I too once was like among men when I had
good fortune in my life.[4]

[3] The Greek expression is foreign to Euripides' idiom and
much doubted; Bothe gives 'poverty, where he is pained by think-
ing of it', Schmidt 'poverty which he bears with pain', Curnis 'is
pained inside his heart', Milo 'is pained inside as he bears it'.
Stobaeus' text in both places is corrupt.   [4] Cf. F 310 and
Homer, *Iliad* 6.155–99 (Introduction above).

286

BELLEROPHON

Does then anyone say there are gods in heaven? There
are not, there are not, if a man is willing not to give foolish
credence to the ancient story. Consider for yourselves,
don't form an opinion on the basis of my words! I say that
tyranny kills very many men and deprives them of posses-   5
sions, and that tyrants break oaths in sacking cities; and in
doing this they prosper more than those who day by day
quietly practise piety. I know too of small cities honouring
the gods which are subject to greater, more impious ones   10
because they are dominated by more numerous arms. I

οἶμαι δ᾽ ἂν ὑμᾶς, εἴ τις ἀργὸς ὢν θεοῖς
εὔχοιτο καὶ μὴ χειρὶ συλλέγοι βίον
<   >
15 τὰ θεῖα πυργοῦσ᾽ αἱ κακαί τε συμφοραί . . .

[Justin], *On Monarchy* 5.6, following citation of F 286b.7

14–15 lacuna marked by Grotius (see note opposite); others
emend 15.

286b (= 292 N)

πρὸς τὴν νόσον τοι καὶ τὸν ἰατρὸν χρεὼν
ἰδόντ᾽ ἀκεῖσθαι, μὴ ᾽πιτὰξ τὰ φάρμακα
διδόντ᾽, ἐὰν μὴ ταῦτα τῇ νόσῳ πρέπῃ.
νόσοι δὲ θνητῶν αἱ μέν εἰσ᾽ αὐθαίρετοι,
5 αἱ δ᾽ ἐκ θεῶν πάρεισιν, ἀλλὰ τῷ νόμῳ
ἰώμεθ᾽ αὐτάς. ἀλλ᾽, ὅ σοι λέξαι θέλω,
εἰ θεοί τι δρῶσιν αἰσχρόν, οὐκ εἰσὶν θεοί.

Stobaeus 4.36.7; vv. 1–3: Stob. 4.36.5; v. 7: Plutarch, *Moralia*
21a and 1049f, [Justin], *On Monarchy* 5.6

2 ἀκεῖσθαι Stob. 4.36.5: ἰᾶσθαι 4.36.7 ἐπιτὰξ Nauck:
ἐπιτακτὰ Stob.   5 ἀλλὰ τῷ νόμῳ obelized by Diggle
6 lacuna of two half-lines after αὐτάς C. W. Müller ἀλλ᾽, ὅ
West: ἀλλὰ Stob.   7 αἰσχρόν Stob., Plut. 1049f: φαῦλον
Plut. 21a (φλαῦρον some mss.), [Justin]

---

[1] Translation of Nauck's textual emendation as 'continually'
or 'summarily' rather than 'by rote' also has ancient support.
Stobaeus' text yields 'giving prescribed remedies'.   [2] This
famously difficult fragment was illuminated by C. W. Müller, *RhM*
136 (1993), 116–21 and W. Luppe in C. F. Collatz et al. (eds.),

think that, if someone lazy were to pray to the gods for a living and not gather it by hand,[1] you would . . . *(text lost)* . . . they exaggerate divine powers tower-high, and their bad disasters . . .[2]

---

[1] This may rely on the identity of the Chorus as farmers: see Introduction. Piety is correlated with industrious farmwork in *Electra* 79–81, cf. *Hippolytus Veiled* F 432.2.   [2] The loss of text makes translation of 15 unsafe; the sense may be '(*missing subject*) exaggerate divine powers tower-high, as do bad disasters'; for the expression cf. *Bacchae* 887 'magnify the gods'. Perhaps 15 belongs elsewhere (Collard). The whole fragment is interpreted at length by C. Riedweg, *ICS* 15 (1990), 39–53.

286b (= 292 N)

As to illness, a doctor too must cure it after examining it, not by giving remedies by rote,[1] in case these do not suit the illness. Human illnesses are some of them self-inflicted, others come from the gods, but we treat them by the rule of practice. This is what I want to say to you, however: if gods do anything shameful, they are not gods.[2]   5

Dissertatiunculae criticae. Festschrift . . . Hansen (Würzburg, 1998), 123–6. The speaker argues that self-inflicted diseases can, and should only, be treated by men and method (v. 2, and v. 5 'by the rule of practice'), while only gods can cure the afflictions which gods themselves cause—and if they do not cure men who revere them, they are not gods (cf. Sophocles, *Philoctetes* 451–2). The relation and progression of the medical analogy ('As to . . . of practice') to the main point ('This is what etc.') is unclear; textual corruption has been supposed (in 'by the rule of practice', Diggle) or loss of text between them conjectured (most lately by Müller). Kannicht moved the fragment closer to F 285 on ground of its affinity.

287

τοῖς πράγμασιν γὰρ οὐχὶ θυμοῦσθαι χρεών·
μέλει γὰρ αὐτοῖς οὐδέν· ἀλλ᾽ οὑντυγχάνων
τὰ πράγματ᾽ ὀρθῶς ἢν τιθῇ, πράσσει καλῶς.

Stobaeus 4.13.14b and 4.44.39, Plutarch, *Moralia* 467a, [Plutarch], *Life of Homer* 153; vv. 1–2: M. Aurelius Antoninus 7.38 and (v. 1 only) 11.6

288

⟨ΒΕΛΛΕΡΟΦΟΝΤΗΣ?⟩

δόλοι δὲ καὶ σκοτεινὰ μηχανήματα
χρείας ἄνανδρα φάρμαχ᾽ ηὕρηται βροτοῖς.

Stobaeus 3.8.1

2 ἄνανδρα Herwerden: ἀνάνδρου Stob.

289

⟨ΒΕΛΛΕΡΟΦΟΝΤΗΣ?⟩

νείκη γὰρ ἀνδρῶν φόνια καὶ μάχας χρεὼν
δόλοισι κλέπτειν· τῆς δ᾽ ἀληθείας ὁδὸς
φαύλη τίς ἐστι· ψεύδεσιν δ᾽ Ἄρης φίλος.

Stobaeus 4.13.20

1 χρεὼν Meineke: χερῶν Stob.

290

⟨ΒΕΛΛΕΡΟΦΟΝΤΗΣ?⟩

ἀεὶ γὰρ ἄνδρα σκαιὸν ἰσχυρὸν φύσει
ἧσσον δέδοικα τἀσθενοῦς τε καὶ σοφοῦ.

Stobaeus 4.13.5

287

One should not get angry at circumstances: they have no concern for anything; but if the person encountering them deals with them correctly, he comes off well.

288
⟨ BELLEROPHON ? ⟩

Men have invented underhand means and dark devices as unmanly remedies for need.[1]

[1] Stobaeus translates with difficulty, 'as remedies for cowardly need'.

289
⟨ BELLEROPHON ? ⟩

Men's bloody feuds and battles should be settled by underhand means. The path of truth is a feeble one, and War is a friend to lies.[1]

[1] Most editors suggest Bellerophon as the speaker, in particular A.-M. Mesturini, *Helikon* 20–21 (1980–1), 301–7, who postpones the fragment (together with F 285 and 286b, remarkably) to his words at play-end.

290
⟨ BELLEROPHON ? ⟩

I always fear a stupid man with natural strength less than a weak and clever one.

291

ὦ παῖ, νέων τοι δρᾶν μὲν ἔντονοι χέρες,
γνῶμαι δ᾽ ἀμείνους εἰσὶ τῶν γεραιτέρων·
ὁ γὰρ χρόνος δίδαγμα ποικιλώτατον.

Stobaeus 4.50.2; vv. 1–2 paraphrased by Cornutus, *Compendium of Greek Theology* 31; v. 2 = [Menander], *Monostichs* 158 Jaekel

1 ἔντονοι Stob.: εὔτονοι Nauck (εὐτονώτεροι χέρες Cornutus)

(292 N = 286b above)

293

τιμή σ᾽ ἐπαίρει τῶν πέλας μεῖζον φρονεῖν.

<   >

θνήσκοιμ᾽ ἄν· οὐ γὰρ ἄξιον λεύσσειν φάος
κακοὺς ὁρῶντας ἐκδίκως τιμωμένους.

Stobaeus 4.42.1; lacuna marked by Meineke, who considered vv. 1 and 2–3 separate fragments: see note opposite.

1 μεῖζον Cobet: μᾶλλον Stob.

294

φθονοῦσιν αὐτοὶ χείρονες πεφυκότες·
εἰς τἀπίσημα δ᾽ ὁ φθόνος πηδᾶν φιλεῖ.

Stobaeus 3.38.13 mss. MA; ms. S has only v. 2, attached to 3.38.12; v. 2 is repeated by ms. M after 3.38.18; Meineke and Hense considered vv. 1 and 2 separate fragments.

291

My son, young men's hands are eager[1] for action, true, but the judgement of their elders is better; for time's teaching is the most subtle.

[1] Or 'well-strung' (Nauck, cf. Cornutus). The thought here is proverbial: cf. *Melanippe* F 508 with note.

(292 N = 286b above)

293

Privilege stirs you to despise your neighbours . . . (*text lost*) . . . If so, I'd gladly die; for it's not worth people's living when they see bad men unjustly privileged.[1]

[1] Even if vv. 1 and 2–3 are given to different speakers (Matthiae), there is no obvious sequence of thought.

294

They are envious, being naturally inferior themselves; envy usually leaps upon distinction.

295

ἤδη γὰρ εἶδον καὶ δίκης παραστάτας
ἐσθλοὺς πονηρῷ τῷ φθόνῳ νικωμένους.

Stobaeus 3.38.19

296

ἀνὴρ δὲ χρηστὸς χρηστὸν οὐ μισεῖ ποτε,
κακὸς κακῷ δὲ συντέτηκεν ἡδονῇ·
φιλεῖ δὲ θοὐμόφυλον ἀνθρώπους ἄγειν.

Stobaeus 2.33.2; v. 1 = [Menander], *Monostichs* 29 Jaekel; v. 2:
Aristotle, *Eudemian Ethics* 1238a34 and 1239b22, cf. [Aristotle],
Magna Moralia 1209b36

297

ὡς ἔμφυτος μὲν πᾶσιν ἀνθρώποις κάκη·
ὅστις δὲ πλεῖστον μισθὸν εἰς χεῖρας λαβὼν
κακὸς γένηται, τῷδε συγγνώμη μὲν οὔ,
πλείω δὲ μισθὸν μείζονος τόλμης ἔχων
5   τὸν τῶν ψεγόντων ῥᾷον ἂν φέροι λόγον.

Stobaeus 3.10.17

2 πλεῖστον suspect: μικρὸν Heath: μείω Jouan
5 ψεγόντων . . . λόγον Jacobs: λεγόντων . . . ψόγον Stobaeus

306

295

In the past I've seen even honourable supporters[1] of justice overcome by that base thing, envy.

[1] A military term (*Children of Heracles* 88, 125) used metaphorically.

296

A good man never hates a good man, and a bad one is pleased to merge with bad. Kinship usually attracts men.

297

Cowardice is innate in all men. Whoever takes a great deal of pay into his hands and proves cowardly, is not condoned; but if he had more pay for greater audacity, he would endure men's censorious talk more easily.[1]

[1] The conjectures 'little' or 'rather little' (pay) in v. 2 create a simpler but much flatter contrast.

298

οὐκ ἂν γένοιτο τραῦμ', ἐάν τις ἐγξέσῃ
θάμνοις ἑλείοις, οὐδ' ἂν ἐκ μητρὸς κακῆς
ἐσθλοὶ γένοιντο παῖδες εἰς ἀλκὴν δορός.

Stobaeus 4.30.10

1 τραῦμ', ἐάν τις Nauck: τραῦμα εἰ Stob.: τραύματ' ἦν
Hense; ἐγξέσῃ Heath: ἐγξύσῃ Stob.   2 θάμνοις ἑλείοις
Stob.: θάλλους ἑλείους Cropp: θαλλοῖς ἐλαίας Diels, Housman

299

πρὸς τὴν ἀνάγκην πάντα τἄλλ' ἔστ' ἀσθενῆ.

Stobaeus 1.4.2b

300

⟨ΒΕΛΛΕΡΟΦΟΝΤΗΣ⟩

οἴμοι· τί δ' οἴμοι; θνητά τοι πεπόνθαμεν.

Diogenes Laertius 4.26, Suda οι 101, Plutarch, *Moralia* 475c,
Synesius, *Letters* 126

301

ὁρᾷς δ' ἀέλπτους μυρίων ἀναστροφάς·
πολλοὶ μὲν οἶδμα διέφυγον θαλάσσιον,
πολλοὶ δὲ λόγχαις πολεμίων ἀμείνονες
ἥσσους γεγῶτες κρείσσον' ἦλθον εἰς τύχην.

Stobaeus 4.47.11

1 ἀέλπτους Nauck: -ων Stob.   2 lacuna after v. 2, Kannicht

298

No wounding would come of it if one whittles in marshy thickets, and a bad mother wouldn't bear fine sons for spear-fighting.[1]

[1] Apparently: as trimmed sapwood from a marsh will yield no spear-shafts sturdy enough to wound, so poor breeding-stock will mother no sons sturdy enough to stand their ground in battle. The conjectures cited for v. 2 attempt to reinforce the first image ('whittles marshy shoots' Cropp, 'whittles with shoots of olive' Diels, Housman). Jouan thinks a proverb may link the two halves, citing *Children of Heracles* 684 'sight (of an enemy) produces no wound if hands do not act'.

299

In the face of necessity everything else is weak.

300

<BELLEROPHON>

Oh me—but why 'Oh me'? For sure, my suffering is human.

301

You see unexpected reversals for countless men: many escape the swelling sea; and many better than their enemies with the spear have been defeated, but come to greater fortune.[1]

[1] Text and translation insecure; v. 1 may mean 'unexpected reversals in countless things' or, with Stobaeus, 'reversals in countless unexpected things'. Some editors think the first term of the antithesis (v. 2) is incomplete, and Kannicht suggests a verse has been lost after it. The accumulation of comparatives in vv. 3–4 is suspicious.

302

θάρσος δὲ πρὸς τὰς συμφορὰς μέγα σθένει.

Stobaeus 3.7.1

303

⟨ΧΟΡΟΣ⟩

οὐδέποτ᾽ εὐτυχίαν κακοῦ ἀνδρὸς ὑπέρφρονά τ᾽
    ὄλβον
βέβαιον εἰκάσαι χρεών,
οὐδ᾽ ἀδίκων γενεάν· ὁ γὰρ οὐδενὸς ἐκφὺς
χρόνος δικαίους ἐπάγων κανόνας
5   δείκνυσιν ἀνθρώπων κακότητας ὅμως.

Stobaeus 3.2.13; Theophilus, *To Autolycus* 2.37, omitting
δικαίους . . . κανόνας and ending at κακότητας

5 ὅμως West: ἐμοί Stob.

304

⟨ΧΟΡΟΣ⟩

ποῦ δὴ τὸ σαφὲς θνατοῖς βιοτᾶς;
θοαῖσι μὲν ναυσὶ πόρον πνοαὶ
    κατὰ βένθος †ἅλιον†
ἰθύνουσι· τύχας δὲ θνατῶν
τὸ μὲν μέγ᾽ ἐς οὐδὲν ὁ πολὺς χρόνος
5   μεθίστησιν, τὸ δὲ μεῖον αὔξων . . .

Stobaeus 4.42.12

2 βένθος Grotius: -ους Stob.   ἅλιον Stob. mss. SM: ἅλιαι
ms. A: ἁλὸς Jouan (the metre is not surely identified)

302

Courage has great strength against disasters.

303

⟨CHORUS⟩

One should never imagine a bad man's good fortune and arrogant prosperity as secure, nor the lineage of unjust men; for Time which has no father applies just standards and demonstrates mankind's villainy all the same.[1]

[1] Time 'has no father' but itself fathers Justice, revealing the bad man (*Antiope* F 222; cf. on *Aeolus* F **38a). This may be the start of an ode, but which 'bad man' is meant: Iobates?

304

⟨CHORUS⟩

Where indeed is the certainty in life for mortal men? Winds steer a path for swift ships over the †ocean's† deep; but as for mortals' fortunes, time in its length changes what is great to nothing, and by increasing what is less . . .

304a (= *Alcmeon in Psophis* F 68 N)

⟨ΜΕΓΑΠΕΝΘΗΣ?⟩

μητέρα κατέκτα τὴν ἐμήν· βραχὺς λόγος.

⟨—⟩

ἑκὼν ἑκοῦσαν ἢ ⟨οὐ⟩ θέλουσαν οὐχ ἑκών;

Aristotle, *Nicomachean Ethics* 1136a13 and two late commentators on Aristotle; assigned to *Bellerophon* by Wagner, earlier to *Alcmeon* by Welcker.

305

. . .

καὶ ξεστὸν ὄχθον Δαναϊδῶν ἑδρασμάτων
στὰς ἐν μέσοισιν εἶπε κηρύκων . . .

Schol. on Euripides, *Orestes* 872

1–2 κἀς ξεστὸν . . . στὰς, Ellis   2 κηρύκων ⟨ὕπο⟩
Cobet

306

⟨ΒΕΛΛΕΡΟΦΟΝΤΗΣ⟩

ἄγ᾽, ὦ φίλον μοι Πηγάσου ταχὺ πτερόν . . .

Schol. on Aristophanes, *Peace* 76b (cf. *Peace* 135), Suda ε 1897

304a (= *Alcmeon in Psophis* F 68 N)

⟨MEGAPENTHES?⟩

He killed my mother; it's briefly said.

⟨—⟩

Willingly, and with her will, or unwillingly, and against her will?[1]

[1] 'My mother' will be Stheneboea. For the problematic ascription of this and the next fragment see the Introduction and especially A. Carlini, *Studi Classici e Orientali* 14 (1965), 201–5, cf. Carlini in M. Cannatà Fera, S. Grandolini (eds.), *Poesia e Religione in Grecia. Studi . . . Privitera* (Naples, 2000), 179–84. The verbal conceit in v. 2 was a Euripidean foible.

305

. . . and the chiselled stone of the lofty Argive tribunal, he stood in their midst and spoke (at the) heralds' (word) . . . [1]

[1] The fragment as transmitted seems to be the end of a sentence (but Ellis made it a beginning with 'Standing at the . . . tribunal, he spoke in the heralds' midst . . . '); '(at the) heralds' (word)' translates Cobet's conjecture, i.e. after they proclaimed silence as Talthybius does at *Hecuba* 531.

F 306–8 have Bellerophon preparing to fly heavenwards, on the theatrical 'crane':

306

⟨BELLEROPHON⟩

Come, my dear Pegasus with your swift wings . . .

307, **307a, 308

⟨ΒΕΛΛΕΡΟΦΟΝΤΗΣ⟩

307   ἴθι χρυσοχάλιν᾽ αἴρων πτέρυγας . . .

* * *

**307a   σπεῦδ᾽, ὦ ψυχή . . .

* * *

308   πάρες, ὦ σκιερὰ φυλλάς, ὑπερβῶ
κρηναῖα νάπη· τὸν ὑπὲρ κεφαλῆς
αἰθέρ᾽ ἰδέσθαι σπεύδω, τίν᾽ ἔχει
στάσιν εὐοδίας.

F 307: Schol. on Aristophanes, *Peace* 154d   F **307a:
Aristophanes, *Wasps* 756 (separated from F 308 by Wilamowitz)
F 308: Aristophanes, *Wasps* 757 (v. 1) and Schol. on 757b (vv. 1–4)

309

ἔπτησσ᾽ ὑπείκων μᾶλλον †ἢ μᾶλλον θέλοι†

Plutarch, *Moralia* 529e and 807e

ἢ: εἰ a few mss. at Plut. 529e, Nauck: ᾗ Munro   second
μᾶλλον omitted by Plut. 529e and most mss. at 807e

309a

τῷ δ᾽ ἐξ ὑδρηλῶν αἰθέρος προσφθεγμάτων . . .

Herodian, *General Prosody* ms. Vienna Hist. Gr. 10.5 ed. H.
Hunger (1967)

ὑδρηλῶν Diggle: ὑδρηρῶν Herodian

BELLEROPHON

307, **307a, 308

⟨BELLEROPHON⟩

(307) Go, my golden-bridled one, lift your wings . . .
(**307a) Hurry, my heart! . . . (308) Give way, shadowy fo-
liage! Let me cross the valleys with their springs! I hurry to
see what state the sky overhead has for a good journey.[1]

[1] It was to become rainy: F 309a with note.

The next two fragments appear to come from a description
of Bellerophon's flight, either his own or a messenger's:

309

(Pegasus) crouched yielding more . . . (*text corrupt*) . . . [1]

[1] Possibly 'if ever he (Pegasus) was more willing' (Nauck); or
'where he (Bellerophon) preferred' (Munro).

309a

. . . but for Pegasus, beneath heaven's watery greetings . . . [1]

[1] Rain—perhaps after Zeus maddens the horse (Jouan).

310 (= 311 N)

⟨ΒΕΛΛΕΡΟΦΟΝΤΗΣ?⟩

ἦσθ᾽ εἰς θεοὺς μὲν εὐσεβής, ὅτ᾽ ἦσθ᾽, ἀεὶ
ξένοις τ᾽ ἐπήρκεις οὐδ᾽ ἔκαμνες εἰς φίλους.

Aelian, *Nature of Animals* 5.34

311 (= 310 N)

κομίζετ᾽ εἴσω τόνδε τὸν δυσδαίμονα.

Schol. on Aristophanes, *Knights* 1249a

κομίζετ᾽: κυλίνδετ᾽ Aristophanes in 1249

312

ὑφ᾽ ἅρματ᾽ ἐλθὼν Ζηνὸς ἀστραπηφορεῖ.

Schol. on Aristophanes, *Peace* 722 and Schol. on Hesiod, *Theogony* 286

ἀστραπηφορεῖ Schol. Ar.: ἀστραπὴν φέρει Schol. Hes.

310 (= 311 N)

⟨BELLEROPHON?⟩

You were always reverent towards the gods, when you lived, and stoutly helped strangers, and did not fail for your friends.[1]

---

[1] The dying Bellerophon addresses his 'soul' heroically (so Aelian, the source—but Milo 309–10 suggests someone else may have addressed the words to him): contrast F **307a. His imminent death restores him to piety: contrast F 286.

311 (= 310 N)

Carry this ill-fated man inside.[1]

---

[1] For such a 'stage-direction' cf. *Stheneboea* F 671. Aristophanes' 'wheel' for 'carry' makes fun of Euripides' perceived indulgence in stage machinery: here (by implication) the wheeled platform (*eccyclema*), earlier the 'crane' for Pegasus (F 306–8).

312

(Pegasus) is harnessed to Zeus's chariot and carries his lightning.[1]

---

[1] See Introduction. This future for Pegasus occurs as early as Hesiod, *Theogony* 285–6; cf. Pindar, *Olympians* 13.92.

BUSIRIS

Pechstein 123–40; Krumeich 413–9; H. Van Looy in ed. Budé VIII.2.37–44.

    LIMC III.i.147–52 'Bousiris'; Gantz 418.

Busiris was a cruel tyrant in 'Egypt' (i.e. the savage East). His habit was to sacrifice strangers to the gods (like the barbarous Thoas in Iphigenia in Tauris*). Heracles came to Egypt after recovering the golden apples of the Hesperides, was fettered by Busiris for sacrifice, but broke free and killed the tyrant and his son. These details are found in Pherecydes FGrH 3 F 17, and more fully in Apollodorus 2.5.11 (neither with attribution to Euripides; both = test. *iii b below; cf. Gantz). The popularity of this story is proved by the survival of twenty or so vase-paintings from the mid-6th to the early 4th centuries* B.C., *concentrated in the 5th, which show the death of Busiris. Scholars single out LIMC no. 9, a Caeretan hydria of c. 530* B.C. *showing Heracles killing Busiris' men and the tyrant himself in bonds, and LIMC no. 2, an Attic red-figure cup of c. 450* B.C. *whose outside has Heracles in bonds being taken by black men (i.e. 'Egyptians') to Busiris while its inside shows Heracles with a satyr: for both see TrGF 5.369. The words 'golden apples' and 'satyrs' in the very scrappy hypothesis P. Oxy. 3651 (= test. iiia) seem to confirm the* *above plot, but nothing further can be known. F 313 gives no clue, for the word 'slave' there only reflects the self-portrayal of satyrs common in their plays, e.g. Eurystheus F 375, Cyclops 31.*

Brief fragments: F 312b 'O deity' (or 'O . . . of the deity': the play's opening words, from the hypothesis), F 314 'offer a holy sacrifice', F 315 'making exact'; F 313a? is missing except for a damaged heading in Stobaeus.   Other proposed ascriptions: F 879, 907 (also ascribed to Syleus), 955h (see note there); adesp. F 33 (Heracles' blazing eyes').

Krumeich 416–7 wonders whether the 'satyric' Heracles of the Attic cup reflects Euripides' Busiris; if so, it will have been one of his earliest productions. No other satyr-play with this subject is known, but there were five comedies entitled Busiris in the 5th and 4th centuries. For Isocrates' propaedeutic 'speech' Busiris (4th. c.) and its mythical and contemporary background, see N. Livingstone, A Commentary on Isocrates' Busiris (Leiden, 2001), 73–90, especially 80–1 on Euripides.

ΒΟΤΣΙΡΙΣ

test. iiib

ὁ δὲ ἔρχεται . . . ἐπὶ τὰ χρυσᾶ μῆλα. ἀφικόμενος δὲ εἰς
Ταρτησσὸν, πορεύεται εἰς Λιβύην, ἔνθα ἀναιρεῖ Ἀνταῖον
τὸν Ποσειδῶνος, ὑβριστὴν ὄντα. εἶτα ἀφικνεῖται ἐπὶ τὸν
Νεῖλον εἰς Μέμφιν παρὰ Βούσιριν τὸν Ποσειδῶνος, ὃν
κτείνει καὶ τὸν παῖδα αὐτοῦ Ἰφιδάμαντα καὶ τὸν κήρυκα
Χάλβην καὶ τοὺς ὀπάονας πρὸς τῷ βωμῷ τοῦ Διός, ἔνθα
ἐξενοκτόνει.

Pherecydes *FrGH* 3 F 17 (from Schol. on Apollonius of
Rhodes 4.1396–9b); slightly expanded in Apollodorus 2.5.11

(312a N–Sn = *Lamia* F 472m)

313

δούλῳ γὰρ οὐχ οἷόν τε τἀληθῆ λέγειν,
εἰ δεσπόταισι μὴ πρέποντα τυγχάνοι.

Stobaeus 4.19.24

320

BUSIRIS

test. iiib

(Heracles) goes . . . after the golden apples (of the Hesperides). Reaching Tartessus he makes his way to Libya, where he kills Poseidon's son Antaeus, who was wantonly violent. Then he comes to the Nile and Memphis, to Poseidon's son Busiris, whom he kills with his son Iphidamas, his herald Chalbes, and his servants, at Zeus's altar where Busiris put strangers to death . . .

(312a N–Sn = *Lamia* F 472m)

313

It is not possible for a slave to speak the truth if it happens not to suit his master (*or* 'if things happen which may not suit his master').

DANAE

H. Van Looy in ed. Budé VIII.2.47–71; I. Karamanou,
Euripides. Danae and Dictys (Munich–Leipzig, 2006).
  Webster 94–5; Aélion (1986) 151–7; *LIMC* III.i.325–
37 'Danae'; Gantz 299–303; Huys, *The Tale*, relevant sec-
tions.

Danae was the virgin daughter of Acrisius, a king of Argos.
Because he had no sons, he consulted an oracle and was
prophesied death at the hands of his daughter's son; he
therefore shut Danae into an underground room to pre-
vent men's access. Zeus however inseminated her after
changing himself into a shower of gold and so entering
the chamber. The baby was Perseus, the future slayer of
the Gorgon and rescuer of Andromeda (see Andromeda
above). Unaware of this parentage, Acrisius in his anger
and fear set mother and child adrift in a chest, but they
came safely ashore on the island of Seriphos, south of the
Attic promontory. This is the myth's outline in Apollodorus
2.4.1, probably derived from Pherecydes, FGrH 3 F 10
(early 5th c.) as paraphrased by the Scholia on Apollonius
of Rhodes 4.1091 (TrGF 5, 371; cf. Gantz). John Malalas
(test. ii below) says of Euripides' plot only (and differently
from above) that Acrisius put Danae in the chest because
she had been raped by Zeus. Danae and Perseus afloat in

the chest were evoked by the 6th c. lyric poet Simonides (F 543 PMG), and Aeschylus dramatized some of Perseus' adventures (see Dictys, Introduction*). Euripides continued the story of Danae and Perseus in* Dictys. *Myth had it that Acrisius indeed lost his life at Perseus' hands, but long afterwards, and accidentally during an athletic contest.*

Although almost all the fragments are sententious, some can be located well enough in Apollodorus. F 316–8 relate to Acrisius' longing for sons; he addresses his wife (F 316). F 320 and perhaps 321 concern his fears of Danae's conceiving a child, no doubt after learning the prophecy (F 330a has the one word 'oracle': for this recurrent narrative motif see Huys, The Tale *130). F 322, certainly 324 and probably 325–8 seem to relate to the discovery of gold in Danae's prison chamber. In F 323 Danae(?) is fantasizing to her father about the joy a baby would bring her; this could be either after the oracle is known or after Zeus has visited her. The mention of Danae's nurse by Pherecydes, and her appearance on an Attic hydria of about 430 B.C. approaching Danae after the shower of gold (LIMC no. 6), have prompted suggestions that the two women attempted to conceal the incident, and possibly also the baby, from Acrisius (a common motif, cf.* Aeolus, Alope, Auge *etc.; see Karamanou 24–9, who adduces F 321 on women's guile). The chorus was of women, who delivered F 329 and possibly F 319; Pollux 4.111 (test. iii below) says that Euripides used them like the chorus of a comedy, to speak in a male voice out of the play directly to the audience. F 330 may be a reflection near the play's end on its ups and downs. While the setting adrift was perhaps reported (by a messenger?), it is wholly uncertain whether the coming ashore on Seriphos, or Perseus' destiny, was prophesied by a god (see especially Karamanou 20–2). The Byzantine 'hypothesis' which precedes the spurious beginning of the play in F 1132 (printed below after the genuine fragments) gives as its final details that the Nereids out of pity put the chest into the nets of Seriphian fishermen, and so both mother and baby were saved for Perseus to grow to manhood; but whether this derives from an authentic ancient hypothesis is an unresolved question (see introductory note on F 1132 below).*

Brief fragments: F 325a 'exceptional' (see note on F 325), F 330a 'oracle' (see above). Other ascriptions: F 1007e+f (cf. F 317); F 1061 (cf. F 320).

Some of the plot's presumable motifs are frequent in myth and in tragedy of all dates, in Euripides especially, e.g. death prophesied at the hand of a descendant and its avoidance attempted (cf. Catreus in Cretan Women), or an infant with a great destiny rescued along with his mother against the odds (e.g. Telephus in Auge).

The metrical criteria indicate a date anywhere between 455 and 425 (Cropp–Fick 78). It is impossible to know the relation in time between this play and Sophocles' Danae and Acrisius (their fragments may in fact all belong to a single play, whether tragedy or satyr-drama). Greek comedy exploited both the golden Zeus and the sea-chest, notably in Eubulus' Danae (4th c.). Livius Andronicus and Naevius produced early Latin adaptations. The rape of Danae by Zeus became a favourite subject for painters (LIMC nos. 1–36), and for artists of all kinds into the modern period (OGCMA I.319–22).

ΔΑΝΑΗ

test. ii

. . . Δανάης . . . περὶ ἧς ἐμυθολόγησεν Εὐριπίδης ὁ
σοφώτατος ἐν τῇ συντάξει τοῦ αὐτοῦ δράματος ἐν κι-
βωτίῳ τινὶ βληθεῖσαν καὶ ῥιφεῖσαν τὴν Δανάην, ὡς
φθαρεῖσαν ὑπὸ Διὸς μεταβληθέντος εἰς χρυσόν.

John Malalas, *Chronicles* 2.11 Thurn = 2.13 Jeffreys–Scott

test. iii

τῶν δὲ χορικῶν ᾀσμάτων τῶν κωμικῶν ἕν τι καὶ ἡ
παράβασις, ὅταν ἃ ὁ ποιητὴς πρὸς τὸ θέατρον βούλεται
λέγειν, ὁ χορὸς παρελθὼν λέγῃ. ἐπιεικῶς δ᾽ αὐτὸ ποι-
οῦσιν οἱ κωμῳδοποιηταί, τραγικὸν δ᾽ οὐκ ἔστιν. ἀλλ᾽
Εὐριπίδης αὐτὸ πεποίηκεν ἐν πολλοῖς δράμασιν. ἐν μέν
γε τῇ Δανάῃ τὸν χορὸν {τὰς γυναῖκας} ὑπὲρ αὐτοῦ τι
ποιήσας παράδειν, ἐκλαθόμενος ὡς ἄνδρας λέγειν ἐποίη-
σε τῷ σχήματι τῆς λέξεως τὰς γυναῖκας.

Pollux 4.111

DANAE

test. ii

Danae . . . The very learned Euripides told the myth about her in the plot of the same play, that she was put into a chest and thrown (into the sea), because she had been violated by Zeus transformed into gold.

test. iii

One part too of the choral songs of comedy is the parabasis, when the chorus comes forward and says what the poet wishes to say to the theatre audience. The comic poets do this with good reason, but it is not tragic practice; yet Euripides has done it in many plays—indeed, in the *Danae*, when he made the chorus come forward and sing something on his own account, he forgot himself and made the women talk like men in the manner of their diction.[1]

[1] Cf. Schol. on the choral ode *Alcestis* 962–1005, at 962, 'the poet wishes to show, through the *persona* of the chorus, how large a share in education he himself had' (the issue is discussed by D. Bain, *CQ* 25 [1975], 14–15); 'in the manner of their diction' has suggested to some scholars that Euripides may have used masculine participles for the women, as some editors allege in the disputed text and voice-division of the ode *Hippolytus* 1102–52. Nothing of such a choral passage survives in the fragments of *Danae*.

316

⟨ΑΚΡΙΣΙΟΣ⟩

γύναι, καλὸν μὲν φέγγος ἡλίου τόδε,
καλὸν δὲ πόντου χεῦμ' ἰδεῖν εὐήνεμον,
γῆ τ' ἠρινὸν θάλλουσα πλούσιόν θ' ὕδωρ,
πολλῶν τ' ἔπαινον ἔστι μοι λέξαι καλῶν·
5 ἀλλ' οὐδὲν οὕτω λαμπρὸν οὐδ' ἰδεῖν καλὸν
ὡς τοῖς ἄπαισι καὶ πόθῳ δεδηγμένοις
παίδων νεογνῶν ἐν δόμοις ἰδεῖν φάος.

Stobaeus 4.24.5

1 καλὸν Herwerden: φίλον Stob.

317

καὶ νῦν παραινῶ πᾶσι τοῖς νεωτέροις
μὴ πρὸς τὸ γῆρας ἀναβολὰς ποιουμένους
σχολῇ τεκνοῦσθαι παῖδας—οὐ γὰρ ἡδονή,
γυναικί τ' ἐχθρὸν χρῆμα πρεσβύτης ἀνήρ—
5 ἀλλ' ὡς τάχιστα· καὶ γὰρ ἐκτροφαὶ καλαὶ
καὶ συννεάζων ἡδὺ παῖς νέῳ πατρί.

Stobaeus 4.22.155; v. 2 is adapted in Menander F 198.8 PCG

2 ἀναβολὰς Körte (from Menander): τοὺς γάμους Stob.

318

γυνὴ γὰρ ἐξελθοῦσα πατρῴων δόμων
οὐ τῶν τεκόντων ἐστίν, ἀλλὰ τοῦ λέχους·
τὸ δ' ἄρσεν ἕστηκ' ἐν δόμοις ἀεὶ γένος
θεῶν πατρῴων καὶ τάφων τιμάορον.

Stobaeus 4.22.148 and 4.24.34

316

⟨ACRISIUS⟩

Wife, this sunlight is beautiful to see,[1] as beautiful as the
sea's flow in a calm, and the earth flowering in spring, and
water rich with fertility;[2] and I can speak the praise of
many beautiful things—but nothing is so brilliant or beau-
tiful to see as is the light of newborn children for those to   5
see in their houses who are childless and gnawed by long-
ing.

[1] Herwerden's 'beautiful' in v. 1 gives a fuller unity to the pas-
sage's repeated theme of beauty than Stobaeus's 'precious'. The
passage is a 'priamel', in which illustrative analogies precede the
statement to be illustrated; F 1059 is a good example, and F 320
below one in miniature; F 324 and 330 are less formal in style.
[2] Praise of rivers' enriching fertility was common.

317

And now I advise all younger men not to delay until old age
and be leisurely in fathering children—for it gives no plea-
sure, and an elderly husband is a hateful thing to a wife[1]—
but (to do it) as soon as possible. For rearing children is
truly good, and a son who shares his youth with a young fa-   5
ther is a pleasing thing.

[1] For the thought cf. *Aeolus* F 23, *Phoenix* F 804 with note.

318

When a woman has left her ancestral home she belongs
not to her parents but to her marriage-bed; but male chil-
dren stand always in a house to protect ancestral gods and
tombs.[1]

[1] A similar sentiment at *Iphigenia in Tauris* 57.

319

⟨ΧΟΡΟΣ?⟩

συμμαρτυρῶ σοι· πανταχοῦ λελείμμεθα
πᾶσαι γυναῖκες ἀρσένων ἀεὶ δίχα.

Stobaeus 4.22.174

320

οὐκ ἔστιν οὔτε τεῖχος οὔτε χρήματα
οὔτ᾽ ἄλλο δυσφύλακτον οὐδὲν ὡς γυνή.

Stobaeus 4.23.13 (but at 4.22.154 attributed to Alexis, fr. dub. 340 *PCG*)

321

ἦν γάρ τις αἶνος, ὡς γυναιξὶ μὲν τέχναι
μέλουσι, λόγχῃ δ᾽ ἄνδρες εὐστοχώτεροι.
εἰ γὰρ δόλοισιν ἦν τὸ νικητήριον,
ἡμεῖς ἂν ἀνδρῶν εἴχομεν τυραννίδα.

Stobaeus 4.22.172

322

ἔρως γὰρ ἀργὸν κἀπὶ τοιούτοις ἔφυ·
φιλεῖ κάτοπτρα καὶ κόμης ξανθίσματα,
φεύγει δὲ μόχθους. ἐν δέ μοι τεκμήριον·
οὐδεὶς προσαιτῶν βίοτον ἠράσθη βροτῶν,
5 ἐν τοῖς δ᾽ ἔχουσιν †ἡβητὴς† πέφυχ᾽ ὅδε.

Stobaeus 4.20.30; v. 1: Plutarch, *Moralia* 757a (with allusion at 760d)

DANAE

319

⟨CHORUS?⟩

I support what you say: everywhere we women are in second place, always at a distance from men.[1]

[1] Almost certainly a choral couplet separating two long speeches. For the idea cf. *Ino* F 401.

320

There is no wall, no wealth, nothing else so difficult to guard as a woman.

321

Now, there was a saying that artful ways are women's concern, while men achieve their aim better with the spear. So if victory's prize had lain with guile, we would possess absolute rule over men.

322

For love is naturally idle and inclined to such things: it likes mirrors and hair dyed blond, and it avoids effort. I have a single proof: no man asking for a livelihood falls in love, but this is naturally †in its prime†[1] among the rich.

[1] For 'in its prime' (unmetrical) Müller cleverly suggested 'a worker', i.e. love is active among the idle rich (v. 1) but the poor cannot entertain it.

---

1 τοιούτοις Plut. 757a: τοῖς ἔργοις Stob.　　5 ἡβητὴς is unmetrical: ἐργάτης G. Müller

323

⟨ΔΑΝΑΗ?⟩

τάχ᾽ ἂν πρὸς ἀγκάλαισι καὶ στέρνοις ἐμοῖς
πίτνων ἀθύροι καὶ φιλημάτων ὄχλῳ
ψυχὴν ἐμὴν κτήσαιτο· ταῦτα γὰρ βροτοῖς
φίλτρον μέγιστον, αἱ ξυνουσίαι, πάτερ.

Stobaeus 4.24.53

2 πίτνων (or πεσὼν) Nauck: πηδῶν Stob.

324

ὦ χρυσέ, δεξίωμα κάλλιστον βροτοῖς,
ὡς οὔτε μήτηρ ἡδονὰς τοίας ἔχει,
οὐ παῖδες ἀνθρώποισιν, οὐ φίλος πατήρ,
οἵας σὺ χοἰ σὲ δώμασιν κεκτημένοι.
5 εἰ δ᾽ ἡ Κύπρις τοιοῦτον ὀφθαλμοῖς ὁρᾷ,
οὐ θαῦμ᾽ ἔρωτας μυρίους αὐτὴν τρέφειν.

P. Ross. Georg. 9 (an anthology, damaged and lacking v. 4),
Stobaeus 4.31.4, Athenaeus 4.159b; vv. 1–4: Sextus Empiricus,
Against the Experts 1.279; vv. 1–3 cited in whole or part else-
where. The fragment is 'translated' by Seneca, *Letters* 115.14
(omitting v. 4) but ascribed to Bellerophon, apparently in
Bellerophon.

3 ἀνθρώποισιν all sources, except ἐν δόμοισιν Ath.

325

κρείσσων γὰρ οὐδεὶς χρημάτων πέφυκ᾽ ἀνήρ,
πλὴν εἴ τις—ὅστις δ᾽ οὗτός ἐστιν οὐχ ὁρῶ.

Stobaeus 3.10.18

2 εἴ τις . . . οὐχ ὁρῶ Stob.: εἷς τις (Porson) . . . οὐκ ἐρῶ
(Badham) Cobet

323

<DANAE?>

Perhaps (he) would fall into and play in my arms and at my breast, and win my heart with a host of kisses: for these things hold the biggest spell over people, their intimacies, father.[1]

[1] A fantasy of a baby son, probably from Danae; 'fall' is due to Nauck, but 'jump about, frolic' in Stobaeus is hardly less apt. For the thought in vv. 3–4 cf. *Alcmene* F 103 with note.

324

O gold, you give mortal man the finest welcome! No mother holds such pleasure for mankind,[1] nor their children, nor a loving father, as you hold for those who possess you in their houses; and if Cypris has a look like gold's in her eyes, it is no wonder she feeds countless passions.[2]

[1] The variant reading in Athenaeus can be defended: Euripides deliberately emphasizes the single location of family joys and the exceptional pleasure of possessing gold 'in their homes'.
[2] Probably Acrisius is speaking, and assuming that a rich man has somehow bribed his way past guards into Danae's prison, and left her some gold as reward or compensation (compare F 325); cf. Huys, *The Tale* 109–10. For the style of this fragment see note on F 316 above.

325

No one is born superior to money, unless (there is) someone—but who this is, I do not see.[1]

[1] Cobet suggested '. . . except one single person—but who this is, I will not say', supposing this fragment to have been lost from Satyrus' *Life of Euripides* where *Danae* is cited for an alleged allusion to Socrates ('one single person') as 'exceptional' in his indifference to gain (this is F 325a: see Introduction, 'Brief fragments').

326

ἆρ᾽ οἶσθ᾽ ὁθούνεχ᾽ οἱ μὲν εὐγενεῖς βροτῶν
πένητες ὄντες οὐδὲν ἀλφάνουσ᾽ ἔτι,
οἳ δ᾽ οὐδὲν ἦσαν πρόσθεν, ὄλβιοι δὲ νῦν,
δόξαν φέρονται τοῦ νομίσματος χάριν
5 καὶ συμπλέκοντες σπέρμα καὶ γάμους τέκνων;
δοῦναι δὲ πᾶς τις μᾶλλον ὀλβίῳ κακῷ
πρόθυμός ἐστιν ἢ πένητι κἀγαθῷ.
κακὸς δ᾽ ὁ μὴ ἔχων, οἱ δ᾽ ἔχοντες †ὄλβιοι†.

Stobaeus 4.31.29 and (with some differences and attribution
to *Hecuba*) 4.31.41

8 †ὄλβιοι†: οὐ κακοί Blaydes: οὐκέτι West: εὐγενεῖς Hense:
verse omitted by Stobaeus 29 mss. MA

327

φιλοῦσι γάρ τοι τῶν μὲν ὀλβίων βροτοὶ
σοφοὺς †ἡγεῖσθαι† τοὺς λόγους, ὅταν δέ τις
λεπτῶν ἀπ᾽ οἴκων εὖ λέγῃ πένης ἀνήρ,
γελᾶν· ἐγὼ δὲ πολλάκις σοφωτέρους
5 πένητας ἄνδρας εἰσορῶ τῶν πλουσίων
καὶ ⟨τοὺς⟩ θεοῖσι μικρὰ θύοντας τέλη
τῶν βουθυτούντων ὄντας εὐσεβεστέρους.

Stobaeus 4.33.14; vv. 6–7: Athenaeus 2.40d

2 †ἡγεῖσθαι† (unmetrical): τίθεσθαι Valckenaer
6 ⟨τοὺς⟩ Meineke: καὶ θεοῖς μικρᾷ (or -ᾳ) χειρὶ θύοντας Stob.:
θεοῖσι μικρὰ θύοντας Ath. (omitting beginning of line)

326

Do you know why, among mankind, those of noble birth
who are poor no longer get any increase, while those who
were nothing before, but are prosperous now, win re-
pute thanks to their money, and by binding together alli-
ances for their offspring and marriages for their children?[1]   5
Everyone is more eager to give to a bad man who is pros-
perous than to one who is poor and virtuous. The man
without money is bad, while those who have it are †pros-
perous†.[2]

[1] For money as a guarantee of 'nobility' and good marriages cf.
Alcmene F 95, *Erechtheus* F 362.14–15, *Thyestes* F 395.
[2] 'Prosperous' makes a false contrast: 'not bad' (Blaydes) suits 6–7;
'no longer (bad)' (West) echoes 3 and suits 6–7 too; for Hense's
'noble', recalling v. 1, cf. *Aeolus* F 22 with note.

327

The truth is, men usually †regard† the words of the pros-
perous as wise, but when some poor man from a modest
house speaks well, they laugh. I often observe that poor
men are wiser than the rich, however, and that those who   5
offer small sacrifices to the gods are more reverent than
those who sacrifice oxen.[1]

[1] With vv. 4–7 compare *Bellerophon* F 286.10–12 and F 986.
In v. 1 'regard' translates both the corrupt verb in Stobaeus and
Valckenaer's conjecture.

328

ὅστις δόμοις μὲν ἥδεται πληρουμένοις,
γαστρὸς δ᾽ ἀφαιρῶν σῶμα δύστηνος κακοῖ,
τοῦτον νομίζω κἂν θεῶν συλᾶν βρέτη
τοῖς φιλτάτοις τε πολέμιον πεφυκέναι.

Stobaeus 3.16.6

329

ΧΟΡΟΣ

φεῦ, τοῖσι γενναίοισιν ὡς ἀπανταχοῦ
πρέπει χαρακτὴρ χρηστὸς εἰς εὐψυχίαν.

Stobaeus 3.7.5

330

ἐς ταὐτὸν ἥκειν φημὶ τὰς βροτῶν τύχας
τῷδ᾽, ὃν καλοῦσιν αἰθέρ᾽, ὅστις ἔστι δή.
οὗτος θέρους τε λαμπρὸν ἐκλάμπει σέλας,
χειμῶνά τ᾽ αὔξει συντιθεὶς πυκνὸν νέφος,
5 θάλλειν τε καὶ μή, ζῆν τε καὶ φθίνειν ποιεῖ.
οὕτω δὲ θνητῶν σπέρμα· τῶν μὲν εὐτυχεῖ
λαμπρᾷ γαλήνῃ, τῶν δὲ συννέφει πάλιν,
ζῶσίν τε σὺν κακοῖσιν, οἳ δ᾽ ὄλβου μέτα
φθίνουσ᾽ ἐτείοις προσφερεῖς μεταλλαγαῖς.

Stobaeus 1.7.8

2 ὅστις ἔστι δή Porson: ᾧ τάδ᾽ ἔστι δή Stob.

328

Whoever delights in a plentiful household but starves his
stomach and harms his body, the wretch, I think would
even plunder god's images;[1] and he is an enemy to his clos-
est kin.

[1] I.e., rob the gods of their rich ornaments or dedications. The
comparison from sacrilege is extreme.

329

CHORUS

Oh! The noble are everywhere distinguished by an excel-
lent character for courage.[1]

[1] Perhaps admiring Danae's courage.

330

I assert that men's fortunes come to the same thing as what
they call the heaven here—whatever indeed it is.[1] This
both shines out summer's bright gleam and gathers thick
cloud to increase winter, and it makes things flourish or
not, to live as well as to die. So it is with the offspring of   5
men: some have theirs prosper in bright calm, some have
theirs back under clouds again; some live with troubles,
others in prosperity die away like the year's changes.[2]

[1] For the nature and naming of 'heaven' cf. F 877, 941.
[2] The natural cycles of fortune and nature compared: *Ino* F 415,
cf. *Chrysippus* F 839.

DANAE, APPENDIX: F 1132

The following appears in a manuscript in the Vatican Library, cod. Pal. Gr. 287 (early 14th c.), fols. 174–8, added by the rubricator who immediately before had added Iphigenia at Aulis 1570–1629 (the final part of its inauthentic Byzantine ending). It has been republished most recently by Kannicht in TrGF 5.1030–4 and Karamanou (2006), 45–56, cf. 225–7. The 65 verses were first condemned by Elmsley in 1811, and were held to be 'medieval' until M. L. West, BICS 28 (1981), 74–6 showed that their vocabulary, style and versification point clearly to the 5th–6th c. A.D. We reproduce the ms. text except for a few minor corrections. See also the introductory note to the translation opposite.

ΔΑΝΑΗ

Ὑπόθεσις Δανάης· Ἀκρίσιος Ἄργους ὢν βασιλεὺς κατὰ
χρησμὸν δή τινα παῖδα Δανάην κατάκλειστον ἐν τοῖς
παρθενῶσιν ἐφύλαττε καλλίστην οὖσαν· ἧς ἐρασθεὶς ὁ
Ζεύς, ἐπεὶ οὐκ εἶχεν ὅπως μιχθείη αὐτῇ, χρυσὸς γενό-
5 μενος καὶ ῥυεὶς διὰ τοῦ τέγους εἰς τὸν κόλπον τῆς
παρθένου ἐγκύμον' ἐποίησεν. ἐξήκοντος δὲ τοῦ χρόνου
βρέφος τὸν Περσέα ἀπέτεκε. τοῦτο μαθὼν Ἀκρίσιος εἰς

338

DANAE, APPENDIX: F 1132

This extraordinary confection has a disputed bearing on the plot and reconstruction of the authentic play. The play-opening (vv. 1–65) has been dated almost certainly to the 5th–6th c. A.D. on grounds of its style and versification, but there is an unresolved argument about the origin, and therefore credibility, of the 'hypothesis' that precedes it; this is very similar to the narrative in Lucian 78.12 telling how the Nereids rescued the chest containing Danae and the infant Perseus. W. Luppe, ZPE 87 (1991),1–7 and 95 (1993), 65–9 argues that it goes back to the 'Tales from Euripides' (see General Introduction). H. Van Looy does not expressly dissent (ed. Budé VIII.2.55–8), but R. Kannicht, ZPE 90 (1992), 33–4 and TrGF 5.1030 maintains that its detail indeed derives from Lucian and cannot safely be used in reconstructing Euripides' play.

DANAE

Hypothesis of *Danae*: Acrisius a king of Argos, responding (as he would) to some oracle, shut up his daughter Danae in her maiden's quarters and kept watch on her; she was very beautiful. Zeus fell in love with her, and as he had no way of having intercourse with her, he changed himself into gold and poured through the roof into the maiden's embrace, and made her   5 pregnant. When her time came, Danae gave birth to a child, Perseus. On learning this Acrisius put both mother and baby

κιβωτὸν ἀμφοτέρους, τήν τε μητέρα καὶ τὸ βρέφος,
ἐνέβαλε καὶ κελεύει ῥίπτειν κατὰ τῆς θαλάσσης. ἰδοῦσαι
10 δὲ ταῦθ' αἱ Νηρηΐδες καὶ κατελεήσασαι τὸ γεγονός,
ἐμβάλλουσι τὸν κιβωτὸν εἰς δίκτυα Σεριφίων ἁλιέων,
κἀντεῦθεν περιεσώθη ἥ τε μήτηρ καὶ τὸ βρέφος, ὅπερ
ἀνδρωθὲν Περσεὺς ὠνομάσθη.

    Τὰ τοῦ δράματος πρόσωπα· Ἑρμῆς Δανάη Τροφὸς
15 Ἀκρίσιος Ἄγγελος Χορὸς Ἀθηνᾶ.

ΕΡΜΗΣ

Δόμοι μὲν οἵδ' εὔπυργά τ' ἐρύματα χθονὸς
οὐκ ἐν πολυχρύσοισιν ἤσκηται χλιδαῖς·
ἀρχὴν δὲ τῶνδε καὶ θεῶν ἱδρύματα
Ἀκρίσιος εἴληχεν τύραννος τῆσδε γῆς·
5 Ἕλλησι δ' Ἄργος ἡ πόλις κικλήσκεται.
οὗτος δ' ἔρωτι παιδὸς ἄρσενος σχεθεὶς
Πυθώδ' ἀφίκτο, καὶ λέγει Φοίβῳ τάδε·
'πῶς ἂν γένοιτο σπέρμα παιδὸς ἐν δόμῳ,
τίνος θεῶν βροτῶν τε πρευμενοῦς τυχών;'
10 κεῖνος δὲ δυσξύμβλητον ἐξήνεγκ' ὄπα·
'ἔσται μὲν ἔσται παιδὸς ἄρσενος τόκος
οὐκ ἐξ ἐκείνου· πρῶτα γὰρ θῆλυν σπορὰν
φῦσαι δεήσει. κᾆτά πως κείνη ποτὲ
εὐνὴν κρυφαίαν γνοῦσα καὶ μὴ γνοῦσα δὴ
15 ὑπόπτερον λέοντα τέξεται πατρί,
ὃς τῆσδέ γ' ἄρξει χἀτέρας πολλῆς χθονός.'
τοιαῦτ' ἀκούσας Λοξίου μαντεύματα
γάμων ἀπείχεθ'· ὅμως δέ γε τίκτει λαθών,
πρὸς τοῦ παρόντος ἱμέρου νικώμενος.

into a chest, and ordered it thrown into the sea. The Nereids
saw this and, from pity at what had happened, put the chest   10
into the nets of fishermen of Seriphos; and then the mother
was saved together with her baby, which when it reached man-
hood was named Perseus.

    Characters of the play: Hermes, Danae, Nurse, Acrisius,
Messenger, Chorus, Athena.   15

HERMES

This house, and the land's well-fortified bulwarks, are not
fashioned with extravagant gold. Rule over them, and over the
gods' shrines, belongs to Acrisius this land's sovereign; Argos
is the city's name among the Greeks. Possessed by desire for a   5
male child Acrisius went to Delphi and said to Phoebus: 'How
might a son be born in my house? Whom among gods or men
might I get to favour me?' The god returned words hard to
comprehend: 'A male child shall come, shall come to birth,   10
but not from that man: for first he will have to get a daughter as
offspring; and then she eventually will know and not know a
secret union, and bear for her father a lion beneath stone,[1]   15
who will rule this land and much else besides.' After hearing
this oracle of Loxias Acrisius refrained from having inter-
course with his wife, but overcome in a moment of desire in-

---

[1] 'Lion' because Perseus was the bold and fierce son of Zeus;
'beneath stone' because conceived and born in Danae's stone-
roofed prison (vv. 39–40); but Bentley altered 'lion beneath stone'
to 'winged lion', to restore normal metre and create an allusion to
Perseus in his winged sandals.

20   Δανάην δέ πως ὠνόμασε τήνδ᾽, ὁθούνεκα
     πολὺς παρῆλθεν εἰς γονὴν παίδων χρόνος.
     ἐν παρθενῶσι δ᾽ εὐθὺς οἷς ἐδείματο
     δίδωσιν Ἀργείαισιν ἔμφρουρον κόραις,
     εἰς ἀνδρὸς ὄψιν εὐλαβούμενος μολεῖν.
25   εἶθ᾽ ὡς ὁ μακρὸς ηὔξανεν ταύτην χρόνος,
     καὶ κάλλος εἶχεν ἔξοχον καθ᾽ Ἑλλάδα,
     φίλτροις ἀφύκτοις Ζεὺς κατασχεθεὶς πατὴρ
     εὐνῇ συνελθεῖν λάθρᾳ πως ἠβούλετο.
     σαφῶς δὲ πείθειν οὐκ ἔχων, εἰς μηχανὴν
30   τοιάνδ᾽ ἐχώρησ᾽, ὡς ἄπυρος χρυσὸς γεγώς—
     ποθεινὸν εἰδὼς κτῆμα τοῦτο τοῖς βροτοῖς—
     διὰ στέγους ῥεύσειεν ἐν χερσὶν κόρης.
     ἡ δ᾽ αὖ μὴ γνοῦσα τὸν κεκρυμμένον δόλον
     κόλποισι τὸν θεὸν εἰσρέοντ᾽ ἐδέξατο.
35   χρόνῳ δ᾽ ἑαυτὴν ὡς κατεῖδ᾽ ἐγκύμονα,
     εἰς θαῦμ᾽ ἐσῄει κἀξεπέπληκτο σαφῶς,
     ὡς εἰς τόδ᾽ ἦλθε, μέμψιν εὐλαβουμένη.
     φυγῇ δὲ λάθρᾳ τῆσδε γῆς ὁρμωμένην
     μαθὼν πατήρ νιν ἐγκατάκλειστον δόμοις
40   ὀργῇ χολωθεὶς καὶ σκότῳ κρύψας ἔχει,
     τἀληθὲς ὄψει προσκοπούμενος μαθεῖν·
     κἂν ταῦτ᾽ ἀληθῆ καὶ σαφῶς ἔχοντ᾽ ἴδῃ,
     ἔγνωκεν ἄμφω ποντίους ἀφιέναι,
     τὴν παῖδα καὶ τὸ τεχθέν. ὧν δέ γ᾽ ἐστάλην,
45   μύθους Δανάῃ τοῦσδ᾽ εὐπροσηγόρους ἄγων
     ἐκ Διός, ἀφίξομαι τάχιστα σημανῶν.
     ὑπηρέτην γὰρ ὄντα τἀπεσταλμένα
     πράσσειν προθύμως, ὅστις ἄν γ᾽ ᾖ νουνεχής.

advertently became a father. He named this daughter Danae,
because a great time had passed before the birth of his child.[2]   20
He at once gave her to Argive girls to guard safely in maidens'
quarters which he built, taking care that she should not come
into a man's sight. Then, after the long passage of time to her
adulthood, and possession of a beauty beyond all others in   25
Greece, father Zeus was seized by her irresistible charms and
wished somehow to lie secretly with her. Having no way to
persuade her openly, he turned to the following means: he
changed himself into unfired gold-dust —knowing that this is   30
a possession desired by men—so as to pour through the roof
into the girl's arms. Not perceiving the hidden trick Danae
welcomed the god in her embrace as he poured in. When after
a time she realised herself to be pregnant, she was astonished   35
and openly distressed that she had come to this, despite her
precautions to avoid blame. She set out to escape secretly
from Argos, but her father learned of it; enraged by anger he
shut her up in the house and kept her hidden in the dark, look-   40
ing to learn the truth through watching her.[3] In case he should
see the truth and certainty of it all, he has determined to set
both mother and child loose on the sea.

As to my errand, however, with comforting words here for
Danae from Zeus, I will go and reveal them to her at once. It is   45
the part of any servant to carry out instructions eagerly, at least
if he has sense.

---

[2] A play upon Danae's name as meaning 'after a long time'
(Greek *dāna-*); cf. e.g. the plays upon names at *Alexander* F 42d
(Alexander), *Antiope* F 181–2 (Zethus and Amphion), *Melanippe*
F *489 (Boeotus), etc.   [3] Note that in this version of the story
Zeus makes Danae pregnant before Acrisius imprisons her; he
keeps watch to see if her lover returns.

EURIPIDES

τίς ὁ καινοτρόπος οὗτος μῦθος
50 κατ' ἐμὰν ἧκεν ἀκουάν;
ἔνθ' ἀσπερχὲς μενεαίνουσα
τοῖσδε δώμασι κοιράνου ἀμφίδοξος πελάζω·
τίς δεσπότιν ἐμὴν Δανάην
βάξις ἔχει κατὰ πτόλιν;
55 ἣν μήποτ' ὤφελ' εἰς ὦτα φέρειν
ὁ πρῶτος τάδε φράσαι τολμήσας,
ὡς ἐγκύμων εἴληπται χρανθεῖσα λέκτροις
ἀνδρός· πατὴρ δέ μιν κλήσας
ἐν παρθενῶσι σφραγῖσι δέμας φυλάσσει.
60 ταῦτ' ἐτήτυμα μαθεῖν θέλω.
ἀλλ' εἰσορῶ γὰρ τύραννον χθονὸς τῆσδ'
Ἀργείας Ἀκρίσιον πρὸ δόμων στείχοντα·
ὀργῇ βαρύς, ὡς δόξαι, κέαρ.

σὺ δ' εἰ κατ' οἴκους εὐνοῶν ἐτύγχανες,
65 οὐκ ἄν ποτ' ἦλθες εἰς τόδε θράσους . . .

344

DANAE

CHORUS
(singing)

What extraordinary story is this that has come to my hearing?   50
It is why I am keenly eager to approach the king's house here
with my doubts. What is this rumour filling the city about my
mistress Danae? If only the first to dare voice it had never
brought it to my ears! — that she has been found pregnant   55
after a defiling union with a man;[4] and that her father has shut
her away in the maidens' quarters and keeps her under sealed
guard. I want to know the truth of this.   60

    But now I see Acrisius, this land's ruler, coming out in front
of his house; he is heavy at heart with anger, it would seem.

ACRISIUS
(addressing a male companion)

You there: if you really were well-intentioned towards the
house, you would never have been this bold . . . [5]

---

[4] 'Defiling union': the rumour hinted therefore at her acquies-
cence.   [5] Acrisius addresses a male: not, therefore, the Cho-
rus, who almost certainly are women (they speak of the segregated
Danae as their mistress, 53), and probably not Hermes (whose
message is for Danae alone, 45), unless he has taken human dis-
guise; and yet the list of characters names only one other male, the
Messenger.

DICTYS

H. Van Looy in ed. Budé VIII.2.73–92; I. Karamanou, *Euripides. Danae and Dictys* (Munich–Leipzig, 2006).

Webster 61–4; Aélion (1983), I.263–70 and (1986), 157–60; Gantz 303–4, 309–10; *LIMC* VII.i.427–8 'Polydektes', cf. III.i.325–37 'Danae'; I. Karamanou, *BICS* 46 (2002–03), 167–75.

The background and outline of the play are safely enough inferred from mythographers who make no express reference to Euripides (Pherecydes FGrH 3 F 10–11, and in more detail Apollodorus 2.4.2–3, duplicated in part in P. Oxy. 2536, a fragmentary commentary by Theon on Pindar, Pythians 12.14), from the fragments themselves (especially F 330b, 332, 342), and from an early 4th c. Apulian volute-crater (LIMC 'Polydektes' no. 6, Todisco Ap 67, Taplin no. 67).[1] The entire mythical background is reviewed by Gantz and by Karamanou (2006), 119–26.

Dictys *continues Danae's story, but many years later than the events in* Danae. *When the chest containing her and the infant Perseus had been cast up on Seriphos, they*

---

[1] On this see Karamanou (2003). The identification of Perseus in a similar scene on a second and slightly earlier Apulian crater (*LIMC* 'Danae' no. 71, Todisco Ap 69) is quite uncertain.

were cared for by Dictys, probably a fisherman (his name means 'Mr. Net': see below on Aeschylus' Dictyulci), but a son nevertheless of Zeus (cf. Hesiod fr. 7 + 8), the very god who is Perseus' father. The scene was set at his hut (Webster; Kannicht in TrGF 5.382) or alternatively in front of the palace on Seriphos with the hut imagined in the foreground (Karamanou [2006], 139–41). His half-brother Polydectes became king of Seriphos, and desired Danae as his wife; but the now grown-up Perseus prevented him. Polydectes then pretended he would marry Hippodamia daughter of Oenomaus instead, and asked for wedding gifts; Perseus said he would not refuse him even the Gorgon's head as a gift, with the clear intention of using it against him. Polydectes charged him to fetch the head, no doubt thinking the challenge would kill him and leave himself free to take Danae (compare the challenge to Bellerophon to kill the Chimaera in Stheneboea). With the aid of his winged sandals and mirror Perseus speedily killed the Gorgon and returned with her head in a bag. He found Danae and Dictys in sanctuary, for Polydectes had attempted violence. They were at a god's shrine, as is narrated by Theon (above), whose damaged text however lacks the god's name (Karamanou [2003] and [2006], 155–6 argues that this was Poseidon as the sea-god who had saved them, using the Apulian crater and her extremely insecure restoration of the name in PSI 1286 fr. B.2, a collection of hypotheses). Perseus showed the head to Polydectes in front of the king's supporters, who were all turned to stone, and installed Dictys as king; just possibly Danae became his queen.

Reconstructions of the plot can offer only a sequence of likely scenes, but a context can be hazarded for some frag-

ments. F 330b, if indeed from this play, began the prologue speech, which narrated how Danae and Perseus came to Seriphos long ago; so the play's action began with a description of Polydectes' intentions for Danae. In F 331 she may express her dependence upon Dictys, and in F 332 Dictys is consoling her against Perseus' expected death when facing the Gorgon; F 344 may just belong here too. These fragments suit either Perseus' absence at the play's beginning (cf. the opening of Heracles with the hero absent in Hades, and especially F 332 with note), or his departure during the play; but Webster 63 gives F 331 to Perseus wishing a life for himself free of troublesome love. F 333–7 appear to come from an agôn scene when Polydectes demands obedience from his 'inferior' brother; the 'old man' addressed in F 337 is Dictys (cf. F 342). This exchange probably preceded a scene including F 338–341, a discussion of Danae's marriage perhaps between Polydectes and an unidentified man: Dictys again, or a courtier, or Perseus' old tutor have all been suggested. F 342 must relate to Perseus' rescue of Danae and Dictys from their sanctuary; Dictys raises her to her feet, and may have offered her marriage (especially if her feelings had been revealed in F 331; but Aélion [1986], 159–60 is notably unconfident of the dénouement). Whether F 343, an exhortation to courage, related to this scene is wholly conjectural. There was almost certainly a role for a messenger, to narrate how Polydectes and his courtiers were turned to stone by the Gorgon's head; and there may have been a final role for a god to announce or sanction the various destinies of Dictys and Danae (marriage and the throne of Seriphos), and of Perseus (a dynasty at Argos); Karamanou (2006), 133–4 again favours Poseidon. No fragment can certainly be at-

tributed to the chorus, and its composition is a guess
(*Danae was too humble to have her own women servants*).
F 345 and 346 may bear on Perseus' sense of duty to his
mother, but their location is unknowable; F 347 is entirely
opaque.

Brief fragment: F 348 ('*I would groan*'?).   Other as-
criptions: F 1048a (*cf.* F 337 and 334.3), F 1107.

The play was produced in 431 B.C. together with
Medea (*of which the hypothesis by Aristophanes of Byzan-
tium survives, giving this date*), Philoctetes *and the satyr-
play* Theristae ('*Harvesters*'). *Dictys is the name-character
because the play traced his noble defence of Danae both
past and present, his rescue with her at the last moment,
and his happy future. Rescue from sanctuary is a frequent
motif in Euripides' plays, like the combination of melodra-
matic danger and 'passion'.*

No other Greek tragedy of this title is known, but the
coming ashore of Danae and Perseus was burlesqued in
Aeschylus' satyr-play Dictyulci ('*Net-fishers*'), *of which
about 100 fragmentary lines survive on papyrus (*Aesch. F
46a–47c*): Dictys may have 'rescued' Danae and the baby
Perseus from the satyrs ('fishermen') who found the chest.
This play may have completed a tetralogy containing a*
Polydectes (*unfortunately a blank*). *There are fragments of
Cratinus' comedy* Seriphians, *perhaps from the late 420's,
only a few years after Euripides' play.*

ΔΙΚΤΥΣ

**330b

Σέριφος ἅλμῃ ποντίᾳ περίρρυτος . . .

Philodemus, *On Poems* P. Herc. 1676 fr. xi col. vii.7–12
Heidmann; assigned to *Dictys* by Koerte, but Aeschylus' tragedy
Polydectes and satyr-play *Dictyulci* (*'Net-fishers'*) have also been
suggested.

331

†φίλος γὰρ ἦν μοι,† καί μ' ἔρως ἕλοι ποτὲ
οὐκ εἰς τὸ μῶρον οὐδέ μ' εἰς Κύπριν τρέπων.

Stobaeus 1.9.4a

ἦν Stob.: εἶ Wilamowitz   ἕλοι Stob.: εἶλεν Herwerden

**332
ΔΙΚΤΥΣ

δοκεῖς τὸν Ἅιδην σῶν τι φροντίζειν γόων
καὶ παῖδ' ἀνήσειν τὸν σόν, εἰ θέλεις στένειν;
παῦσαι· βλέπουσα δ' εἰς τὰ τῶν πέλας κακὰ
ῥάων γένοι' ἄν, εἰ λογίζεσθαι θέλοις
5 ὅσοι τε δεσμοῖς ἐκμεμόχθηνται βροτῶν
ὅσοι τε γηράσκουσιν ὀρφανοὶ τέκνων,

DICTYS

**330b

Seriphos surrounded by the ocean's salty flow . . . [1]

[1] The play's first line, if correctly attributed: see note opposite, and Introduction above.

331

†For he was dear to me†, and may a love one day seize me that does not turn me towards folly, or to Cypris.[1]

[1] V. 1 is incoherent (Wilamowitz's 'you are dear to me' does not help, even with Herwerden's 'and love one day seized me'); and the end of v. 2 is puzzling since 'love' and 'Cypris' are synonyms. Perhaps Danae is speaking, and 'he' is Dictys (see Introduction).

**332

DICTYS

(consoling Danae)

Do you think that Hades is concerned at all for your laments, and will send your son back up if you will go on grieving?[1] Stop! You'd feel easier if you looked at the troubles of those near at hand, if you'd be willing to consider how many of mankind have been exhausted by struggling with bonds, how many grow old bereft of children, and

[1] Similarly *Heracles* 145–6, the tyrant Lycus taunting the family of the supposedly dead Heracles.

351

τοὺς δ᾽ ἐκ μέγιστον ὀλβίας τυραννίδος
τὸ μηδὲν ὄντας· ταῦτά σε σκοπεῖν χρεών.

Plutarch, *Moralia* 106a

7 μέγιστον Elmsley: μεγίστης Plut.

333

φεῦ φεῦ, παλαιὸς αἶνος ὡς καλῶς ἔχει·
οὐκ ἂν γένοιτο χρηστὸς ἐκ κακοῦ πατρός.

Stobaeus 4.30.5; v. 2: Chrysippus fr. 180.15 von Arnim

334

πολλοῖς παρέστην κἀφθόνησα δὴ βροτῶν
ὅστις κακοῖσιν ἐσθλὸς ὢν ὅμοιος ἦν,
λόγων ματαίων εἰς ἅμιλλαν ἐξιών.
τὸ δ᾽ ἦν ἄρ᾽ οὐκ ἀκουστὸν οὐδ᾽ ἀνασχετόν,
5 σιγᾶν κλύοντα δεινὰ πρὸς κακιόνων.

Stobaeus 4.42.2; v. 4: *Anecdota Graeca* I.373.5 Bekker = Photius, *Lexicon* a 818 Theodoridis

335

τυραννικόν τοι πόλλ᾽ ἐπίστασθαι λέγειν.

Stobaeus 3.36.15

336

εἰς δ᾽ εὐγένειαν ὀλίγ᾽ ἔχω φράσαι καλά·
ὁ μὲν γὰρ ἐσθλὸς εὐγενὴς ἔμοιγ᾽ ἀνήρ,
ὁ δ᾽ οὐ δίκαιος κἂν ἀμείνονος πατρὸς
Ζηνὸς πεφύκῃ, δυσγενὴς εἶναι δοκεῖ.

Stobaeus 4.29.1; vv. 1–2 paraphrased in Aristotle fr. 94 Rose

those who are nothing after ruling in the greatest prosperity: these are the things you should contemplate.

333

Alas, alas, how well the old saying has it: a good son will never be born from a bad father.

334

I've stood beside many a man, and been truly indignant at any who, though honourable, was like base men in coming out for a contest of wild words. What proved past hearing or bearing, however, was listening in silence to dreadful abuse from baser men.[1]

[1] Polydectes standing on his dignity as king?

335

It is the quality of a ruler, I tell you, to know how to say much.[1]

[1] For kings' god-given eloquence see Hesiod, *Theogony* 81–90.

336

When it comes to noble birth I have few good things to say. The honourable man in my eyes is the noble one, but the unjust man, even if he has a father better than Zeus, seems to me ignoble.[1]

[1] Zeus is the guarantor of royalty first at Hesiod, *Theogony* 96. Dictys is probably the speaker, attacking Polydectes' rule (cf. F 337). For criticism of identifying nobility with 'good birth' see on *Alexander* F 61b.

337

μὴ νεῖκος, ὦ γεραιέ, κοιράνοις τίθου·
σέβειν δὲ τοὺς κρατοῦντας ἀρχαῖος νόμος.

Stobaeus 4.2.2

1 κοιράνοις Salmasius: τυράννοις (unmetrical) Stob.

338

ὄντων δὲ παίδων καὶ πεφυκότος γένους
καινοὺς φυτεῦσαι παῖδας ἐν δόμοις θέλεις,
ἔχθραν μεγίστην σοῖσι συμβάλλων τέκνοις;

Stobaeus 4.26.21; punctuated at end as a question by Collard.

339

πατέρα τε παισὶν ἡδέως συνεκφέρειν
φίλους ἔρωτας ἐκβαλόντ᾽ αὐθαδίαν,
παῖδάς τε πατρί· καὶ γὰρ οὐκ αὐθαίρετοι
βροτοῖς ἔρωτες οὐδ᾽ ἑκουσία νόσος.
5 σκαιόν τι δὴ τὸ χρῆμα γίγνεσθαι φιλεῖ,
θεῶν ἀνάγκας ὅστις ἰᾶσθαι θέλει.

Stobaeus 4.26.16

340

Κύπρις γὰρ οὐδὲν νουθετουμένη χαλᾷ,
ἤν τ᾽ αὖ βιάζῃ, μᾶλλον ἐντείνειν φιλεῖ,
κἄπειτα τίκτει πόλεμον· εἰς δ᾽ ἀνάστασιν
δόμων περαίνει πολλάκις τὰ τοιάδε.

Stobaeus 4.20.48; vv. 1–2: Chrysippus fr. 475 von Arnim

1 οὐδὲν Nauck: οὐδὲ Stob., Chrysipp.

337

Don't start a quarrel, old man, with kings: it's an ancient law to respect those in power.

338

When you have sons born, and descendants, do you want to sire fresh ones in your house, and concert great enmity between your children?

339

. . . a father (should) be pleased to put away stubborn objections, and help his sons achieve their fond passions, as (should) sons their father; for men's passions really aren't self-chosen, or a voluntary affliction. The thing usually becomes quite stupid when anyone wants to cure what gods impose.[1]

[1] Tolerance of sons' love affairs recommended: F 951. A cure unwisely attempted for involuntary or divine affliction in the matter of love: *Bellerophon* F 286b with note.

340

Cypris, you see, relents when not admonished at all;[1] if you force her, on the other hand, she usually presses harder, and then generates conflict; and such things often end in upheaval for homes.

[1] Translation as 'does not relent at all when admonished' makes a poor contrast with 'if you force her etc.', as does Stobaeus' 'does not relent even when admonished'.

341

μή μοί ποτ᾽ εἴη χρημάτων νικωμένῳ
κακῷ γενέσθαι, μηδ᾽ ὁμιλοίην κακοῖς.

Stobaeus 4.31.57, repeated at 4.31.96

342

ΔΑΝΑΗ

τί μ᾽, ὦ γέραιε, πημάτων λελησμένην
ὀρθοῖς;

Schol. on Sophocles, *Ajax* 787–8

1 restored by Kannicht: τί μ᾽ ἄρτι πημάτων λελησμένην |
ὀρθοῖς Schol. ms. L: τί μ᾽, ὦ γέραιε, πημάτων πεπαυμένην |
ὀρθοῖς Schol. ms. G

343

θάρσει· τό τοι δίκαιον ἰσχύει μέγα.

Stobaeus 3.13.5

344

νέος, πόνοις δέ γ᾽ οὐκ ἀγύμναστος φρένας.

Stobaeus 4.11.10

345

ἐγὼ νομίζω πατρὶ φίλτατον τέκνα
παισίν τε τοὺς τεκόντας, οὐδὲ συμμάχους
ἄλλους γενέσθαι φήμ᾽ ἂν ἐνδικωτέρους.

Stobaeus 4.26.18

DICTYS

341

May it never happen to me to be mastered by money and become evil, nor to associate with evil men!

342

DANAE

(to Dictys)

Why make me stand up, old man, when I have forgotten my miseries?[1]

[1] Compare Sophocles, *Ajax* 787–8, 'Why make me stand up when I had just got rest from inexhaustible misery?'

343

Take heart! There is great power in justice, I tell you.

344

Young, yes, but with a mind not untested by hard tasks.[1]

[1] Perseus: see Introduction. Possibly an answer in stichomythia.

345

I think myself that for a father his children are the dearest thing, and for sons their parents; and I declare that none could be more rightful allies.

346

εἷς γάρ τις ἔστι κοινὸς ἀνθρώποις νόμος—
θεοῖσι τοῦτο δόξαν, ὡς σαφῶς λέγω—
θηρσίν τε πᾶσι, τέκν’ ἃ τίκτουσιν φιλεῖν·
τὰ δ’ ἄλλα χωρὶς χρώμεθ’ ἀλλήλων νόμοις.

Stobaeus 4.26.17

2 Verse deleted by West.

347

εἰ δ’ ἦσθα μὴ κάκιστος, οὔποτ’ ἂν πάτραν
τὴν σὴν ἀτίζων τήνδ’ ἂν ηὐλόγεις πόλιν·
ὡς ἔν γ’ ἐμοὶ κρίνοιτ’ ἂν οὐ καλῶς φρονεῖν
ὅστις πατρῴας γῆς ἀτιμάζων ὅρους
5 ἄλλην ἐπαινεῖ καὶ τρόποισιν ἥδεται.

Stobaeus 3.39.7 (vv. 1–2) + 8 (vv. 3–5)

4 ὅρους Stob.: νόμους Nauck

346

There is one single law common to men—this having the
gods' agreement, as I say with certainty[1]—and to all beasts,
to love the offspring they bear. For the rest, we have differ-
ent laws from one another.

[1] West deleted v. 2 as an irrelevant intrusion.

347

If you were not very bad, you would never be slighting your
fatherland and praising this city; because in my eyes at
least, a man would be judged wrong-headed who scorns
the confines of his ancestral land, to commend another and
take pleasure in its ways.[1]

[1] This fragment is impossible to locate in the play: some edi-
tors doubt even its attribution to the play.

EPEUS (ΕΠΕΙΟΣ)

Pechstein 29–34, 141–4; H. Van Looy in ed. Budé VIII.2.93–4; Krumeich 420–1.

The play is known only through a list of Euripidean ti-tles partially preserved in the so-called Monumentum Albanum *now in the Louvre (= IG XIV.1152: see TrGF 5 pp. 57–8, T 6). Its placing in the list shows it was a satyr play, and its inclusion there should mean that the text was preserved in the Alexandrian Library; but the complete ab-sence of other evidence suggests it may have been one of several Euripidean satyr plays that were lost before that collection was made. Epeus is best known as the builder of the Trojan Horse (Homer,* Odyssey *8.493, 11.523). In Achilles' funeral games he excels as a boxer but not as a dis-cus thrower, and admits to being no fighter (Homer,* Iliad *23.664ff., 838ff.). Later he was reputed to have been a mere water-carrier for the Atreidae (Stesichorus F 200 PMGF), and became proverbial for cowardice. A suitable subject for a satyr play, then, perhaps concerning the construction of the Horse.*

For F 988, assigned by Welcker to Epeus, *see* Cretans, *after F 472g.*

ERECHTHEUS

Austin, *NFE* 22–40; A. Martínez Díez, *Euripides: Erecteo* (Madrid, 1976); P. Carrara, *Euripide: Eretteo* (Florence, 1977); M. Cropp in *SFP* I.148–94, 286–7 (~ II.366–7); Diggle, *TrGFS* 101–10 (F 360, 362, 369, 370); F. Jouan in ed. Budé VIII.2.95–132; cf. J. C. Kamerbeek, *Mnemosyne* 23 (1970), 113–26, and in H. Hofmann and A. Harder, *Fragmenta Dramatica* (Göttingen, 1991), 111–6. See also on F 370.

Webster, *Euripides*, 127–30; H. Van Looy in *Hommages à Marie Delcourt* (Brussels, 1970), 115–22; V. di Benedetto, *Euripide: teatro e società* (Turin, 1971), 145–53; C. Clairmont, *GRBS* 12 (1971), 485–95; M. Treu, *Chiron* 1 (1971), 115–31; M. Lacore, *REA* 85 (1983), 215–234 and *Kentron* 11.2–12.1 (1995–6), 89–107; Aélion (1986) 198–216; R. Parker in J. N. Bremmer (ed.), *Interpretations of Greek Mythology* (London, 1986), 187–214; E. O'Connor-Visser, *Aspects of Human Sacrifice in the Tragedies of Euripides* (Amsterdam, 1987), 148–76; *LIMC* IV.i.923–8, 938–41, 949 'Erechtheus'; E. Kearns, *The Heroes of Attica* (London, 1989), 59–63, 113–5, 160, 201–2; J. Wilkins in A. Powell (ed.), *Euripides, Women and Sexuality* (London, 1990), 177–94; Gantz 233–5, 242–4; R. E. Harder, *Die Frauenrolle bei Euripides* (Stuttgart, 1993), 172–6, 336–42; F. Jouan in V. Pirenne-Delforge and E.

Suárez de la Torre (eds.), *Héros et héroines dans les mythes et les cultes grecques* (Liège, 2000), 29–39; Matthiessen 258–60.

The Homeric Erechtheus was born from the soil of Athens, nurtured by Athena, and given cult in Athena's own temple (Iliad 2.546–51, Odyssey 7.80–1). In Athenian tradition he was to some extent identified with the semi-serpentine figure of Erichthonius, but in the 5th century he was also one of the ten tribal heroes under the Cleisthenic constitution, and remembered for defeating Eumolpus in war. Eumolpus was the legendary ancestor of the Eumolpidae, the chief priestly family at Eleusis, and in early accounts was himself an Eleusinian; the story of the war then accounted for Athens' control of Eleusis and its Mysteries (cf. Thucydides 2.15.1). In Euripides' play, however, he is a Thracian invader whose descendants will become established at Eleusis (F 370.100ff.), and his purpose is to claim control of Attica in the name of his father Poseidon, thus reversing the outcome of the legendary contest in which the Athenians chose Athena over Poseidon as their protecting deity. This version of the story, possibly invented by Euripides, conveniently changed its focus from internal strife to the repulsion of a barbarian invasion sponsored by an elemental god, with a providential outcome in the incorporation of the god and the barbarians' descendants into the Athenian state and its religious system.

The play's conclusion is now known from the extensive Sorbonne papyrus (F 370), which shows that it was set on the Acropolis and culminated with the victory of Athens at the cost of the lives of Erechtheus and his three daughters. What went before can be inferred to some extent from a

*summary of the story (test. ii below) in the speech deliv-
ered in 330 by the anti-Macedonian politician Lycurgus
against Leocrates, who was accused of abandoning Athens
after the battle of Chaeronea. Lycurgus cites Erechtheus'
obedience to the Delphic oracle in sacrificing his daughter
to save the city as an ideal example of patriotism, and he
goes on to quote the whole of the speech in which queen
Praxithea persuaded Erechtheus of the need for the sacri-
fice (F 360). The speech reads as if Erechtheus was reluc-
tant to kill his daughter (F 360.1–3, 17–18, 34–7), and
other sources ([Plutarch] and 'Demaratus': see apparatus
to test. ii below) speak of him discussing the oracle with
Praxithea. This and other hints suggest that the play's early
scenes were broadly similar to those of another patriotic
play,* Children of Heracles. *After a prologue in which Po-
seidon told of Eumolpus' birth and upbringing (F 349) and
gave the context of the war, Erechtheus probably returned
from Delphi to find Praxithea preparing a supplication
of Athena (F 350, perhaps preceded by F 351). Some or
all of F 352–6 seem to come from a scene in which Erech-
theus confronted a herald or some other representative of
Eumolpus demanding the surrender of Athens, and F 357–
8 suggest a scene in which the mutual affection of king,
queen and daughters was expressed. The order of these
scenes and the moment when Erechtheus revealed the ora-
cle are unclear, but this part of the play culminated with
Praxithea's speech (F 360), a subsequent dialogue (F 360a),
and the decision to proceed with the sacrifice of one of
the daughters.*[1] *After this there is more uncertainty. One*

---

[1] 'Demaratus' (see app. to test. ii below) says the eldest of
the three daughters was sacrificed, and Persephone the recipi-

might expect a report of the sacrifice, but there is no direct evidence of this (compare perhaps the absence of a report of the sacrifice of Heracles' daughter in Children of Heracles*). In F 370 (36–8, 68–70) it becomes clear that the other two daughters also killed themselves after making a suicide pact with their sister,[2] but it is (again) possible that the pact and their deaths were only revealed to Praxithea after the battle. F 369 comes from a stasimon in which the Chorus prays for peace, probably just before the battle (cf.* Cresphontes *F 453). Most puzzling is Erechtheus' sententious farewell speech (F 362) delivered to a son who has not reached military age, and who has been ignored by Praxithea (note especially F 360.36–7). It would seem that Erechtheus has adopted an heir, perhaps recently or even in the course of the play; the dismissive remark about adopted children in F 359 may come from Praxithea, insisting on the purity of her own family and unaware that she will soon lose them all. The identity of this heir remains quite uncertain; a younger Cecrops, Xuthus and Ion all figure as heirs of Erechtheus in some versions of the highly artifical mythology of early Athens, but none fits the part well in the context of this play.*

F 370 gives the arrival of a messenger with news of the battle (the report speech itself is lost), then part of Praxithea's lament for her husband and daughters, Poseidon's last assault on Athens in the form of an earthquake, and Athena's intervention and instructions concerning the

---

ent. Probably none of the daughters was named, although later mythographers provided a variety of names. [2] Cf. Apollodorus 3.15.4 (= test. *via); Hyginus, *Fab.* 46; Aristides, *Orations* 1.85ff. (= test. *iv).

cults of the Erechtheids and Erechtheus himself (now to be known respectively as the Hyacinthids and Poseidon Erechtheus), the appointment of Praxithea as priestess of Athena Polias, and the future establishment of the Eumolpidae at Eleusis. For these details see F 370.65ff. with the accompanying notes.

The placing and relevance of F 363–7 are unknown (but see notes on F 366 and 367). Brief fragments: F 368 'pollution of the oak', F 369a 'unbetrothed union(s)', F 369b 'without exit', F 369d 'sounds of the Asian (lyre)'. Other ascriptions: F 981 (combined with F 360.7–10 in Plutarch, Moralia 604d), F 1053.

Plutarch's citation of F 369.1 in his Life of Nicias *suggests that* Erechtheus *was performed during the Athenian–Spartan truce of 423–2, so probably at the Dionysia of 422, but this literary allusion may be historically inaccurate, and the metrical evidence suggests a date a few years later; there are probable allusions to* Erechtheus *in Aristophanes' plays of 411 (Lysistrata 1135, cf. F 363; Women at the Thesmophoria 120, cf. F 369d), and in the possibly earlier Horae ('Seasons': F 580, 586 PCG, cf. Eur. F 357, 366). The play may have been inspired by the planning or building of the Erechtheum in this period (cf. F 370.90ff. with note), but the chronological guidance this provides is at best vague. At any rate the play can confidently be classed with other 'patriotic' plays of the Peloponnesian War period, especially the extant* Children of Heracles *and* Suppliant Women, *and its myth with others in which Athens was saved from foreign aggression by the self-sacrifice of a king (Codrus) or a group of noble daughters (those of Leos, and those of Hyacinthus with whom the Erechtheids are actually identified in F 370.73–4). It seems unlikely that in dramatizing a myth of this kind Euripides presented it in an ambivalent light (as Lacore 1995–6 amongst others has argued), although he no doubt emphasized the tragic character of the episode and its human costs.*

Euripides' dramatization of the story is unique in Attic tragedy and seems to have had no impact in figurative art,[3] but the account of a purely Thracian invasion of Attica led by Eumolpus son of Poseidon became influential in Athenian patriotic rhetoric (besides Lycurgus' speech mentioned above see e.g. Plato, Menexenus 239a–b, Isocrates 4.68: TrGF test. v) and in the later mythographic tradition. The play's only poetic descendants are Ennius' Latin Erechtheus *(2nd c.* B.C., *now almost completely lost) and* Swinburne's Erechtheus *(1876).*

[3] The identification of the subject in a late 5th c. Lucanian vase (*TrGF* test. *vii) is very doubtful, as is the suggestion of J. Breton Connelly (*AJA* 100 (1996), 53–80) that the sacrifice is represented in the Parthenon Frieze.

ΕΡΕΧΘΕΥΣ

test. ii

φασὶ γὰρ Εὔμολπον τὸν Ποσειδῶνος καὶ Χιόνης μετὰ
Θρᾳκῶν ἐλθεῖν τῆς χώρας ταύτης ἀμφισβητοῦντα, τυ-
χεῖν δὲ κατ᾽ ἐκείνους τοὺς χρόνους βασιλεύοντα Ἐρε-
χθέα, γυναῖκα ἔχοντα Πραξιθέαν τὴν Κηφισοῦ θυγα-
τέρα. (99) μεγάλου δὲ στρατοπέδου μέλλοντος αὐτοῖς
εἰσβάλλειν εἰς τὴν χώραν, εἰς Δελφοὺς ἰὼν ἠρώτα τὸν
θεόν, τί ποιῶν ἂν νίκην λάβοι παρὰ τῶν πολεμίων.
χρήσαντος δ᾽ αὐτῷ τοῦ θεοῦ, τὴν θυγατέρα εἰ θύσειε πρὸ
τοῦ συμβαλεῖν τῷ στρατοπέδῳ, κρατήσειν τῶν πολεμίων,
ὁ δὲ τῷ θεῷ πιθόμενος τοῦτ᾽ ἔπραξε, καὶ τοὺς ἐπιστρα-
τευομένους ἐκ τῆς χώρας ἐξέβαλε. (100) διὸ καὶ δικαίως
ἄν τις Εὐριπίδην ἐπαινέσειεν, ὅτι τά τ᾽ ἄλλ᾽ ἦν ἀγαθὸς
ποιητής, καὶ τοῦτον τὸν μῦθον προείλετο ποιῆσαι, ἡγού-
μενος κάλλιστον ἂν γενέσθαι τοῖς πολίταις παράδειγμα
τὰς ἐκείνων πράξεις, πρὸς ἃς ἀποβλέποντας καὶ θεω-
ροῦντας συνεθίζεσθαι ταῖς ψυχαῖς τὸ τὴν πατρίδα

Lycurgus, *Against Leocrates* 98–101. The same story is briefly
summarized and attributed to Euripides' *Erechtheus* in [Plu-
tarch], *Moralia* 310d (= test. iiia), and without attribution in
'Demaratus', *Stories from Tragedy*, FGrH 42 F 4 (= test. iiib).

ERECHTHEUS

test. ii

They say that Eumolpus, son of Poseidon and Chione, came
with the Thracians to lay claim to this country, and that at
that time Erechtheus happened to be king, being married to
Praxithea, daughter of Cephisus.[1] (99) As a great army was
about to invade their land, Erechtheus went to Delphi and
asked the god what he should do to get victory over his ene-
mies. The god replied that if he sacrificed his daughter be-
fore the two armies met, he would defeat the enemy; and
Erechtheus obeyed him and did this, and expelled the invad-
ers from the country. (100) Accordingly it would be proper to
praise Euripides for being a good poet in other ways, and es-
pecially for choosing to compose this story, reckoning that the
deeds of those men would be an excellent example for our citi-
zens, which they could look to and contemplate, and thus ha-
bituate their souls to love of their country. And it is of value . . .

---

[1] God of the local river Cephisus.

φιλεῖν. ἄξιον δὲ . . . καὶ τῶν ἰαμβείων ἀκοῦσαι ἃ
πεποίηκεν λέγουσαν τὴν μητέρα τῆς παιδός . . . (F 360)
. . . (101) ταῦτα ὦ ἄνδρες τοὺς πατέρας ὑμῶν ἐπαίδευε.
φύσει γὰρ οὐσῶν φιλοτέκνων πασῶν τῶν γυναικῶν, ταύ-
την ἐποίησε τὴν πατρίδα μᾶλλον τῶν παίδων φιλοῦσαν
(cf. F 360a) . . .

349
⟨ΠΟΣΕΙΔΩΝ⟩

Αἰθιοπίαν νιν ἐξέσωσ᾽ ἐπὶ χθόνα.

Stephanus of Byzantium, ʻΑἰθίοψʼ (p. 47.12 Meineke)

350
⟨ΕΡΕΧΘΕΥΣ?⟩

καί μοι—πολὺν γὰρ πελανὸν ἐκπέμπεις δόμων—
φράσον σελήνας τάσδε πυρίμου χλόης . . .

Suda α 2082, cf. β 458

351
⟨ΠΡΑΞΙΘΕΑ?⟩

ὀλολύζετ᾽, ὦ γυναῖκες, ὡς ἔλθῃ θεὰ
χρυσῆν ἔχουσα Γοργόνʼ ἐπίκουρος πόλει.

Schol. on Aristophanes, *Peace* 97

to hear also the verses which he represented the girl's mother as speaking . . . (*Lycurgus quotes* F 360) . . . (101) This, gentlemen, was what he taught your fathers; for while all women are devoted to their children, he represented this one as loving her fatherland more than her children (cf. F 360a).

349
⟨POSEIDON⟩

I took him to safety in the Ethiopian land.[1]

[1] According to Apollodorus 3.15.4, Eumolpus of Thrace was the son of Poseidon and Chione ('Snow Maiden'), daughter of the North Wind. His mother threw him into the sea to conceal his birth, and Poseidon rescued him and had him raised by a sea-nymph in 'Ethiopia' (for this location see note on *Andromeda* F 145).

350
⟨ERECHTHEUS?⟩

And as you are bringing much sacred mixture from the house, tell me (why/where you are taking) these moons made from young wheat . . . [1]

[1] A mixture of wheat-meal, oil and honey was used for pouring libations and for making sacrificial cakes (here 'moons' because of their special shape).

351
⟨PRAXITHEA?⟩

Raise a cry, women, so the goddess may come to the city's aid, wearing her golden Gorgon.[1]

[1] Athena's protective mantle (aegis) decorated with a Gorgon's head.

352

⟨ΕΡΕΧΘΕΥΣ?⟩

ὡς σὺν θεοῖσι τοὺς σοφοὺς κινεῖν δόρυ
στρατηλάτας χρή, τῶν θεῶν δὲ μὴ βίᾳ.

Stobaeus 4.13.12

353

⟨ΕΡΕΧΘΕΥΣ?⟩

οὐδεὶς στρατεύσας ἄδικα σῶς ἦλθεν πάλιν.

Stobaeus 4.13.13

354

⟨ΕΡΕΧΘΕΥΣ?⟩

τὰς οὐσίας γὰρ μᾶλλον ἢ τὰς ἁρπαγὰς
τιμᾶν δίκαιον· οὔτε γὰρ πλοῦτός ποτε
βέβαιος ἄδικος . . .

Stobaeus 4.31.105

355

⟨ΚΗΡΤΞ?⟩

ναῦς ἡ μεγίστη κρεῖσσον ἢ σμικρὸν σκάφος.

Stobaeus 4.17.13

356

⟨ΕΡΕΧΘΕΥΣ?⟩

⟨ἐσθλοὺς ἐγὼ⟩
ὀλίγους ἐπαινῶ μᾶλλον ἢ πολλοὺς κακούς.

Stobaeus 4.10.19

⟨ἐσθλοὺς ἐγὼ⟩ Hense

352
⟨ERECHTHEUS?⟩

For wise commanders should go to war with the gods on their side, not in spite of them.

353
⟨ERECHTHEUS?⟩

No one who goes to war unjustly returns unscathed.

354
⟨ERECHTHEUS?⟩

It is right to value property rather than plunder. For neither is wrongly acquired wealth ever secure . . .

355
⟨HERALD?⟩

The biggest ship is stronger than a little skiff.

356
⟨ERECHTHEUS?⟩

I (myself) approve a few (brave) men rather than a host of cowards.

357

ζεῦγος τριπάρθενον

Hesychius ζ 125 Latte

358

οὐκ ἔστι μητρὸς οὐδὲν ἥδιον τέκνοις.

* * *

ἐρᾶτε μητρός, παῖδες, ὡς οὐκ ἔστ' ἔρως
τοιοῦτος ἄλλος ὅστις ἡδίων ἐρᾶν.

Stobaeus 4.25.4; Orion, Euripidean Appendix 9–10 Haffner.
Vv. 2–3 were considered a separate fragment by Ed. Fraenkel and
others, and are so marked in Orion ms. V.

359

θετῶν δὲ παίδων ποῦ κράτος; τὰ φύντα γὰρ
κρείσσω νομίζειν τῶν δοκημάτων χρεών.

Stobaeus 4.24.28

360

ΠΡΑΞΙΘΕΑ

τὰς χάριτας ὅστις εὐγενῶς χαρίζεται,
ἥδιον ἐν βροτοῖσιν· οἱ δὲ δρῶσι μέν,
χρόνῳ δὲ δρῶσι, δυσγενέστερον <τόδε>.
ἐγὼ δὲ δώσω παῖδα τὴν ἐμὴν κτανεῖν.
5   λογίζομαι δὲ πολλά· πρῶτα μὲν πόλιν
οὐκ ἄν τιν' ἄλλην τῆσδε βελτίω λαβεῖν·

Lycurgus, *Against Leocrates* 100 (see test. ii above); vv. 7–10:
Plutarch, *Moralia* 604d, with F 981 subjoined

357

a team of three maidens[1]

[1] The daughters of Erechtheus and Praxithea (see Introduction).

358

Nothing brings children more joy than their mother.

* * *

Love your mother, children; no other love brings more joy than this.

359

Where is the advantage in adopted children? We should consider those truly born better than mere pretences.[1]

[1] Against adoption see also *Melanippe* F 491.

360

PRAXITHEA
(to Erechtheus)[1]

People find it more pleasing when someone gives favours generously—but to act yet take one's time is considered ill-bred. I for my part shall offer my daughter to be killed.

My reasons are many, and the first of them is that I could get no other city better than this. In the first place, 5

[1] In v. 36 'you' must be Erechtheus.

ἣ πρῶτα μὲν λεὼς οὐκ ἐπακτὸς ἄλλοθεν,
αὐτόχθονες δ' ἔφυμεν· αἱ δ' ἄλλαι πόλεις
πεσσῶν ὁμοίως διαφοραῖς ἐκτισμέναι
10 ἄλλαι παρ' ἄλλων εἰσὶν εἰσαγώγιμοι.
ὅστις δ' ἀπ' ἄλλης πόλεος οἰκήσῃ πόλιν,
ἁρμὸς πονηρὸς ὥσπερ ἐν ξύλῳ παγείς,
λόγῳ πολίτης ἐστί, τοῖς δ' ἔργοισιν οὔ.

ἔπειτα τέκνα τοῦδ' ἕκατι τίκτομεν,
15 ὡς θεῶν τε βωμοὺς πατρίδα τε ῥυώμεθα.
πόλεως δ' ἁπάσης τοὔνομ' ἕν, πολλοὶ δέ νιν
ναίουσι· τούτους πῶς διαφθεῖραί με χρή,
ἐξὸν προπάντων μίαν ὑπὲρ δοῦναι θανεῖν;
εἴπερ γὰρ ἀριθμὸν οἶδα καὶ τοὐλάσσονος
20 τὸ μεῖζον, †ἑνὸς† οἶκος οὐ πλέον σθένει
πταίσας ἁπάσης πόλεος οὐδ' ἴσον φέρει.

εἰ δ' ἦν ἐν οἴκοις ἀντὶ θηλειῶν στάχυς
ἄρσην, πόλιν δὲ πολεμία κατεῖχε φλόξ,
οὐκ ἄν νιν ἐξέπεμπον εἰς μάχην δορός,
25 θάνατον προταρβοῦσ'; ἀλλ' ἔμοιγ' εἴη τέκνα
⟨ἃ⟩ καὶ μάχοιτο καὶ μετ' ἀνδράσιν πρέποι,
μὴ σχήματ' ἄλλως ἐν πόλει πεφυκότα.
τὰ μητέρων δὲ δάκρυ' ὅταν πέμπῃ τέκνα,
πολλοὺς ἐθήλυν' εἰς μάχην ὁρμωμένους.
30 μισῶ γυναῖκας αἵτινες πρὸ τοῦ καλοῦ
ζῆν παῖδας εἵλοντ' ἢ παρῄνεσαν κακά.

20 †ἑνὸς†: οὕνὸς Emperius: οὑμὸς Bekker   σθένει Lycurg.:
στένει Blass   31 εἵλοντ' ἢ Matthiae: εἵλοντο καὶ Lycurg.

we are not an immigrant people from elsewhere but born
in our own land,[2] while other cities are founded as it were
through board-game moves, different ones imported from
different places. But someone who settles in one city from 10
another is like a bad peg fixed in a piece of wood: he's a citi-
zen in name, but not in reality.

Next, we bear our children for this reason, to protect
the gods' altars and our homeland. The city as a whole has a 15
single name, but many inhabit it: why should I destroy
them when I can give one child to die for all? If I know my
numbers and can tell greater from smaller, †one person's†[3]
family falling into misfortune does not weigh more[4] than 20
an entire city, nor does it have an equal impact.

If our house had a crop of males instead of females, and
the flame of war was besetting our city, would I be refusing
to send them out to battle for fear of their deaths? No, give
me sons (who) would fight and stand out amongst the men, 25
not mere figures raised uselessly in the city. When moth-
ers' tears accompany their children, they soften many as
they set off to battle. I detest women who choose life for
their sons ahead of honour, or encourage them to coward- 30

---

[2] This claim of 'autochthony' was a commonplace of Athenian
patriotic rhetoric, e.g. Eur. *Ion* 589–90, Thucydides 2.36.1,
Isocrates 4.24.   [3] This is the sense of both Stobaeus' unmetrical
word and Emperius' adjustment of it; Bekker suggested 'my fam-
ily'.   [4] Some editors prefer Blass's 'does not grieve more'.

καὶ μὴν θανόντες γ’ ἐν μάχῃ πολλῶν μέτα
τύμβον τε κοινὸν ἔλαχον εὐκλειάν τ’ ἴσην·
τῇ μῇ δὲ παιδὶ στέφανος εἷς μιᾷ μόνῃ
35 πόλεως θανούσῃ τῆσδ’ ὕπερ δοθήσεται,
καὶ τὴν τεκοῦσαν καὶ σὲ δύο θ’ ὁμοσπόρω
σώσει· τί τούτων οὐχὶ δέξασθαι καλόν;
    τὴν οὐκ ἐμὴν <δὴ> πλὴν φύσει δώσω κόρην
θῦσαι πρὸ γαίας. εἰ γὰρ αἱρεθήσεται
40 πόλις, τί παίδων τῶν ἐμῶν μέτεστί μοι;
οὔκουν ἅπαντα τοὐν γ’ ἐμοὶ σωθήσεται;
{ἄρξουσί τ’ ἄλλοι, τήνδ’ ἐγὼ σώσω πόλιν.}
    ἐκεῖνο δ’ οὗ <τὸ> πλεῖστον ἐν κοινῷ μέρος,
οὐκ ἔσθ’ ἑκούσης τῆς ἐμῆς ψυχῆς ἄτερ
45 προγόνων παλαιὰ θέσμι’ ὅστις ἐκβαλεῖ·
οὐδ’ ἀντ’ ἐλαίας χρυσέας τε Γοργόνος
τρίαιναν ὀρθὴν στᾶσαν ἐν πόλεως βάθροις
Εὔμολπος οὐδὲ Θρῆξ ἀναστέψει λεὼς
στεφάνοισι, Παλλὰς δ’ οὐδαμοῦ τιμήσεται.
50 χρῆσθ’, ὦ πολῖται, τοῖς ἐμοῖς λοχεύμασιν,
σῴζεσθε, νικᾶτ’· ἀντὶ γὰρ ψυχῆς μιᾶς
οὐκ ἔσθ’ ὅπως οὐ τήνδ’ ἐγὼ σώσω πόλιν.
    ὦ πατρίς, εἴθε πάντες οἳ ναίουσί σε
οὕτω φιλοῖεν ὡς ἐγώ· καὶ ῥᾳδίως
55 οἰκοῖμεν ἄν σε κοὐδὲν ἂν πάσχοις κακόν.

42 deleted by Busche   44 ἄτερ Stob.: ποτε Austin

ice. Consider this too: sons who die in battle with many others get a communal tomb and glory equally shared— but my daughter, when she dies for the city, will be given a single crown for herself alone, and will save her mother, and you, and her two sisters:[5] which of these things is not a fine reward?   35

This girl—not mine (in fact) except in birth—I shall offer for sacrifice to defend our land. For if the city is taken, what share in my children have I then? Shall not all, then, be saved, so far as is in my power? {Others shall govern, I shall save this city.}   40

As for that duty which we share above all, no one shall without(?) my heart's consent[6] cast out the ancient ordinances of our forefathers, nor shall Eumolpus or his Thracian folk replace the olive and the golden Gorgon[7] by planting a trident upright in the city's foundations and crowning it with garlands, leaving Pallas dishonoured.   45

Citizens, use the offspring of my womb, be saved, be victorious! At the cost of just one life I surely shall not fail to save our city.   50

My homeland, would that all your inhabitants loved you as I do; then we could dwell in you easily, and you would suffer no harm.

[5] Praxithea's confidence is tragically misplaced: her husband and all three daughters will die (F 370.16–44).   [6] An oddly pleonastic phrase; Austin's 'no one shall ever with my heart's consent' is one of several suggested improvements.   [7] The olive tree was Athena's gift to Athens when she competed for patronage of the city with Poseidon, who offered a salt spring. For the Gorgon see F 351 above.

EURIPIDES

360a

φιλῶ τέκν', ἀλλὰ πατρίδ' ἐμὴν μᾶλλον φιλῶ.

Plutarch, *Moralia* 809d; paraphrased by Lycurgus, *Against Leocrates* 101 (see test. ii above), and in part by Cicero, *Letters to his Friends* 12.14.7.

(361 N = 370.21–2 below)

362

⟨ΕΡΕΧΘΕΥΣ⟩

ὀρθῶς μ' ἐπήρου· βούλομαι δέ σοι, τέκνον,
(φρονεῖς γὰρ ἤδη κἀποσώσαι' ἂν πατρὸς
γνώμας φράσαντος, ἢν θάνω) παραινέσαι
κειμήλι' ἐσθλὰ καὶ νέοισι χρήσιμα.
5 βραχεῖ δὲ μύθῳ πολλὰ συλλαβὼν ἐρῶ.
  πρῶτον φρένας μὲν ἠπίους ἔχειν χρεών·
τῷ πλουσίῳ τε τῷ τε μὴ διδοὺς μέρος
ἴσον σεαυτὸν εὐσεβῆ πᾶσιν δίδου.
  δυοῖν παρόντοιν πραγμάτοιν πρὸς θάτερον
10 γνώμην προσάπτων τὴν ἐναντίαν μέθες.
  ἀδίκως δὲ μὴ κτῶ χρήματ', ἢν βούλῃ πολὺν
χρόνον μελάθροις ἐμμένειν· τὰ γὰρ κακῶς
οἴκους ἐσελθόντ' οὐκ ἔχει σωτηρίαν.

Stobaeus 3.3.18; vv. 11–13: Stob. 4.31.97; vv. 14–17: Stob. 4.31.25 and 36; vv. 18–20: Plutarch, *Moralia* 63a, Stob. 3.14.3; vv. 21–3: Stob. 4.50.3; v. 21 = [Menander], *Monostichs* 572 Jaekel; vv. 24–7: Stob. 3.17.6; vv. 28–31: Stob. 4.2.4; vv. 29–31: Plut. *Mor.* 337f

ERECHTHEUS

360a

PRAXITHEA

I love my children, but I love my homeland more.

(361 N = 370.21–2 below)

362

⟨ERECHTHEUS⟩

You asked me rightly, and now I wish, my son—since you
have understanding and, if I should die, will observe these
father's precepts that I shall explain—to give you a store of
advice that is honourable and valuable to the young. In a
brief statement I shall sum up much.   5

First, you should maintain a gentle frame of mind; give
equal weight to rich and poor alike, and show yourself re-
spectful to everyone.

When two courses of action are before you, apply your
mind to one and dismiss the other.   10

Do not get possessions unjustly if you want them to stay
for long in your house; those that come into it dishonestly
do not have security.[1] Try, though, to have possessions, for
this bestows nobility and the means to make the best mar-
riages;[2] poverty brings disrepute and low esteem in life,   15
even if one is wise.

---

[1] Cf. especially Solon F 13.7–13 *IEG;* Eur. *Ino* F 417.1–2.
[2] Cf. *Aeolus* F 22, *Danae* F 326.1–5 with notes.

ἔχειν δὲ πειρῶ· τοῦτο γὰρ τό τ' εὐγενὲς
15 καὶ τοὺς γάμους δίδωσι τοὺς πρώτους ἔχειν.
ἐν τῷ πένεσθαι δ' ἐστὶν ἥ τ' ἀδοξία,
κἂν ᾖ σοφός τις, ἥ τ' ἀτιμία βίου.

   φίλους δὲ τοὺς μὲν μὴ χαλῶντας ἐν λόγοις
κέκτησο· τοὺς δὲ πρὸς χάριν σὺν ἡδονῇ
20 τῇ σῇ πονηροὺς κλῇθρον εἰργέτω στέγης.

   ὁμιλίας δὲ τὰς γεραιτέρων φίλει,
ἀκόλαστ<α δ>' ἤθη λαμπρὰ συγγελᾶν μόνον
μίσει· βραχεῖα τέρψις ἡδονῆς κακῆς.

   ἐξουσίᾳ δὲ μήποτ' ἐντρυφῶν, τέκνον,
25 αἰσχροὺς ἔρωτας δημοτῶν διωκαθεῖν·
ὃ καὶ σίδηρον ἀγχόνας τ' ἐφέλκεται,
χρηστῶν πενήτων ἤν τις αἰσχύνῃ τέκνα.

   καὶ τοὺς πονηροὺς μήποτ' αὔξαν' ἐν πόλει·
κακοὶ γὰρ ἐμπλησθέντες ἢ νομίσματος
30 ἢ πόλεος ἐμπεσόντες εἰς ἀρχήν τινα
σκιρτῶσιν, ἀδόκητ' εὐτυχησάντων δόμων.

   ἀλλ' ὦ τέκνον μοι, δὸς χέρ', ὡς θίγῃ πατήρ,
καὶ χαῖρ'· ὑπ' αἰδοῦς δ' οὐ λίαν <σ'> ἀσπάζομαι·
γυναικόφρων γὰρ θυμὸς ἀνδρὸς οὐ σοφοῦ.

20 πονηροὺς Stob.: λέγοντας Herwerden
24 ἐντρυφῶν Kock: ἐξουσίαν . . . εὐτυχῶν Stob. 3.3.18: ἐξουσίᾳ
. . . εὐτυχῶν Stob. 3.17.6, whence ἐντυχῶν Gesner (and ed.
Trincavelli?)   30 ἀρχήν τινα Stob.: τιμάς τινας Plut.
31 ἀδόκητ' Plut., Stob. 4.2.4: ἀδίκως Stob. 3.3.18

Make friends of those who do not give way in discussions, and bar your door to those (who are) mischievous for your gratification and pleasure.[3]   20

Welcome the company of older men, and scorn unbridled behaviour which wins acclaim only by raising laughs: there's brief enjoyment in dishonourable pleasure.[4]

Never indulge your power,[5] my son, by pursuing shameful desires for commoners; this brings in its train cold steel   25
and knotted cords,[6] when someone shames the children of the worthy poor.

Never give villains advancement in the city. Scoundrels gorged with money, or falling into some office[7] in the city,   30
become unruly as their house prospers unexpectedly.[8]

And now, my son, give your hand to your father's touch, and fare well; restraint forbids me to embrace you excessively. It's an unwise man who shows a woman's spirit.

[3] Vv. 18–20 contrast good associates who speak out for the ruler's benefit with bad ones who speak only to please him: cf. Isocrates 1.30. For 'mischievous' ($\pi o \nu \eta \rho o i$) associates of bad rulers cf. Xenophon, *Education of Cyrus* 5.4.36. But the syntax here is awkward, hence Herwerden's 'those speaking'.   [4] On the influence of good and bad companions cf. *Andromache* 683–4, *Aegeus* F 7, *Peliades* F 609, *Phoenix* F 812.7–9, F 1024; and against laughter-seeking behaviour, *Melanippe Captive* F 492.
[5] Literally 'Never, luxuriating in your power, pursue . . . ' (Kock). Stob. 3.3.18 has 'Never, prospering as to power'; Gesner inferred 'Never, having chanced upon power' from Stob. 3.17.6. For the thought cf. *Suppliant Women* 452–5.   [6] Literally 'iron and nooses': the victims of the tyrant's sexual abuse will be driven to suicide.   [7] 'some office', Stobaeus; 'some privileges', Plutarch.   [8] Stobaeus in one place has 'unjustly' rather than 'unexpectedly'.

363

εἷς μὲν λόγος μοι δεῦρ᾽ ἀεὶ περαίνεται.

Aristophanes, *Lysistrata* 1135 with schol., and lexica

364

ἐκ τῶν πόνων τοι τἀγάθ᾽ αὔξεται βροτοῖς.

Stobaeus 3.29.9 and 3.29.22; Orion 7.2 Haffner; elsewhere in several places as a proverb. Stob. 3.29.22 and Orion add two verses identified by Stobaeus elsewhere with *Archelaus* (F 239).

365

⟨ΕΡΕΧΘΕΥΣ?⟩

αἰδοῦς δὲ καὐτὸς δυσκρίτως ἔχω πέρι·
καὶ δεῖ γὰρ αὐτῆς κἄστιν αὖ κακὸν μέγα.

Clement of Alexandria, *Miscellanies* 6.2.9.5

366

τοὐνθένδ᾽ ἀπίχθυς βαρβάρους οἰκεῖν δοκῶ.

Eustathius on Homer, *Odyssey* 12.251 citing Aristophanes of Byzantium F 48A Slater

367

ἐν ἀστρώτῳ πέδῳ
εὕδουσι, πηγαῖς δ᾽ οὐχ ὑγραίνουσιν πόδας.

Clement of Alexandria, *Miscellanies* 6.2.7.1; v. 2 πηγαῖς . . . πόδας: Eustathius on Homer, *Iliad* 16.235

363

One argument of mine extends thus far.

364

Men's goods increase because of their own efforts.

365

⟨ERECHTHEUS?⟩

I also am of two minds about self-restraint. It is needed, but it is also a great evil.[1]

[1] The contrast between 'good' *aidôs* (proper restraint) and 'bad' *aidôs* (disabling inhibition) goes back to Hesiod, *Works & Days* 318 (cf. Homer, *Iliad* 24.44–5); cf. also the enigmatic *Hippolytus* 385–7.

366

The region beyond is inhabited, I believe, by barbarians who eat no fish.[1]

[1] This seems comparable with Homer's description of men who know nothing of the sea because they live far from it (*Odyssey* 11.122–5), but the context is unknown: possibly from a description of Eumolpus' Thrace?

367

They sleep on uncovered ground and do not wet their feet with water.[1]

[1] A description of the Helloi or Selloi, priests of Zeus's oracle at Dodona: cf. Homer, *Iliad* 16.233–5; Sophocles, *Women of Trachis* 1166–8. The reference here has been variously explained: Erechtheus consulting Dodona, or the Dodonaean seer Skiros assisting Eumolpus, or Erechtheus thinking of Dodona as a refuge for his daughter (cf. *Phoenician Women* 977–85)?

EURIPIDES

369

ΧΟΡΟΣ

κείσθω δόρυ μοι μίτον ἀμφιπλέκειν ἀράχναις·
μετὰ δ' ἡσυχίας πολιῷ γήρᾳ συνοικῶν
ᾄδοιμι κάρα στεφάνοις πολιὸν στεφανώσας,
Θρηκίαν πέλταν πρὸς Ἀθάνας
5   περικίοσιν ἀγκρεμάσας θαλάμοις,
δελτῶν τ' ἀναπτύσσοιμι γή-
ρυν ᾷ σοφοὶ κλέονται.

Stobaeus 4.14.4; v. 1: Plutarch, *Life of Nicias* 9

2 συνοικῶν Cropp: συνοικοίην or -είην Stob.: σύνοικος Page

(370 N = 369d, brief fragment)

370

col. i *remains of two lines, then:*

<ΚΟΡΥΦΑΙΟΣ ἢ ΠΡΑΞΙΘΕΑ>

τί]ς ἂν πρὸς ἀγμοῖς Παλλάδος σταθεὶς‹ς› ποδὶ
κ]ῆρυξ γένοιτ' ἂν τῶν κατὰ στ‹ρ›ατόν, φίλοι;

<ΧΟΡΟΣ>

5   ἢ ποτ' ἀνὰ πόλιν ἀλαλαῖς 'ἰὴ παιὰν'
κ]αλλίνικον βοάσω μέλος

P. Sorbonne 2328, ed. C. Austin, *Recherches de Papyrologie* 4 (1967), 11–67 with Plates 1–2; some new readings by M. Fassino in *TrGF* 5.1161; vv. 21–2: Stobaeus 4.53.16

1–11 assigned to Chorus by Austin: 1–2, 5–11 to Chorus, 3–4 to Praxithea by Martínez

369

CHORUS

Let my spear lie idle for spiders to entangle in their webs;
and may I dwell peacefully with grey old age, singing my
songs, my grey head crowned with garlands, after hanging
a Thracian shield upon Athena's columned halls;[1] and may   5
I unfold the voice of the tablets in which the wise are cele-
brated.[2]

[1] A dedication in the Parthenon to mark retirement from mili-
tary service at the age of sixty; 'Thracian' suggests a shield cap-
tured from the invaders. For the association of song with old age
cf. *Heracles* 676–9.   [2] An allusion to books, unusual in trag-
edy: cf. *Alcestis* 962–9, *Hippolytus* 954.

(370 N = 369d, brief fragment)

370

remains of two lines, then:

⟨CHORUS LEADER *or* PRAXITHEA⟩

(Who) has stood by Pallas' cliffs,[1] my friends, and can be
our herald of how things stand with the army?

⟨CHORUS⟩
(chanting)

Shall I ever shout through the city the glorious victory
song, crying *Iē paiān*,[2] taking up the task of my aged hand,   5

[1] The steep north face of the Acropolis, overlooking the bat-
tlefield. This call for news raises expectation of the theatrical mes-
senger's arrival: cf. *Electra* 759, Aeschylus, *Seven against Thebes*
36–8.   [2] A cry appealing for or celebrating deliverance, usu-
ally directed to Apollo with whom the healing god Paieon had
come to be identified.

ἀναλαβόμενος [ἔρ]γον γεραιᾶς χερὸς,
Λίβυος ἀχάεντος [λω]τοῦ
κιθάριδος βοαῖς .... ε[..] ι τροχαλὸς
    ἐπομέναις;
10   ἆρα νέα γέροντι [κοι]νώσεται χοροῦ παρθένος;

ἀ]λλ᾽ εἰσορῶ γὰρ τόνδ᾽ ἀπὸ στρατοῦ πέλ[ας
        (about nine lines missing)

⟨ΑΓΓΕΛΟΣ⟩

col. ii μη.[... Ἐρεχθ]εὺς ὡς τροπαῖα[
         ἔστη[σε χώρ]ᾳ τῇδε βαρβά[ρ

⟨ΠΡΑΞΙΘΕΑ⟩

καλῶ[ς ἔλεξ]ας· ἀλλὰ τίς γαρειθ[

⟨ΑΓΓΕΛΟΣ⟩

15 πέπτ[ωκε..]......π.ρευ[

⟨ΠΡΑΞΙΘΕΑ⟩

πόσις δ᾽ Ἐρεχθεύς ἐστί μοι σεσ[ωμένος;

⟨ΑΓΓΕΛΟΣ⟩

μακάριός ἐστ᾽ ἐκεῖνος εὐδαίμων [τ᾽ ἀνήρ.

⟨ΠΡΑΞΙΘΕΑ⟩

εἰ ζῇ γε πόλεώς τ᾽ εὐτυχῆ νίκ[ην φέρει.

13 βαρβά[ρων κάτα Austin: βαρβά[ρου δορός (or στρα-
τοῦ) Reeve   15 πέπτ[ωκε δ]ὴ πρὸς ἧπαρ Εὔ[μολπος
τυπείς (e.g.) Austin and Page   17 [τ᾽ ἀνήρ Diggle: [θ᾽ ἅμα
Austin   18 φέρει Martínez, West: ἄγει Austin

the Libyan (lotus) pipe sounding to the cithara's cries . . .
wheeling along (with?) . . . following? Shall young girl
share with aged man in the dance?   10

⟨CHORUS LEADER⟩
But look, I see approaching here from our army . . .
                    (*about nine lines missing*)

⟨MESSENGER⟩
Do not(?) . . . for (Erechtheus) has set up a trophy . . . for   12
this (land over the) barbarian(s) (*or* the barbarian army).

⟨PRAXITHEA⟩
(You have spoken) well—but who . . .

⟨MESSENGER⟩
. . . has fallen . . . [3]   15

⟨PRAXITHEA⟩
And my husband Erechtheus—is he safe?

⟨MESSENGER⟩
He is a blessed and a fortunate (man).

⟨PRAXITHEA⟩
Yes, if he lives and (brings) our city's happy victory.

[3] Perhaps 'Eumolpus has fallen, struck to the heart' (Austin
and Page).

‹ΑΓΓΕΛΟΣ›

ὥστ' αὐτὰ ταῦτα .(.)ε.λα λειφθ[ῆναι

‹ΠΡΑΞΙΘΕΑ›

20 τί φῄς; τέθνηκεν ἢ φάος βλέπε[ι τόδε;

‹ΑΓΓΕΛΟΣ›

τέθνηκ'· ἐγὼ δὲ τοὺς καλῶς τεθνηκότας
ζῆν φημὶ μᾶλλον †τοῦ βλέπειν τοὺς μὴ καλῶς†.

*traces of one more line, then about 8 lines missing from end
of column*

(4 columns = about 80 lines missing)

col. iii *ten lines missing at top of column, then ends of ten lines
(23–32), some or all lyric, 25 and 28 at least delivered by
Praxithea, including the words* 23 δυστήνου μόρον, 25
ἐμὰς κόρας, 27 (ἐ)πίπτετε, 28 ἀπύουσα, 30 δωμάτων, 32
πρόσοψιν τέκνων

col. iv *about ten lines missing, then:*

‹ΧΟΡΟΣ›

traces of one line

Δηιοῦς κάρα· φερόμεθ' ἀγόμεθ' ἐπὶ δάκρυα·
35 σὲ δ'—αἰαῖ—διῆλθέ σ', οἴμοι.

19 .(.)ε.λα read by Fassino: σκῦλα Austin   λειφθ[ῆναι
μόνον Austin (πόλει Kamerbeek, θεοῖς Cropp)   22 so
Stobaeus (κοὐ Diels, τ' οὐ Tucker): possibly ζῆν .[. . .] μᾶλλον
καὶ οὐ[P. Sorb.   32 τέκνων read by Fassino: .ει . . . . . Austin
34 κάρα: κόρα Diggle, Collard

⟨MESSENGER⟩

He brings it, so that just these . . . (have been) left . . . ⁴

⟨PRAXITHEA⟩

What are you saying? He is dead, or still sees (this) light?   20

⟨MESSENGER⟩

He is dead—but those who have died nobly, I declare, live
more (than those who survive ignobly).⁵

*about one hundred lines lost including four whole columns
with the Messenger's report and beginning of the reaction
to it; then ends of ten lyric lines of Praxithea, or perhaps
Praxithea with Chorus, including* 23 wretched . . . 's *fate,*
25 *my daughters,* 27 *you are (or were) falling,* 28 *crying out
(or calling on),* 30 *the house,* 32 *sight of (my) children; then
about ten more lines missing; then:*

⟨CHORUS⟩

. . . head(?)⁶ of Deio. We are borne, we are driven, to tears.
But you—alas!—you it has pierced—o woe!   35

⁴ With Austin's reading (doubted by Fassino), 'just these spoils
(alone have been) left' ('left for the city', Kamerbeek; 'left for the
gods', Cropp).   ⁵ This is the likely sense of the original text,
but the wording is uncertain. Stobaeus has 'live more than those
who have died ignobly live'. The papyrus may have had 'live more,
and those who have died ignobly do not live'. For the sentiment
see on *Meleager* F 518.   ⁶ Perhaps part of an address to
Demeter (= Deio), phrased as for example Sophocles, *Antigone* 1.
But 'daughter of Deio' (Diggle, Collard) may well be right, i.e.
Persephone to whom Erechtheus' daughter was probably sacri-
ficed.

⟨ΠΡΑΞΙΘΕΑ⟩

αἰαῖ· τίν᾽ ἐπὶ πρῶτον, †ἢ σὲ τὰν {ἢ σὲ τὰν} ἢ σὲ
    τὰν φίλαν
παρθένων δραμων φρ . . μανει τάφῳ
. ακ . . α μέλεα προσεῖδον† . . . . ι . . . ν
κάτω πόσιν ἐμὸν στένω . . . .

40 φόνια φυσήματ᾽; ἢ σὲ τὰν πρὸ πόλεως
τόδ᾽ ἱερὸν ἀνίερον ὅσιον ἀνόσιον
. αι κορυφὴν απαταιθ[
οἱ]χόμεθ᾽ οἰχόμεθ᾽, ὦ π[

col. v   ὡς ἄδ]ακρύς τις ὠμόφρων ⟨θ᾽⟩ ὃς κακοῖς ἐμοῖς
    οὐ στένει.

⟨ΧΟΡΟΣ⟩

45 φεῦ φε]ῦ, ἰὼ Γᾶ, φεύγετε . . . . . . ν . . . .
πόνων] εἴ τί μοί ποτ᾽ εἴη τελευτά.
    ]γετε χώρας χθόνιος μ . . . . . . νοις
    ]ατας· ὀρχεῖται δὲ π[ό]λεος πέδον σάλῳ·
ἔνοσι]ν ἐμβάλλει Ποσειδῶν πόλει
50]ηπερ δυστανοτατα . . . . . . εμοι
    ]ων πόνοι πάρεισι, συμπίπτει στέγη·

36 so read (with deletion) by Fassino: ἢ σὲ τὰν πάτραν ἢ σὲ
τὰν φίλαν Austin: τὰν φιλᾶν Kamerbeek   37 δράμων P.
Sorb.: δράμω Collard: φρενομανεῖ (declined by Austin) Kamer-
beek: φρενομανὴς ἀφῶ | δάκρυα Diggle   38 τακερά? Aus-
tin: δάκρυα Diggle (see above)   41 τόδε read by Fassino,
τὸν by Austin   ἱερὸν ἀνίερον Diggle: ἀνίερον ἀνίερον P. Sorb.
49 ἔνοσι]ν Diggle   51 βάθρ]ων Austin: σεισμ]ῶν Diggle

<CPRAXITHEA>

Alas! To whom first, †to you or to you the dear one of my
daughters . . . in (my) . . . funeral rite . . . I have looked upon
your . . . limbs (?) . . . † (Or) shall I lament my husband be-
low . . . murderous blasts, or you, who for the city . . . this   40
holy and unholy, hallowed and unhallowed . . . the height
. . . ?[7] We are lost, we are lost, O . . . (how) incapable of
tears, and cruel, is anyone who does not lament my suffer-
ings.

(The earth trembles)

<CHORUS>

(Oh, Oh!) O Earth! Flee . . . if there could ever be any end   45
(of my sufferings) . . . the land's subterranean . . . The city's
ground dances with the quaking! Poseidon is hurling (an
earthquake) on the city . . . most miserabl(y?) . . . for me(?)   50
Here are tribulations . . . [8] the roof is falling in . . . we are

---

[7] The text of vv. 36–42 is very uncertain. In 36 Austin's reading
gave awkward sense, 'to you my fatherland, or to you the dear one
amongst my daughters'. Probably Praxithea addresses first the two
daughters who have killed themselves and whose bodies may now
lie before her (36–8, cf. 68–70), then her husband Erechtheus
who was swallowed up into the earth (38–40), then the daughter
who was sacrificed and whose body will not have been brought
back to the palace (40–2). Fassino's reading in 36 and the sugges-
tions of Collard and Kameerbeek in 36–7 might then give: 'To
which—to you, or to you—of my dear daughters shall I run in my
distraught funeral rite'. Diggle suggests in 37–8 '. . . shall I, dis-
traught, release my tears'. In v. 41 we translate Diggle's adjust-
ment; the papyrus has 'this unholy, unholy, hallowed and unhal-
lowed . . .'   [8] 'troubles for foundations', Austin; 'troubles
from quakes', Diggle.

].ασενστρααος οἰχόμεθα....πάσαις

one line largely illegible

....].ας πόδα δὲ βακχεύων.

⟨ΑΘΗΝΑ⟩

55 αὐδῶ τρία⟨ι⟩ναν τῆσδ᾽ ἀπο⟨σ⟩τρέφειν χθονός,
πόντιε Πόσειδον, μηδὲ γῆν ἀναστατοῦν
πόλιν τ᾽ ἐρείπειν τὴν ἐμὴν ἐπήρατον·
μὴ δεύτερόν σοι δοῖεν ....οι·
οὐχ εἷς ἄδην σ᾽ ἔπλησεν; οὐ κατὰ χθονὸς

60 κρύψας Ἐρεχθέα τῆς ἐμῆς ᾔψω φρενός;
κἄπε]ιτα μέλλεις ταῦτα ....ρα
... ν]ερτεροι[.............].σεν θεά;
σὺ δ᾽,] ὦ χθονὸς [σώτειρα Κηφισοῦ] κόρη,

col. vi ἄκου᾽ Ἀθάνας τῆς ἀμήτορο[ς λό]γους·

65 καὶ πρῶτα μέν σοι σημανῶ παι[δὸς] πέρι
ἣν τῆσδε χώρας σὸς προθύεται [πόσι]ς·
θάψον νιν οὗπερ ἐξέπνευσ᾽ ο[ἰκτ]ρὸν βίον,
καὶ τάσδ᾽ ἀδελφὰς ἐν τάφῳ τ[αὐτ]ῷ χθονὸς
γενναιότητος οὕνεχ᾽, αἵτιν[ες φί]λης

70 ὅρκους ἀδελφῆς οὐκ ἐτόλμησα[ν λι]πεῖν.
ψυχαὶ μὲν οὖν τῶνδ᾽ οὐ βεβᾶσ᾽ [Ἅιδ]ην πάρα,
εἰς δ᾽ αἰθέρ᾽ αὐτῶν πνεῦμ᾽ ἐγὼ [κ]ατῴκισα·

52 begining so read by Fassino:].ασεν στρατός, Austin
54 so read by Fassino: ἐν δώ]μασι⟨ν⟩ πάλαι βακχεύων Austin
58 μὴ δεύτερόν read by Fassino: μηδ᾽ εὐτυχῆ, and perhaps at end
θεοί, Austin: μὴ δεύτερόν σοι δοῖεν εὐτυχεῖν θεοί Collard
61 end δὴ τελεσφόρα? Austin: σωφρονέστερα Fassino

lost . . . all . . . (*one illegible line*) . . . and dancing in frenzy.[9]

(*The goddess Athena appears above*)

<ATHENA>

I call on you to avert your trident from this country, sea god   55
Poseidon; do not uproot my land, nor ruin my fair city. May
. . . not give you a second . . . [10] Has one (victim) not satis-
fied you? Have you not clutched at my heart by confining
Erechtheus below the earth? (And) do you (then) intend   60
(*or* wait) . . . these . . . [11] (for?) the nether powers . . . god-
dess . . . ?

(And you, daughter of Cephisus),[12] saviour of this land,
hear now the words of motherless Athena.[13] First I shall in-
struct you concerning your child whom your (husband)   65
caused to be sacrificed for this country. Bury her where
she breathed out her (lamented) life, and these sisters also
in (the same) earth tomb, in recognition of their nobility,
as they did not allow themselves to forsake their pledges to
their dear sister. Therefore these girls' souls have not gone   70
down to (Hades), but I have lodged their spirits in the

---

[9] Austin's reading gives 'dancing in frenzy long since in the pal-
ace'.   [10] With Austin's readings, 'May the gods not give you a
successful . . . ' Collard suggests 'May the gods not permit you to
succeed a second time'.   [11] Perhaps 'these effectual (ac-
tions)' (Austin), or 'these more temperate (actions)' (Fassino).
[12] See test. ii above with note.   [13] Athena was born from the
head of Zeus after he swallowed her mother Metis (Hesiod, *The-
ogony* 886–900). The reference here seems to emphasize her de-
tachment from Praxithea's maternal grief.

ὄνομα δὲ κλεινὸν θήσομαι κα[θ᾽ Ἑλλ]άδα
Ὑακινθίδας βροτοῖσι κικλή[σκε]ιν θεάς.

75 ἐπει..........κα.οιχετητ[....]μένη
τοῦ συ........... ὑακίν[θου γ]άνος
καὶ γῆν ἔσωσε, τοῖς ἐμοῖς ἀστο[ῖς λέγ]ω
ἐνιαυσίαις σφας μὴ λελησμ[ένους] χρόνῳ
θυσίαισι τιμᾶν καὶ σφαγαῖσι [βουκ]τόνοις

80 κοσμοῦ[ντας ἱ]εροῖς παρθένων [χορεύ]μασιν·
γνον[..... ἐ]χθρ. εἰς μάχη[ν
κινῇ [......]ας ἀσπίδα στρατ[

col. vii πρώταισι θύειν πρότομα πολεμίου δορὸς
τῆς οἰνοποιοῦ μὴ θιγόντας ἀμπέλου

85 μηδ᾽ εἰς πυρὰν σπένδοντας ἀλλὰ πολυπόνου
καρπὸν μελίσσης ποταμίαις πηγαῖς ὁμοῦ·
ἄβατον δὲ τέμενος παισὶ ταῖσδ᾽ εἶναι χρεών,
εἴργειν τε μή τις πολεμίων θύσῃ λαθὼν
νίκην μὲν αὐτοῖς, γῇ δὲ τῇδε πημονήν.

81–2 γνόν[τας δ᾽ ὅτ᾽ ἐ]χθρὸς εἰς μάχη[ν ὁρμώμενος | κινῇ
[πρὸς ὑμ]ᾶς ἀσπίδα στρατ[ηλατῶν (e.g.) Austin (γνόν[τας
δ᾽ Kamerbeek, ὅτ᾽ Treu)

14 This recognition of the girls' valour recalls part of the epitaph
for Athenian soldiers fallen at Poteidaia (*IG* I³ 1179), 'Heaven has
received their souls, and earth their bodies'. The idea that the soul
or spirit might naturally escape to the heavens after death was also
current in Euripides' time; cf. *Chrysippus* F 839.8–14 with note.
15 The Attic historian Phanodemus (4th c. B.C., cited in *TrGF* test.
*vib) said the burial site was on the 'Hyacinthus Hill', perhaps the

heaven,[14] and shall establish for them a renowned name—
'Hyacinthid goddesses'—which mortals shall call them by
throughout all Greece.[15] (And) since . . . the hyacinth's   75
sheen and preserved the land, I (instruct) my citizens to
honour them—never forgetting this over time—with an-
nual sacrifices and slayings of (oxen), adorning these ritu-
als with sacred maiden dances.[16] (I instruct them also,   80
whenever they) learn (that an) enemy (is setting forth) for
battle and moving his army (against you on campaign), to
offer to these maidens first the pre-campaign sacrifice, not
touching the wine-producing vine nor pouring wine on the
altar,[17] but rather the produce of the industrious bee mixed   85
with stream-water. These maidens should have a sanctuary
that is untrodden, and no enemy should be allowed to
make covert offerings there, getting victory for them and
affliction for this land.[18]

one now known as the Hill of the Nymphs. The identification of
the Erechtheids with the Hyacinthids replaced the identification
of the latter as daughters of a Spartan immigrant, Hyacinthus, who
in myth had also sacrificed themselves for Athens (cf. Apollodorus
3.15.8). In reality Hyacinthus and Hyacinthides were originally
names for deities promoting vegetation and perhaps child-
growth.   [16] The festival prescribed may be the Panatheaea:
cf. *Children of Heracles* 777–83. On the rituals for the Hya-
cinthids in vv. 79–80 and 83–6, and for Erechtheus in v. 94, see G.
Ekroth, *The Sacrificial Rituals of Greek Hero-Cults* (Liège, 2002),
172–6, 186–9.   [17] Vine-wood and wine were excluded from
use in the fuel and libations for sacrifices to some deities (e.g. the
Furies in Aeschylus, *Eumenides* 107).   [18] For this guarding
of the heroized girls' protective power cf. *Children of Heracles*
1030–44 (Eurystheus' tomb) and Sophocles, *Oedipus at Colonus*
1520–35 (Oedipus' tomb).

πόσει δὲ τῷ σῷ σηκὸν ἐν μέσῃ πόλει
τεῦξαι κελεύω περιβόλοισι λαΐνοις·
κεκλήσεται δὲ τοῦ κτανόντος οὕνεκα
Σεμνὸς Ποσειδῶν ὄνομ' ἐπωνομασμένος
ἀστοῖς Ἐρεχθεὺς ἐν φοναῖσι βουθύτοις.

σοὶ δ', ἢ πόλεως τῆσδ' ἐξανώρθωσας βάθρα,
δίδωμι βωμοῖς τοῖς ἐμοῖσιν ἔμπυρα
πόλει προθύειν ἱερέαν κεκλημένην.

ἃ μὲν κατ' αἶαν τήνδε ⟨δεῖ⟩ 'κπονεῖν κλύεις,
ἃ δ' αὖ δικάζει Ζεὺς πατὴρ ἐν οὐρανῷ
100   λέγοιμ' ἄν· Εὔμολπος γὰρ Εὐμόλπου γεγὼ[ς
col. viii   *beginnings of 17 lines completing Athena's speech, then be-*
ginning of Praxithea's reply:

101 τοῦ κατθ[ανόντος	105 μίαν δε.[
102 Δημητρ[	106 καὶ τὴν τ
103 ὃν χρὴ γεν[έσθαι	107 Ὑάσιν δεμ.[
104 γήμαντ[	108 ἄ..(.)ων λ.[

98 τηνδεεκ- (hence τήνδε ⟨δεῖ⟩'κ-) Austin: τοισιδεκ-
(hence τοῖσδε ⟨δεῖ⟩'κ-) Fassino   101 end τοῦδε πέμπτος
ἔκγονος (e.g.) West   108 ἄστρων read by Austin, ἄρτων
by Fassino

19 Athena's instructions give an origin for the 'Erechtheum',
also known as the temple of Athena Polias (Pausanias 1.26.6; J. M.
Hurwit, *The Acropolis in the Age of Pericles* [Cambridge, 2004],
164–80 with CD-ROM images 120–32). This complex structure
in its classical form was planned or under construction when

For your husband I command that a precinct be built in
mid-city, with stone surrounds; and on account of his killer   90
he shall be called August Poseidon surnamed Erechtheus,
by the citizens in their sacrifices of oxen.[19]

To you, Praxithea, who have restored this city's founda-
tions, I grant the right to make burnt sacrifices for the city   95
on my altars, and to be called my priestess.[20]

You have heard what (must) be brought to pass in this
land; and now I shall tell you the judgement that Zeus my
father in heaven passes.[21] Eumolpus, born from Eumolpus
who (has died) . . . [22] Demeter . . . he is (to become) . . . mar-   100
rying . . . and one (*fem.*) . . . and the (*fem.*) . . . and to (*or* for)   105

Erechtheus was produced. It incorporated Athena's olive tree,
Poseidon's salt spring with the marks of his trident blow, and an
altar of Erechtheus. In it the cults of Athena Polias, Poseidon
and Erechtheus were all administered by the family of the Eteo-
boutadai. The identification of Erechtheus with Poseidon here re-
flects their strong association as chthonic powers in Athenian cult
and ideology: cf. Lacore 1983 (bibl. above), M. Christopoulos
in R. Hägg, *Ancient Greek Cult Practice from the Epigraphical
Evidence* (Stockholm, 1994), 123–30. For the sacrifices of oxen
see Ekroth (n. 16 above).   [20] Praxithea becomes the first
priestess of Athena Polias (see previous note). The rituals at the
beginning of the play foreshadow this (F 350–1).   [21] Zeus's
authority is needed to settle the dispute over the ownership of
Attica, and to assign to Eumolpus and his descendants their des-
tined role in connection with the cult of Demeter and Persephone
at Eleusis (see Introduction above).   [22] West suggests 'born
as fifth descendant from Eumolpus who died here', comparing
the genealogy given by Andron, *FGrH* 10 F 13.

109 Δηιοῦς μι[
110 ἄρρητά γε[
111 πόνος τε.[
112 σεμνῶν .[
113 Ἑρμοῦ το[

114 Κήρυκες [
115 ἀλλ᾽ ἴσχε .
116 οἰκτρὰς ἀν[τ
117 καὶ ταπε[

⟨ΠΡΑΞΙΘΕΑ⟩

118 δέσποινα .[119 ο]ἰκτροὶ με[

the Hyades[23] . . .[24] of/from Deio[25] . . . (things) not to be ut-
tered . . . toil (or trouble) . . . of/from the holy . . . of/from   110
Hermes . . . Heralds . . . [26] But restrain . . . piteous (cries?)   115
. . . and . . .

⟨PRAXITHEA⟩

Mistress . . . (we are?) pitiable . . .

[23] According to a scholiast on Aratus, *Phaenomena* 172, Eurip-
ides here identified the Erechtheids/Hyacinthids with the Hyades
(rain nymphs, and stars in the constellation Taurus). The associa-
tion may validate Athena's assurance that she has 'lodged their
spirits in the heaven (*aether*)', v. 72. The Hyades also had a child-
nursing role similar to that of the Hyacinthides (n. 15 above): cf.
Kearns 61, J. Larson, *Greek Heroine Cults* (Madison, 1995), 189–
90 n. 5.   [24] Austin's reading 'stars' can be associated with the
mention of the Hyades; Fassino's 'loaves' is less easy to accommo-
date.   [25] Demeter, as in v. 34.   [26] Vv. 110–4 referred
to the secrets of the Eleusinian mysteries (110) and the priestly
family of the Kerykes ('Heralds') who claimed descent from Keryx
son of Hermes.

EURYSTHEUS

Pechstein 145–76; Krumeich 422–30; H. Van Looy in ed. Budé VIII.2.133–41.

Gantz 381, 389–90; *LIMC* V.i.92 (cf. 44–6) under 'Herakles' and VIII.i.580 'Eurystheus'.

Through the hostility of the goddess Hera to many irregular children of her husband Zeus, his son Heracles performed the famous Twelve Labours for Eurystheus king of Mycenae (how Hera tricked Zeus, so that a mere mortal dominated his own son, is told in Homer, Iliad *19.95–124; cf. on* Alcmene *F 89 above).*

The satyr play Eurystheus *burlesqued the story of the Twelfth Labour, the fetching from Hades of the dog Cerberus (this is part of the background to the deeply tragic* Heracles, *and* Children of Heracles *ends with Eurystheus' eventual fall and death).* Eurystheus *intended the task to be fatal (cf.* Heracles *22–5, 610–7 etc., also Polydectes' plot against Perseus in* Dictys, *and Proetus' against Bellerophon in* Stheneboea). *F 372 has Heracles taking orders from Eurystheus, presumably soon after the play's start; but the other fragments give no clear idea of the plot, which we must guess from the outline known in myth and inferred from many vase-paintings of Heracles' feat with Cerberus (LIMC 'Herakles' nos. 2097–2136). F 371 is ad-*

dressed to Silenus as 'father' of the satyrs, but this is regular in such plays (e.g. Cyclops 84). If F 377 refers not to Heracles' own 'bastardy' (for his 'mixed' parentage see Introduction to Alcmene*) but to Theseus' doubtful parentage (Pechstein 158; cf.* Aegeus *F 1 and 2), this hero will have figured in the play too, for myth generally had Heracles not only returning with Cerberus but at the same time saving Theseus (*Heracles *619, 1169–70), who had gone there unsuccessfully to retrieve his friend Pirithous (see* Pirithous *in the Appendix at the end of this edition).*

The scene must be Mycenae; Heracles goes to Hades (cf. F 379a, 380) and returns with Cerberus; Eurystheus is doubly thwarted in his design, perhaps comically, for the dog may have terrified him (F 372 may even point to a giant theatrical dog, perhaps two men inside a kind of 'working model' or mock-up like a pantomime horse): a Caeretan hydria of c. 530–20 B.C. *has Heracles bringing Cerberus to Eurystheus, who then hides in panic in a great jar (LIMC 'Herakles' no. 2616). So Euripides may not be original in diverting to this Twelfth Labour Eurystheus' panic when Heracles brings him either the Erymanthine boar or the Nemean lion (cf. Gantz 389–90). At any rate the play would have ended probably with some means of dealing with Cerberus and certainly with Heracles' release from bondage to the humiliated Eurystheus, and with that of the satyrs themselves from their slavery to him (such release is common in satyr plays; cf. Cyclops 679, 701–9).*

Brief fragments: F 379 'a deep cup' and F 380 'Tartarean'. Other ascriptions: F 863 (also ascribed to Syleus), 936 (also to Pirithous); adesp. F 658 (two damaged papyrus fragments with 24 lines relating to Heracles fetching Cerberus: see under Pirithous, Other ascriptions.

There is no evidence for the date, but Krumeich 430, noting that the delivery of Cerberus to Eurystheus is anticipated in Heracles (610–7, 1386–7), suggests that Eurystheus *may have been the satyr play in the same production, near 415* B.C. *The only other play perhaps with this subject was Sophocles'* Cerberus, *of which there is only one fragment and the plot is a complete blank.*

ΕΥΡΥΣΘΕΥΣ

371

ΗΡΑΚΛΗΣ

πέμψεις δ᾽ ἐς Ἅιδου ζῶντα κοὐ τεθνηκότα·
καί μοι τὸ τέρθρον δῆλον οἷ πορεύομαι.

Erotian τ 29

372

οὐκ ἔστιν, ὦ γεραιέ, μὴ δείσῃς τάδε·
τὰ Δαιδάλεια πάντα κινεῖσθαι δοκεῖ
βλέπειν τ᾽ ἀγάλμαθ᾽· ὧδ᾽ ἀνὴρ κεῖνος σοφός.

Schol. on *Hecuba* 838: vv. 2–3: Tzetzes, *Chiliades* 1.521–2

3 βλέπειν Schmidt: λέγειν Schol.

373

πᾶς δ᾽ ἐξεθέρισεν ὥστε πύρινον ⟨στάχυν⟩
σπάθῃ κολούων φασγάνου μελανδέτου.

Pollux 10.145

1 πᾶς δὲ φασγάνῳ ἐξεθέρισεν ὥστε πύρινον Pollux: corr.
and suppl. Pierson: τὰς δὲ (sc. κεφαλάς) Weil

EURYSTHEUS

371
HERACLES

You will be sending a living man into Hades, and not a dead one; and the end towards which I make my way is clear to me.

372

They are not real, old man; do not fear them: all the figures made by Daedalus seem to move and look, so clever is that man![1]

[1] Daedalus was the mythical constructor of lifelike, and seemingly alive, figures; cf. also Euripides, *Hecuba* 838, where the Scholia cite this fragment with 'move and speak', since the figures are evoked there for their artificial voices. Daedalus constructs an artificial cow for Pasiphae in *Cretans*: see Introduction with F 988 there.

373

Everyone made harvest, as if of ears (of corn), slashing with the blades of their black swords.[1]

[1] A reference to the killing of the many-headed Hydra, one of Heracles' earlier Labours—but 'everyone' makes sense only if Silenus the father of the satyrs is claiming that they helped Heracles (as Dionysus does in *Cyclops* 5–8). Weil conjectured 'He made harvest of them (i.e. the heads) . . . '

374

ἢ κύαθον ἢ χαλκήλατον
ἠθμὸν προσίσχων τοῖσδε τοῖς ὑπωπίοις.

Pollux 10.108

375

†πιστὸν μὲν οὖν εἶναι χρὴ τὸν διάκονον
τοιοῦτον τ᾽ εἶναι† καὶ στέγειν τὰ δεσποτῶν.

Stobaeus 4.19.6 (text unmetrical and tautologous)

376

οὐκ οἶδ᾽ ὅτῳ χρὴ κανόνι τὰς βροτῶν τύχας
ὀρθῶς ἀθρήσαντ᾽ εἰδέναι τί δραστέον.

Stobaeus 4.34.41

2 τί Meineke: τὸ Stob.

377

μάτην δὲ θνητοὶ τοὺς νόθους φεύγουσ᾽ ἄρα
παῖδας φυτεύειν· ὃς γὰρ ἂν χρηστὸς φύῃ,
οὐ τοὔνομ᾽ αὐτοῦ τὴν φύσιν διαφθερεῖ.

Stobaeus 4.24.44

374

. . . applying a ladle or a hammered strainer to these black eyes of mine.[1]

[1] Treatment for contusion like cupping: Aristophanes, *Peace* 541–2.

375

†So a servant must be faithful and be such† and keep his master's business secret.

376

I do not know by what measure one rightly considers the fortunes of men, and knows what is to be done.

377

So it is vain for men to avoid getting bastard sons; the name will not corrupt the nature of anyone born virtuous.[1]

[1] Compare *Antigone* F 168, *Andromeda* F 141 with note.

378

νῦν δ᾽ ἤν τις οἴκων πλουσίαν ἔχῃ φάτνην,
πρῶτος γέγραπται τῶν κακιόνων κράτει·
τὰ δ᾽ ἔργ᾽ ἐλάσσω χρημάτων νομίζομεν.

Stobaeus 4.31.42

2 τῶν κακιόνων κράτει Stob.: τῶν τ᾽ ἀμεινόνων κρατεῖ
Herwerden

379a (= 933 N)

†βάσκανον μέγιστον ψυχαγωγόν†

Lexicon Vindobonense ψ 6; possibly alluded to at Photius,
Lexicon β 81 Theodoridis

378

Now if anyone keeps a rich board[1] at his house, he is listed first on the authority of his inferiors;[2] and we regard his actions less than we do his money.

[1] Literally 'manger', possibly a colloquialism: cf. *Stheneboea* F 670.2.   [2] Because they sponge on him; alternatively, 'he is listed first and is (judged) superior to his betters' (Herwerden).

379a (= 933 N)

† . . . sorcerer, very great, conjuring up the dead . . . †[1]

[1] In this play a reference to Heracles, possibly to his recovery of Theseus from Hades (see Introduction above). The Greek is corrupt, however, and the word translated 'conjuring up the dead' is paraphrased with the adjectives 'malicious' and 'dreadful'.

THERISTAE, 'HARVESTERS'
(ΘΕΡΙΣΤΑΙ)

Pechstein 284–6; H. Van Looy in ed. Budé VIII.2.143–4; Krumeich 476.

This satyr play was lost except as a title by about 200 B.C., the approximate date of the hypothesis (by Aristophanes of Byzantium) to Medea, *which notes that it was produced with* Medea, Dictys *and* Philoctetes *in the year 431 but 'is not preserved'. There have been attempts to infer its content from comparisons with (1) Sositheus'* Daphnis or Lityerses *(early 3rd c. B.C.: TrGF 99 F 1a–2a), a satyr play in which Lityerses compelled passers-by to join him in harvesting his crops and at the end of the day cut off their heads and bound their bodies in with the sheaves; and with (2) Euripides' satyric* Syleus, *in which the name-character compelled passers-by to dig up his vines before killing them and burning them with the roots. It was suggested in the 19th century that* Syleus *had a chorus of harvesters and acquired the name* Harvesters *as an alternative. For an account of such speculations see Pechstein (above).*

THESEUS

H. Van Looy in ed. Budé VIII.2.145–65.

E. Simon, *Antike Kunst* 6 (1963), 14–16; Webster 105–9, 303; Trendall–Webster III.3.50–1; Aélion (1986) 223–30; Gantz 260–70; *LIMC* III.i.1050–77 'Ariadne', VII.i.922–55 'Theseus' (esp. 940–3); S. Mills (1997: see bibl. for *Aegeus*), 252–5.

King Minos of Crete compelled the Athenians to send him seven youths and seven maidens every ninth year as an of- fering to the Minotaur, the monstrous offspring of his wife Pasiphae whose story Euripides used in Cretans. *On the third occasion the young Theseus volunteered himself and succeeded in killing the Minotaur and escaping from the Labyrinth with the help of Ariadne, who had fallen in love with him, and of Daedalus, architect of the Labyrinth. Theseus had promised to marry Ariadne but on the home- ward voyage he left her on the island of Naxos where Dio- nysus claimed her as his bride; Theseus later married an- other daughter of Minos, Phaedra. This story is well known from mythographic summaries such as Diodorus 4.61.4–5 and Apollodorus,* Epit. *1.7–9, and from the lengthy ac- count in Plutarch,* Theseus *17–23. It is mentioned in early epic, appears frequently on archaic vases, and was proba- bly given its canonical Athenocentric shape by a 6th c. epic*

Theseis *(now entirely lost) and the 5th c. Athenian my-*
thographer Pherecydes (FGrH 3 F 148). The fragmentary
hypothesis in P. Oxy. 4640 (= test. iiia below) confirms that
it was the subject of Euripides' Theseus.

The hypothesis and fragments suggest only a broad
dramatic outline. The play was probably set before Minos'
palace with the Labyrinth close by. A chorus of Cretan men
or women associated with Minos or Ariadne is likely, while
Theseus' companions (F 385–6) made a secondary chorus.
The arrival of Theseus' ship (test. iiia.1) was probably re-
ported by the Herdsman in the first episode (F 382: cf. the
herdsman in Iphigenia in Tauris). *Theseus and his com-*
rades would then have been brought to Minos, and the la-
ment of Theseus' companions (F 385–6) sung at some point
before they were taken to the Labyrinth. How Theseus en-
countered Ariadne is unclear, but the hypothesis suggests
that the two of them jointly obtained Daedalus' assistance
(test. iiia.3–7). The action in the Labyrinth must have been
reported by an eye-witness (F 386a, *386aa, **386b?),
perhaps to Minos himself (test. iiia.8) by one of his ser-
vants. Ariadne then persuaded her angered father to ac-
cept the fait accompli *and departed with Theseus (test.*
iiia.8–14; F 387?). Her separation from him and Theseus'
later marriage with Phaedra were probably announced
by a god instructing Minos at the end of the play (test.
iiia.14–17), perhaps by Athena herself who in some ac-
counts ordered Theseus to abandon Ariadne. E. Simon
plausibly suggested that F 388 recommending 'temperate'
love comes from Athena's speech at the end of the play, and
that this ending is reflected in a late 5th c. vase (LIMC
'Ariadne' no. 94, Trendall–Webster III.3.50, Todisco A 63)
which shows Athena crowning Theseus as he boards his

ship under Poseidon's supervision, while Dionysus calmly approaches Ariadne to claim her as his destined bride.

Ascription of F **386b to Theseus is uncertain (see note there). Brief fragment: F 390 'fellow citizen' (Theseus appealing to Daedalus?). Other ascriptions: Aegeus F 7 and 7a (ascriptions confused in the sources), F 926 (see apparatus for F **386b.7), F 964. P. Oxy. 2452 has fragments of an unidentified play on the same subject which are tentatively ascribed to Sophocles' Theseus in TrGF 4 (F **730); cf. Lloyd-Jones in the Loeb Sophocles Fragments, 344–5, Mills 245–52.

Parodies in Aristophanes' Wasps (F 385–6) place Theseus before 422 B.C. Sophocles' Theseus is a blank except perhaps for P. Oxy. 2452, and nothing is known of the plays with this title produced in the same period by Achaeus and Hera(clides?) (TrGF nos. 20 and 37).

The character of Euripides' play is hard to establish from the fragments, but he may have given the love-struck Ariadne a pivotal role (cf. test. iiia.5–6, 10–13) while also treating her love for Theseus with some ambivalence so as to justify their final separation (see above on F 388, and Mills 254–5). Eroticization of the story is evident in art from the late 5th century onwards and in later poetry (especially Catullus 64.52–264 and Ovid, Heroides 10 and Ars Amatoria 1.527–64, all discussed by R. Armstrong, Cretan Women [Oxford, 2006], 187–260). It has inspired countless works of European art, literature and music down to the present day (OGCMA I.204–14).

ΘΗΣΕΥΣ

test. iiia (Hypothesis)

　　　　　　]ν ὑπομείνας· ἐπεὶ δ᾽ εἰς τὴν Κρήτην
μετὰ τῶν ἄλλων π]αρεγενήθη παίδων, εἰσαχθεὶς εἰς τὸν
λαβύρινθον τὸν Με]ινώταυρον ἀπέκτεινεν καὶ ῥᾳδί-
ως τὴν ἔξοδον ηὗρε]ν Δαιδάλου βοηθήσαντος αὐτῷ·
5　ἐγένετο γὰρ ἐκεῖν]ος Ἀθηναῖος, καὶ τῆς τοῦ βασιλέως
θυγατρὸς Ἀριάδνης] Θησεῖ συναγωνιώσης πρὸς εὐσεβῆ
　　　　　　]υχθεὶς διακονεῖν οὐκ ἀπώκνησεν·
ὁ δὲ Μείνως τὴν ἀπ]ώλειαν αἰσθόμενος τοῦ Μεινωταύ-
ρου　　　　　]ω τοὺς περὶ Θησέα τὸν κίνδυνον
10　　　　　　]ως τῆς Ἀριάδνης ἐπιθυμίας ὑπη-
ρέτην?　　ἡ δὲ τ]ὸν μὲν πατέρα πρῶτον ἔπεις σ᾽εν τὸν
　　　　　ἀ]ξιῶσαι, τὸν δὲ Θησέα παρεστήσατο
　　　　　]εντος ἀποπλεῖν ἑαυτὴν ἀναλαβόν-
τα· Θησεὺς μὲν οὖν] Ἀθήνας εὐπλόησεν, Ἀ[ρ]ιάδνην
15　δὲ　　　　] ἔγημε· Μείνω δεθυμ......με
　　　　　] κελεύσασα γάμῳ τὴν ὁ[ρ]γὴν μεσο-
λαβεῖν/-όντα?　　] τὴν νεωτέραν θυγατέρα π[

P. Oxy. 4640 col. i.1–18 (followed by hypothesis of *Hippolytus Veiled*), ed. M. van Rossum-Steenbeek (2003) with cooperation of R. Kannicht and J. Diggle; supplements in ed. pr. (vv. 2, 5, 11 Diggle)

418

THESEUS

test. iiia (Hypothesis)

... enduring ... And when he arrived in Crete (with the other) children, after being taken into the (Labyrinth), he killed the Minotaur and easily (found the way out) with the help of Daedalus; for (Daedalus was born) Athenian, and as the king's (daughter Ariadne) was aiding Theseus in his struggle, he did not shrink from ... towards a righteous ... and assisting them.[1] When (Minos) learned of (the) destruction of the Minotaur (and) ... (that) Theseus and his companions (had escaped) the danger ... Ariadne's desire ... But she first persuaded her father to consider ... deserving of ..., and induced Theseus ... to sail away with herself on board. (Now Theseus) made a fair voyage to Athens, but ... (he did not) marry (or Dionysus married?) Ariadne. And when Minos ... (Athena?) ordered him (to put an end to) his anger with a marriage ... his younger daughter ... 5 10 15

[1] 'he did not shrink from being bound by an oath and assisting them towards a righteous accomplishment (or bloodshed)' van Rossum, Kannicht; 'when summoned to a righteous transgression he did not shrink from assisting them', Diggle.

---

7 ... (ἐν) ὅρκῳ ζε]υχθεὶς (e.g.) van Rossum (πρᾶξιν or φόνον preceding, Kannicht): παρανομίαν εἰσκηρ]υχθεὶς (e.g.) Diggle   9–10 ἐπέγνω ... | φυγόντας (e.g.) van Rossum   14 or (e.g.) καὶ πεμφθεὶς ὑπ'] Ἀθηνᾶς Kannicht   15 ἐν Νάξῳ λιπὼν οὐκ] Diggle: ἐν Νάξῳ Διόνυσος] Kannicht

381

σχεδὸν παρ᾽ αὐτοῖς κρασπέδοις Εὐρωπίας

Stephanus of Byzantium, Ἐυρώπη᾽ (p. 287.11 Meineke)

382

ΠΟΙΜΗΝ

ἐγὼ πέφυκα γραμμάτων μὲν οὐκ ἴδρις,
μορφὰς δὲ λέξω καὶ σαφῆ τεκμήρια.
κύκλος τις ὡς τόρνοισιν ἐκμετρούμενος,
οὗτος δ᾽ ἔχει σημεῖον ἐν μέσῳ σαφές·
5 τὸ δεύτερον δὲ πρῶτα μὲν γραμμαὶ δύο,
ταύτας διείργει δ᾽ ἐν μέσαις ἄλλη μία·
τρίτον δὲ βόστρυχός τις ὡς εἰλιγμένος·
τὸ δ᾽ αὖ τέταρτον ἡ μὲν εἰς ὀρθὸν μία,
λοξαὶ δ᾽ ἐπ᾽ αὐτῆς τρεῖς κατεστηριγμέναι
10 εἰσίν· τὸ πέμπτον δ᾽ οὐκ ἐν εὐμαρεῖ φράσαι·
γραμμαὶ γάρ εἰσιν ἐκ διεστώτων δύο,
αὗται δὲ συντρέχουσιν εἰς μίαν βάσιν·
τὸ λοίσθιον δὲ τῷ τρίτῳ προσεμφερές.

Athenaeus 10.454b

(383 + 384 N = 386c below)

385 + 386

ΠΑΙΔΕΣ ΑΘΗΝΑΙΟΙ

385   τί με δῆτ᾽, ὦ μελέα μᾶτερ, ἔτικτες;

* * *

386   ἀνόνατον ἄγαλμ᾽, ⟨ὦ⟩ πάτερ, οἴκοισι τεκών

Aristophanes, Wasps 312, 314 with Schol.

THESEUS

381

Nearly on the very fringes of Europe.[1]

[1] Probably referring to Crete.

382

HERDSMAN

I am not acquainted with letters, but will tell you their
shapes and identify them clearly: a circle such as is mea-
sured out with compasses, that has in its centre a conspicu-
ous mark; the second, first of all a pair of lines, and another
one holding these apart at their middles; third, something 5
like a curly lock of hair, and then the fourth has one part
standing upright, and three more that are fastened cross-
wise on it; the fifth is not an easy one to explain—there are
two lines that begin from separate points, and these run to-
gether into a single base; and the last of all is similar to the 10
third.[1]

[1] The letters spell Theseus' name (ΘΗΣΕΥΣ), perhaps seen
on his ship as it approached the Cretan shore. Athenaeus says that
this description was imitated by Agathon and Theodectas (*TrGF*
39 F 4 and 72 F 6).

(383 + 384 N = 386c below)

385 + 386

ATHENIAN CHILDREN
(singing)

Why, then, O my poor mother, did you bear me . . .

* * *

. . . begetting this ornament for your house in vain, O
father.

386a

⟨ΑΓΓΕΛΟΣ?⟩

κἂν τῷδ᾽ ἔπεισι νυκτὸς ἀμβλωπὸν σέλας.

Photius, *Lexicon* α 1164 Theodoridis

*386aa (= 1001 N)

⟨ΑΓΓΕΛΟΣ?⟩

. . . λίνου κλωστῆρα περιφέρει λαβών.

Pollux 7.31

**386b

⟨ΑΓΓΕΛΟΣ⟩

      ]θε κιόνω[ν
      ].ατ᾽ εἶχον [.
      ]ακρον καὶ δα[
      ]ων θεατὴς ἀσφ[αλ-
5 λεύσσω] δὲ τὸν μὲν βο[υ-
      ν]τα κυρτόν, εἰς κ[έρας θυμούμενον,
      ]ι διαψαίροντα.[
      ]τι θαρσοῦντ(α).[
      ν]τα μηρῶν εντοσ[
10 ὁ δ᾽ Αἰγέ]ως μὲν τῷ λόγῳ [κεκλημένος,
   ἔργῳ] δὲ Θησεὺς [ἐ]κ Ποσε[ιδῶνος γεγώς
      ]ματ᾽ ἐκδὺς θηρὸς [
   κο]ρύνῃ δεξιὰν ὡ[πλισμένος

P. Oxy. 3530, ed. P. J. Parsons (1983). Supplements in ed. pr.

386a

⟨MESSENGER?⟩

Meanwhile the sombre glow of night came on.

*386aa (= 1001 N)

⟨MESSENGER?⟩

He carries about with him a skein of thread.

**386b[1]

⟨MESSENGER⟩

. . . (before *or* behind?) the pillars . . . I had . . . (top-
most *or* distant) and . . . a spectator . . . (taking a safe posi-
tion?). And (I caught sight of) the (bull, bull-formed, bull-
horned?) . . . curved, (tossing his horns in anger), sweeping   5
(with his tail?) . . . [2] . . . full of courage . . . of his thighs . . .
(But) Theseus (who is called the son of Aegeus) in name,
but (in reality is sprung from) Poseidon, threw off (his gar-   10
ments and approached?) the beast, (armed) with his . . .
club in his right hand . . .

---

[1] Ascription to Euripides is probable on linguistic grounds.
Theseus seems a more likely source than *Aegeus* (Theseus facing
the Marathonian bull) since 'pillars' in v. 1 suggests an interior
scene (cf. *Heracles* 971–80).   [2] Identification with F 926
(where the participle is feminine) is not likely.

---

1 πρόσ]θε or ὄπισ]θε (e.g.) Parsons   3 ἄκρον or
μ]ακρὸν Parsons   4 ἀσφ[αλῆ λαβὼν ἕδραν (e.g.) Parsons
(cf. *Suppl.* 653)   5 βο[ῦν or a compound Parsons
(βο[υγενῆ, βο[υκέρων Kannicht)   6 Parsons compares
Bacchae 743, ταῦροι δ' ὑβρισταὶ κἀς κέρας θυμούμενοι . . .
7 κέρκω]ι Parsons (while tentatively identifying v. 7 with F 926)
12 τἀσθή]ματ' ἐκδὺς θηρὸς [ἔρχεται πέλας (e.g.) Parsons

EURIPIDES

386c (= 383 + 384 N)

⟨ΘΗΣΕΥΣ ἢ ΜΙΝΩΣ⟩

κάρα τε γάρ σου συγχέω κόμαις ὁμοῦ
†ῥαναί τε δ᾽† ἐγκέφαλον· ὀμμάτων δ᾽ ἄπο
αἱμοσταγεῖς πρηστῆρες οἴσονται κάτω.

Schol. on Aristophanes, *Frogs* 473

2 ῥανῶ τε πέδοσ᾽ Hermann (but πέδοσ᾽ is metrically un-
likely): ῥανεῖ τε γῆν ἐγκέφαλος Kannicht (ῥανεῖ τε γῆν
Grotius, ἐγκέφαλος Matthiae)   3 οἴσονται Herwerden:
ῥεύσονται Schol. (then πρηστῆρε ῥεύσονται Barnes)

387

καίτοι φθόνου μὲν μῦθον ἄξιον φράσω.

Schol. on Euripides, *Hecuba* 288

THESEUS

386c (= 383 + 384 N)
⟨THESEUS or MINOS⟩

I will crush your head together with your hair, †and . . . pour . . . † your brain;[1] and jets of blood will be carried down from your eyes.[2]

[1] The Greek text is defective in metre and sense. Hermann's 'and I will pour your brain onto the ground' is plausible (cf. *Cyclops* 402, Soph. *Women of Trachis* 781) except for a metrical difficulty in 'onto the ground'. Kannicht suggests 'and your brain will pour to the ground'.   [2] The exaggerated tone of these threats is surprising, but compare e.g. *Heracles* 565–73. The scholia on *Frogs* 465–7, while quoting these lines for comparison, suggest that the Underworld Gatekeeper's speech threatening Heracles there contains further elements of Theseus' speech threatening Minos. For refutation of this see Rau, *Paratragodia* 116–7.

387

And yet I will tell you something that deserves reproach.[1]

[1] Ariadne confessing her love for Theseus? The scholiast on *Hecuba* 288 cites this verse to illustrate the use of the word φθόνος to mean 'reproach'.

388

ἀλλ' ἔστι δή τις ἄλλος ἐν βροτοῖς ἔρως
ψυχῆς δικαίας σώφρονός τε κἀγαθῆς.
καὶ χρῆν δὲ τοῖς βροτοῖσι τόνδ' εἶναι νόμον,
τῶν εὐσεβούντων οἵτινές τε σώφρονες
ἐρᾶν, Κύπριν δὲ τὴν Διὸς χαίρειν ἐᾶν.

Stobaeus 1.9.4b; vv. 1–2: Stobaeus 3.5.61; [Plutarch], *Moralia* 11e

(389 N = *Aegeus* F 7a)

388

But there is another kind of love amongst mortals, belonging to a soul that is just and temperate and good. And indeed it would be better if this were their rule, to love those who practise piety and temperance, and leave Zeus's daughter Cypris well alone.[1]

[1] Perhaps from a speech of Athena at the end of the play: see Introduction above. Plutarch gives these lines a Platonic sense as validating male homosexual love, but they probably only reformulated a commonplace distinction between moderate and uncontrolled love, the former being associated with wisdom, temperance and virtue: cf. *Melanippe* F 503, *Stheneboea* F 661.22–5, also F 897, 929a, 967, and *Medea* 627–44, 835–45, *Hippolytus* 525–42, *Iphigenia at Aulis* 543–57. Aphrodite is usually identified with both kinds but sometimes especially with uncontrolled sexual desire as in v. 5 here: cf. *Dictys* F 331, *Ino* F 400.

(389 N = *Aegeus* F 7a)

THYESTES

H. Van Looy in ed. Budé VIII.2.167–83.

A. Lesky, *Wiener Studien* 43 (1922–3), 172–98 = *Gesammelte Schriften* (Munich, 1966), 519–40; Webster 113; Aélion (1983) I.84–90; Gantz 545–52; *LIMC* VIII.i.20–2 'Thyestes'.

Our knowledge of the story of Pelops' sons Atreus and Thyestes in early Greek literature is surprisingly incomplete, but it is clear that it was and remained subject to continual variation and elaboration. The essentials are that Thyestes seduced Atreus' wife Aerope and obtained from her a divinely sent golden-fleeced lamb which entitled its owner to the kingdom of Mycenae; but Zeus reversed the course of the sun to confirm Atreus' title (accounts of this event vary greatly: see below on F *397b), and Atreus killed Aerope and banished Thyestes. Later Thyestes returned with his sons seeking a reconciliation, or lured by Atreus into expecting one, but Atreus killed the sons, served their flesh to Thyestes at a feast, and sent the broken man again into exile. The story to this point is well known in extant 5th c. tragedies (see especially Aeschylus, Agamemnon 1217ff., 1583ff. and Euripides, Electra 699ff., Orestes 807ff., 995ff.). Thyestes' youngest son Aegisthus, who killed Atreus' son Agamemnon on his return from

Troy, is said in Agamemnon *1605–6 to have escaped the banquet as a baby, but in another account he was born later out of incest between Thyestes and his daughter Pelopia and as a young man assisted Thyestes in killing Atreus. The story of his conception and/or birth must have been in some form the subject of Sophocles'* Thyestes at Sicyon *(the incest was located there) and is represented— not necessarily in its Sophoclean form—on a fine Apulian vase by the Darius Painter of about 340 B.C. (LIMC 'Thyestes' no. 1, Todisco Ap 144, Taplin no. 30). The slaying of Atreus by Thyestes and Aegisthus appears in another tragedy-inspired picture by the Darius Painter (LIMC 'Thyestes' no. 2, Todisco Ap 137, Taplin no. 95) and in a summary of a (perhaps later) tragic plot in* Hyginus, *Fab. 88.5–11. Pelopia appears in both of these vase paintings, and in Hyginus she is said to have been married to Atreus while pregnant with Aegisthus, who thus grew up believing he was Atreus' son and was recognized by his true father only when sent by Atreus to kill him; this led both to the killing of Atreus and to Pelopia's suicide on learning of her incestuous union with her father.*

Sophocles composed three or four tragedies dealing with this series of stories, but there is very little direct evidence for their content, or for Euripides' plot, or for six other recorded 5th–4th c. Thyestes *tragedies (including plays by Agathon, Carcinus and Chaeremon). Lesky argued plausibly that Sophocles treated the golden lamb story in his* Atreus *or* Women of Mycenae, *the banquet in a play recorded as either* Thyestes *or* Second Thyestes, *and the incest in one recorded as either* Thyestes at Sicyon *or* First Thyestes. *A* Third Thyestes *mentioned in one late documentary source might perhaps be identical with*

Atreus, *or a mirage. In Euripides'* Thyestes, *Thyestes was one of Euripides' ragged heroes (test. ii below), and Atreus was also a character (F 396, *397b), so the play presumably involved either Thyestes' first return from exile and the banquet, or his second return and the killing of Atreus. Scholars have generally favoured the first of these, and it would be confirmed if Bergk was right in supposing that a parody of Thyestes' reaction to the banquet in Aristophanes'* Proagon *(of 422 B.C.) alluded to Euripides' play. On the other hand, as Kannicht notes, the apparent reference to Atreus as an 'old man' in F 396 (cf. also F 397a?) would better suit the later event; but uncertainties over the text of F 396 and of the ancient commentary identifying its context leave some room for doubt. Some of the other fragments can be fitted well enough into either scenario, F 391–3 perhaps coming from a disillusioned and 'philosophical' Thyestes, and F 394 from an Atreus devoted to action above all. This encourages the supposition (likely enough in itself) that Euripides' Thyestes was something like the complicated and relatively sympathetic character that we find in Seneca's play.*

Brief fragments: none. Other ascriptions: F 941, F 953b.

The play was probably produced before 425 B.C., when Aristophanes mentioned Euripides' 'Thyestean rags' in Acharnians *(cf. test. ii); the metrical character of the fragments (no resolutions in sixteen trimeters) is consistent with this. In addition to the many Greek tragedies mentioned above, we know of eight relevant Latin tragedies (cf. Van Looy 173) all of whose antecedents are uncertain, as are their plots except in the case of Accius'* Atreus *and the extant* Thyestes *of Seneca which both focused on the* banquet. *Lesky's view that Seneca's* Thyestes *contains substantial Euripidean elements is attractive but subject to the many uncertainties mentioned above. For discussions of Ennius'* Thyestes *(169 B.C.) see Jocelyn 412–9, of Accius'* Atreus *Dangel 275–83, of Varius'* Thyestes *(29 B.C.) E. Lefèvre,* Der Thyestes des Lucius Varius Rufus *(Wiesbaden, 1976), and for a concise survey of Seneca's possible antecedents R. J. Tarrant,* Seneca's Thyestes *(Atlanta, 1985), 40–3. A number of 17th and 18th c. tragedies deal with the quarrels of Atreus and Thyestes, most of them with the banquet under Seneca's influence* (OGCMA I.256).

ΘΥΕΣΤΗΣ

test. ii (= *Cretan Women* test. iv)

῾τῶν Θυεστείων ῥακῶν᾿· ἢ τῶν Κρησσῶν ἢ αὐτοῦ τοῦ
Θυέστου.

Schol. on Aristophanes, *Acharnians* 433

391

οὐκ ἔστιν οὐδὲν χωρὶς ἀνθρώποις θεῶν·
σπουδάζομεν δὲ πόλλ᾽ ὑπ᾽ ἐλπίδων, μάτην
πόνους ἔχοντες, οὐδὲν εἰδότες σαφές.

Orion 5.7 Haffner; vv. 1 and 2–3 separately: Theophilus of
Antioch, *To Autolycus* 2.8. F 391 and 397 are attributed to Euripi-
des by Theophilus, simply to *Thyestes* by Orion; Haffner prefers
to attribute them to Sophocles.

392

εἰ δ᾽ ἄτερ πόνων
δοκεῖς ἔσεσθαι, μῶρος εἶ, θνητὸς γεγώς.

Stobaeus 4.34.20

THYESTES

test. ii (= *Cretan Women* test. iv)
'Thyestes' rags': either in *Cretan Women* or in *Thyestes* itself.[1]

[1] The reference to Thyestes' rags is made by Aristophanes'
character Euripides as he helps Dicaeopolis to make himself piti-
able in his forthcoming trial. The scholiast's comment suggests
that Thyestes appeared in rags in both *Cretan Women* (see Intro-
duction there) and *Thyestes*, and that both were produced before
Acharnians (425 B.C.).

391

Nothing in human affairs is independent of the gods.
Prompted by hopes we pursue many schemes, but our toils
are in vain since we have no sure knowledge.[1]

[1] This may have been the beginning of the play's prologue
speech, as Kannicht suggests. It encapsulates the thought ex-
pounded at length in Solon fr. 13.33–70 *IEG*.

392

If you expect to be free of troubles you are a fool, seeing
that you are mortal.[1]

[1] A commonplace of Greek ethical thought from Homer (*Iliad*
24.525–33) onwards.

393

γνώμης γὰρ οὐδὲν ἀρετὴ μονουμένη.

Orion 7.4 and Euripidean Appendix 20 Haffner

394

οὐ πώποτ' ἔργου μᾶλλον εἱλόμην λόγους.

Stobaeus 2.15.17

395

πλούτου δ' ἀπορρυέντος ἀσθενεῖς γάμοι·
τὴν μὲν γὰρ εὐγένειαν αἰνοῦσιν βροτοί,
μᾶλλον δὲ κηδεύουσι τοῖς εὐδαίμοσιν.

Stobaeus 4.31.37; vv. 2–3: Aristotle fr. 92 Rose (cited in Stobaeus 4.29.25)

396

ΘΤΕΣΤΗΣ(?)

ἀλλ' εἴπερ ἐστὶν ἐν βροτοῖς ψευδῆ, γέρον,
πιθανά, νομίζειν χρή σε καὶ τοὐναντίον,
ἄπιστ' ἀληθῆ πολλὰ συμβαίνειν βροτοῖς.

Aristotle, *Rhetoric* 1397a17, with anonymous commentary in *CAG* XXI.2. 133.21; the commentary seems to indicate (in a corrupt sentence) that the speaker was Thyestes addressing Atreus.

1 ψευδῆ, γέρον Nauck: ψευδηγέρον Aristot. ms. A: ψευδηγορεῖν ms. A later correction, several later mss., and anon. comm.

393

Excellence is worth nothing if it is not combined with judgement.

394

I have never preferred words to action.

395

People get weaker marriages when their wealth has drained away. Men pay lip-service to nobility, but they prefer to ally themselves with those who are prospering.[1]

[1] Cf. *Danae* F 326.1–5 with note.

396

THYESTES
(to Atreus?)

But if, old man, there are falsehoods amongst men that are persuasive, you should recognize the opposite—that many truths turn out to be unpersuasive to them.[1]

[1] Aristotle uses these lines to illustrate the rhetorical ploy of 'demonstration from opposites'. For a similar argument cf. *Helen* 309–10, and on persuasive falsehoods *Antiope* F 206. In v. 1 the reading 'if, old man, there are falsehoods' is supported (against the alternative 'if it is possible to speak falsely') by the word pattern 'falsehoods . . . persuasive . . . , truths . . . unpersuasive'; but the 'old man' and his likely identification as Atreus make an interpretative difficulty: see apparatus opposite and Introduction above.

397

θεοῦ θέλοντος κἂν ἐπὶ ῥιπὸς πλέοις.

Orion 5.6 Haffner; Theophilus of Antioch, *To Autolycus* 2.8; Plutarch, *Moralia* 405b; and elsewhere as a proverb. On the attribution of this fragment to Euripides see under F 391 above.

397a

ἀμβλῶπας αὐγὰς ὀμμάτων ἔχεις σέθεν.

Photius, *Lexicon* α 1164 Theodoridis

*397b (= 861 N)

ΑΤΡΕΤΣ

δείξας γὰρ ἄστρων τὴν ἐναντίαν ὁδόν,
δόμους τ᾽ ἔσωσα καὶ τύραννος ἱζόμην.

Achilles, *Introduction to Aratus'* Phaenomena 1 and 20 (E. Maass, *Commentariorum in Aratum Reliquiae*, pp. 29.1–2 and 48.11–12)

δόμους Achill. 20: δήμους Achill. 1

397

If God willed it, you could sail even on a straw mat.

397a

The brightness of your eyes is dulled.[1]

[1] Literally, 'You have the rays of your eyes dull-eyed'; for the phrasing cf. *Heracles* 131–2, Sophocles, *Ajax* 69–70.

*397b (= 861 N)

ATREUS

By showing the contrary course of the stars, I saved my house and established myself as ruler.[1]

[1] Achilles cites this fragment as showing that Euripides credited Atreus with discovering the retrograde 'movement' along the ecliptic of the Sun and planets ('stars' here). Atreus' discovery is mentioned also by Strabo 1.2.15 (citing Polybius) and Lucian 48.12, and seems to have become a standard part of astronomical lore. It is more accurately credited to Oenopides of Chios (41 A 7 DK) in the later 5th century. It appears then that Euripides here ascribes the validation of Atreus' kingship to a scientific revelation by Atreus himself rather than a miracle supplied by Zeus. He may have described the same phenomenon as brought about by Zeus on Atreus' behalf in *Electra* 727–36 and *Orestes* 1001–06, but the texts of these passages are corrupt and their sense uncertain. Accounts of the miracle vary greatly: Plato makes it a permanent reversal of the Sun's daily course from eastward to westward rather than a one-time event; in some later accounts it is Zeus's response to Atreus' banquet rather than to Thyestes' theft.

INO

H. Van Looy in ed. Budé VIII.2.185–209.

W. Luppe, *Philologus* 128 (1984), 41–4, 57–9; Webster 98–101; *LIMC* II.i.950–3 'Athamas' and V.i.657–61 'Ino'; Gantz 176–9, 472–3, 478; C. Pache, *Baby and Child Heroes in Ancient Greece* (Urbana, 2004), 135–80, esp. 140–1, 148–9.

The mythography of Ino and her husband Athamas is un-usually confused (Gantz 176–9, Pache 135–80; see also on Phrixus A and B), and evidence for the play itself is very limited. Apart from two brief but definite allusions in Aris-tophanes (below) and the quite numerous but chiefly gno-mological and therefore contextless fragments, the only other matter ascribed to Euripides comes in Hyginus, Fab. *4 (= test. iii below). Headed 'Euripides' Ino', its narrative is ostensibly based on the play,*[1] *and reconstructors have little choice but to use it, approximately as follows:*

Athamas king of Thessaly (where the play is set) had two sons by Ino (his second wife, after Nephele: see on F

---

[1] *Fab*. 4's relation to a narrative hypothesis is constantly de-bated. Luppe 57–9 is much more confident of such derivation and therefore reliability than M. Huys, *APF* 42 (1996), 172–3; Kannicht in *TrGF* (test. iii) follows Luppe. Cf. on *Antiope* with reference to Hyginus, *Fab*. 8 (= *Antiope* test. iii (a)) and 7.

438

**399); they were Learchus and Melicertes. She disap-
peared and, believing her dead, he married Themisto, who
bore him twin boys; Ino's two sons were still in his house.
Much later he learned that Ino had gone to Mt. Parnassus
above Delphi to join the permanent rites of Dionysus; she
had been the god's 'nurse' (Apollodorus 3.4.3) after his
mother Semele, her sister, died when simultaneously in-
seminated, delivered of the child, and incinerated by Zeus's
lightning (Bacchae 2–3); in anger, Zeus's jealous wife
Hera maddened Ino and sent her wandering (Medea
1284–5—in fact to Delphi); Athamas recalled Ino. Thus far
cf. test. iii.1–2, and for the dramatic action (next para-
graph) cf. 3–5.

The play began with Ino's return (possibly F **399),
following a prologue which gave the background (F *398,
speaker unknown: a god is possible; but the fragment itself
is doubted for the play); F 401–3 may all be Ino's, the first
two early in the play, the third perhaps later. Athamas con-
cealed Ino from Themisto, disguising her (possibly in the
rags mocked by Aristophanes, Acharnians 434 = test. iia)
as a captive serving-woman who was now to look after all
four boys. F 404–7 come from an argument about nobility
(Van Looy 194, cf. also F 414), perhaps in the same episode
in which Athamas commends the disguised but 'honest' Ino
to Themisto (F 410 and 412? See Webster 101). Plutarch in
citing F 413.1–2 notes Ino's 'freedom of speech' in the play
as a quality of noble upbringing; so this fragment too may
belong here (cf. Webster 99–100)—or, rather, to the play's
ensuing and critical turn. Themisto learned that Ino had
returned, but could not identify her; she became jealous of
Ino's two sons (a dramatic motif like Merope's jealousy in
Alcmeon in Corinth or the Queen's in Melanippe Captive),

and planned their death (as if they were a 'stepmother's children', as the brief allusion in Nonnus, Dionysiaca *9.320 has it). She used the 'captive' Ino as her accomplice, probably enjoining secrecy upon her (F 410, 411 and 413 may refer to this), and ordering her to clothe her twins in white, and Ino's own two sons in black (symbolizing their intended death, cf.* Melanippe Wise *test. i.21–4). Ino interchanged the colours, however, and Themisto killed her own twins; on discovering her mistake, she took her life (despite consolation, F 415, cf. 418). Though Ino had cleverly saved her own sons, disaster now struck (possibly F *398) with cruel irony (compare the sequence in e.g.* Heracles*), for Athamas while hunting was visited by madness, a further consequence of Hera's hatred for Ino, and killed his son Learchus; furthermore, Ino in grief leapt into the sea carrying her other son Melicertes (Hyginus 2.4–5 and Apollodorus 1.9.2, cited by Kannicht on test. iii.[5]).[2] F 421–2 likely come from a messenger's report of Learchus' death, or of the other two deaths, or of both. It is guesswork how the play had moved from Themisto's death to Athamas' madness, but it probably ended with Dionysus foretelling Ino's deification under the name Leucothea, 'White Goddess', and her son's as Palaemon (Webster 101 suggests that adesp. F 100 + 101 referring to these events belongs here). It is impossible to place F 408–9, 416–7, 419.*

Brief fragment (doubtful): F 423, particles meaning 'and so in fact'. Other ascriptions: F **953m (a woman has apparently threatened and then committed infanti-

---

[2] At *Medea* 1283–9 Ino, maddened, kills both her sons. R. M. Newton, *AJP* 106 (1985), 496–502 suggests that Euripides deliberately adapted the story to match Medea's double infanticide.

cide, and a boy's body is brought on stage: see note there), F 972; adesp. F 100 + 101 (see above).

The play was produced before 425 B.C. (the date of Aristophanes' Acharnians: above); the metrical criteria do not help to suggest how long before (Cropp–Fick 81). The only other Ino known is Livius Andronicus' fragmentary Latin tragedy, perhaps a derivative; Ennius' Athamas may have been dependent for some incidents. Athamas' killing of Learchus and Ino's leap into the sea left marks in vase-painting and other art from the 4th century (see LIMC 'Athamas' no. 5, 'Ino' nos. 14–19). Plutarch, Moralia 556a (citing F 399) and Philostratus, Life of Apollonius 7.5 (citing F 420.1–3) attest performances of the play in the 1st century A.D., the latter at Ephesus.

INΩ

INO EURIPIDIS. Athamas in Thessalia rex cum Inonem
uxorem, ex qua duos filios ‹susceperat›, perisse putaret, duxit
nymphae filiam Themistonem uxorem; ex ea geminos filios
procreauit. (2) Postea resciit Inonem in Parnaso esse, quam
bacchationis causa eo peruenisse; misit qui eam adducerent;
quam adductam celauit. (3) Resciit Themisto eam inuentam
esse, sed quae esset nesciebat. Coepit uelle filios eius necare;
rei consciam quam captiuam esse credebat ipsam Inonem
sumpsit, et ei dixit ut filios suos candidis uestimentis operiret,
Inonis filios nigris. (4) Ino suos candidis, Themistonis pullis
operuit; tunc Themisto decepta suos filios occidit; id ubi
resciit, ipsa se necauit. (5) Athamas autem in uenatione per
insaniam Learchum maiorem filium suum interfecit; at Ino
cum minore filio Melicerte in mare se deiecit et dea est facta.

Hyginus, *Fab.* 4

(1) ‹*susceperat*› Muncker

INO

EURIPIDES' INO. When Athamas king of Thessaly came to think that his wife Ino, by whom (he had had) two sons, had died, he took Themisto, a nymph's daughter, as wife; with her he fathered twin sons. (2) Later he discovered that Ino was on Mount Parnassus, and that she had gone there for bacchic rites;[1] he sent men to fetch her, and when that was done, disguised her. (3) Themisto discovered that the woman had been found, but did not know who she was. She formed a wish to murder Ino's sons; as accessory to the act she took Ino herself, whom she believed to be a captive, and told her to veil her own sons in white vestments, and Ino's sons in black. (4) Ino veiled her own sons in white, Themisto's in black; then Themisto was deceived and killed her own sons. When she discovered this, she slew herself. (5) Athamas moreover while hunting killed his elder son Learchus through madness; but Ino threw herself into the sea together with her younger son Melicertes, and was deified.[2]

[1] For Ino's bacchic wanderings on Mount Parnassus near Delphi, see Introduction above.   [2] The details in (5) are given more fully by Hyginus in *Fab*. 2.4, where Athamas' madness too is attributed to the goddess Hera's antipathy to Ino.

*398

εὔδουσα δ᾽ Ἰνοῦς συμφορὰ χρόνον πολὺν
νῦν ὄμμ᾽ ἐγείρει.

Schol. on Pindar, *Isthmians* 3/4.40

1 εὔδουσα . . . συμφορὰ Musgrave: ἰδοῦσα . . . συμφορὰν
Schol.

**399

ΙΝΩ

φίλαι γυναῖκες, πῶς ἂν ἐξ ἀρχῆς δόμους
Ἀθάμαντος οἰκήσαιμι τῶν πεπραγμένων
δράσασα μηδέν;

Plutarch, *Moralia* 556a

400

ὦ θνητὰ πράγματ᾽, ὦ γυναικεῖαι φρένες·
ὅσον νόσημα τὴν Κύπριν κεκτήμεθα.

Stobaeus 4.22.183

401

φεῦ,
ὅσῳ τὸ θῆλυ δυστυχέστερον γένος
πέφυκεν ἀνδρῶν· ἔν τε τοῖσι γὰρ καλοῖς
πολλῷ λέλειπται κἀπὶ τοῖς αἰσχροῖς πλέον.

Stobaeus 4.22.182

*398

Though for a long while asleep, Ino's misfortune[1] now wakes and stirs.

[1] The long-standing hatred of Hera (see Introduction).

**399

INO

Dear women, how I wish I could live from the beginning again in Athamas' house, and have done nothing of what I have done![1]

[1] If this fragment is from the play's opening, 'what I have done' refers either to her disappearance after bearing Athamas' two sons (test. iii.1–2 above) or to her attempt on the children of Athamas' first wife Nephele (*Phrixus A* test. iia–b, cf. *Phrixus B* test. iia–b and *Phrixus A/B* F 824). But it could well come later and refer to Ino's killing of Themisto's children (test. iii.3–4).

400

Oh, mankind's dealings! Oh, women's hearts! What a great affliction we have acquired in love!

401

Alas! How much more unfortunate the female sex is by nature than that of men: it is left far behind in good conduct, and yet further in bad.

402

νόμοι γυναικῶν οὐ καλῶς κεῖνται πέρι·
χρῆν γὰρ τὸν εὐτυχοῦνθ᾽ ὅπως πλείστας ἔχειν
{γυναῖκας, εἴπερ ⟨ἡ⟩ τροφὴ δόμοις παρῆν},
ὡς τὴν κακὴν μὲν ἐξέβαλλε δωμάτων,
5 τὴν δ᾽ οὖσαν ἐσθλὴν ἡδέως ἐσῴζετο.
νῦν δ᾽ εἰς μίαν βλέπουσι, κίνδυνον μέγαν
ῥίπτοντες· οὐ γὰρ τῶν τρόπων πειρώμενοι
νύμφας ἐς οἴκους ἑρματίζονται βροτοί.

Stobaeus 4.22.36

2 ὅπως Erfurdt: ὅτι Stobaeus   3 deleted by Mekler ⟨ἡ⟩
Gesner: ⟨δὴ⟩ Stob. ms. Paris 1985

403

τίς ἆρα μήτηρ ἢ πατὴρ κακὸν μέγα
βροτοῖς ἔφυσε τὸν δυσώνυμον φθόνον;
ποῦ καί ποτ᾽ οἰκεῖ σώματος λαχὼν μέρος;
ἐν χερσὶν ἢ σπλάγχνοισιν ἢ παρ᾽ ὄμματα;
5 †ἔσθ᾽ ἡμῖν ὡς ἦν† μόχθος ἰατροῖς μέγας
τομαῖς ἀφαιρεῖν ἢ ποτοῖς ἢ φαρμάκοις
πασῶν μεγίστην τῶν ἐν ἀνθρώποις νόσων.

Stobaeus 3.38.8; vv. 3–4: Satyrus, *Life of Euripides* P. Oxy.
1176 fr. 39 col. xvii.1–7

3 ποῦ καί ποτ᾽ Stob.: ποῖόν ποτ᾽ West   6 φαρμάκοις
Stob.: χρίμασιν West

402

Laws are not well made concerning wives: the prosperous
man should be having as many as possible {if his house
could maintain them}, so he could throw the bad one out of
his home and be pleased at keeping the one who actually is
good. Now, however, they look to one wife, and risk much   5
on the throw; for people take wives into their houses like
ballast, with no experience of their ways.[1]

[1] The metaphors 'on the throw' (from dicing) and 'as ballast'
(from seafaring) are remarkably combined; the point of the
second seems to be that no one takes care to check the content of
ballast when they take it on board.

403

What mother or father gave life to ill-named envy, as a
great evil for men? Wherever does it actually have a part in
the body, and live—in the hands or entrails or close by the
eyes? †There is for us as there was†[1] a great labour for
doctors to remove by surgery or potions or remedies this
greatest of all mankind's afflictions.[2]

[1] The text is plainly corrupt, and unmetrical.   [2] I.e. ex-
ternal medicaments ('ointments' is substituted by West; 'or by
remedial potions', Barnes).

404

τό τ᾽ εὐγενὲς
πολλὴν δίδωσιν ἐλπίδ᾽ ὡς ἄρξουσι γῆς.

Stobaeus 4.29.48

405

τὴν εὐγένειαν, κἂν ἄμορφος ᾖ γάμος,
τιμῶσι πολλοὶ προσλαβεῖν τέκνων χάριν,
τό τ᾽ ἀξίωμα μᾶλλον ἢ τὰ χρήματα.

Stobaeus 4.29.49

2 πρὸς τέκνων χάριν λαβεῖν Stob., corrected by Hense

406

μὴ σκυθρωπὸς ἴσθ᾽ ἄγαν
πρὸς τοὺς κακῶς πράσσοντας, ἄνθρωπος γεγώς.

Stobaeus 4.48.4

407

ἀμουσία τοι μηδ᾽ ἐπ᾽ οἰκτροῖσιν δάκρυ
στάζειν· κακὸν δέ, χρημάτων ὄντων ἅλις,
φειδοῖ πονηρᾷ μηδέν᾽ εὖ ποιεῖν βροτῶν.

Stobaeus 3.16.5; vv. 1–2: Stob. 4.48.20

408

ἐν ἐλπίσιν χρὴ τοὺς σοφοὺς ἄγειν βίον.

Stobaeus 4.46.3

404

Their high birth gives great hope that they will rule the land.

405

Many men value acquiring a wife of high birth, even if she is not handsome, for the children's sake,[1] and reputation more than money.

[1] 'Father well-born children from noble stock', *Antiope* F 215.2.

406

Don't scowl too much at those who do badly: you are human too.

407

Just as it's boorish, I tell you, to shed no tear even for those deserving pity, so it is bad, when there is money enough, not to help any man through cheap thriftiness.

408

The wise should live their life amid hopes.

409

μήτ᾽ εὐτυχοῦσα πᾶσαν ἡνίαν χάλα,
κακῶς τε πράσσουσ᾽ ἐλπίδος κεδνῆς ἔχου.

Stobaeus 4.46.5

410

τοιάνδε χρὴ γυναικὶ προσπολονεῖν ἀεί
ἥτις τὸ μὲν δίκαιον οὐ σιγήσεται,
τὰ δ᾽ αἰσχρὰ μισεῖ καὶ κατ᾽ ὀφθαλμοὺς ἔχει.

Stobaeus 4.28.2

1 προσπολεῖν Musgrave ἀεί Collard: πρόσπολον ἐᾶν Stob.:
πρόσπολον νέμειν Dobree

411
⟨ΘΕΜΙΣΤΩ?⟩

ἴστω δὲ μηδεὶς ταῦθ᾽ ἃ σιγᾶσθαι χρεών·
σμικροῦ γὰρ ἐκ λαμπτῆρος Ἰδαῖον λέπας
πρήσειεν ἄν τις, καὶ πρὸς ἄνδρ᾽ εἰπὼν ἕνα
πύθοιντ᾽ ἂν ἀστοὶ πάντες {ἃ κρύπτειν χρεών}.

Stobaeus 3.41.1; vv. 2–4 Plutarch, *Moralia* 507b; vv. 2–3
(μικροῦ . . . τις): Schol. on Pindar, *Pythians* 3.66

4 ἃ κρύπτειν χρεών (unmetrical) Stob.: omitted by Plutarch,
deleted by Herwerden.

INO

409

Neither slacken every rein in good fortune—and when you
do badly, keep hold of fine hope.[1]

[1] Addressed to a woman; either Themisto or Ino is possible.

410

A wife should always be served[1] by such a woman as will
not be silent over what is right, but who hates what is
shameful and keeps it before the eyes.

[1] Collard adapts Musgrave's 'a wife should be allowed such a
maid as . . .' ('should be assigned': Dobree). Stobaeus' Greek is
unmetrical.

411

⟨THEMISTO?⟩

And let no one know these things which ought to be kept
quiet. Just as one could set fire to the slopes of Ida[1] from a
small torch, so from one's word to a single man all citizens
could find out {what one ought to conceal}.[2]

[1] Probably the great mountain above Troy rather than Zeus'
birth place and cult site in Crete.   [2] The speaker may be
Themisto, confiding in Ino (whom she has not identified) about
killing Ino's children: see Introduction.

412

ἐμοὶ γὰρ εἴη πτωχός, εἰ δὲ βούλεται
πτωχοῦ κακίων, ὅστις ὢν εὔνους ἐμοὶ
φόβον παρελθὼν τἀπὸ καρδίας ἐρεῖ.

Stobaeus 3.13.12; Plutarch, *Moralia* 63a

1 γὰρ εἴη Plut.: γένοιτο Stob.

413

ΙΝΩ

ἐπίσταμαι δὲ πάνθ᾽ ὅσ᾽ εὐγενῆ χρεών,
σιγᾶν θ᾽ ὅπου δεῖ καὶ λέγειν ἵν᾽ ἀσφαλές,
ὁρᾶν θ᾽ ἃ δεῖ με κοὐχ ὁρᾶν ἃ μὴ πρέπει.
<   >
γαστρὸς κρατεῖν δέ· καὶ γὰρ ἐν κακοῖσιν ὢν
5 ἐλευθέροισιν ἐμπεπαίδευμαι τρόποις.

Stobaeus 4.29.62; vv. 1–3: Orion 1.5 Haffner; vv. 1–2: Plutarch, *Moralia* 506c (attributing the words to Ino); v. 2 is frequently cited or paraphrased, e.g. Plutarch, *Moralia* 606a, Aulus Gellius 13.19.4.

3 πρέπει Orion: χρεών Stob.   4–5 omitted by Orion, separated from 1–3 and suggested for a different speaker by Matthiae; deleted by some editors. Kannicht suggests a lemma has been lost in Stobaeus before 4–5.

414

φειδώμεθ᾽ ἀνδρῶν εὐγενῶν, φειδώμεθα,
κακοὺς δ᾽ ἀποπτύωμεν, ὥσπερ ἄξιοι.

Stobaeus 4.29.8

412

Give me a beggarman—worse than a beggarman if he will—who has good will towards me and will set fear aside and speak what comes from the heart!

413

INO

I know all that one well-born should, to keep silent where necessary and to speak where safe, and to see what is necessary and not to see what is unfitting . . . and to control appetite; for though I am in the midst of troubles, I have been schooled in freeborn ways.[1]

[1] See Introduction above on this fragment. Vv. 4–5 probably come from another fragment which has lost both lemma and beginning in Stobaeus (Kannicht). They do not cohere with vv. 1–3, and 'control appetite' is unapt to Ino's circumstances. The Greek masculine singular participle used of herself by a woman in v. 4 is very doubtful (the plural is not rare, e.g. *Cretans* F 472e.40).

414

Let us spare well-born men, yes, spare them—but spurn bad ones as they deserve.

415

ἄνασσα, πολλοῖς ἔστιν ἀνθρώπων κακά,
τοῖς δ' ἄρτι λήγει, τοῖς δὲ κίνδυνος μολεῖν.
κύκλος γὰρ αὐτὸς καρπίμοις τε γῆς φυτοῖς
θνητῶν τε γενεᾷ· τῶν μὲν αὔξεται βίος,
5 τῶν δὲ φθίνει τε καὶ θερίζεται πάλιν.

Stobaeus 4.41.19; vv. 3–5: [Plutarch], *Moralia* 104b

3 κύκλος γὰρ αὐτὸς [Plut.]: κύκλῳ γὰρ ἔρπει Stob. (= *Aeolus* F 22.3)　　5 καὶ θερίζεται Stob.: κἀκθερίζεται [Plut.]

416

πολλοί γε θνητῶν τῷ θράσει τὰς συμφορὰς
ζητοῦσ' ἀμαυροῦν κἀποκρύπτεσθαι κακά.

Stobaeus 3.4.9

417

κέκτησο δ' ὀρθῶς ἂν ἔχῃς ἄνευ ψόγου,
κἂν σμικρὰ σῴζου τοὐνδικον σέβων ἀεί,
μηδ' ὡς κακὸς ναύκληρος εὖ πράξας ποτὲ
ζητῶν τὰ πλείον', εἶτα πάντ' ἀπώλεσεν.

Stobaeus 4.31.102; vv. 1–2: Stobaeus 3.9.2

1 ἂν ⟨τ'⟩ Madvig: ἂν ⟨δ'⟩ Dindorf　　2 so Nauck (but reading σέβουσ': σέβων ἃ δεῖ Hense): καὶ (or κἂν) σμικρὰ σῴζων τοὐνεχ' ὃν σέβειν πρέπει Stob. 4.31.102: καὶ μικρὰ σῴζου τῇ δίκῃ ξυνοῦσ' ἀεί Stob. 3.9.2

415

My queen, many men have troubles; for some they have just ceased, for others there is danger of their coming. The cycle is the same for earth's green crops as for generations of men: the life of some increases, of others it dies off again and is harvested.[1]

[1] For the whole sentiment cf. *Danae* F 330.

416

Many mortals seek by their audacity to keep their disasters dark and hide their troubles away.[1]

[1] Reversing the usual maxim (*Cretan Women* F 460 with note).

417

Make sure that you have acquired what you have properly, without censure, and if (it be) small, preserve it while always respecting what is right, and not as a bad ship's captain after a past success seeks more, and then loses everything.[1]

[1] The Greek phrasing in v. 1 is difficult, but for the sense cf. *Erechtheus* F 362.11 with note. Vv. 2–4 seem to say that one should not risk ruin by trying to increase one's wealth beyond its proper measure. In v. 2 Stobaeus has either 'saving even(?) small things for the man(?) whom it is fitting to respect' (4.31.102) or 'and save small things, keeping ever on the side of justice' (3.9.2). Nauck's restoration (adopted and slightly modified here) combines elements of both but remains insecure.

418

γίγνωσκε τἀνθρώπεια μηδ' ὑπερμέτρως
ἄλγει· κακοῖς γὰρ οὐ σὺ πρόσκεισαι μόνη.

Stobaeus 4.56.7

419

βίᾳ νυν ἕλκετ' ὦ κακοὶ τιμὰς βροτοί,
καὶ κτᾶσθε πλοῦτον πάντοθεν θηρώμενοι,
σύμμικτα μὴ δίκαια καὶ δίκαι' ὁμοῦ·
ἔπειτ' ἀμᾶσθε τῶνδε δύστηνον θέρος.

Stobaeus 3.10.23 and 4.31.56

1 βίᾳ νυν ἕλκετ' Stob. 3.10.23: καὶ νῦν ἐφέλκετ' Stob.
4.31.56

420

ὁρᾷς τυράννους διὰ μακρῶν ηὐξημένους,
ὡς σμικρὰ τὰ σφάλλοντα, καὶ μῖ' ἡμέρα
τὰ μὲν καθεῖλεν ὑψόθεν, τὰ δ' ἦρ' ἄνω.
ὑπόπτερος δ' ὁ πλοῦτος· οἷς γὰρ ἦν ποτε,
5 ἐξ ἐλπίδων πίπτοντας ὑπτίους ὁρῶ.

Stobaeus 4.41.1; vv.1–2, 4–5: P. Cairo 65445 (badly damaged);
many partial quotations, paraphrases and reflections in prose
writers.

1 ηὐξημένους Grotius, sufficiently confirmed by Ariston of
Ceos fr. 13 Wehrli: αὐξηθέντας Philostratus, Life of Apollonius
7.5: ἠσκημ(μ)ένους Stob.: P. Cair. is defective.

418

Understand mankind's condition and do not grieve beyond measure: you are not alone in being visited by evil fortune.[1]

[1] Consolation for Themisto or Ino (a woman is addressed).

419

Now use force to draw privilege your way, you wicked mankind, and possess yourselves of wealth by hunting it everywhere, through actions just and unjust mixed together—then reap their unhappy harvest!

420

Do you see how small the things are that bring down tyrants whose power has long increased, and how one day brings some down from a height, and lifts others up? Wealth has wings![1] Those who once had it, I see dashed from their hopes, backs laid to the ground.

[1] A proverb, cf. *Meleager* F 518.2. In v. 1 Stobaeus' plausible 'promoted, preened themselves' is a mere error of transcription.

421

κοίλοις ἐν ἄντροις ἄλυχνος, ὥστε θήρ, μόνος

Pollux 7.178

422

πολλοὶ παρῆσαν, ἀλλ᾽ ἄπιστα Θεσσαλῶν.

Schol. on Aristophanes, *Wealth* 521; Schol. on Euripides, *Phoenician Women* 1408 cite both *Wealth* 521 and the paraphrase of Euripides' line by Demosthenes 1.21.

ἄπιστα Θεσσαλῶν Hemsterhuis: ἄπιστοι Θεσσαλοί Schol. Aristoph.: πολλοὶ γάρ εἰσιν, ἀλλ᾽ ἄπιστα Θεσσαλοῖς Schol. Eur.

421

... in a hollow cave, without a lamp, like a beast, alone ... [1]

[1] The fragment describes probably Athamas, in flight or helpless imprisonment after killing his son (see Introduction).

422

... many were present, but what Thessalians say is unreliable.[1]

[1] Thessalians' mendacity, especially as exploitative slave dealers, was proverbial (so the Scholia on Aristophanes).

IXION

H. Van Looy in ed. Budé VIII.2.211–9.

Webster 160–1, 303; Aélion (1983) I.273–5; *LIMC* V.i.857–62 'Ixion'; Gantz 718–21; Sourvinou-Inwood 472–80.

Ixion is one of Greek myth's great sinners greatly punished. He committed the first homicide when he treacherously killed his father-in-law in order to avoid paying him the bride-gifts he had promised. No human or god would purify him until Zeus did so and gave him refuge amongst the gods. He then attempted to rape Hera, but Zeus foiled him by replacing her with a cloud by whom he fathered Kentauros, the father of the Centaurs. Zeus punished Ixion by having him tied to a wheel which revolved eternally in the aether (or in some Hellenistic and later accounts, the Underworld). Ixion's story is summarized by Pindar, Pythians 2.21–48 and explained extensively in the scholia there and on Apollonius of Rhodes 3.62 (citing the mythographers Pherecydes and Asclepiades), and in Diodorus 4.69.3–5. Ixion was usually regarded as the father of Pirithous, although in the Iliad (14.317–8) Zeus claims to be the father, having seduced Ixion's wife. Pirithous himself relates his father's crime and punishment in Pirithous (F 5).

Aeschylus' Women of Perrhaebia (Ixion's homeland near Mount Olympus) and his Ixion seem to have dramatized respectively the homicide and the attempted rape and *its punishment, perhaps as two parts of a trilogy; little survives from either play (there are also references to Ixion's purification in Aeschylus, Eumenides 441, 717–8). Nothing is known about the plots of Sophocles' Ixion (one fragment, date unknown) or Callistratus' Ixion (known only from a record of its production at the Lenaea in 418). According to the Athenian historian Philochorus (FGrH 328 F 217 = test. i), Euripides' play alluded to the death of Protagoras which occurred probably around 420, so it could be the latest of all these. Test. iii (below) shows that it culminated in the punishment of Ixion for his sins, and suggests that Ixion defended his immorality with sophistic arguments (cf. F 426, **426a?), like for example Laius in Chrysippus. F 427 speaks of his pollution inspiring fear amongst those he encountered, but this could have been a reference back to his past rather than to his condition at the time of the play's action. Some scholars infer from test. iii that Ixion was nailed to his wheel on stage at the end, and then exited on the eccyclema, or upwards to the sky on the crane. Sourvinou-Inwood suggests alternatively that the crane was used to show him already suspended on the wheel in the sky, accompanied by a god (perhaps Hephaestus) who spoke the closing speech.*

Other ascriptions: Ino F 403; adesp. F 5 (from an unattributed Ixion), 'The man is my enemy, yet I respect justice'.

Later dramatic treatments include a tragic Ixion by Timesitheus (title only, date uncertain), and a comic one by Eubulus (mid-4th c., one fragment). A few vase paintings have been speculatively associated with Aeschylus' and Euripides' plays (LIMC 'Ixion' no. 1 and nos. 2, 3, 14, 15 respectively), but none of them has theatrical features.

ΙΞΙΩΝ

test. iii

αὗται μὲν οὖν αἱ τῶν λόγων ἀποφάσεις καὶ δόξαι παντός
εἰσι κατιδεῖν τοῦ προσέχοντος· ἑτέρας δ' ἐκ τῶν πραγμά-
των αὐτῶν παρέχουσι μαθήσεις, ὥσπερ ὁ Εὐριπίδης
εἰπεῖν λέγεται πρὸς τοὺς τὸν Ἰξίονα λοιδοροῦντας ὡς
ἀσεβῆ καὶ μιαρόν, 'οὐ μέντοι πρότερον αὐτὸν ἐκ τῆς
σκηνῆς ἐξήγαγον ἢ τῷ τροχῷ προσηλῶσαι.'

Plutarch, *Moralia* 19d–e

424

Φλεγύαντος υἱέ, δέσποτ' Ἰξίων . . .

Schol. on Apollonius of Rhodes 3.62

425

ὅστις γὰρ ἀστῶν πλέον ἔχειν πέφυκ' ἀνήρ
{οὐδὲν φρονεῖ δίκαιον οὐδὲ βούλεται·}
φίλοις τ' ἄμεικτός ἐστι καὶ πάσῃ πόλει.

Stobaeus 3.10.7 (vv. 1–3) and 3.22.2 (vv. 1, 3 without lemma).

1 ἀστῶν Stob. 3.22.2: ἐπὶ τὸ Stob. 3.10.7 ms. S (ἐπὶ τῷ mss.
MA)   2 omitted by Stob. 3.22.2, deleted by Wecklein

IXION

test. iii

Now these judgments and opinions conveyed in the words (of
a poet) are easy to notice for anyone who pays attention. But
they (i.e. the poets) also provide lessons from the actions
themselves (that they portray). Thus Euripides is said to have
answered those who criticized his Ixion for being impious and
impure by saying, 'But I did not bring him off the stage before
I had nailed him to the wheel.'

424

Son of Phlegyas,[1] lord Ixion . . .

[1] A son of Ares, and father of Coronis the mother of Asclepius
(Pindar, *Pythians* 3.8). His name suggests 'Fiery'. Several alterna-
tive fathers of Ixion are named in ancient sources, including Zeus:
see Gantz 719.

425

Anyone who is inclined to have more than his fellow-
citizens {neither thinks nor wants anything just;} is uncon-
genial to his friends and all his community.

426

τά τοι μέγιστα πάντ᾽ ἀπείργασται βροτοῖς
τόλμ᾽ ὥστε νικᾶν· οὔτε γὰρ τυραννίδες
χωρὶς πόνου γένοιντ᾽ ἂν οὔτ᾽ οἶκος μέγας.

Stobaeus 4.10.14

1 ἀπείργασται Heath, Musgrave: ἀπεργάζεται Stob.

**426a (= adesp. 4 N)

τοῦ μὲν δικαίου τὴν δόκησιν ἄρνυσο,
τὰ δ᾽ ἔργα τοῦ πᾶν δρῶντος ἔνθα κερδανεῖ.

Plutarch, *Moralia* 18d; Stobaeus 3.3.38 (ed. Trincavelli only, without lemma)

2 τοῦ πᾶν δρῶντος ἔνθα κερδανεῖ Nauck, following Heath and Musgrave: τοῦ πᾶν δρῶντος· ἔνθα κερδανεῖς Plut., Stob.

427

οἱ δὲ τοῖς ἐναγέσι προσφθεγγόμενοι καὶ αὐτοὶ δοκοῦσι
μιαίνεσθαι, ὡς καὶ ἐν Ἡρακλεῖ καὶ Ἰξίονι δέδεικται.

Schol. on Euripides, *Orestes* 73

426

Boldness is the means for men to win all the greatest prizes. Neither tyrannies nor great domains can be gained without striving.

**426a (= adesp. 4 N)

Aim for the reputation of a just man, but the deeds of one who does anything when he will gain by it.

427

Those who address polluted people think they become polluted themselves, as is shown in *Heracles* and *Ixion*.[1]

[1] Cf. *Heracles* 1155–62, 1198–1234 (where the enlightened Theseus in fact dismisses Heracles' fear of polluting him). For Ixion's pollution cf. test. iii above.

HIPPOLYTUS VEILED

W. S. Barrett, *Euripides. Hippolytos* (Oxford, 1964), 18–26; M. R. Halleran, *Euripides. Hippolytus* (Warminster, 1995), 25–37; H. Van Looy in ed. Budé VIII.2.221–48.

For the ever-expanding literature on this play and its relation to the extant *Hippolytus*, Sophocles' *Phaedra*, and Seneca's *Phaedra* see Barrett 10–45; Webster 64–71; B. Snell, *Szenen aus griechischen Dramen* (Berlin, 1971), 25–51; *LIMC* V.i.445–64 'Hippolytos I'; G. Danek, *Wiener Studien* 105 (1992), 19–37; O. Zwierlein, *Senecas Phaedra und ihre Vorbilder nach dem Fund der neuen Hippolytos-Papyri* (Mainz, 1987), revised in *Lucubrationes Philologae I* (Berlin–New York, 2004), 57–136, esp. 57–90; Gantz 285–8; J. Gibert, *CQ* 47 (1997), 85–97; W. Luppe, articles cited under test. iia and F **953f below; H. Roisman, *Hermes* 127 (1999), 397–409; G. O. Hutchinson, *ZPE* 149 (2004), 15–28; M. Magnani, *Eikasmos* 15 (2004), 227–40.

There is no certain evidence for Hippolytus' story before tragedy of the mid-5th century. In Euripides' surviving play, Hippolytus, son of Theseus king of Athens and the Amazon Hippolyte, falls victim to the anger of Aphrodite because he rejects sexuality and devotes himself at Troezen to hunting and the virgin goddess Artemis. Aphrodite fills Theseus' new wife Phaedra with desire for Hippolytus;

when she comes to Troezen, she fails to conceal her desire, and her nurse betrays it to Hippolytus. He rejects it violently. Although he undertakes, indeed swears, not to disclose it to Theseus, Phaedra fears he yet may; in a letter to Theseus she falsely accuses Hippolytus of making the first advance, and hangs herself. Theseus arrives, finds the letter, believes it at once, condemns Hippolytus to exile but adds a death curse in the name of Poseidon. Hippolytus will not defend himself, merely protest his innocence. As he drives away into exile, in a chariot along the seashore, the god sends a monstrous bull from the sea which bolts his horses, and he is fatally injured. When he is brought back dying, Artemis appears and discloses Aphrodite's work, and forecasts a cult in his memory. Before he dies, Hippolytus absolves the broken Theseus from blame.

That is the plot of the surviving play, known to ancient scholars as Hippolytus Stephanephoros ('Garland-bearer': he brings a garland to Artemis, Hipp. 82–3) to distinguish it from the now fragmentary play which they named Kalyptomenos ('Veiling Himself': Schol. on Theocritus 2.10 = test. iv; Pollux 9.50 citing F 442). The hypothesis of Aristophanes of Byzantium (= test. i below, about 200 B.C.) states that the extant play was the second in time (see below on the date), and that what was 'unseemly and reprehensible' in the earlier one was 'put right' in it. Modern scholars have almost all believed that the 'unseemly and reprehensible' was a direct approach to Hippolytus by Phaedra herself. Asclepiades (FGrH 12 F 28 = test. *iic (1)) has 'she decided to persuade the young man to have sex with her'; F 430 has Phaedra speaking of 'Eros . . . (my) teacher of daring': these are tones inconsistent with the initially tormented Phaedra of the extant play, in which Phaedra does *not speak face to face with Hippolytus at all. These scholars believe too that it was this directness of Phaedra, rather than the nurse's oblique approach to Hippolytus in the extant play, that lay behind Aristophanes' depiction of Phaedra as a typical Euripidean 'whore'* (Frogs 1043, 1052–4 = test. iiia; cf. Women at the Thesmophoria 491–8). *There was at least one further and major difference between the plays: in the lost play Phaedra killed herself only after the truth came out and Hippolytus had been injured or killed; this is strongly implied by Asclepiades (above) and by Apollodorus,* Epit. 1.19 (= test. *iic (2)).

Greater differences still are argued by Danek, Roisman, Luppe, Van Looy, Hutchinson and Magnani. All suggest reconstructions of various fullness, but so differently that no consensus seems achievable; for example, they are at variance over the location, nature and success of Phaedra's approach to Hippolytus (test. iia.6–15, iib throughout), the identity of the killer and victim (test. iia.1), the cause of the 'veiling' and even the identify of the 'veiler', and whether Phaedra rather than Hippolytus is punished by Aphrodite. Hutchinson and Magnani usefully review the state of the problem. Our own discussion ignores the most dangerous temptation of all: to reconstruct Euripides' play from reference to the scanty remains of Sophocles' Phaedra *(date unknown) and through back-projection from Seneca's tragedy; Seneca's debt to either Greek tragedian, his independent invention, or the balance between them, cannot be surely established (see especially Zwierlein 2004).*

The few fragments of Hippolytus Veiled *in fact mostly suggest, or are consistent with, a plot and general character like those of the extant* Hippolytus. *F 428 contrasts Hippolytus' aversion to sex with Phaedra's desire, and probably is a warning to him (cf.* Hipp. *88–120); F 429 (a* *comment from the chorus of women), F 430 (Phaedra's response?) and F 432–4 (she may herself speak F 433–4) relate to her boldness in satisfying her desire; it is inferred from the Scholia on Theocritus 2.10 (test. iv) that she had invoked the moon in conventional love magic. F 430 and 432–4 indeed attest the very 'direct' Phaedra surmised from the Aristophanic hypothesis; so too may F 435, by which time she has approached Hippolytus; the fragment itself hints that she has either supplicated or induced an oath of silence from him (cf. the nurse's manoeuvre at Hipp. 601–15), and defies him to break it; F 436 expresses his disgust, and may be the moment when he veils himself, in the conventional gesture of shame and repudiation. F 437–8 may belong to this scene, or come already from Theseus' condemnatory argument with Hippolytus; F 439 certainly does, abusing Hippolytus' hypocrisy (cf. Hipp. 925–31); F 440 probably also belongs here, with the chorus (or a servant) protesting at Theseus' credulity, like F 441, another protest. F **953f would fit here if it belongs to the play (see after the other fragments below); it would be Theseus' sentence of banishment. F 442 is almost certainly from a messenger's report of the chariot disaster. By F 443 the truth is clear, and Phaedra (rather than Hippolytus) bids farewell to life (but some reconstructors see this fragment as a greeting to life's joys from Phaedra on her initial entry, or from Theseus returning from Hades); F 444 and 445 may be her own further bitter comments (when Plutarch, Moralia 28a [test. v] has Euripides' Phaedra rebuking Theseus for his sexual transgressions as the cause of her own, such a moment can come only from Hippolytus Veiled, either in this scene or in her earlier letter). F 446 is the play's end; the chorus' satisfaction at Hippolytus' cult after death implies that Artemis has come to predict it (cf.*

Hipp. 1423–9). *All these book fragments however contain no allusion to Phaedra's false accusation (and neither Asclepiades nor Apollodorus explicitly mentions a letter), nor to Theseus' curse which led to the fatal attack of the bull.*

Filling out this action, and perhaps reshaping it, from the papyrus hypotheses is hazardous; despite their promising overlaps, they yield no certain spans of sense, even short ones, and supplementation of their many incomplete words is seldom convincing. For instance, it remains mere speculation that Phaedra killed someone as part of her attempt to seduce or incriminate Hippolytus (test. iia col. ii.1). On the other hand, that she fabricated his breaking into her chamber (test. iib.10–14) gets implicit support from Apollodorus ('Phaedra splintered the doors of her chamber and tore her dress apart and falsely accused Hippolytus of violence': test. *iic (2)(c)). It seems certain that Theseus ordered some kind of scrutiny of Phaedra's accusation and Hippolytus' real conduct, probably after condemning him to exile and in response to criticism that he was too credulous (test. iia col. ii.13–17; test. iib.34–7), but before the messenger reported the chariot disaster: this forms a major difference between the plays. P. Mich. gives an apparent role in the scrutiny to '(one of?) Hippolytus' slaves' (test. iib.21); Luppe's supplement has this man ordered to 'cover himself' in (the now absent) Hippolytus' clothing (test. iib.29–31), and he suggests that such a trick to detect Phaedra's true mind would lead to a 'sensational' reinterpretation of the play's title—rather, it must be said, an impossible one, for the title Hippolytus Veiled *or* Veiling Himself *cannot connote an action by an impersonator. It is possible however that a 'scrutiny' was reported to Theseus and reversed his satisfaction at Hippolytus' injuries, per-*

*haps before news of them came, whereas in the extant play
the goddess Artemis herself disillusions him.*

*There are some similarities of motif, character, plot and
sequence with* Stheneboea, *close in date, in which Stheneboea
unsuccessfully tries to seduce the morally upright
Bellerophon (but with the aid of her nurse), and fails both
in this and with retaliation; but she meets her death at
Bellerophon's own hands. Zwierlein (2004) has made
much of these similarities in reconstructing* Hippolytus
Veiled.

Brief fragment: F 447 'ship's captain'. Other ascriptions: Theseus *F 386; F 897, 898, 929a, 964, 987, 1067, and
particularly **953f printed below after F 446. Sophocles,*
Phaedra *F 684, five lines about love's universal power over
men and gods, was once ascribed (= Eur. F 431 N).*

*The date of the play is again in dispute, after Gibert's
contention (1997) that the long-trusted test. i (below) may
be unreliable in dating the lost play before the extant one, a
view accepted by Hutchinson, Zwierlein and (hesitantly)
Kannicht at TrGF 5.460, but rejected by Van Looy and
Luppe (most recently (2005), 111–12; see further on test. i
below). Hutchinson's argument for dating the extant play
much earlier than 428 on metrical grounds is rebutted by
M. Cropp and G. Fick, ZPE 154 (2006), 43–5.*

Apart from Sophocles' fragmentary Phaedra *and Seneca's surviving* Phaedra, *only Lycophron's* Phaedra *is
known, and solely by title. Fifth-century tragedy introduced the story to art; the first certain representations are
from the 4th century (LIMC lists 126 all told). See R.
Armstrong,* Cretan Women *[Oxford, 2006], 261–98 and
OGCMA II.883–8 for the extraordinary life of this story in
the modern era.*

471

ΙΠΠΟΛΥΤΟΣ ΚΑΛΥΠΤΟΜΕΝΟΣ

test. i

ἡ σκήνη τοῦ δράματος ὑπόκειται ἐν †Θήβαις†. ἐδιδάχθη
ἐπὶ Ἐπαμείνονος ἄρχοντος ὀλυμπιάδι πζ΄ ἔτει δ΄. πρῶτος
Εὐριπίδης, δεύτερος Ἰοφῶν, τρίτος Ἴων. ἔστι δὲ οὗτος
Ἱππόλυτος δεύτερος, ⟨ὁ⟩ καὶ Στεφανίας προσαγορευ-
όμενος. ἐμφαίνεται δὲ ὕστερος γεγραμμένος· τὸ γὰρ
ἀπρεπὲς καὶ κατηγορίας ἄξιον ἐν τούτῳ διώρθωται τῷ
δράματι . . .

Hypothesis of Aristophanes of Byzantium to the extant *Hip-
polytus*, preserved in medieval mss. W. Luppe, *Philologus* 142
(1998), 173–5 suggests that text has been lost before ἔστι δὲ
οὗτος: see note opposite.

472

HIPPOLYTUS VEILED

test. i
Hypothesis of Aristophanes of Byzantium to the extant Hippolytus:

The play's scene is set in †Thebes†. It was produced in the archonship of Epameinon in the fourth year of the eighty-seventh Olympiad (428 B.C.). The first prize went to Euripides, the second to Iophon, the third to Ion. This *Hippolytus* is the second and is also named *The Garland-bearer*; and it is clearly written later, for what was unseemly and reprehensible has been put right in this play.[1]

[1] In the first sentence 'Thebes' is usually corrected to 'Troezen', where the extant *Hippolytus* is in fact set. Luppe however (most lately, 2005) maintains that the hypotheses to two different plays are here conflated, and that the location and date given belong to an unnamed play while those for the extant *Hippolytus* have vanished.

test. iia (Hypothesis, P. Oxy.)

Beginnings from lines of 40–42 letters each (underlining marks words found also in test. iib):

col. i 19 Ἱππόλυ]τος ε[

(about seven lines lost)

col. ii 1 <u>των κατέσφαξ</u>[2 <u>χαράξασα παρ</u>. .[3 Ἱππολύτου δι[
4 μετὰ βίας τον[5 <u>παρθενων</u> . . .[6 πλείονος γει . [
7 <u>πιστεύσας</u> α[8 <u>καὶ μετ᾽ οὐ π</u>[ολὺ 9 <u>τὸν ἀσεβήσα</u>[ντα
10 λειπομεν[11 πον ἐκελ[ευ 12 .οβον απ[
13 .ιδ᾽ ἀποτυχ[<u>ἐκέ-</u>] 14 <u>λευσεν</u> του[<u>κα-</u>] 15 θ[ί]σαι
<u>λημ</u>[ἐ-] 16 <u>λεγχον</u> ων[17 <u>ἐζήτει</u> π[18 *(a few letters)*

P. Oxy. 4640 col. i.19–20 and col. ii, ed. M. van Rossum-Steenbeek (2003); overlapped by a fuller version in P. Mich. inv. 6222A (= test. ii b below), ed. G. Schwendner (diss. U. Michigan, 1988), re-ed. W. Luppe, ZPE 102 (1994), 23–39. Both papyri are reconsidered and correlated by van Rossum; see further Hutchinson and Magnani (bibl. above) and W. Luppe, ZPE 151 (2005), 11–14 (cf. 156 [2006], 38) and in Bastianini–Casanova, *Euripide e i papiri* 87–96.

5 παρθενῶνος . [Luppe   12 φ]όβον (eds.) seems inevitable but fits the traces uncertainly.

test. iia

*Remains of a narrative hypothesis, P. Oxy. 4640 (under-
lined words are found also in test. iib):*

col. i: *Hippolytus* . . . *(about seven lines lost)* . . . col. ii:
(Phaedra) slew . . . <u>scratching (on?)</u>[1] . . . of Hippolytus . . . vio-
lently . . . <u>of the maidens'</u> rooms[2] . . . (of?) more . . . (Theseus)   5
<u>trusting</u> (Phaedra's accusation) . . . <u>not long after</u> . . . <u>the un-
chaste</u> (*i.e.* Hippolytus) . . . being left . . . (Theseus) ordered . . .   10
fear(?) . . . fail(ing?) . . . (Theseus) <u>ordered</u> . . . <u>to sit</u> (*or* <u>to seat</u>)
. . . scrutiny . . . <u>was seeking</u> . . .   15

[1] I.e. on a writing tablet, a false accusation, probably of
Hippolytus as in *Hipp.* 856–9.   [2] So Luppe: just 'of maidens'
ed. pr., exactly matching the letters preserved in test. iib.13.

475

test. iib (Hypothesis, P. Mich.)

*Three larger fragments from a single column (and three
very small ones omitted here), with letters from near the
ends of lines of about 30 letters each; the last two lines of
fr. C appear to contain letters which originally stood early
in the first two lines of fr. B. Underlining marks words
found also in test. iia:*

fr. A   1–2 *(a few letters each)*   3 ἐ]ζήτησε[4]ν τυχεῖν οὐκ
ἠ[δύνατο   5]εμφανη[6]θειν ἀπο[7]Θετταλι[
8 *(7 letters)*   9 οἰ]κετῶν κ[10]λαμοις[11]ενχαρ[

(two lines missing before the start of fr. C)

fr. C   12 *(7 letters)*   13]παρθενων[14]ον καὶ βοη[
15 Τρ]οιζῆν[α γ]ενομ[ε   16] ὁ Θησεὺς πιστ[εύσας
17]κατὰ τοῦ παιδ[ὸς   18 Ποσειδ]ῶνι· καὶ μετ' οὐ πολ[ὺ
19 κα]ταξιώσας αὐτὸ[ ]μ[20 τὸ]ν ἀσεβήσαντα τω[
21]τῶν δ' Ἱππολύτου δούλων ἕν[α   22 ἱ]ππο[*(more
traces)*   23–26 *(a few letters each)*

fr. B   27–28 *(a few letters each)*   29 Ἱπ]πολύτου στολὴν[
30]λιαν ἐκέλευσε[31 κα]λυψάμενον το[ ][32]τθιας
καθίσαι λη[33]ς ἀληθῆ τῶν π[34 ἔλ]εγχον γενομε[ν
35] ἡ μὲν Φαίδρα[36]ν ἐζή(τει)   37 θερ]άπων

38–41 *(a few letters each)*

P. Mich. inv. 6222A: see on test. iia above.

10 θα]λάμοις ed. pr.   11 perhaps] ἐγχαρ[αξ-
Kannicht   19 αὐτὸ[s] μ[ὲν Luppe   30 νεα]νίαν
Luppe

test. iib

*Remains of a similar but fuller hypothesis, P. Mich. inv.
6222A (underlined words are found also in test. iia):*

fr. A: (Theseus) . . . sought . . . not (able?) to achieve . . . clear(?)   5
. . . from(?) . . . Thessalian (*or* Thessaly) . . . of(?) house ser-
vants . . . bedrooms(?) . . . <u>scratching (on?)</u> . . .   10

fr. C: . . . <u>of maidens</u> . . . shout(ing?) . . . Troezen . . . (becom-
ing?) . . . Theseus <u>trust</u>(ing?) . . . against his son . . . to (Posei-   15
don?); and <u>not long after</u> . . . demanding[1] . . . <u>the unchaste</u> (i.e.
Hippolytus) . . . and (one of?) Hippolytus' slaves . . . horses . . .   20

fr. B: . . . Hippolytus' clothing . . . (Theseus) <u>ordered</u> . . . [2] . . .   30
veiling himself . . . <u>to sit</u> (*or* <u>to seat</u>) . . . truth(?) of the . . . <u>scru-</u>
<u>tiny</u> (happening?) . . . Phaedra . . . . . . <u>(was) seek(ing)</u> . . . ser-   35
vant . . .

[1] 'himself demanding', Luppe.   [2] 'ordered (the young
man)', Luppe.

428

οἱ γὰρ Κύπριν φεύγοντες ἀνθρώπων ἄγαν
νοσοῦσ᾽ ὁμοίως τοῖς ἄγαν θηρωμένοις.

Stobaeus 4.20.3; Plutarch, *Moralia* 778b

2 τοῖς ἄγαν θηρωμένοις one late ms. of Plut.: τοῖς ἀγαθὰ
ᾑρημένοις the rest: τοῖς διώκουσιν ἄγαν Stob.

429

⟨ΧΟΡΟΣ⟩

ἀντὶ πυρὸς γὰρ ἄλλο πῦρ
μεῖζον ἐβλάστομεν γυναῖ-
   κες πολὺ δυσμαχώτερον.

Stobaeus 4.22.176; Clement of Alexandria, *Miscellanies*
6.2.12.1–2 (word order adapted); later allusions.

430

⟨ΦΑΙΔΡΑ⟩

ἔχω δὲ τόλμης καὶ θράσους διδάσκαλον
ἐν τοῖς ἀμηχάνοισιν εὐπορώτατον,
Ἔρωτα, πάντων δυσμαχώτατον θεόν.

Stobaeus 4.20.25

(431 N = Sophocles, *Phaedra* F 684)

428

Those of mankind who flee too much from Cypris are similarly at fault to those who hunt after her too much.

429
<CHORUS>

In place of fire we women were born, a different fire, greater and much harder to fight.[1]

[1] Aristophanes F 469 *PCG* employs the proverb 'adding fire to fire' to describe giving a man a Phaedra as wife, almost certainly an allusion to our fragment.

430
<PHAEDRA>

I have a teacher of daring and audacity who is most inventive amid difficulties—Eros, the hardest god of all to fight.

(431 N = Sophocles, *Phaedra* F 684)

432

αὐτός τι νῦν δρῶν εἶτα δαίμονας κάλει·
τῷ γὰρ πονοῦντι καὶ θεὸς συλλαμβάνει.

Schol. on Homer, *Iliad* 4.249; v. 1: Suda α 4525; v. 2 is frequently cited (e.g. Stobaeus 3.29.33) or alluded to: see also *Temenos* F *746a.

1 δρῶν εἶτα Sud.: δρᾷ χοὔτως Schol.

433

‹ΦΑΙΔΡΑ?›

ἔγωγέ φημι καὶ νόμον γε μὴ σέβειν
ἐν τοῖσι δεινοῖς τῶν ἀναγκαίων πλέον.

Stobaeus 3.12.10

434

‹ΦΑΙΔΡΑ?›

οὐ γὰρ κατ᾽ εὐσέβειαν αἱ θνητῶν τύχαι,
τολμήμασιν δὲ καὶ χερῶν ὑπερβολαῖς
ἁλίσκεταί τε πάντα καὶ θηρεύεται.

Stobaeus 4.10.13

435

τί δ᾽, ἢν λυθείς με διαβάλῃς, παθεῖν σε δεῖ;

Erotian δ 7

436

ὦ πότνι᾽ Αἰδώς, εἴθε τοῖς πᾶσιν βροτοῖς
συνοῦσα τἀναίσχυντον ἐξῃροῦ φρενῶν.

Stobaeus 3.31.3

432

Do something *now* yourself, and then invoke the gods; for god adds his assistance to the man who strives.[1]

---

[1] The entire sentiment is proverbial, e.g. Aeschylus, *Persians* 742.

433

⟨PHAEDRA?⟩

I myself say, do not give even law greater respect amid dangers than necessity.

434

⟨PHAEDRA?⟩

Mortal men's fortunes are not in accord with their piety, but everything falls captive when hunted down by acts of daring and superior force.

435

And what must you suffer if you are released and traduce me?[1]

---

[1] Translation insecure: 'traduce' is the verb's normal sense in Euripides, but Erotian cites the fragment for the meaning 'deceive'. Nor is 'released' clear: is this from an oath of silence which Hippolytus swears to Phaedra (as to her Nurse in the extant *Hipp.* 611–2, 657–8), or from her supplication to secure one? See Introduction.

436

O shame our revered goddess, if only you accompanied all men and took Shame out of their hearts!

437

ὁρῶ δὲ τοῖς πολλοῖσιν ἀνθρώποις ἐγὼ
τίκτουσαν ὕβριν τὴν πάροιθ᾽ εὐπραξίαν.

Stobaeus 4.41.43

438

ὕβριν τε τίκτει πλοῦτος, οὐ φειδὼ βίου.

Stobaeus 4.31.55; [Menander], *Monostichs* 792 Jaekel

1 οὐ Nauck: ἢ Stob., [Men.]

439

⟨ΘΗΣΕΤΣ⟩

φεῦ φεῦ, τὸ μὴ τὰ πράγματ᾽ ἀνθρώποις ἔχειν
φωνήν, ἵν᾽ ἦσαν μηδὲν οἱ δεινοὶ λέγειν.
νῦν δ᾽ εὐρόοισι στόμασι τἀληθέστατα
κλέπτουσιν, ὥστε μὴ δοκεῖν ἃ χρὴ δοκεῖν.

Stobaeus 2.2.8; vv. 1–2: Plutarch, *Moralia* 801f; vv. 3–4 (νῦν
. . . δοκεῖν): Clement of Alexandria, *Miscellanies* 1.8.41.1

440

Θησεῦ, παραινῶ σοὶ τὸ λῷστον, ⟨εἰ⟩ φρονεῖς,
γυναικὶ πείθου μηδὲ τἀληθῆ κλύων.

Stobaeus 4.22.180

441

χρόνος διέρπων πάντ᾽ ἀληθεύειν φιλεῖ.

Stobaeus 1.8.25

437

I can see that for many people previous success generates arrogance.[1]

[1] Perhaps Theseus reproving Hippolytus' presumption after his prominence at Athens (see note on F 438 and Introduction).

438

Wealth in life, not thrift, generates arrogance.[1]

[1] Perhaps Hippolytus defends himself by asserting his own probity and simplicity, as in *Hipp.* 994–1006 etc.

439

⟨THESEUS⟩

Oh alas that facts have no voice for men (to hear) so that clever speakers would be nothing! Now, as things are, these disguise the veriest truth with fluent tongues, so that what should seem so, does not.

440

Theseus, I advise you for the best, ⟨if⟩ you are sensible: don't trust a woman even when you hear the truth from her.

441

Time as it passes usually gives all the truth.[1]

[1] Part of a warning to Theseus, and so an ironic riposte to F 439? Cf. Hippolytus to Theseus at *Hipp.* 1051–2; *Aeolus* F ** 38a with note.

442

⟨ΑΓΓΕΛΟΣ?⟩

. . . πρὸς ἵππων εὐθὺς ὁρμήσας στάσιν . . .

Pollux 9.50

443

ὦ λαμπρὸς αἰθὴρ ἡμέρας θ᾽ ἁγνὸν φάος,
ὡς ἡδὺ λεύσσειν τοῖς τε πράσσουσιν καλῶς
καὶ τοῖσι δυστυχοῦσιν, ὧν πέφυκ᾽ ἐγώ.

Stobaeus 4.52.12

444

ὦ δαῖμον, ὡς οὐκ ἔστ᾽ ἀποστροφὴ βροτοῖς
τῶν ἐμφύτων τε καὶ θεηλάτων κακῶν.

Stobaeus 4.34.50

445

ἀλλ᾽ οὐ γὰρ ὀρθῶς ταῦτα κρίνουσιν θεοί . . .

[Justin], *On Monarchy* 5.5

446

⟨ΧΟΡΟΣ⟩

ὦ μάκαρ, οἵας ἔλαχες τιμάς,
Ἱππόλυθ᾽ ἥρως, διὰ σωφροσύνην·
οὔποτε θνητοῖς
ἀρετῆς ἄλλη δύναμις μείζων·
ἦλθε γὰρ ἢ πρόσθ᾽ ἢ μετόπισθεν
τῆς εὐσεβίας χάρις ἐσθλή.

Stobaeus 3.5.2

442
⟨MESSENGER?⟩
. . . setting out at once towards the stables . . .

443
O bright heaven, and day's holy light, how sweet you are to see, both for those who prosper and those who are unfortunate, of whom I am one.[1]

[1] For possible speakers and context see Introduction.

444
O you deity, how mortal men have no way to avert their inborn or godsent[1] troubles!

[1] 'Godsent' is used of Phaedra's mother Pasiphae's sinful passion for the bull at *Cretans* F 472e.30 (a passion deplored by Phaedra at *Hipp*. 337).

445
But as the gods are not determining this correctly . . .

446
⟨CHORUS⟩
O blessed hero Hippolytus, what honours you have won, because of your chastity! Men have no other power as great as virtue; for sooner or later pure conduct receives a fine reward.[1]

[1] Almost certainly from the play's final lines; for 'hero', a reference to Hippolytus' cult after death, see Introduction.

HIPPOLYTUS VEILED,
UNCERTAIN FRAGMENT

**953f

fr. 1 col. 1   *remnants of 7 lines (1–7)*

col. ii   *beginnings of 20 dialogue trimeters, probably part of a single speech which continues into fr. 2:*

ἐᾶτε δ᾽ αὐτὸ[ν
ἐᾶθ᾽ ὑβρίζε[ιν
10   μήτ᾽ εἰ κακ[
ὁριζέτω πρ[
καὶ γῆς ὁπο[ῦ
ἱππευέτω· π[
γύης ἀροτρο[
15   ἀλλ᾽ ἔρπ᾽ ἐς ἀγ[ροὺς
φίλως καταρ[

P. Oxy. 4639, ed. A. Kerkhecker (2003), frs. 1–2 (frs. 3 and 4 yield only a few letters and are omitted here). Kerkhecker suggests ascription to *Hippolytus Veiled*; Kannicht in *TrGF* ascribes it just to Euripides.

9 ὑβρίζε[ιν· μήτε γάρ Kannicht   16 κατ᾽ ἀρ[χὴν
or καταρ[ξας Kerkhecker

HIPPOLYTUS VEILED,
UNCERTAIN FRAGMENT

**953f

*From an angry scene in which a king sends a man riding
into exile and is then addressed by the chorus. The papy-
rus' editor A. Kerkhecker suggests this is Theseus banish-
ing the chariot-driving Hippolytus (cf. Hipp. 893, 973,
1173ff.); but Kannicht in* TrGF *leaves the fragment unat-
tributed:*

fr. 1 col. ii: . . . Leave him . . . leave him to be arrogant! (For
let him neither . . .) nor if . . . bad . . . (but?) let him traverse   10
(*or* separate *or* define) . . . and where on the earth . . . let
him ride . . . ploughed(?) fields . . . So make your way into
the country . . . in a friendly way (from the beginning?) . . .   15

χὤταν παρῇ[ς
νικᾶν ἐπιστ[α
ἦ ταῦτα βουλ[
20 καὶ μηδενα[
ἄγ᾽ εἶά μοι κ[
ἐχθρῶν κα[
ἦ καὶ δοκῶ σ[οι
ἐπίσταμαι [
25 εἰ γὰρ παθει.[
τοὐμὸν μελ[
ὡς οὔτε παιδ[

fr. 2 *remnants of the centres of 12 lines (28–39), including:*
29   ]ν . . κρε‹ι›σσόνων[
30   ]ἐμαυτὸν ἐξεπί[σταμαι
31   ]ντα καὶ καθ᾽ ἡμέ[ραν
32   ] . τρίβοντα μη[
          (*change of speaker*)
33   (*line centre blank*)
34   ]νων, δέσποτ᾽, ἐξ[
35   ]ώμεσθα· μ.[.]εστ[

18 ἐπίστ[ασ᾽ Parsons   19 ἦ ταῦτα βούλ[ῃ Kannicht
25 παθεῖν [or πάθει .[P. Oxy.

488

and when (you?) are present . . . (know how?) to win . . . Is
this (what you wish?) . . . and no . . . Go on, go, I tell you . . .   20
of (my?) enemies . . . Do I really seem to you . . . I know . . .
For if . . . suffer (*or* by suffering) . . . my . . . since neither . . .   25

fr. 2: . . . of stronger . . . I know myself well . . . (daily?) . . .   30
spending time . . .

(*Chorus*?) . . . , master! . . . we . . .   35

[CADMUS (ΚΑΔΜΟΣ)]

A Cadmus *by Euripides is attested only in the late classical commentary of 'Probus' on Virgil, Eclogues 6.31 (Servius III.2, p. 333.29 Thilo–Hagen), in a discussion which also cites* Antiope *F 182a and F 941. The fragment attributed to* Cadmus, *F [448], is cited to illustrate the use of the word* χάος *'chaos' as equivalent to* ἀήρ *'air':*

οὐρανὸς ὑπὲρ ἡμᾶς †καινῶς φοτῶν† ἕδος
δαιμόνιον, τὸ δ' ἐν μέσῳ τοῦ οὐρανοῦ τε καὶ
χθονός, οἱ μὲν ὀνομάζουσι χάος . . .

'Heaven, seat of the gods † . . . † over us; and what lies between heaven and earth some call 'chaos' . . .

This is metrically defective and either very corrupt or a paraphrase rather than a direct quotation; but in any case it is not in itself sufficient to confirm that Euripides composed such a play. Valckenaer's suggestion that F 930 might be assigned to Cadmus *is not persuasive (see note there). Buecheler's assignment of* TrGF *adesp. F 536 ('You immigrant—without even being a native you hold this ⟨land?⟩ in slavery!') is even less plausible.*

CRESPHONTES

Austin, *NFE* 41–8; O. Musso, *Euripide: Cresfonte* (Milan, 1974); A. Harder, *Euripides' Kresphontes and Archelaos* (Leiden, 1985), 1–122; M. Cropp in *SFP* I.121–47, 286 (~ II.366); Diggle, *TrGFS* 111–4 (F 448a, 449, 453.15–26); H. Van Looy in ed. Budé VIII.2.257–87. See also on F 448a below.

S. Cengarle, *Dioniso* 40 (1966), 63–76; Webster 136–43; Z. Vysoký, *Strahovská Knihovna* 5–6 (1970–1), 5–18 (German summary, 19–21); Gantz 735–6; Matthiessen 263–6. Myth, political aspects: J. N. Bremmer, *ZPE* 117 (1997), 13–17; N. Luraghi in H.-J. Gehrke (ed.), *Geschichtsbilder und Gründungsmythen* (Würzburg, 2001), 37–63, esp. 51–7.

The hero is a son of the Cresphontes who established the Dorian kingdom of Messenia after the so-called Return of the Heraclidae (see Introduction to Archelaus*). According to the play, the elder Cresphontes and his two older sons were killed by a usurper Polyphontes, who forced the murdered king's widow, Merope, to become his own wife. The younger Cresphontes survived the murders, being an infant at the time, and was raised in exile by Merope's father or some other family ally. He then returned in disguise, pretending to be his own murderer and claiming the price*

493

which Polyphontes had put on his head. The king welcomed him, but Merope, unaware of his true identity and believing his story, resolved to kill him as he slept. She entered the guest chamber with an axe and was about to strike the death blow when an old servant who had acted as messenger between Merope and her son intervened and identified Cresphontes. Mother and son now plotted to kill the usurper. Merope falsely offered reconciliation, Cresphontes attacked Polyphontes unawares as he offered a celebratory sacrifice, and so vengeance and restoration were achieved.

This plot is inferred largely from Hyginus, Fab. 137 (= test. iia below: cf. Apollodorus 2.8.5, Aristotle, Poetics 1454a4–7 and Nicomachean Ethics 1111a11–12, and Palatine Anthology 3.5, which are test. iib–d). The papyri in F 448a give the end of the prologue and beginning of the parodos: Cresphontes, who has reached Polyphontes' palace in disguise and probably spoken the prologue speech, learns the local situation from (probably) a palace servant, delivers a monologue about the challenge he faces, and then exits, making way for the Chorus of old and oppressed Messenians to enter. Other fragments certainly or probably represent Cresphontes contemplating his challenge (F 450), the false reconciliation (F 449, 454, 455, 458), the same or an earlier confrontation between Merope and Polyphontes (F 451, 452), and Merope's attack on Cresphontes (F 456). A recently published Cologne papyrus enlarges F 453 and shows that the previously known choral ode praising Peace and deploring civil strife followed the preparation of the tyrant's death; its additional text comes from a scene-closing speech in which Cresphontes addresses the exiting (and unsuspecting) Polyphontes and an-

CRESPHONTES

<MEROPE.> Polyphontes, king of Messenia, killed Cresphontes son of Aristomachus and took possession of his kingdom and his wife Merope. (2) Merope however secretly entrusted the infant son she had borne to Cresphontes to a family friend in Aetolia. Polyphontes sought this child very vigorously, promising gold to whoever might kill him. (3) When he had grown up, Cresphontes planned to avenge the death of his father and brothers; so he came to king Polyphontes requesting the gold and claiming to have killed the son of Cresphontes and Merope, Telephontes.[1] (4) The king told him to stay in a guest room for the moment so that he might enquire further about him. Cresphontes fell asleep through fatigue, and an old man who had been a messenger between mother and son came to Merope weeping and saying he was not with the family friend and had disappeared. (5) Merope, believing the sleeping man to be her son's murderer, came into the chamber with an axe, unwittingly intending to slay her own son. But the old man recognized him and restrained the mother from her crime. (6) Realizing that her enemy had given her the opportunity of avenging herself,

---

[1] The name Telephontes suggests 'Killer from afar' (while Polyphontes suggests 'Killer of many'). Perhaps Cresphontes used it to disguise his real identity, and the point has become slightly confused in the summary.

datam esse ab inimico se ulciscendi, redit cum Polyphonte in
gratiam. Rex laetus cum rem diuinam faceret, hospes falso si-
mulauit se hostiam percussisse, eumque interfecit, pa-
triumque regnum adeptus est.

448a

P. Oxy.
col. i
P. Oxy.
col. ii

1–12 *remains of line ends, then 27 lines lost*

⟨ΚΡΕΣΦΟΝΤΗΣ⟩

μ[ῶν ἄδικο]ς οἴκων δε[σ]πότης περὶ ξένους;

⟨ΘΕΡΑΠΩΝ?⟩

ὁ [ζῶν γ'], ὁ δ' οὐκ ὢν πᾶσι προσφιλέστατος.

⟨ΚΡΕΣΦΟΝΤΗΣ⟩

15   τ[ίς δ' ἔσ]τι; τὸν δὲ μηκέτ' ὄντ' αὖθις φράσον.

⟨ΘΕΡΑΠΩΝ?⟩

ἀ[φ' Ἡ]ρ[α]κλειδῶν, ὄνομα Πολυφόντης, ξένε.

⟨ΚΡΕΣΦΟΝΤΗΣ⟩

[ὁ κα]τθανὼν δὲ δεσπότης τίς ἦν δόμων;

⟨ΘΕΡΑΠΩΝ?⟩

ταὐτοῦ γένους τοῦδ' οἶσθα Κρεσφόντην κλύων;

⟨ΚΡΕΣΦΟΝΤΗΣ⟩

κτιστῆρά γ' ὄντα τῆσδε γῆς Μεσσηνία[ς.

⟨ΘΕΡΑΠΩΝ?⟩

20   τοῦτον κατακτὰς δῶμα Πολυφόντης [ἔ]χει.

Vv. 1–68, 71–81: P. Oxy. 2458, frs. 1–3 (further scraps in frs. 4–
6), ed. E. G. Turner (1962); vv. 51–64, 69–93: P. Mich. Inv. 6973,
ed. S. Bonnycastle and L. Koenen (forthcoming): interim texts

CRESPHONTES

Merope made things up with Polyphontes. As the joyful king was performing a religious ceremony his guest, falsely pretending to have killed the victim, killed Polyphontes and regained his father's kingdom.

448a

1–12 *remains of line ends, then 27 lines lost*

⟨CRESPHONTES⟩
You mean the master of the house (abuses) strangers?

⟨SERVANT?⟩
The (living one) does, though the one now dead was most friendly to all.

⟨CRESPHONTES⟩
Who is he? And tell me also who it was that died.   15

⟨SERVANT?⟩
One of the Heraclids; his name is Polyphontes, stranger.

⟨CRESPHONTES⟩
And the master of the house that died—who then was he?

⟨SERVANT?⟩
You have heard of Cresphontes, one of this same family?

⟨CRESPHONTES⟩
I have—the settler of this Messenian land.

⟨SERVANT?⟩
Polyphontes killed him, and now possesses his house.   20

---

in *SFP* I (Cropp), *TrGFS* (Diggle), ed. Budé (Van Looy), *TrGF* (Kannicht).

13–30, 52: P. Oxy. identifies the speakers as $\bar{a}$ and $\bar{\gamma}$, i.e. first and third actor.

⟨ΚΡΕΣΦΟΝΤΗΣ⟩

πότερα βιαίως ἢ τύχαις ἀκουσίοις;

⟨ΘΕΡΑΠΩΝ?⟩

βίᾳ δολώσας, ὡς τυραννεύοι χθονός.

⟨ΚΡΕΣΦΟΝΤΗΣ⟩

ἄπαιδά γ' ὄντα καὶ γυναικὸς ἄζυγα;

⟨ΘΕΡΑΠΩΝ?⟩

οὔκ, ἀλλὰ δισσοὺς συγκ[ατέ]κτεινεν κόρους.

⟨ΚΡΕΣΦΟΝΤΗΣ⟩

25 ἢ πᾶσ' ὄλωλε δῆτα κα[ὶ] τέκνων σπορά;

⟨ΘΕΡΑΠΩΝ?⟩

εἷς ἐστὶ παίδων λοιπ[ός], εἴπερ ἔστ' ἔτι.

⟨ΚΡΕΣΦΟΝΤΗΣ⟩

πῶς τόν γε θάνατο[ν καὶ] τύχας ὑπεκφυγών;

⟨ΘΕΡΑΠΩΝ?⟩

μαστοῦ 'πὶ θηλῆς σμ[ικρ]ὸς ὢν ἐτ[.]'[..].[

⟨ΚΡΕΣΦΟΝΤΗΣ⟩

ἔκδημο[ς] ὢν τῆσ[δ' ἢ 'πιχ]ώριος χθ[ονός;

⟨ΘΕΡΑΠΩΝ?⟩

30 μητρ[ὸ]s [π]ατήρ νιν[

31 *has traces only; then a brief gap; then 32–38 with only
a few legible words; then a further brief gap before 39
(traces only) and line-ends in 40–47; the dialogue proba-
bly continued to 45, followed by the Servant's(?) exit
speech 46–51, then Cresphontes' monologue:*

⟨CRESPHONTES⟩
Violently, or through some unintended accident?

⟨SERVANT?⟩
Through a violent plot, so that he could rule the land.

⟨CRESPHONTES⟩
Was the one he killed childless, not wedded to a wife?

⟨SERVANT?⟩
No; the usurper killed two sons of his with him.

⟨CRESPHONTES⟩
All of his offspring, then, are dead as well?   25

⟨SERVANT?⟩
One son remains—if indeed he still lives.

⟨CRESPHONTES⟩
And how did he escape the deadly fate of the others?

⟨SERVANT?⟩
Being a small child, (still feeding?) at the breast.

⟨CRESPHONTES⟩
Away from this country, or living here in it?

⟨SERVANT?⟩
His mother's father . . . him . . .   30

thirteen fragmentary or lost lines, then conclusion of the dialogue with exit speech of the Servant(?) probably starting at 46:

---

28 end ἔτ[ι]᾿[έν] τ[ροφαῖς Radt

40 δ]άμαρτ᾽ ἔχειν   41]‥ πόσιν   42]η πάρος δέρην
43]εις ἐχθροὺς ἔχει   44]‥ας ἀντιτείσετα[ι   45]ε ἂν
γένοιτ᾽ ἐμ[46] ἑστίας ἴθι

P. Oxy. *remains of one more line-end (47), then:*
col. iii γυνὴ δε‥[
       πόσιν θ᾽ ὐ[
50   ξέναι δ᾽ ε‥[

P. Mich.
col. i κλαίουσα· χαῖρε[   ]ατα

〈ΚΡΕΣΦΟΝΤΗΣ〉

αἰαῖ· τί δράσω;‥[   ]‥
πῶς δ᾽ ἀθλίοισι ‥‥‥‥[   ]‥‥s
δεῖ σ᾽, ὦ τάλαινα καρδ[ία   ]η
55 ξίφος τε θηκτόν, ὦ ταλ[   ]‥α
ὦ νερτέρα χθὼν ‥‥[   ]‥‥ ἄπο
Ἅιδη θ᾽ ὃς ἄρχει[s]‥‥[   ]‥κάτω
‥ν‥‥λεν ἐχθρα[   ]‥[

then further line-beginnings:

59, 60 (*a few letters each*) 61 νῦν εἴ ποτε‥[62 ὑμεῖς τ᾽
ἐάσατ[63 μνησθέντες ει‥‥[64 σφ[65 ὦ φίλτατε [
66 ‥‥]πηστα[67 κ]αὶ νῦν μ[

traces of one line-beginning, then about five lines missing,
then:

P. Mich.
col. ii οὐκ ἔστι τό[λ]μης τῆσδ᾽ ὅπως ἀφέξομ[αι]
70   σὺν μητρὶ [τ]ὸν ἐμὸν ἐχθρὸν ὥστε μὴ [κτανεῖν.

... to have (as his?) wife ... husband ... (her?) throat be-   40
fore that ... has enemies ... will take vengeance ... might
come to pass (for me?) ... go (from this?) hearth ... *(one*   45
line) ... wife ... and (her?) husband ... but alien (women?)
... weeping *(sing.)*. Farewell ...   50

<CRESPHONTES>

Alas, what shall I do ... and how ... wretched ... O (my)
long-suffering heart, you must ... [1] and a sharpened sword,
O long-suffering ... O land below ... from ... and you,   55
Hades, who rule ... beneath ... (whom?) hatred (*or* hos-
tile) ... (destroyed?) ... *(two lines)* ... now, if ever ... and   61
you, permit ... remembering ... *(one line)* ... O dearest ...   65
(one line) ... now too ... *(six lines)* ... Nothing shall make
me shirk this deed of daring and fail (to kill) my foe with

---

[1] With the supplement suggested by Bonnycastle–Koenen: 'O
(my) long-suffering heart (and arm), you must . . . ' (cf. esp.
Alcestis 837); but a completion of 'you must . . . ' seems needed in
this verse. On the reconstruction and rhetoric of Cresphontes'
monologue see E. Medda, *Eikasmos* 13 (2002), 67–84.

---

45 end ἐμ[οί Mette   46 τῆσδ᾽ ἀφ᾽] ἑστίας Koenen
(ἀφ᾽ Harder)   51 κλαίουσα P. Oxy.: κλαύ]σασα P. Mich.
54 καρδ[ία καὶ χεὶρ ἐμ]ή (e.g.) Bonnycastle–Koenen
58 ὃν εἷλεν Bonnycastle–Koenen   64 ⟦πατρὸς⟧ σφ[P.
Oxy. (πατρὸς perhaps belonged at the end of the previous line)

Ζεῦ, Ζεῦ, σὺ [δ'] ἡμᾶς εὐτυχεστέρους πατ[ρὸς
θὲς ἀλλ' ἐπειδὴ μονογενεῖς λελείμμεθα.

ΧΟΡΟΣ

73a   αἰαῖ· φεῦ·
73b   ὦ γεραιοί, πρόβατε τᾷδε,
        βάρεα γουνάτων φέροντες
75   πολυετ[έα], μακροβίοτα
        μέλεα· δίκετε βάκτρ['] ἐς οὖδας.
        ἔκλαυσα τάδε μέλαθρα [...]....[.]..ιλων
        τυράννου μόνα[ ] μόνου στερέντα
        τοῦ πάλαι ποτε[.]...[..ν.[.].[.]ς
80   ὁ πολυδάκρυτος·
        ὅσιον ἄφατο[ν] ἔμ' αὐ[δ]ᾶ[ν]·
        φεῦ, φεῦ· ὦ γῆρας, ὦ πα.δι.[
        τάλα[ι]να [......].ιμως πτερου[σ]σα
        ἀείδο[υσ......].η φιλοπροσῳδ[ί]ᾳ
85   ἀλέᾳ [.........]στρεφει παρα[ἀπο-
        ζυγεῖ[σα .. παιδ]ὸς οὗ πόθῳ στ[έ]νεις·

72 ἀλλ' P. Mich.: τὰ ἄλλα above line, altered to τὰ δ'
ἄλλα P. Oxy.: θὲς τἄλλ', ἐπειδὴ Slings: θὲς· τἄλλ' ἐπειδὴ
Kannicht   73–81 colometry as in P. Oxy. (colometry appears
to be lacking in P. Mich.)   76 δίκετε βάκτρ[α Kannicht:
δίκε τὸ βάκτρ[ον P. Mich.: δ'ι[P. Oxy.?   77 ἔκλαυσα[P.
Oxy.: ἔκλυον P. Mich.   82–3 ὦ Πανδίο[νος] τάλα[ι]να
[παῖς Haslam   84 ἀείδο[υσ' ὀξέα μέ]λη (e.g.)
Bonnycastle–Koenen   85 [φωνᾷ τ' ἐπι]στρεφεῖ Haslam

my mother's aid. Zeus, Zeus, make me more fortunate than   70
my father, now at least when I am left as his only son![2]

Alas, woe! Old men, step forward this way . . . bearing the
years-old weight that loads your knees . . . long-lived limbs.   75
Plant your staffs on the ground. I weep for[3] this house . . .
alone, deprived of its former ruler's only (son?) . . . the
much-weeping (*or* much-wept) one . . . a sacrosanct, un-   80
mentionable thing for me to utter. Alas, alas! O old age, O
wretched (daughter of Pandion?)[4] . . . feathered, sing(ing
your shrill songs?) with vain tunefulness (and modulating
voice?) separated from your son, in yearning for whom you   85

[2] P. Oxy.'s wording (before its unmetrical correction: see app.
opposite) could give 'Make me more fortunate than my father in
other regards, seeing that I am left . . . ' (Slings), or 'Make me more
fortunate than my father, especially because . . . ' (Kannicht).
[3] P. Mich. has 'I heard that . . . '   [4] As Haslam observed, this
sentence seems to have referred to Procne, daughter of king
Pandion of Athens, who became a nightingale after killing her son
to punish her husband Tereus for raping and mutilating her sister
(cf. *Phaethon* 67–70). Sophocles dramatized the story in his
Tereus.

δεινα[........]αζε. συγγόνου δ[ ]δεασθε[
χερὶ σφ[........]ν τέκνοισι φονίω[ι
ἅμ' αἴτ[ιος τοσῶν]δ' ἐμοὶ κακῶν ὤ[ν.

*remains of four further lines, perhaps the beginning of
an antistrophe, including* 90 πατρὸς τέκνων, 92 τάδ'
ἐπαφεθ[έντα, 93 τυ]ράννων κυσίν τε

87–88 συγγόνου δ'[ὅ]δ' ἀσθε[νέσι] χερὶ σφ[αγεὺς ἐπῆ]ν
τέκνοισι φονίῳ Bonnycastle–Koenen

449

traces of two lines in the papyrus
ἐχρῆν γὰρ ἡμᾶς σύλλογον ποιουμένους
τὸν φύντα θρηνεῖν εἰς ὅσ' ἔρχεται κακά,
5 τὸν δ' αὖ θανόντα καὶ πόνων πεπαυμένον
χαίροντας εὐφημοῦντας ἐκπέμπειν δόμων.
remains of three more lines in the papyrus

P. Fayum, ed. R. A. Coles, *ZPE* 6 (1970), 247–8 (fragmentary
lines, perhaps from an anthology, so vv. 1–2, 7–9 may not be from
Cresphontes); vv. 3–6: Sextus Empiricus, *Outlines of Pyrrhonism*
3.230; Clement of Alexandria, *Miscellanies* 3.3.15.2; Stobaeus
4.52.42; Schol. on Hermogenes, *On Invention*, ed. C. Walz, *Rhet.
Gr.* VII.765.17; Latin translation in Cicero, *Tusculan Disputa-
tions* 1.115; vv. 4–6: Strabo 11.11.8; Plutarch, *Moralia* 36f;
Menander Rhetor p. 413.27–9 Spengel (p. 162 Russell–Wilson);
and elsewhere in whole or part.

3 ἐχρῆν Sext., Stob., others: ἔδει Clement., Schol. Hermog.,
others: *decebat* Cicero

moan . . . But (this man) with bloody hand (stood as executioner over?) his brother's (feeble) children, (being) the cause (of these great evils) for me as well . . . father's children . . . these(?) . . . discharged at . . . tyrants' . . . and for dogs . . .

449

. . . *(traces of two lines)* . . . We would do better to assemble and bewail a newborn child for all the troubles he is entering, and when a man dies and has his rest from hardships to see him from his home with joy and cries of gladness[1] . . . *(remains of three lines)* . . .

---

[1] Euripides may have borrowed this idea from Herodotus 5.4, where the practice of mourning births and celebrating deaths is ascribed to the Thracian Trausi. For the sentiment 'better not to be born' cf. *Bellerophon* F 285.1–2, F 908.1, Sophocles, *Oedipus at Colonus* 1224–5.

EURIPIDES

450

ΚΡΕΣΦΟΝΤΗΣ

εἰ μὲν γὰρ οἰκεῖ νερτέρας ὑπὸ χθονὸς
ἐν τοῖσιν οὐκέτ᾽ οὖσιν, οὐδὲν ἂν σθένοι.

[Plutarch], *Moralia* 110b

451

ΜΕΡΟΠΗ

εἰ γάρ σ᾽ ἔμελλεν, ὡς σὺ φής, κτείνειν πόσις,
χρῆν καὶ σὲ μέλλειν, ὡς χρόνος παρήλυθεν.

Aulus Gellius 6.3.28

452

< ΠΟΛΥΦΟΝΤΗΣ? >

ἐκεῖνο γὰρ πέπονθ᾽ ὅπερ πάντες βροτοί·
φιλῶν μάλιστ᾽ ἐμαυτὸν οὐκ αἰσχύνομαι.

Schol. on *Medea* 84

453

Line-ends from a scene-ending speech by Cresphontes:

1] συμφορας [2].ον..φοινιο[3 μά]χαιραν ἤ σ᾽
ἀποκτενεῖ 4]...ν μαθήσομαι 5] τὴν ἐμὴν

P. Köln 398, ed. M. Gronewald (2003), has vv. 1–14 and parts of
vv. 15–26 (and a few further lines) without colometry; vv. 15–26:
Stobaeus 4.14.1; vv. 15–22: Polybius 12.26.5 (= Timaeus *FGrH*
566 F 22); vv. 15–16 were parodied in Aristophanes, *Farmers*
F 111 *PCG*

508

450
CRESPHONTES

If he dwells in the land below with those who are no more,
he can have no strength.[1]

[1] The source indicates that Cresphontes refers to Heracles,
who could be thought of as either a ghost in the underworld or a
god in heaven. Cresphontes might expect help from his ancestor
if he were a god, but not if he were a ghost (cf. *Heracles* 145–6,
296–7).

451
MEROPE

If, as you claim, my husband was waiting to kill you, you
should have waited too, since time had passed.[1]

[1] Merope exploits alternative meanings of the verb μέλλειν,
either 'intend' or 'delay'. Gellius says that she 'outwitted' Poly-
phontes with this riposte, so it may have occurred in the false rec-
onciliation scene.

452
⟨POLYPHONTES?⟩

My experience is the same as every man's: I feel no dis-
grace in loving myself above all.

453
⟨CRESPHONTES⟩
(to Polyphontes, exiting)[1]

. . . misfortune(s) . . . bloody . . . knife which will kill you . . .
I shall learn . . . my unmanliness . . . I . . . gods . . . rather, and   5

[1] Polyphontes does not hear Cresphontes' words as he leaves
for the sacrifice at which he expects to celebrate the death of
Merope's son: cf. *Electra* 1139–46, *Heracles* 726–33, *Bacchae*
847–61.

ἀνανδρίαν 6]. ἐγὼ θεοί 7] μᾶλλον ἐσθίων τε σῶν
8]ε πρόσπολοι δόμων 9].. μαθη τὸ σωφρονεῖν
10]τε νῦν φέρει με... 11]α παῖδα.......υσφ[
12]γ᾽ ἱερεύω δ᾽ ἐγώ 13 λ]έγει μήτηρ ἐγώ
14]. συμβούλους θέλει.

ΧΟΡΟΣ

στρ.   Εἰρήνα βαθύπλουτε καὶ
16   καλλίστα μακάρων θεῶν,
    ζῆλός μοι σέθεν ὡς χρονίζεις.
    δέδοικα δὲ μὴ πρὶν πόνοις
    ὑπερβάλῃ με γῆρας,
20   πρὶν σὰν χαρίεσσαν προσιδεῖν ὥραν
    καὶ καλλιχόρους ἀοιδὰς
    φιλοστεφάνους τε κώμους.
    ἴθι μοι, πότνια, πόλιν.

ἀντ.   τὰν δ᾽ ἐχθρὰν Στάσιν εἶργ᾽ ἀπ᾽ οἴ-
25   κων τὰν μαινομέναν τ᾽ Ἔριν
    θηκτῷ τερπομέναν σιδάρῳ.

parts of a few more lines in the papyrus, colometry uncertain, including the words πόλεος, στάσιν, πόλιν

18 δέδοικα Stob., Polyb.: δέδια (for metre) Rupprecht
20 προσιδεῖν χαρίεσσαν (for metre) Austin   23 <ἴθ᾽ > ἴθι
(for metre) Diggle   πότνα (for metre) Bergk   24 τὰν δ᾽
ἐχθρὰν στάσιν Stob.: ἐχθρ]ὰν δὲ στάσι[ν P. Köln

eating (from?) your . . . servants . . . of/from the house . . . he may learn(?) self-control . . . now carries . . . son . . . and I   10
perform the sacrifice . . . (as?) my mother says, I . . . wants . . . advisers.

Peace, with your depths of wealth, fairest of the blessed   15
gods, I pine for you, so long you are in coming; I fear old age may overwhelm me with hardships before I can look upon your graceful beauty, your songs adorned with   20
dancing, your garland-loving revels. Come, mistress, to my city!

Ban from our homes the hateful Discord, and raging Strife that delights in whetted iron . . . city . . . discord . . . city . . .   25

454

ΜΕΡΟΠΗ

τεθνᾶσι παῖδες οὐκ ἐμοὶ μόνῃ βροτῶν
οὐδ᾽ ἀνδρὸς ἐστερήμεθ᾽, ἀλλὰ μυρίαι
τὸν αὐτὸν ἐξήντλησαν ὡς ἐγὼ βίον.

[Plutarch], *Moralia* 110d

455

⟨ΜΕΡΟΠΗ⟩

καὶ δὶς ἔπτ᾽ αὐτῆς τέκνα
Νιόβης θανόντα Λοξίου τοξεύμασιν

Schol. on *Phoenician Women* 159

456

ΜΕΡΟΠΗ

†ὠνητέραν† δὴ τήνδ᾽ ἐγὼ δίδωμί σοι
πληγήν.

Plutarch, *Moralia* 998e

1 †ὠνητέραν† δὴ: ὁσιωτέραν δὴ Turnebus: ὦ νέρτερ᾽ Ἅιδη
Porson: τῷ νερτέρῳ δὴ Collard

457

αἰδὼς ἐν ὀφθαλμοῖσι γίγνεται, τέκνον.

Stobaeus 3.31.15

454

MEROPE

I am not alone amongst mortals in having had children die,
nor in being bereft of my husband. Countless women have
drained the same life as I.

455

⟨MEROPE⟩

. . . and the twice seven children of Niobe herself, killed by
Loxias' arrows . . .[1]

---

[1] Niobe is an example of extreme maternal loss and grief. Her
many children were killed by Apollo and (in some accounts) Arte-
mis when she boasted of having more children than their mother,
the goddess Leto. Both Aeschylus and Sophocles produced fa-
mous *Niobe* tragedies.

456

MEROPE

A . . . blow is this that I give to you![1]

---

[1] Plutarch describes the scene to which these words belong:
'Look at Merope in the tragedy, lifting an axe against her son in the
belief that he is her son's murderer. What a commotion she causes
in the theatre, bringing them all to their feet together, and what
terror that she will hurt the boy before the old man gets hold of
her!' The first word of the quotation as transmitted is meaningless:
'A more righteous blow is this . . .', Turnebus; 'O Hades below, to
you I give this blow', Porson; 'To you below (i.e. her supposedly
dead son) do I give this blow', Collard.

457

Modesty is born in the eyes, my child.[1]

---

[1] A proverbial thought: see Aristotle, *Rhetoric* 1384a34.

458

ΜΕΡΟΠΗ

αἱ τύχαι δέ με
μισθὸν λαβοῦσαι τῶν ἐμῶν τὰ φίλτατα
σοφὴν ἔθηκαν.

Plutarch, *Moralia* 90a

459

κέρδη τοιαῦτα χρή τινα κτᾶσθαι βροτῶν,
ἐφ᾽ οἷσι μέλλει μήποθ᾽ ὕστερον στένειν.

Stobaeus 4.31.95 (followed without new heading by a repetition of 4.31.57 = *Dictys* F 341)

514

458

MEROPE

My misfortunes, taking as their fee the dearest of my loved ones, have taught me wisdom.

459

A man should get the kind of profits that he will never lament later.

CRETAN WOMEN

H. Van Looy in ed. Budé VIII.2.289–301.

Wilamowitz, *Analecta* 255; Webster 37–9; M. Gronewald, *ZPE* 33 (1979), 1–5, and (with W. Luppe) *ZPE* 115 (1997), 47–9 (see test. *v below); Gantz 545–7, 554–6; C. Collard in McHardy, *Lost Dramas*, 52–7 (written in 1996, but taking account of Gronewald–Luppe 1997).

*Euripides' plot is summarized with extreme concision in the Scholia on Sophocles, Ajax 1297a (= test. iiia below): when the Cretan king Catreus discovered that his daughter Aerope had slept with a servant, he handed her to Nauplius to drown, but instead Nauplius married her to Pleisthenes. Aerope's behaviour in the play is described by the scholiast on Aristophanes, Frogs 849 (= test. iiib) as 'like a whore's'; since Frogs 1043 uses the word 'whore' of Phaedra (see Hippolytus Veiled) and Stheneboea (Stheneboea), who are other 'wicked' women in this early phase of Euripides' career, it looks as if Aerope was an important character here. Apollodorus 3.2.1–2 and 5 (= test. *iiic), however, tells Aerope's story differently, with no sexual wrongdoing (and without mention of Euripides): Catreus received an oracle that he would die at the hands of one of his children and tried to prevent this by giving his two daughters Aerope and Clymene to Nauplius to sell into*

*slavery (see note on F 466); but Pleisthenes married Aerope
and she bore him Menelaus and Agamemnon. Apollodorus
is at least consistent with the Sophocles scholiast in this
last detail; myth more commonly has Atreus as Aerope's
husband, and Menelaus and Agamemnon their sons, not
Pleisthenes as the husband and father (see further our
Introduction to* Pleisthenes*). The fragments themselves
confirm Nauplius as a character (F 466) but also Atreus
(source of F 465; cf. test. *v below). Next, Aristophanes,*
Acharnians *433 and the scholiast there (= test. iv) attest
the presence in the play of Thyestes 'in rags', as also in*
Thyestes *(see test. ii there); Thyestes is Atreus' brother and
in all accounts seduces his wife Aerope, drawing on himself
the hideous retaliation of being served the flesh of his chil-
dren (Aeschylus,* Agamemnon *1582–1602 etc.; again, see*
Thyestes*).*

*Catreus and Aerope are Cretan; Atreus, Thyestes and
Nauplius are from (near) Argos. The presence in the plot of
Atreus, let alone Thyestes (and 'in rags'), is one problem,
particularly if Aerope is destined to end the play married to
Pleisthenes. A second problem is the play's location: the
emphasis in the Sophocles scholiast on Aerope's behaviour
at home on Crete, and the play's name from its chorus,
strongly suggest Crete as the scene (cf. Wilamowitz 255);
but test. *v, a fragmentary papyrus commentary appar-
ently on this play, suggests illogicalities in the dramaturgy
both if Catreus sends the women away from Crete and if
they leave voluntarily (i.e. go to Argos), and if the chorus
fails to recognise Atreus from his royal retinue. The papy-
rus breaks off here, but presumably it condemned failure of
recognition in either Crete or Argos.*

What can be done with all this? A plot is feasible whose

essence is the discovery of Aerope's improper liaison (F 460?), Catreus' harsh reaction and commission to Nauplius to get rid of her (F 466: see note on the translation), and Atreus' perhaps uncomfortable presence (F 465: see note on the translation) as the father of Pleisthenes, all perhaps leading to the latter's marriage to Aerope and her happy escape (cf. Kannicht, TrGF 5.496). F 463 and 464 may be Catreus' cynical observations on the marriage. The scene would indeed be not Argos but Crete; the chorus may (illogically: test. *v) not recognise Atreus there; Nauplius and Atreus may be 'convenient' visitors to Crete, or (Kannicht suggests) Nauplius may have been summoned by Catreus and have brought Atreus with him. Thyestes would fill out this rather thin plot—but why is he in it, and in rags? Has Euripides brought him wandering to Crete after losing the throne at Argos to Atreus (Agamemnon 1585–6)? Does F 462 express his misery? Has Euripides daringly clothed him 'in rags' as the servant who in the Sophocles scholiast seduces Aerope, a seduction Euripides transfers from the time when she is Atreus' wife (Eur. Electra 720–2)? This suggestion was first made by Wilamowitz. Does Thyestes here 'leave quietly'? What then of F 467–9, an evocation of a lavish banquet, which reconstructors who locate the play in Argos, and at the seduction there, must relate to Atreus' cannibal retaliation upon Thyestes (e.g. Webster 39). F 467–9 better suit a feast on Crete celebrating Aerope's future. Lastly, F 461 and 470 cannot be located in any reconstruction.

A succinct history of attempts on the play is given by Van Looy 294–6. His own is most cautious, but he sets the play at Argos, where Nauplius arrives with Aerope and recounts Catreus' orders to him. Van Looy discards Thyestes altogether, and leaves Atreus' role in the obscurity of test. *v, discarding him from F 465 (but on p. 293 n. 7 he suggests intriguingly that test. *v relates not to Euripides but to Agathon or Carcinus: see below). Most questions asked here were posed, and some answered differently, by Collard (2005, but written before Van Looy and TrGF and overlooking Wilamowitz).

Other ascription: F 470a, a now residual heading in Stobaeus from which a quotation on the instablity of fortune has been lost.

The play was produced in 438 B.C. (test. ii: see on Alcmeon in Psophis). Aeschylus wrote a Cretan Women, and Agathon and Carcinus an Aerope: all are of unknown content. The apparent story of Euripides' play has left no trace in art.

ΚΡΗΣΣΑΙ

test. iiia

'αὐτὸς δὲ μητρὸς ἐξέφυς Κρήσσης, ἐφ' ᾗ | λαβὼν
ἐπακτὸν ἄνδρ' ὁ φιτύσας πατὴρ | ἐφῆκεν ἐλλοῖς ἰχθύσιν
διαφθοράν'· ἡ ἱστορία ἐν ταῖς Κρήσσαις Εὐριπίδου, ὅτι
διαφθαρεῖσαν αὐτὴν λάθρᾳ ὑπὸ τοῦ θεράποντος ὁ πατὴρ
Ναυπλίῳ παρέδωκεν ἐντειλάμενος καταποντῶσαι· ὁ δὲ
οὐκ ἐποίησεν, ἀλλ' ἠγγύησε Πλεισθένει.

Sophocles, *Ajax* 1295–7 and Schol. on 1297a

(test. iv: see *Thyestes* test. ii)

test. *v

(a few letters legible) ἄλογον
τὸ γυναῖκας ἐκ [Κρήτης] ὑπὸ Κατρέ-
ως πέμπεσθαι, ἄ[λογον] δὲ καὶ τὸ αὐ-
τὰς ἀφ' αὐτῶν ἀφ[ικνεῖσ]θαι καταλι-
πούσας το[*c. 8 letters* τ]υφλὸς δὲ
κ]αὶ ὁ χορὸ[ς *c. 9 letters*] τὸν Ἀτρέ[α
.]. βασιλικ[*c. 10 letters*] καὶ δορυφό[
] ἀλλὰ καὶ .[.

P. Harris 13 col. i, frs. 1 and 2, ed. M. Gronewald, *ZPE* 33
(1979), 1–5, re-ed. with W. Luppe, *ZPE* 115 (1997), 47–9

CRETAN WOMEN

test. iiia

'You (Menelaus) were yourself born from a Cretan mother, whom her own father (Catreus) caught with a man taken into her bed, and sent her to death and destruction by dumb fishes':[1] the story is in Euripides' *Cretan Women*, that when (Aerope) had been secretly violated by her servant her father handed her over to Nauplius with orders to drown her; Nauplius did not do this, however, but pledged her in marriage to Pleisthenes.

[1] 'Dumb fishes': to consume her totally, so that nothing of her disgrace should ever be told.

(test. iv: see *Thyestes* test. ii)

test. *v

. . . illogical that the women should be sent from (Crete) by Catreus, (illogical) too that they should (come) of their own accord leaving . . . and the chorus (would be?) blind . . . (not to recognise?) Atreus . . . royal . . . armed (i.e. guard) . . .

460

λύπη μὲν ἄτη περιπεσεῖν αἰσχρᾷ τινι·
εἰ δ' οὖν γένοιτο, χρὴ περιστεῖλαι καλῶς
κρύπτοντα καὶ μὴ πᾶσι κηρύσσειν τάδε·
γέλως γὰρ ἐχθροῖς γίγνεται τὰ τοιάδε.

Stobaeus 4.45.7

461

οὐκ ἂν δύναιο μὴ καμὼν εὐδαιμονεῖν,
αἰσχρόν τε μοχθεῖν μὴ θέλειν νεανίαν.

Stobaeus 3.29.23

462

ἐπίσταμαι δὲ καὶ πεπείραμαι σαφῶς
ὡς τῶν ἐχόντων πάντες ἄνθρωποι φίλοι.
οὐδεὶς γὰρ ἔρπει πρὸς τὸ μὴ τροφὴν ἔχον,
ἀλλ' εἰς τὸ πλοῦτον καὶ συνουσίαν ἔχον.
5 καὶ τῶν ἐχόντων ηὐγένεια κρίνεται·
ἀνὴρ δ' ἀχρήμων εἰ θάνοι πράσσει καλῶς.

Florentine Gnomology PSI 1476 no.1 Bartoletti (= Austin,
NFE fr. 152: without attribution); vv. 1–2: Stobaeus 4.31.11; v. 2:
Stobaeus 4.31.39, [Menander], *Monostichs* 854 Jaekel

1 end: [σ]αφ[ω]ς read insecurely in PSI by Kannicht ([λί]α[ν]
ed. pr.): λίαν Stob.

460

It is painful to have a shaming disaster befall one; but if it should happen, one must conceal and cover it well, and not proclaim it to all.[1] Such things become a mockery for one's enemies.

[1] Cf. *Cretans* F 472e.2–3, 29–33, *Oedipus* F 553, *Scyrians* F 683, and contrast *Ino* F 416.

461

You can't prosper without effort; and it is shameful for a young man to be unwilling to work hard.

462

I know, and have definite experience, that all men are friends of the rich; for no one goes where there is no sustenance, but where there is wealth and company. Also, nobility is judged a quality of the rich, while a man without property does well if he should die.[1]

[1] Thyestes in the guise of a beggar ('in rags'?) may be speaking. The rich credited with nobility: *Aeolus* F 22 with note. In v. 1 Stobaeus offers '(have) too much (experience)'.

463

οὐ γάρ ποτ᾽ ἄνδρα τὸν σοφὸν γυναικὶ χρὴ
δοῦναι χαλινοὺς οὐδ᾽ ἀφέντ᾽ ἐᾶν κρατεῖν·
πιστὸν γὰρ οὐδέν ἐστιν· εἰ δέ τις κυρεῖ
γυναικὸς ἐσθλῆς, εὐτυχεῖ κακὸν λαβών.

Stobaeus 4.23.2

464

γαμεῖτε νυν, γαμεῖτε, κᾆτα θνῄσκετε
ἢ φαρμάκοισιν ἐκ γυναικὸς ἢ δόλοις.

Stobaeus 4.22.121

465

ΑΤΡΕΥΣ

⟨Ἅιδης⟩ κρινεῖ ταῦτ(α) . . .

Schol. on Aristophanes, *Wasps* 762–3, naming Atreus as speaking to Aerope; ⟨Κ⟩ΑΤΡΕΥΣ Wilamowitz (see note opposite)

466

ἐγὼ χάριν σὴν παιδά σου κατακτάνω;

Apollonius Dyscolus, *On Prepositions* p. 246.32 Schneider (*Gramm. Gr.* II.1) = Tryphon fr. 56 von Velsen

παιδά σου Apollon.: παῖδας οὐ Bekker   κατακτάνω (as question) Schmidt: κατακτενῶ Apollon. (as statement or question, eds.)

463

The wise man should never ease the reins on his wife, nor
relax them and let her take control; for there is nothing
trustworthy about her. If anyone gets a virtuous wife, he
enjoys good fortune from a bad possession.[1]

1 Similarly F 1056–7.

464

Well, go on and get married, get married, and then die
either through poison or plot from your wife!

465

ATREUS[1]

(to Aerope)

⟨Hades⟩ will judge this . . .

1 Wilamowitz, locating the play in Crete, removed Atreus
from the cast-list and assigned this fragment to Catreus; but see
the Introduction, and test. *v.6.

466

Am I to kill your child as a favour to you?[1]

1 Almost certainly Nauplius addressing Catreus about the pro-
posed killing of Aerope. If Bekker's 'I will not kill your children'
is read, the children are Aerope and Clymene (cf. Apollodorus
3.2.2. = test. *iiic).

467

τί γὰρ ποθεῖ τράπεζα; τῷ δ᾽ οὐ βρίθεται;
πλήρης μὲν ὄψων ποντίων, πάρεισι δὲ
μόσχων τέρειναι σάρκες ἀρνεία τε δαὶς
καὶ πεπτὰ καὶ κροτητὰ τῆς ξουθοπτέρου
5 πελάνῳ μελίσσης ἀφθόνως δεδευμένα.

Athenaeus 14.640b; vv. 2–3 (πάρεισι . . . σάρκες): Eustathius
on Homer, *Odyssey* 5.247; vv. 4–5: Plutarch, *Moralia* 1097d

3 ἀρνεία Meineke: χηνεία (unmetrical) Ath., Eustath.

468

τὰ δ᾽ ἄλλα χαῖρε κύλικος ἑρπούσης κύκλῳ.

Athenaeus 11.504b

469

. . . νόμος δὲ λείψαν᾽ ἐκβάλλειν κυσίν.

Athenaeus 3.97a

νόμος δὲ ⟨δείπνου⟩ Mekler

470

†πρὶν ἂν ἐκφλῆναί με καὶ μαθεῖν λόγον†

Etymologicum Genuinum B and (slightly varied) *Etym. Magnum* p. 796.6 Gaisford under the word φλήναφος 'idle babbling'.
Syntax and meaning are faulty; one or more words have been lost.

467

What is there missing on the table? What is it not laden with? It's full of broiled seafood, and with it are tender meats of veal and a feast of lamb; and cakes and biscuits, drenched without stint in thick honey from the buzzing bee.[1]

[1] Athenaeus uses the passage to illustrate the joys of 'second courses' served occasionally on feast days by masters to their servants, after themselves eating the 'first course'; he prefaces it with *Hippolytus* 436 'second thoughts are somehow wiser'. The implication for the plot may be that Catreus has had second thoughts about Aerope and was now content to marry her off (F 464?).

468

Be cheerful about the rest of things while the cup goes round.

469

It is the custom to throw the leavings . . . to the dogs.[1]

[1] 'the leavings (of a meal)', Mekler.

470

†Before I should babble and learn the tale . . . †

CRETANS

Austin, *NFE* 49–58; C. Collard in *SFP* I.53–78, 282–4
(~ II.364–5); Diggle, *TrGFS* 115–9 (F 472, 472b, 472e);
H. Van Looy in ed. Budé VIII.2.303–32; A.-T. Cozzoli,
Euripide: Cretesi (Pisa–Rome, 2001), reviewed by V. di
Benedetto, *RFIC* 129 (2001), 210–30. See also under F
472, 472b, 472e.

M. Croiset, *Revue des Études Grecques* 28 (1915), 217–
33; A. Rivier, *Études de littérature grecque* (Geneva,
1975), 43–60 (orig. 1958); Webster 87–92, 299; M.
Schmidt in H. Froning et al. (eds.), *Kotinos. Festschrift für
E. Simon* (Mainz, 1992), 306–11 with Plate 69; *LIMC*
VI.i.574–81 'Minotauros', VII.i.193–200 'Pasiphae'; Gantz
260–1, 273–5; C. Abadie-Reynal, *CRAI* (Avr.–Juin 2002),
743–71, esp. 751–3 with Fig. 6; E. Simon, *Archäologischer
Anzeiger* 2004.2, 419–32, esp. 429–30.

*Minos claimed the kingship of Crete, asserting it was the
gods' gift to him; he said that Poseidon would send him a
confirmatory sign. He then prayed to the god to send a bull
from the sea, vowing to sacrifice it in return. A magnificent
animal appeared, and Minos took the throne; but he kept
the bull and sacrificed another. Poseidon angrily punished
him by afflicting his wife Pasiphae with a lust to mate with
the bull. She persuaded the marvellous builder and crafts-*

EURIPIDES

man Daedalus to make her an artificial cow, inside which
she put herself and was served by the bull. She gave birth to
the Minotaur, bull-headed upon a human body (F 472a,
472b.31).

   Thus Apollodorus 3.1.3–4 (test. *iiia below), without
reference to Euripides; but F 472e.21–6 summarizes
Minos' offence and punishment by Poseidon through
Pasiphae. The play survives in only a very few fragments,
mostly on badly damaged papyrus. It was set at Minos' pal-
ace on Crete, and began—probably after an introductory
prologue speech (perhaps the god Poseidon himself: Van
Looy 310)—with the discovery of the Minotaur's birth.
The Chorus of Cretan priests of Zeus makes a stately entry
(F 472); Minos may have summoned them for consultation
after learning of the monstrous birth, for their opening
words are addressed to him. They appeal to Apollo for
help, and are present when Minos interrogates Pasiphae's
Nurse(?) about the creature (F 472b); they react with lyric
alarm before Minos resumes—only for the text to break off
(F 472c).

   If Apollodorus 3.1.4 and Hyginus, Fab. 40.3 (together =
test. *iiia) reflect the play's course, Minos then ordered
Daedalus to build the famous labyrinth in which to confine
the Minotaur; but these two sources hint nothing of what
the one large fragment (F 472e) suggests was the play's cen-
tral episode: Pasiphae's behaviour and secrecy have been
uncovered, and she is arraigned before Minos. She excul-
pates herself by blaming his offence against Poseidon for all
the misery. The Chorus nevertheless fails to prevent Minos
from instantly sentencing her to death by underground im-
prisonment (F 472e.42–51: the fragment stops short here).

   The remaining action is guesswork, for Hyginus 40.4

continues with details apparently contradicting Pasiphae's punishment: when Minos imprisons Daedalus too for making the cow, she releases him; he then devises the famous wings to carry himself and (vainly) his son Icarus away from Crete. Some Etruscan relief-urns of c. 100 B.C. (LIMC 'Pasiphae' nos. 8, 10, 23, 28–31 = test. *iiib) seem to support Hyginus' narrative, with various scenes of Daedalus and Pasiphae supplicating at an altar or entreating Minos, or of Daedalus and Icarus in bonds; and an Apulian crater of c. 350 B.C. (Schmidt 1992; cf. under LIMC 'Pasiphae' no. 4; Todisco Ap 155; Taplin no. 90) may reflect the play in a composite scene including a named Daedalus, recognizably Icarus and Pasiphae, possibly Nurse and Minos (see also below on the Zeugma mosaic). That Euripides' play ended with on-stage roles for Daedalus and Icarus is also arguable from hints in the scholia on Aristophanes, Frogs 1356–64 that the parodic monody there drew upon one in Cretans (see F 472f); certainly F 988 (printed below after F 472g) looks like an exchange between Minos and Daedalus. Also, the scholia to Frogs 849 (= F 472g) state that 'Euripides had Icarus sing a monody in Cretans . . . his character seems to be rather bold'. This could have been before his fatal flight (although Van Looy 318 suggests he lamented Daedalus' imprisonment). The flight itself may have been shown at its start (like Bellerophon's flight with Pegasus in Bellerophon, and possibly in Stheneboea), and the disaster narrated by a messenger, or 'reported' by a god at the end. While most scholars posit such a god, at least to tell of Pasiphae's future, there is much doubt whether the play ended with Daedalus and Icarus at all, e.g. M. Huys, APF 43 (1997), 13–14; Cozzoli 13: see Kannicht, TrGF 5, 516; such an end-

531

ing is however supported by Schmidt (1992) and Simon (2004). Certainly the flight is more often linked in both myth and art with Daedalus' escape after aiding Theseus and Ariadne to escape from the fully grown Minotaur (see LIMC III.i.313–21 'Daidalos et Ikaros').

Despite the play's broken outline we can appreciate how the portrayal of Minos contributed to his harsh stereotype in tragedy (Plato, Minos 318d and others: test. *iv, *v). His abrupt condemnation of Pasiphae is like that of Hippolytus by Theseus in Hippolytus 882–9, 893–8. Pasiphae's wonderful counter-attack (F 472e) shows Euripides in his early career already a master of law-court rhetoric; but we cannot know whether there was a full agôn scene (cf. Van Looy 313). The dramatic needs of Pasiphae's speech excluded a self-analysis like that of another early 'bad woman' of Euripides, Phaedra in Hippolytus (Pasiphae's own daughter), with whom scholars compare her and who fears her evil inheritance from her mother (Hipp. 337–8).

Other ascriptions: F 893, F 912 (also ascribed to Oedipus or Pirithous), adesp. F 60 'But what if (s)he falls into the ocean's watery depth?' (also ascribed to Bellerophon or Stheneboea).

The metrical criteria for dating (Cropp–Fick 70, 82), and particularly the anapaestic parodos (F 472), point before 430. No other ancient tragedy with this plot is certainly known, but there were many involving Minos (above), Daedalus and Icarus; see also Euripides' Polyidus. The comic playwright Alcaeus wrote a Pasiphae, Aristophanes and three others a Daedalus, and both Apollophanes and Nicochares a Cretans: some of these may have used the Minotaur and Pasiphae for crude humour, and there were

Roman adaptations (on all these plays see Van Looy 307–8, Cozzoli 15–17). A superbly preserved Roman mosaic of about A.D. *200 at Zeugma on the upper Euphrates appears to represent* Cretans *and may show most of the characters.[1] The story was very popular in post-classical art: see OGCMA II.666–9, 842–4.*

[1] See Abadie-Reynal (Bibl. above). Pasiphae, veiled and seated on the viewer's left, looks at other figures, all of them named, towards whom a female servant points; at Pasiphae's feet is an Eros playing with a bull's head. In the centre is a Nurse, also looking to the right where Daedalus, with carpenter's tools, looks back at Pasiphae but is moving towards Icarus, who is seated and also looking off right while shaping a branch of wood. Interpretation remains insecure; the scene may be composite and allude to the myth rather than the play, but another mosaic from the same room has composite scenes from *Menander's Women Lunching Together* (named: Abadie-Reynal 763–9 with Figures 17–19); it is possible that Pasiphae is directing Daedalus (and Icarus) to make the artificial cow.

ΚΡΗΤΕΣ

test. *iiia

Ἀστερίου δὲ ἄπαιδος ἀποθανόντος Μίνως βασιλεύειν
θέλων Κρήτης ἐκωλύετο. φήσας δὲ παρὰ θεῶν τὴν βασι-
λείαν εἰληφέναι, τοῦ πιστευθῆναι χάριν ἔφη, ὅ τι ἂν
εὔξηται, γενέσθαι. καὶ Ποσειδῶνι θύων ηὔξατο ταῦρον
ἀναφανῆναι ἐκ τῶν βυθῶν, καταθύσειν ὑποσχόμενος τὸν
φανέντα. τοῦ δὲ Ποσειδῶνος ταῦρον ἀνέντος αὐτῷ δια-
πρεπῆ τὴν βασιλείαν παρέλαβε, τὸν δὲ ταῦρον εἰς τὰ
βουκόλια πέμψας ἔθυσεν ἕτερον . . . (4) ὀργισθεὶς δὲ
αὐτῷ Ποσειδῶν ὅτι μὴ κατέθυσε τὸν ταῦρον, τοῦτον μὲν
ἐξηγρίωσε, Πασιφάην δὲ ἐλθεῖν εἰς ἐπιθυμίαν αὐτοῦ
παρεσκεύασεν. ἡ δὲ ἐρασθεῖσα τοῦ ταύρου συνεργὸν
λαμβάνει Δαίδαλον, ὃς ἦν ἀρχιτέκτων, πεφευγὼς ἐξ
Ἀθηνῶν ἐπὶ φόνῳ. οὗτος ξυλίνην βοῦν ἐπὶ τροχῶν κατα-
σκευάσας . . . ἐκδείρας τε βοῦν τὴν δορὰν περιέρραψε,
καὶ θεὶς ἐν ᾧπερ εἴθιστο ὁ ταῦρος λειμῶνι βόσκεσθαι,
τὴν Πασιφάην ἐνεβίβασεν. ἐλθὼν δὲ ὁ ταῦρος ὡς ἀλη-
θινῇ βοῒ συνῆλθεν. ἡ δὲ Ἀστέριον ἐγέννησε τὸν κλη-
θέντα Μινώταυρον. οὗτος εἶχε ταύρου πρόσωπον, τὰ δὲ
λοιπὰ ἀνδρός· Μίνως δὲ ἐν τῷ λαβυρίνθῳ κατά τινας
χρησμοὺς κατακλείσας αὐτὸν ἐφύλαττεν . . .

Apollodorus 3.1.3–4

534

CRETANS

When Asterius died childless, Minos wanted to be king of Crete but was prevented. He claimed that he had received the kingship from the gods and, to gain credence, that whatever he prayed for would happen. While sacrificing to Poseidon he prayed for a bull to appear from the depths, promising to sacrifice the bull that appeared. When Poseidon sent him up a splendid bull, however, he seized the kingship but sent the bull to his herds and sacrificed another . . . (4) Angry that he had not sacrificed the bull, Poseidon maddened it and made Pasiphae come to desire it. In her passion for the bull she took Daedalus as her accomplice, who was a builder and in exile from Athens because of bloodshed. This man constructed a wooden cow on wheels . . . flaying a cow he stitched its hide round it; setting it in a meadow in which the bull was accustomed to graze, he had Pasiphae go inside it. The bull came and mounted it as if it was a real cow. Pasiphae gave birth to Asterius, called the Minotaur; he had the features of a bull, but the rest was a man. Minos in obedience to certain oracles shut him in the labyrinth and kept him secure . . .

The narrative of Apollodorus above is overlapped by Hyginus' briefer summary which ends:

535

. . . Minos re cognita Daedalum in custodiam coniecit, at Pasiphae eum uinculis liberauit. Itaque Daedalus pennas sibi et Icaro filio suo fecit et accommodauit, et inde auolarunt. Icarus altius uolans, a sole cera calefacta, decidit in mare, quod ex eo Icarium pelagus est appellatum. Daedalus peruolauit ad regem Cocalum in insulam Siciliam . . .

Hyginus, *Fab.* 40.4

(471 N = 472f below)

*471a

ἡ Κρήτη . . . εἶχεν ἐν μέσῳ θαλάσσης ὑπαρχούσας πόλεις ἑκατόν, καθὼς περὶ τῆς αὐτῆς νήσου ἐξέθετο ὁ σοφώτατος Εὐριπίδης.

John Malalas, *Chronicles* 14.12 Thurn = 14.12 Jeffreys–Scott

472

ΧΟΡΟΣ
Φοινικογενοῦς τέκνον Εὐρώπης
καὶ τοῦ μεγάλου Ζηνός, ἀνάσσων
Κρήτης ἑκατομπτολιέθρου·
ἥκω ζαθέους ναοὺς προλιπών,
5   οὓς αὐθιγενὴς στεγανοὺς παρέχει

Porphyry, *On Abstinence* 4.19; vv. 4–8 (ἥκω . . . ἁρμούς): Erotian α 4 (these two texts re-edited by Cozzoli 47–50); vv. 12–15: P. Oxy. 2461, fr. 4 (very damaged: for P. Oxy. 2461 see under F 472b below); v. 12 (in part): Hesychius ω 218 Schmidt

1 after Φοινικογενοῦς Porphyry has παῖ τῆς Τυρίας (deleted by Bothe)   5 οὓς Porphyry, Erotian: οἷς Bentley

. . . Learning of the thing (i.e. the Minotaur's birth), Minos put Daedalus under guard, but Pasiphae freed him from his bonds; and so Daedalus made wings for himself and his son Icarus, and fitted them, and they flew off. Icarus flew too high, and when the wax warmed from the sun, fell into the sea, which is called the Icarian sea for him. Daedalus flew across to King Cocalus in Sicily . . .

(471 N = 472f below)

*471a

Crete . . . in mid-ocean had one hundred cities in it, as the most learned Euripides expounded about the same island.[1]

[1] See F 472.3; probably dependent on Homer, *Iliad* 2.649.

472[1]

CHORUS

Son of Phoenician-born Europa[2] and of great Zeus—you who rule Crete and its hundred cities! I have come here from the most holy temple whose roof is provided from na- 5

[1] This remarkable fragment is densely allusive; its text and interpretation generate constant discussion: see esp. B. Gallistl, *Würzburger Jahrbücher für die Altertumswissenschaft* n.s. 7 (1981), 235–47; G. Casadio, *Didattica del Classico* 2 (1990), 278–310; Collard in *SFP* I.67–70; Cozzoli 18–26, 79–93; di Benedetto 211–9; A. Bernabé in J. A. López Férez, *La tragedia griega en sus testos* (Madrid, 2004), 257–86.   [2] I.e. Minos. Europa was abducted by Zeus in the form of a bull (cf. *Phrixus B* F 820). Myth made her father either Agenor of Phoenician Tyre or his son Phoenix (cf. *Hypsipyle* F 752g.21).

τμηθεῖσα δοκοὺς Χαλύβῳ πελέκει
καὶ ταυροδέτῳ κόλλῃ κραθεῖσ᾽
    ἀτρεκεῖς ἁρμοὺς κυπάρισσος.
ἁγνὸν δὲ βίον τείνομεν ἐξ οὗ
10   Διὸς Ἰδαίου μύστης γενόμην
καὶ νυκτιπόλου Ζαγρέως βούτης
τὰς ὠμοφάγους δαῖτας τελέσας,
Μητρί τ᾽ ὀρείᾳ δᾷδας ἀνασχὼν
μετὰ Κουρήτων
15   βάκχος ἐκλήθην ὁσιωθείς.
πάλλευκα δ᾽ ἔχων εἵματα φεύγω
γένεσίν τε βροτῶν καὶ νεκροθήκας
οὐ χριμπτόμενος, τήν τ᾽ ἐμψύχων
βρῶσιν ἐδεστῶν πεφύλαγμαι.

5–6 word-order von Arnim, Austin: στεγανοὺς παρέχει after
Χαλύβῳ πελέκει, Porphyry, Erotian   7 κόλλῃ κραθεῖσ᾽
Hermann: κολληθεὶς Erotian: κρηθεῖσ᾽ Porphyry
8 κυπάρισσος Bentley: -ίσσου Porphyry   11 καὶ Grotius:
καὶ μὴ Porphyry   βούτης Diels, Nauck: βρο(ν)τὰς Porphyry
12 τὰς Cantarella: τάς τε Porphyry   14 μετὰ Blaydes,
Wilamowitz: καὶ P. Oxy., Porphyry   17 νεκροθήκας
Wecklein: -ης Porphyry: -αις, with lacuna before καὶ and τ᾽ de-
leted in 19, Wilamowitz   18 lacuna before οὐ χριμπτό-
μενος Diggle

tive cypress-wood cut into beams with Chalybean axe and
bonded in exact joints with ox-glue.[3] Pure is the life I have
led since I became an initiate of Idaean Zeus and a servitor 10
of night-ranging Zagreus,[4] performing his feasts of raw
flesh; and raising torches high to the mountain Mother
among the Curetes, I was consecrated and named a cele-
brant.[5] In clothing all of white I shun the birthing of men, 15
and the places of their dead I do not go near;[6] against the
eating of animal foods I have guarded myself.

[3] Euripides describes skilled carpentry: see A. T. Hodge, *The
Woodwork of Greek Roofs* (Cambridge, 1960). The Chalybeans
were an iron-working people of northern Asia Minor.   [4] In v.
11 Porphyry's apparent reading 'thunders' (instead of 'a servitor')
is defended by some editors as alluding to thunder imitated dur-
ing the rites of Zagreus-Dionysus, on whose birth amid lightning
see *Bacchae* 3, 6–8. The reading creates very great further prob-
lems in the text.   [5] Vv. 9–15 refer to the cult of Zeus at his
birthplace on Mt. Ida in Crete. The Curetes (*Kourētes*) were
'(guardians) of the boy (*kouros*)', i.e. Zeus, both divinities them-
selves and worshippers impersonating them. But Euripides
brings in elements from other cults: Zagreus ('The Great Hunter')
was a son of Zeus and seemingly merged with Dionysus; 'moun-
tain Mother' here seems to be Rhea, Zeus' own mother, merged
with an original Phrygian fertility goddess Cybele (cf. *Palamedes*
F 586). Their rites were ecstatic, often nocturnal, sometimes in-
volving dismemberment and ingestion of animals, literally or sym-
bolically (historical at Plutarch, *Moralia* 417c; poetic cf. Eur.
Bacchae 734–47). 'Initiate', 'servitor' (lit. 'herdsman', a metaphor
from an outdoor cult) and 'celebrant' are loosely synonymous.
[6] White clothing and the avoidance of birth (e.g. *IT* 380–3) and
death were widespread religious purities. The apparent contra-
diction between flesh-eating (12) and vegetarianism (18–19, cf. F
1004 below) shows reality subordinated to the poetic; the latter
practice was associated with Orphism (e.g. *Hippolytus* 952–4).

EURIPIDES

472a (= 996 N)

σύμμικτον εἶδος κἀποφώλιον βρέφος

Plutarch, *Life of Theseus* 15.2 (with F 472b.29) and *Moralia* 520c

κἀποφώλιον Plut.: κἀποφύλιον Musgrave, Housman   βρέφος Plut.: τρέφος Nauck

472b

fr. 2 col. i   *Ends of eight lyric lines (metre uncertain):*
1 νέμ?]εσις ὅτ᾽ ἐπιπνεῖ, 2]ος Λυκίας ἄπο, 3 Λα]τώε
παῖ, 4]ν ὦναξ, 5].α μέλπων, 6].ψ.ασε μέγαν,
7 Δελ?]φοις, 8 εὐ]πάτειρα

(at least twenty-seven lines missing)

fr. 2 col. ii   9–17: *beginnings of seven lines (metre unclear) with no in-
dication of speaker, then two lines each preserving only a
marginal note of the speakers* 16 Χο., 17 Μι., *then an un-
known number of lines missing.*

fr. 1   18–28: *words from near the centres of eleven dialogue
trimeters including* 25 θ]εοῖσι προσβ[ολ]ὴν [, *then (29–
43):*

P. Oxy. 2461, ed. E. G. Turner (1962); frs. 2 and 1 re-ed. H.
Lloyd-Jones, Gnomon 35 (1963), 447–9; cf. di Benedetto (Bibl.
above), 219–27: frs. 2 and 1 (so ordered by Turner, Lloyd-Jones
and most editors) = F 472b; fr. 3 = F 472c; fr. 4 = F 472.12–15
above; fr. 5 = F 472d (exiguous, not printed here).

540

CRETANS

472a (= 996 N)

. . . an infant of mixed appearance, born to sterility . . . [1]

[1] ἀποφώλιον 'born to sterility' is a rare word, used to stress through contrast the gods' own fecundity at Homer, *Odyssey* 11.249. Musgrave's ἀποφύλιον means '*sui generis*, from no species, unique'.

472b

fr. 2 col. i: . . . when (retribution?)[1] blasts . . . from Lycia . . . , son of Leto![2] . . . lord! . . . singing . . . great . . . (at Delphi?)   5
. . . daughter of a splendid father[3] . . .

(*at least twenty-seven lines missing*)

fr. 2 col. ii: *beginnings of seven lines (9–15), then two lines each preserving only a marginal note of the speakers,* 16 Chorus, 17 Minos, *then an unknown number of lines missing before the next fragment:*

fr. 1: *remains of a dialogue in 18–28, stichomythic at least from 26; 25 preserves* '(with?) the gods' . . . onslaught'; *then* (29–43):

[1] If 'retribution' is correctly conjectured, this refers to the punishment of Minos' offence against Poseidon through the gods' 'onslaught' (25).   [2] Apollo, called 'Lycian', e.g. *Telephus* F 700.   [3] Artemis, Apollo's sister; their father was Zeus.

---

1 νέμ]εσις Cantarella   6 μὲ τὰν Austin: σε μέγαν
Cantarella   7 perhaps Δελ]φοῖς Cozzoli

541

EURIPIDES

⟨ΤΡΟΦΟΣ⟩

ταύρου μέμεικται καὶ βροτοῦ διπλῇ φύσει.

⟨ΜΙΝΩΣ⟩

30 ἤκ]ουσα καὶ πρίν· πῶς δ' ο[

⟨ΤΡΟΦΟΣ⟩

στέ]ρνοις ἔφεδρον κρᾶτα τ[αύρειον φέρει.

⟨ΜΙΝΩΣ⟩

τετρ]ασκελὴς γὰρ ἢ δίβαμ[ος ἔρχεται;

⟨ΤΡΟΦΟΣ⟩

δίπ]ους [μ]ελαίνη δασκ[

⟨ΜΙΝΩΣ⟩

ἢ κ]αί τι πρὸς τοῖσδ' ἄλλο [

⟨ΤΡΟΦΟΣ⟩

35 μύ]ωπος οἴστρου κέρκον [

⟨ΜΙΝΩΣ⟩

c. 10 letters]υ γῆρυν [

⟨ΤΡΟΦΟΣ⟩

c. 11 letters] φορβάδος [

29–41 ⟨ΤΡΟΦΟΣ⟩, ⟨ΜΙΝΩΣ⟩ Cantarella: ⟨ΤΡΟΦΟΣ⟩, ⟨ΧΟΡΟΣ⟩
Page; ⟨ΧΟΡΟΣ⟩, ⟨ΜΙΝΩΣ⟩ Lloyd-Jones   29 = F 997N (see
under F 472a)   33 δίπ]ους Page: δίπ]λους P. Oxy.?, Lloyd-
Jones   34 ἢ κ]αί τι Barrett:]ντι Turner   35 μύ]ωπος
οἴστρου Barrett:]ωπος ε . . .ου Turner

CRETANS

⟨NURSE⟩

It is mixed, with a twofold nature, of bull and human.

⟨MINOS⟩

I have (heard) that before too; but how . . . ?   30

⟨NURSE⟩

(It bears a bull's?) head set above its breast.

⟨MINOS⟩

So (does it go) on four legs or walk on two?

⟨NURSE⟩

On (two?) . . . dark with black . . .[4]

⟨MINOS⟩

And is there anything further . . . ?

⟨NURSE⟩

. . . a tail . . . (against?) the maddening cattle-fly.[5]   35

⟨MINOS⟩

. . . voice . . .

⟨NURSE⟩

. . . grazing . . .

[4] 'On (two?) feet', Page; '(On two feet?) dark with black (hair?), Lloyd-Jones.   [5] For the Minotaur's active tail cf. *Theseus* F 386b.7.

⟨ΜΙΝΩΣ⟩

μ]αστ[ὸς] δὲ μ[η]τρὸς ἢ βοὸς . [

⟨ΤΡΟΦΟΣ⟩

τρ]έφ[ου]σιν οἱ τεκόντες ου . [

40–43: *scraps of four more (stichomythic?) trimeters including* 40 δωμάτων, 41 τοῖς τεκο[ῦσι

38 μ]αστ[ὸς] Page, then end θ[ήλη τρέφει Diggle (τρέφει Collard): μ]αστ[ῷ] . . . βοὸς θ[ηλάζεται Luppe

472c

fr. 3 1–3: *traces of three lines ending a lyric passage (metre unclear), the last beginning* ἀπείρου μι[*, then the start of a dialogue episode, speaker unknown:*

Κρήτης απα[

5 φόβος τὰ θεῖ[α τοῖσι σώφροσιν βροτῶν

πολλὴ γὰρ . [

ἐμοὶ δ . . . [

P. Oxy. 2461 fr. 3 (see under F 472b above); v. 5 = adesp. F 356 (so Barrett: 'perhaps', Kannicht)

CRETANS

<MINOS>

. . . a mother's breast, or a cow's . . . ?[6]

<NURSE>

Its parent[7] feeds it . . .

Four more lines (stichomythic?) including 40 'of the house' *and* 41 'to its parent'.

[6] '(Does) a mother's breast or a cow's (teat feed it)?', Diggle, Collard; '(Is it suckled by) a mother's breast or a cow's?', Luppe.
[7] Pasiphae.

472c

Traces of three lyric lines, the last beginning 'inexperienced' *(or* 'limitless' *or* 'mainland'), *then beginnings of four dialogue lines:*

. . . of Crete . . . The gods' actions are a terror (to the wise among men?). For in her greatness[1] . . . but to me . . .

[1] Perhaps Aphrodite (whom this phrase describes at *Hippolytus* 443, *Iphigenia at Aulis* 557), if she aided Poseidon's retribution by filling Pasiphae with desire for the bull.

EURIPIDES

472e

<ΧΟΡΟΣ>
οὐ γάρ τιν' ἄλλην φημὶ τολμῆσαι τάδε.
σὺ †δ' ἐκ κακῶν†, ἄναξ,
φρόνησον εὖ καλύψαι.

ΠΑΣΙΦΑΗ
ἀρνουμένη μὲν οὐκέτ' ἂν πίθοιμί σε·
5 πάντως γὰρ ἤδη δῆλον ὡς ἔχει τάδε.
  ἐγ[ὼ] γὰρ εἰ μὲν ἀνδρὶ προύβαλον δέμας
  τοὐμόν, λαθραίαν ἐμπολωμένη Κύπριν,
  ὀρθῶς ἂν ἤδη μάχ[λο]ς οὖσ' ἐφαινόμην·
  νῦν δ', ἐκ θεοῦ γὰρ προσβολῆς ἐμηνάμην,
10 ἀλγῶ μέν, ἐστὶ δ' οὐχ ἑκο[ύσ]ιον κακόν.
  ἔχει γὰρ οὐδὲν εἰκός· ἐς τί γὰρ βοὸς
  βλέψασ' ἐδήχθην θυμὸν αἰσχίστῃ νόσῳ;
  ὡς εὐπρεπὴς μὲν ἐν πέπλοισιν ἦν ἰδεῖν,
  πυρσῆς δὲ χαίτης καὶ παρ' ὀμμάτων σέλας
15 οἰνωπὸν ἐξέλαμπε περ[καί]νων γένυν;
  οὐ μὴν δέμας γ' εὔρ[υθμον   ν]υμφίου·
  τοιῶνδε λέκτρω[ν οὕνεκ' εἰς] πεδοστιβῆ
  ῥινὸν καθισ .[   ]ται;
  ἀλλ' οὐδὲ παίδων .[   ] πόσιν
20 θέσθαι. τί δῆτα τῇ[δ' ἐμαι]νόμην νόσῳ;

P. Berlin 13217, ed. U. von Wilamowitz and W. Schubart (1907); re-ed. Page, *GLP* 70–7 (no. 11), Cozzoli 42–3 with Plates III, IV. The parchment was lost in 1945 and rediscovered in Warsaw in 1992.

546

CRETANS

472e

<CHORUS>

. . . for I say that no other woman dared this. Now you, my lord—think how to conceal (trouble?) following trouble!

PASIPHAE

Denials from me will no longer convince you; for the facts are now quite clear. 5

If I had thrown myself at a man in love's furtive commerce, I should rightly now be revealed as lascivious. As it is, because my madness was a god's onslaught, I hurt, but my trouble is not voluntary. Why, it has no probability! 10 What did I see in a bull to have my heart eaten away by a most shaming affliction? Was it that it was handsome to the eye in robes, and threw out a bright gleam from its ruddy hair and eyes, the beard on its cheeks darkly red? Certainly 15 it wasn't the (lissom *or* well-formed?) body of a bridegroom! Was it for a union like that . . . of an animal's hide[1] . . . ? Nor (to get)[2] children . . . to make it my husband! Why then was I (maddened) by this affliction? It was this man's 20

[1] 'Animal' is literally '(animal) walking the ground', a clear allusion to Daedalus' artificial cow; 'walking' may imply that it moved: cf. F 988 and note on *Eurystheus* F 372. Roberts' supplement gives 'Was it for a union like that that (Minos) thinks I put myself into an animal's hide?'   [2] 'to get' is the approximate sense of all the supplements.

---

1 <ΧΟΡΟΣ> ed. pr: 1 <ΜΙΝΩΣ>, 2–3 <ΧΟΡΟΣ> Körte
2 σὺ δ<ὲ κάκ'> ἐκ κακῶν Cropp   16 εὔρ[υθμόν ἐστι ed. pr.:
εὔ[μορφον Kannicht   18 καθιστ[άναι με σῶμ' ὅδ' οἴε]ται
(e.g.) Roberts   19 φ[ύτορ' εἰκὸς ἦν ed. pr. (ο[ὕνεκ' Collard):
ἐ[ς σπορὰν ἔδει Cropp

δαίμων ὁ τοῦδε κἄμ᾽ ἐ[νέπλησεν κα]κῶν,
μάλιστα δ᾽ οὗτος οισε[   ]ων·
ταῦρον γὰρ οὐκ ἔσφαξ[εν ὅνπερ ηὔ]ξατο
ἐλθόντα θύσειν φάσμα [πο]ντίῳ [θε]ῷ.
25 ἐκ τῶνδέ τοί σ᾽ ὑπῆλθ[ε κἀ]πετείσ[ατο
δίκην Ποσειδῶν, ἐς δ᾽ ἔμ᾽ ἔσκηψ[εν νόσον.
κἄπειτ᾽ αὐτεῖς καὶ σὺ μαρτύρῃ θεοὺς
αὐτὸς τάδ᾽ ἔρξας καὶ καταισχύνας ἐμέ;
κἀγὼ μὲν ἡ τεκοῦσα κοὐδὲν αἰτία
30 ἔκρυψα πληγὴν δαίμονος θεήλατον,
σὺ δ᾽, εὐπρεπῆ γὰρ κἀπιδείξασθαι καλά,
τῆς σῆς γυναικός, ὦ κάκιστ᾽ ἀνδρῶν φρονῶν,
ὡς οὐ μεθέξων πᾶσι κηρύσσεις τάδε.
σύ τοί μ᾽ ἀπόλλυς, σὴ γὰρ ἡ ᾽ξ[αμ]αρτία,
35 ἐκ σοῦ νοσοῦμεν. πρὸς τάδ᾽ εἴτε ποντίαν
κτείνειν δοκεῖ σοι, κτε[ῖ]ν᾽· ἐπίστασαι δέ τοι
μιαιφόν᾽ ἔργα καὶ σφαγὰς ἀνδροκτόνους·
εἴτ᾽ ὠμοσίτου τῆς ἐμῆς ἐρᾷς φαγεῖν
σαρκός, πάρεστι· μὴ ᾽λλίπῃς θοινώμενος.
40 ἐλεύθεροι γὰρ κοὐδὲν ἠδικηκότες
τῆς σῆς ἔκατι ζημ[ία]ς ὀλούμεθα.

22 οἴσε[ται ψόγον βροτ]ῶν Zuntz   26 νόσον Collard
(νόσος previously Austin)   39 μὴ ᾽λλίπῃς Murray: μὴ
λίπῃς P. Berl.   41 ὀλούμεθα Kannicht: ὀνούμεθα P. Berl.:
θανούμεθα ed. Pr.

destiny that (brought) me too (my fill) of trouble, and
he especially . . . [3] since he did not slaughter (that) bull
(which) he vowed to sacrifice to the sea-god when it was
manifested. This is the reason, I tell you, why Poseidon un-
dermined you and exacted punishment, but launched (the   25
affliction) upon me.[4]

And then you cry out and call the gods to witness, when
you did this yourself and brought shame upon me? While
I, who gave birth and was at fault in nothing, concealed the
god's stroke launched by heaven, you—fine and splendid   30
things to put on show!—you proclaimed them to all as if
you want no part in your wife, you worst of men (or hus-
bands) in your intention![5] It is you who have destroyed me!
Yours was the wrongdoing! You are the cause of my afflic-
tion! So either, if you have decided to kill me by drowning,   35
go on and kill me—indeed you understand acts of foul
murder and the slaughtering of men!—or, if you desire to
eat my flesh raw,[6] here it is: don't go short[7] on your ban-
quet! Because of the punishment upon you, we are to die,
who are free and quite innocent of wrongdoing.   40

[3] 'and he especially (will bear men's blame)', Zuntz.
[4] The essence of the plot: see Introduction. Austin preferred 'the
affliction fell on me.'   [5] Concealment of shame for sexual
misbehaviour: cf. *Cretan Women* F 460 with note, and Introduc-
tion to *Hippolytus Veiled*.   [6] A horror first found in Achilles'
wish against Hector at Homer, *Iliad* 22.347; in Euripides cf. es-
pecially *Hecuba* 1072–3.   [7] Murray's simple correction of
'Don't leave (me) as you banquet' (which Kannicht retains).

ΧΟΡΟΣ

πολλοῖσι δῆλον [ὡς θεήλατον] κακὸν
τόδ᾽ ἐστίν· ὀργη[   ].ς, ἄναξ.

ΜΙΝΩΣ

ἆρ᾽ ἐστόμωται; .[   ]. βοᾷ.
45 χωρεῖτε, λόγχη[   ]υμενη,
λάζυσθε τὴν πανο[ῦργον, ὡ]ς καλῶς θάνῃ,
καὶ τὴν ξυνεργὸν [τήνδε, δ]ωμάτων δ᾽ ἔσω
ἄγο]ντες αὐτὰς εἴρ[ξατ᾽ ἐς κρυπτ]ήριον,
ὡς μ]ηκέτ᾽ εἰσίδ[ωσιν ἡλίου κ]ύκλον.

ΧΟΡΟΣ

50 ἄ]ναξ, ἐπίσχ[ες· φρο]ντί[δος] γὰρ ἄξιον
τὸ πρ[ᾶγ]μα· [...].. δ᾽ ο[ὔτις] εὔβουλος βροτῶν.

ΜΙΝΩΣ

κ[αὶ δὴ] δ[έδοκται] μὴ ἀναβάλλεσθαι δίκην.

43 ὀργῇ [μὴ λίαν εἴξῃ]ς ed. pr.   44 at end, .ς written
above —οα in P. Berl. ('perhaps a variant βοῆς or βοαῖς', Hunt)
51 [θερ]μὸς Collard: [νηλ]ὴς ed. pr. (too short?)

472f

<ΜΙΝΩΣ?>

ἀλλ᾽, ὦ Κρῆτες, Ἴδας τέκνα . . .

Aristophanes, *Frogs* 1356 with Schol. ascribing the words to
Euripides' *Cretans*

CHORUS

It is clear to many that this trouble (was launched by heaven. Do not yield . . . to) anger . . . my lord!

MINOS

Has she had her tongue sharpened?[8] · · · is/are shouting (*or* with shouts?*) . . . (*to his attendants*) Come . . . spear(men?) . . . , seize this evil woman so she may get a fine death, and 45 her accomplice here, and take them inside the palace and shut them in (a hidden prison?),[9] so they will no longer see the orb (of the sun).

CHORUS

My lord, hold back! The matter deserves thought; no 50 (hasty?)[10] man is well-advised.

MINOS

It is (quite) decided: no deferment of penalty!

[8] A metaphor for (over-) clever rhetoric: Aristophanes, *Clouds* 1108. [9] Pasiphae will be left to die (John Malalas, *Chronicles* 4a.16 Thurn = 4.21 Jeffreys-Scott), like Antigone in Sophocles' *Antigone*. [10] 'hasty', Collard; 'ruthless', Wilamowitz.

472f

⟨MINOS?⟩

You Cretans, children of Ida![1]

[1] The fragment is unlocatable, but Kannicht well observes that tragic style would not permit it to precede the Chorus' anapaestic entry-song (F 472), where most editors place it.

EURIPIDES

472g

ἐν γὰρ τοῖς Κρησὶν Ἴκαρον μονῳδοῦντα ἐποίησεν (ὁ
Εὐριπίδης) . . . θρασύτερον γὰρ δοκεῖ εἶναι τὸ πρόσωπον.

Schol. on Aristophanes, *Frogs* 849

472g

For (Euripides) has Icarus singing a monody in Cretans ... his character seems to be rather bold.[1]

[1] For the importance of this fragment see Introduction, at end.

ALMOST CERTAINLY
FROM *CRETANS*

988

⟨ΜΙΝΩΣ⟩

τέκτων γὰρ ὢν ἔπρασσες οὐ ξυλουργικά.

Plutarch, *Moralia* 812e

1004

. . . παντάπασιν ἂν οἰκεῖον εἴη καὶ συγγενὲς ἡμῖν τὸ τῶν
λοιπῶν ζῴων γένος. καὶ γὰρ τροφαὶ αἱ αὐταὶ πᾶσιν
αὐτοῖς καὶ πνεύματα, ὡς Εὐριπίδης, καὶ

φοινίους ἔχει ῥοὰς

τὰ ζῷα πάντα,

καὶ κοινοὺς ἁπάντων δείκνυσι γονεῖς οὐρανὸν καὶ γῆν.

Porphyry, *On Abstinence* 3.25; the fragment has also been
ascribed to *Melanippe Wise* (cf. F 484).

ALMOST CERTAINLY
FROM *CRETANS*

988
⟨MINOS⟩

You are a builder but what you did was not carpentry.[1]

[1] An allusion to Daedalus and the artificial cow: see Introduction.

1004

. . . the family of other living creatures would be altogether close to us, and related to us. For all of them have the same sustenance, and (all draw) breath, as Euripides (says), and

all living things have blood flowing in them,[1]

and (Euripides) shows heaven and earth as parents common to all.

[1] If from *Cretans*, this may have justified abstinence from eating meat (cf. F 472.18–19, which Porphyry also cites); alternatively from *Melanippe Wise*, in association with F 484.2–6.

LAMIA

Pechstein 177–84; H. Van Looy in ed. Budé VIII.2.333–6; Krumeich 475–6.   *LIMC* VI.i.189 'Lamia'.

Lamia was a beautiful Libyan girl seduced by Zeus; in jealousy Zeus's wife Hera destroyed the children she bore. Lamia's grief made her hideous, and she became a killer of others' children (Duris FGrH 76 F 17, whence Scholia to Aristophanes, Peace 758 and Wasps 1035 etc.). Such a bogey figure would suit comedy (Crates wrote a play with her name) or satyric drama.

While the Alexandrian cataloguers of Euripides' works did not list the play, there was a much repeated testimony of the 1st c. B.C. Roman antiquarian Varro about 'the second of the Sibyls, a Libyan, whom Euripides mentioned in the prologue of his Lamia' (F 56a Cardauns = test. i), and Diodorus cites two verses (F 472m below) which may have provided the basis for Varro's information. Further, Pausanias 10.12.1 records a tradition that the most ancient Sibyl at Delphi was a daughter of Zeus and Lamia, and called Sibylla by the Libyans. Whether Pausanias reflects Euripides in any way is not known, but it seems likely that there was a Euripidean satyr play of this name which was lost very early; if so, its plot can only be guessed (cf. H. W. Parke, Sibyls and Sibylline Prophecy in Classical Antiquity [London, 1988], 104–5).

ΛΑΜΙΑ

472m (= 922 N, 312a N–Sn)

<ΛΑΜΙΑ>

τίς τοὐ⟨μὸν ὄ⟩νομα τοὐπονείδιστον βροτοῖς
οὐκ οἶδε Λαμίας τῆς Λιβυστικῆς γένος;

Diodorus 20.41.6

1 τοὐ⟨μὸν ὄ⟩νομα Meineke

LAMIA

472m (= 922 N, 312a N–Sn)

〈LAMIA〉

Who does not know 〈my〉 name that men revile, Lamia,
the Libyan by race?[1]

---

[1] The play's opening words (see Varro above). The fragment
was for a time held by those who doubted a Euripidean *Lamia* to
be the opening of the satyric *Busiris*, set in 'Egypt' (i.e. 'Libya');
but that play's first line has since been recovered: F 312b.

LICYMNIUS

H. Van Looy in ed. Budé VIII.2.337–46.   Webster 36–7.

Licymnius was Electryon's son by a second wife, and survived the conflict in which his half-brothers were killed by the Taphians (see on Alcmene above). When his father was killed by Amphitryon, he went with the latter and Alcmene (his half-sister) into exile at Thebes, married a sister of Amphitryon, and later took part in some of Heracles' exploits. Two episodes involving him look like subjects for tragedy. In one of these, told in the scholia on Iliad 1.52, Licymnius allowed Heracles to take his second son Argeus on his expedition against Laomedon's Troy, but since his first son had died on a previous campaign with Heracles, he made Heracles swear that he would bring Argeus home to him. Argeus was somehow killed, and Heracles fulfilled his promise by burning his body—thus inventing cremation—and bringing Licymnius the remains. In the other episode, Licymnius in his later years was killed accidentally or in anger by Heracles' son Tlepolemus, who then went into exile and founded the Greek cities on the island of Rhodes (Homer, Iliad 2.653ff., cf. Pindar, Olympians 7.27ff.). This was the subject of a barely known Licymnius by Euripides' younger contemporary Xenocles (see TrGF 33 F 2), but the references to Heracles in F 473 (and possi-

bly F 474 and 475) and to the region of Mysia near Troy in F 476 make the Argeus story a little more likely for Euripides; Webster offers a tentative reconstruction accordingly. All this is very uncertain, as are attempts to date the play before 448 (or at least before the late 420s) through Cratinus' use of the word ἄκομψον in his Archilochoi (see F 473, Cratinus F 15 PCG). The reference to lightning as 'Licymnian bolts' in Aristophanes, Birds 1242 (= test. *iia) might be relevant, but Callimachus (fr. 455, cited in the Aristophanes scholia = test. iib) seems to have denied this, and the one thing that is clear from the Aristophanes scholia is that ancient scholars could neither explain the phrase nor trace its source.

Brief fragments: F 477a 'will take(?)'; F 478 'to be possessed'.   Other ascription: F 982.

ΛΙΚΤΜΝΙΟΣ

473
φαῦλον ἄκομψον, τὰ μέγιστ᾿ ἀγαθόν,
πᾶσαν ἐν ἔργῳ περιτεμνόμενον
σοφίαν, λέσχης ἀτρίβωνα

Diogenes Laertius 3.63; v. 1: Plutarch, *Cimon* 4.5 and *Marcellus* 21.6, and frequently in lexica

474
πόνος γάρ, ὡς λέγουσιν, εὐκλείας πατήρ.

Stobaeus 3.29.7

475
τὸ τῆς ἀνάγκης οὐ λέγειν ὅσον ζυγόν

Stobaeus 1.4.6

The sentence as it stands is incomplete; perhaps add e.g. οἷός τ᾿ ἂν εἴης, Kannicht: οὐχ ὁρᾷς for οὐ λέγειν, F. W. Schmidt

476
Τευθράντιον δὲ σχῆμα Μυσίας χθονός

Stephanus of Byzantium, ᾿Τευθρανία᾿ (p. 618.15 Meineke)

LICYMNIUS

473

. . . plain and straightforward, virtuous in the extreme, putting aside all artfulness in action, unversed in gossip.[1]

  [1] The sources indicate that this was a description of Heracles.

474

Toil, as they say, is the father of fame.

475

(One could?)[1] not express how strong the yoke of compulsion is.

  [1] This translates the supplement suggested by Kannicht. F. W. Schmidt's alteration gives 'Do you not see how strong' (cf. *Antiope* F 217).

476

. . . and Teuthrania, adornment[1] of the land of Mysia . . .

  [1] The sense of σχῆμα (lit., 'form', 'outward appearance') is uncertain: cf. Eur. *Andromache* 1, Ἀσιατίδος γῆς σχῆμα Θηβαία πόλι, 'City of Thebe, adornment(?) of the land of Asia'. Teuthrania was named after Teuthras, the Mysian king who married Auge the mother of Telephus: see Introduction to *Auge*, and *Telephus* F 696.

EURIPIDES

477

<ΧΟΡΟΣ>

δέσποτα φιλόδαφνε Βάκχε, παιὰν Ἄπολλον
εὔλυρε

Macrobius, *Saturnalia* 1.18.6

479 (= 920a N–Sn)

φιμώσ[α]τ᾿ αὐτοῦ κἀποκλείσατ[ε σ]τόμα,
δεσμοῖ[ς] δὲ [.....]ς ἀντὶ [

Demetrius Laco, *On Poems* 2, in P. Herc. 1014 col. 30.5–9
(pp. 108–9 Romeo)

LICYMNIUS

477

<CHORUS>

Laurel-loving lord Bacchus, healer Apollo skilled with the lyre . . . [1]

[1] Macrobius cites this lyric fragment as identifying Dionysus and Apollo as 'one and the same god'.

479 (= 920a N–Sn)

Muzzle him and close up his mouth, and . . . with fetters . . . instead of (*or* in return for) . . .

MELANIPPE WISE *and*
MELANIPPE CAPTIVE

Van Looy (1964), 185–304 and in ed. Budé VIII.2.347–96;
M. Cropp in *SFP* I.240–80, 289 (~ II.368–9); Diggle,
TrGFS 120–7 (test. i, F 481, 484, 494–5, 506).

Wilamowitz, *Kleine Schriften* I.440–60; Z. Vysoký,
Listy Filologické 87 (1964), 17–32; Webster 147–57; G.
Mengano Cavalli, *RAAN* 52 (1977), 165–83; Gantz 734–5;
LIMC VIII.i.829–30 'Melanippe I'; Matthiessen 266–8.
Mel. Capt. myth, political aspects: D. Giacometti, *Annali
della Facoltà di lettere e filosofia, Univ. di Perugia* 28
(1990–1), 277–96; M. Nafissi, *Ostraka* 6 (1997), 337–57.

*For pairs of similarly named plays see the introductory
note to* Alcmeon. *The fragments of the two* Melanippe
*plays are followed by those which cannot be assigned with
certainty to one or other (but see 'Other ascriptions' in the
Introductions below, and notes to the translations).*

MELANIPPE WISE

*Melanippe ('Black-Mare') belongs to the complicated my-
thology of Thessaly and Boeotia, but her story is obscure in
origin and varies considerably in extant accounts; her only
notable appearance in Greek poetry is in Euripides' plays.
According to the incomplete hypothesis and prologue of
Melanippe Wise (test. i and F 481 below), she was a daugh-
ter of Aeolus (ancestor of the Aeolian Greeks) and Hippo or
Hippē ('Mare', a daughter of the centaur Chiron), and
mother by Poseidon of twins named Aeolus (identified with
migrant Aeolians) and Boeotus (identified with Boeotia)—
though in some genealogies the mother of these twins was
Arne rather than Melanippe. Melanippe Wise, so called
because of the wisdom its heroine inherited from Chiron
and Hippo and displayed in the play (test. i, iia, F 482–4),
was about the illicit birth and survival of the twins (cf. the
plots of Alope, Auge, Danae, and probably Sophocles' first
Tyro). Melanippe was seduced or raped by Poseidon in her
father's absence, and when he returned she hid her re-
cently born sons in a stable where herdsmen discovered
them and brought them to Aeolus, superstitiously thinking
they were the unnatural offspring of a cow. Aeolus' father
Hellen agreed and encouraged him to destroy them, but
Melanippe defended them by arguing rationally that they
must be the natural children of an unidentified girl. This*

*early part of the play—probably the prologue and first
two or three episodes—is represented by test. i–iia and F
482–5, and by a magnificent Apulian vase published in
1986 (LIMC no. 1 = test. iv; Todisco Ap 221, Taplin no. 68)
which is the only known 'illustration' of the play; it pictures
a herdsman showing the twins to Hellen in Aeolus' pres-
ence while Melanippe and her nurse observe from one side.
The remainder of the plot is almost completely unknown,
the only other certain fragments being F 486 (a choral
praise of justice), F 487 (probably Melanippe protesting
her innocence), and test. va mentioning a horse mask worn
by Hippo, presumably in a divine intervention at the end of
the play (the Apulian vase painting includes Melanippe's
half-brother Cretheus crowning a horse which may pos-
sibly represent Hippo; Kannicht includes Cretheus as a
character in the play). It must be assumed that, as in other
plays on this pattern, Melanippe's guilt was somehow re-
vealed and she and her sons subjected to further suffering.
Melanippe Captive presupposes that they were all some-
how brought to southern Italy, like Telephus and Auge to
Mysia, Danae and Perseus to Seriphos; but this does not
necessarily reflect Melanippe Wise (that the two plays
were part of the same production is a possibility, but no
more than that: see below on the dates of the two plays).
Hyginus' syncretic and rather confused Fab. 186 (=
Melanippe Captive test. iii) begins by saying that Melanip-
pe's father blinded and imprisoned her and exposed her in-
fant sons who were then suckled by a cow and raised by
herdsmen, but again the relevance of this to Melanippe
Wise is doubtful; it seems more likely that Hippo appeared
in time to rescue both mother and sons from further vio-
lence.*

Brief fragments: none specifically ascribed to Melanippe Wise. *Other ascriptions:* Melanippe F 497, 500, 506, 508–10 *(see notes to the translations below), and F 514 'Adonis gardens' (young plants allowed to die in honour of Adonis, perhaps a metaphor for the condemned babies in this play); also F 928, 1004.*

Quotations in Aristophanes' plays of 411 (F 482, 487) show that Melanippe Wise *was composed before that year, while its trimeter resolutions make a date earlier than the mid-420s somewhat unlikely (Cropp–Fick 83–4); it probably preceded its 'sequel'* Melanippe Captive. *Melanippe's cleverness and rhetorical skill made her a 'pernicious woman' for Aristophanes (Women at the Thesmophoria 546–8 = test. iiib), and an example of unsuitable characterization for Aristotle (Poetics 1454a22–31 = test. iiia). The later testimonia show that the play remained noted for these features, but there is no evidence of a wider afterlife except a Latin version by Ennius, of which six brief fragments survive.*

Bibliography: see p. 567.

ΜΕΛΑΝΙΠΠΗ Η ΣΟΦΗ

test. i (Hypothesis)

Με[λανίππη ἡ Σοφή, ἧς ἀρχή·
Ζεὺς δ.[
[ἡ δὲ ὑπόθεσις·]
Ἕλληνος τοῦ Διὸς Αἴολος τεκνωθεὶς
5 ἐκ μὲν Εὐρυδίκης ἐγέννησε Κρηθέα καὶ
Σαλμωνέα καὶ Σίσυφον, ἐκ δὲ τῆς Χείρω-
νος θυγατρὸς Ἵππης κάλλει διαφέρου-
σαν Μελανίππην. αὐτὸς μὲν οὖν φόνον
ποιήσας ἐπ᾽ ἐνιαυτὸν ἀπῆλθε φυγάς,
10 τὴν δὲ Μελανίππην Ποσειδῶν διδύμων
παίδων ἔγκυον ἐποίησεν. ἡ δὲ διὰ τὴν προσ-
δοκίαν τῆς τοῦ πατρὸς παρουσίας τοὺς γεν-
νηθέντας εἰς τὴν βούστασιν ἔδωκε τῇ
τροφῷ θεῖναι κατὰ τὴν ἐντολὴν τοῦ κα-
15 τασπείραντος. ὑπὸ δὲ τὴν κάθοδον τοῦ
δυνάστου τὰ βρέφη τινὲς τῶν βουκόλων
φυλαττόμενα μὲν ὑπὸ τοῦ ταύρου, θη-
λαζόμενα δὲ ὑπὸ μιᾶς τῶν βοῶν ἰδόντες,
ὡς βουγενῆ τέρατα τῷ βασιλεῖ προσή-
20 νεγκαν. ὁ δὲ τῇ τοῦ πατρὸς Ἕλληνος γνώ-
μῃ πεισθεὶς ὁλοκαυτοῦν τὰ βρέφη κρί-

572

MELANIPPE WISE

test. i (Hypothesis)

Me(lanippe Wise, which begins,) 'Zeus . . . *(remainder of first line lost: cf. F 481.1 below)* . . .'; (the plot is as follows):

Aeolus, son of Hellen son of Zeus, fathered Cretheus, Sal- 5
moneus and Sisyphus by Eurydice, and by Chiron's daughter
Hippe (he fathered) the exceedingly beautiful Melanippe.
Now he himself went into exile for a year after committing a
murder, and Poseidon made Melanippe pregnant with twin
sons. Expecting her father's return, she gave the infants she 10
had borne to her nurse to put in the ox-stable, as their father
(i.e. Poseidon) had instructed. About the time of the king's re-
turn, some of the herdsmen saw the babies being watched 15
over by the bull and suckled by one of the cows, and think-
ing they were the cow's monstrous offspring they brought
them to the king. He took his father Hellen's advice and de- 20
cided to burn the babies alive, and so he instructed his daugh-

---

P. Oxy. 2455, ed. E. Turner (1962), frs. 1–2 (parts of vv. 1–2, 5–
19); P. Leiden inv. 145, ed. R. Daniel (1991: parts of vv. 18–23);
vv. 4–25: Ioannes Logothetes, Commentary on [Hermogenes],
Means of Rhetorical Effectiveness (ed. H. Rabe, *RhM* 63 [1908],
145), 28; Gregory of Corinth, Commentary on the same treatise,
Rhet. Gr. VII.1313 Walz. See also van Rossum-Steenbeek 199,
206–7, Diggle, *TrGFS* 120.   v. 2 = F 481.1

νας Μελανίππη τῇ θυγατρὶ προσέταξεν
ἐνταφίοις αὐτὰ κοσμῆσαι. ἡ δὲ καὶ τὸν
κόσμον αὐτοῖς ἐπέθηκε καὶ λόγον εἰς
25   παραίτησιν ἐξέθηκε φιλότιμον.

test. iia

ἡ Μελανίππη σοφὴ . . . ἐπιγέγραπται μὲν Σοφή, ὅτι
φιλοσοφεῖ, καὶ διὰ τοῦτο τοιαύτης μητρός ἐστιν, ἵνα μὴ
ἀπίθανος ᾖ ἡ φιλοσοφία . . . ἡ δὲ Μελανίππη ἐπεράνθη
μὲν ὑπὸ τοῦ Ποσειδῶνος, γέγονε δὲ ταύτῃ παιδία· ἐξέθη-
κεν δὲ αὐτὰ εἰς τὰ τοῦ πατρὸς βουφόρβια. ὁ δὲ πατὴρ
ἡγεῖται ἐκ βοὸς εἶναι, καὶ ὡς τέρας βούλεται κατακαῦ-
σαι. βοηθοῦσα αὐτῇ ἡ Μελανίππη ἀποφαίνεσθαι πει-
ρᾶται, ὅτι τέρας οὐδέν ἐστιν. οὕτω τὸ δρᾶμα ὅλον ἐσχη-
μάτισται· καὶ ἅμα διδάσκει ἡμᾶς Εὐριπίδης, ὅτι τὸν
σχηματίζοντα ἐγγυτάτω δεῖ εἶναι τοῦ λῦσαι τὸ σχῆμα
μετὰ τῆς ἀσφαλείας τοῦ σχήματος. περιερχομένη γὰρ
πάσας αἰτίας τοῦ σῶσαι τὰ παιδία λέγει, 'εἰ δὲ παρθένος
φθαρεῖσα ἐξέθηκε τὰ παιδία . . . σὺ φόνον δράσεις;' (= F
485)· ὥστε καὶ τὸ αὐτῆς πρᾶγμα λέγει ἐν σχήματι συμ-
βουλῆς.

[Dionysius of Halicarnassus], *Art of Rhetoric* 9.11 (and more
briefly in 8.10 = test. iib)

test. va

τὰ δ' ἔκσκευα πρόσωπα Ἀκταίων ἐστὶ κερασφόρος, ἢ
Φινεὺς τυφλός . . . ἢ Ἵππη ἡ Χείρωνος ὑπαλλαττομένη
εἰς ἵππον παρ' Εὐριπίδῃ . . .

Pollux 4.141

ter Melanippe to dress them in funeral clothing. Melanippe clothed them and made a feisty speech in their defence.

test. iia

The *Melanippe Wise* has the title 'Wise' because she argues philosophically, and she is the daughter of such a mother (i.e. Hippo) so that her philosophizing will not be implausible . . . Melanippe was raped by Poseidon and gave birth to sons whom she put in her father's ox-stable. Her father thinks they are a cow's offspring and wants to burn them as a monstrosity. Melanippe defends herself and tries to show that they are no monstrosity. Thus the whole action of the play is disguised; and Euripides teaches us that the disguiser should come very close to revealing the disguise while still maintaining it. For while going through all the reasons for sparing the children she says, 'But if a girl who had been raped exposed the children . . . will you then commit murder?' (= F 485 below). Thus she actually pleads her own case in the guise of giving advice.

test. va

Special masks are Actaeon wearing horns, or Phineus blind . . . or Chiron's daughter Hippe transformed into a horse in Euripides . . .

EURIPIDES

test. vb (a) (~ F 488 N)

Ἵππος· . . . Ἄρατος μὲν οὖν φησὶ τὸν ἐπὶ τοῦ Ἑλικῶνος
εἶναι ποιήσαντα κρήνην τῇ ὁπλῇ . . . , ἄλλοι δὲ τὸν
Πήγασον εἶναι . . . , Εὐριπίδης δὲ ἐν τῇ Μελανίππῃ
Ἱππὼ εἶναι τὴν Χείρωνος καὶ ἀπατηθεῖσαν ὑπ᾽ Αἰόλου
φθαρῆναι, καὶ ἕως μὲν τινὸς κρύπτειν, ἐπειδὴ δὲ κατα-
φανὴς ἦν διὰ τὸν ὄγκον τῆς γαστρός, φυγεῖν εἰς τὰ ὄρη·
κἀκεῖ ὠδινούσης αὐτῆς τὸν πατέρα ἐλθεῖν κατὰ ζήτησιν,
τὴν δὲ εὔξασθαι καταλαμβανομένην πρὸς τὸ μὴ γνωσθῆ-
ναι μεταμορφωθῆναι· καὶ οὕτως γενέσθαι ἵππον τεκοῦ-
σαν τὸ παιδίον· διὰ δὲ τὴν εὐσέβειαν αὐτῆς καὶ τοῦ
πατρὸς εἰς τὰ ἄστρα ὑπὸ τῆς Ἀρτέμιδος τεθῆναι.

Schol. on Aratus, *Phaenomena* 205; similarly [Eratosthenes],
Catasterisms 18 and in Latin (stating Artemis' role differently: see
note opposite) Hyginus, *Astronomy* 2.18 (= test. vb (b)).

480

Ζεύς, ὅστις ὁ Ζεύς, οὐ γὰρ οἶδα πλὴν λόγῳ . . .

Plutarch, *Moralia* 756b; Lucian 21.41; [Justin], *On Monarchy*
5.8

test. vb (a) (~ F 488 N)

The Horse (i.e. the constellation): . . . Aratus says it is the horse that made the spring on Mount Helicon (i.e. Hippocrene) with its hoof . . . , others that it is Pegasus . . . , and Euripides in *Melanippe* says it is Chiron's daughter Hippo, and that she was deceived and raped by Aeolus, and concealed it for a time, but when her pregnancy became evident because of the swelling of her belly she fled to the mountains; while she was in labour there her father came in search of her, and as she was caught she prayed to be transformed so as not to be recognized; thus she became a horse after giving birth to her child, and because of her and her father's piety she was placed by Artemis amongst the stars.[1]

1 The explanation of Hippo's horse transformation is not Euripidean; contrast F 481.14–19 below. Her catasterism may be, but the mythographic sources are confused. Hyginus, *Astronomy* 2.18 attributes her prophetic activities and punishment to other authors (unnamed), and connects Artemis with Callimachus, not Euripides.

480

Zeus, whoever Zeus is—for I know this only by report . . .[1]

1 Plutarch claims this was the play's original first line and was replaced by F 481.1 because it caused offence, but it is very unlikely that such a sceptical statement (cf. *Heracles* 1263) opened this or any other tragedy.

EURIPIDES

481

(Beginning of the play)

ΜΕΛΑΝΙΠΠΗ

Ζεύς, ὡς λέλεκται τῆς ἀληθείας ὕπο,
Ἕλλην' ἔτιχθ' ὃς ἐξέφυσεν Αἴολον·
οὗ χθών, ὅσην Πηνειὸς Ἀσωποῦ θ' ὕδωρ
ὑγροῖς ὁρίζων ἐντὸς ἀγκῶσι στέγει,
5 σκήπτρων ἀκούει πᾶσα καὶ κικλήσκεται
ἐπώνυμος χθὼν Αἰολὶς τοὐμοῦ πατρός.
ἐν μὲν τόδ' ἐξέβλαστεν Ἕλληνος γένος·
πτόρθον δ' ἀφῆκεν ἄλλον εἰς ἄλλην πόλιν
⟨   ⟩
κλεινὰς Ἀθήνας Ξοῦθον, ᾧ νύμφη ποτὲ
10 θυγάτηρ Ἐρεχθέως Κεκροπίας ἐπ' αὐχένι
Ἴων' ἔτικτεν. ἀλλ' ἀνοιστέος λόγος
†ὄνομά τε τοὐμὸν† κεῖσ' ὅθενπερ ἠρξάμην.
καλοῦσι Μελανίππην ⟨με⟩, Χείρωνος δέ με
ἔτικτε θυγάτηρ Αἰόλῳ· κείνην μὲν οὖν
15 ξανθῇ κατεπτέρωσεν ἱππείᾳ τριχὶ
Ζεύς, οὕνεχ' ὕμνους ᾖδε χρησμῳδοὺς βροτοῖς
ἄκη πόνων φράζουσα καὶ λυτήρια.

Ioannes Logothetes (see under test. i above); vv. 1–2 (ἔτικτεν):
Gregory of Corinth (see under test. i above); v. 1: Aristophanes,
Frogs 1244 with Schol. (see also test. i.2 above); v. 11 (last three
words): Plutarch, *Moralia* 390c and 431a (= F 970 N)

8–9 lacuna proposed by Wilamowitz   12 ἐπ' ὄνομα
τοὐμὸν Wilamowitz

578

481
(Beginning of the play)

MELANIPPE

Zeus, as is told by reliable tradition,[1] fathered Hellen who
was father to Aeolus. All of the land that Peneus and
Asopus bound and enclose within their watery arms[2] ac-
knowledges his rule and is named Aeolia after my father.   5
This is one of the families that descended from Hellen, and
he sent forth other offspring to other areas ... *(probably a
line or two lost)* ... [3] to glorious Athens Xuthus, whose
bride, Erechtheus's daughter, bore Ion to him on Cecro-
pia's ridge.[4]   10

But I must bring my account †and my name†[5] back to
where I started from. My name is Melanippe; Chiron's
daughter bore me to Aeolus. Now Zeus gave her a coat of
tawny horse-hair because she sang oracular songs to men,   15
telling them cures and ways to relieve their pains;[6] and

---

[1] The first line (partially preserved at the start of test. i above)
is identical with Critias' or Euripides' *Pirithous*, F 1.9 (see Appen-
dix at the end of this edition). Such a repetition is not unlikely.
[2] Thessaly was bounded to the north by the river Peneus, and
Boeotia to the south by the Asopus.   [3] Wilamowitz's lacuna
allows for a mention of Dorus, traditionally brother of Aeolus and
Xuthus, who migrated to Doris and became the ancestor of the
Dorians.   [4] The Acropolis of Athens, where the royal palace
of heroic times was supposed to have been. In *Ion* Euripides made
Apollo Ion's real father.   [5] Probably corrupt, though ac-
cepted by some as '(the explanation of) my name'. Wilamowitz's
conjecture leaves the sentence slightly incoherent ('to my name,
to where ... ').   [6] Hippo is described as an *iatromantis* or
'healing seer', like Asclepius (also punished for usurping divine
prerogatives) in Pindar, *Pythians* 3.45–53.

πυκνῇ θυέλλῃ δ' αἰθέρος διώκεται
Μουσεῖον ἐκλιποῦσα Κωρύκιόν τ' ὄρος.
20 νύμφη δὲ θεσπιῳδὸς ἀνθρώπων ὕπο
Ἱππὼ κέκληται σώματος δι' ἀλλαγάς.
μητρὸς μὲν ὧδε τῆς ἐμῆς ἔχει πέρι.

εἶτα λέγει καὶ ὅτι Ποσειδῶνι μιγεῖσα τέτοκε τοὺς διδύ-
μους παῖδας.

482 (= 483 N)

ΜΕΛΑΝΙΠΠΗ

ἐγὼ γυνὴ μέν εἰμι, νοῦς δ' ἔνεστί μοι.

Aristophanes, *Lysistrata* 1124 with Schol.

483 (= 482 N)

⟨ΜΕΛΑΝΙΠΠΗ⟩

ἢ πρῶτα μὲν τὰ θεῖα προυμαντεύσατο
χρησμοῖσι σαφέσιν ἀστέρων ἐπ' ἀντολαῖς.

Clement of Alexandria, *Miscellanies* 1.15.73.5; Cyril of Alex-
andria, *Against Julian* 4 (*PG* LXXVI.705c)

driven in a dense squall of mist she left the Corycian mountain,[7] her place of inspiration. This young prophetess is called by men Hippo because of her change of body. 20 Such are the facts concerning my mother.

Then she adds that she (Melanippe) has had intercourse with Poseidon and borne the twin sons.

[7] Mount Parnassus, where the Corycian Cave was sacred to the Nymphs.

F 482–5 are from Melanippe's famous speech (test. i.23–5 and test. ii above):

482 (= 483 N)

MELANIPPE

I am a woman, but I have intelligence.

483 (= 482 N)

⟨MELANIPPE⟩

. . . who first proclaimed divine knowledge in accurate prophecies based on the risings of the stars.[1]

[1] One of the first references in Greek literature to astrology (actually an import from Babylonia), although astronomical observations had long been used to predict seasons and weather (Hesiod, *Works & Days* 383–7, 414ff.).

EURIPIDES

484

ΜΕΛΑΝΙΠΠΗ

κοὐκ ἐμὸς ὁ μῦθος, ἀλλ' ἐμῆς μητρὸς πάρα,
ὡς οὐρανός τε γαῖά τ' ἦν μορφὴ μία,
ἐπεὶ δ' ἐχωρίσθησαν ἀλλήλων δίχα,
τίκτουσι πάντα κἀνέδωκαν εἰς φάος,
5 δένδρη, πετεινά, θῆρας, οὕς θ' ἅλμη τρέφει,
γένος τε θνητῶν.

vv. 1–2: Dionysius of Halicarnassus, *Art of Rhetoric* 9.11 (cf.
test. iia: v. 1 also in 8.10); v. 1 adapted by Plato, *Symposium* 177a.3
(cf. Aristides, *Oration* 2.132) and often elsewhere; vv. 2–6:
Diodorus 1.7.7; vv. 2–4: Tzetzes, *Exegesis of Homer's Iliad*. p.
41.18 Hermann; v. 2 (οὐρανός . . . μία) appears amongst Orphic
inscriptions on a late antique alabaster bowl (R. Delbrueck, W.
Vollgraff, *JHS* 54 [1934], 129–39).

485

ΜΕΛΑΝΙΠΠΗ

εἰ δὲ παρθένος φθαρεῖσα ἐξέθηκε τὰ παιδία καὶ
φοβουμένη τὸν πατέρα, σὺ φόνον δράσεις;

Dionysius of Halicarnassus, *Art of Rhetoric* 9.11 (cf. test. iia
above)

484

MELANIPPE

The account is not my own, but comes from my mother,[1]
that Heaven and Earth were once a single form, but when
they were parted from each other into two, they bore and
delivered into the light all things—trees, winged things,
beasts, creatures of the sea, and the race of mortals.[2]   5

[1] Cf. test. iia and F 481.13–17 above. Hippo was supposed to
have taught natural science to Aeolus as well: cf. Clement cited in
the apparatus to F 483.   [2] For the separation of Sky from
Earth see especially Hesiod, *Theogony* 154–206, and for Heaven
and Earth jointly propagating life Aeschylus F 44, Eur. *Antiope* F
182a and elsewhere (see further on *Chrysippus* F 839).

485

MELANIPPE

But if a girl exposed the children because she had been
raped and was in fear of her father, will you then commit
murder?

EURIPIDES

486

<ΧΟΡΟΣ>

(a) δικαιοσύνας τὸ χρύσεον πρόσωπον

(b) οὔθ᾽ ἕσπερος οὔθ᾽ ἑῷος οὕτω θαυμαστός.

(a) Anonymous Commentary on Aristotle, *Nicomachean Ethics* 1129b28 in *CAG* XX.210.9; Athenaeus 12.546b (= Aristoxenus F 50 Wehrli); (b) Aristotle, *Nic. Eth.* 1129b28 with Commentary as for (a). There are several derivative adaptations of both phrases.

487

<ΜΕΛΑΝΙΠΠΗ?>

ὄμνυμι δ᾽ ἱερὸν αἰθέρ᾽, οἴκησιν Διός.

Aristophanes, *Women at the Thesmophoria* 272 with Schol., and Schol. on Aristophanes, *Frogs* 100

(488 N = test. vb (a) above)

486
⟨CHORUS⟩

(a) . . . Justice's golden countenance . . .
(b) Neither evening nor morning (star) is so wonderful.

487
⟨MELANIPPE?⟩

I swear by sacred heaven, Zeus's dwelling.

(488 N: see test. vb (a) above)

MELANIPPE CAPTIVE

*The story that Melanippe was transported to Metapontium
in southern Italy and became the wife of the city's founder
Metapontus exists in various forms (e.g. Diodorus 4.67,
Strabo 6.1.15), but Euripides' version is not directly re-
flected in any of them. It must have been similar in some re-
spects to Hyginus, Fab. 186 (= test. iii) in which, along
with much ill-digested detail, Metapontus' childless wife
Theano secretly adopted Melanippe's baby sons but then
bore sons of her own and later encouraged them to kill
Melanippe's sons during a hunting expedition; when her
own sons were killed instead she committed suicide, the
twins rescued their mother from imprisonment, and
Metapontus married Melanippe. In Euripides' play, how-
ever, the Queen was probably called Siris (see test. iib be-
low with note), and in F 495 it is the Queen's brothers who
attack Melanippe's sons; the latter regard themselves as the
Queen's sons (F 495.7, 15), and their uncles seems to be
jealous of their position as Metapontus' heirs (F 495.18–21
as reconstructed). At the same time their slave birth seems
to be an issue (F 495.40–3, cf. 20–3 as reconstructed; prob-
ably also F 511), as are a childless father's adoption of
sons (F 491) and a husband's conflict with a wife of supe-
rior rank (probably F 502–3). All this suggests that in Eu-
ripides' play Melanippe's sons have been brought up in*

Metapontus' household and adopted as his heirs, and that his high-born Queen resents this because of her own child-lessness and loyalty to her natal family; this leads her to plot the attack which brings about her own brothers' deaths (F 495) and probably her suicide. Her plot may have been precipitated by the discovery that the twins were the sons of the slave Melanippe, but how they and Melanippe reached Italy, how the twins came to be adopted by the King and Queen, and how Melanippe her-self has been living can only be guessed. The one certainty is that Melanippe's imprisonment gave the play its sur-name, but it is unclear whether she was imprisoned many years before as in Hyginus, or (more likely) only recently—even in the course of the play—by the jealous Queen in whose household she has served as a slave. Either way, Melanippe's adult sons must be unaware of her identity, and she is probably unaware of theirs; thus their rescue of her would lead to recognition and reunion. Probably a closing speech by their divine father Poseidon (who seems to protect them during the fight: F 495.27) ordered the Queen's funeral and commemoration (test. iib with note), the marriage of Metapontus and Melanippe, and the mi-grations of Boeotus (to Boeotia) and Aeolus (to the Aeolian Islands?).

Also unclear is the occasion for the defence of women in one of the play's most notable fragments, F 494 (cf. F 493, 498). The speaker is more likely the eloquent Melanippe than the erring Queen, and Van Looy attractively suggests that she is responding to her son Boeotus, who might then be the misogynistic speaker of F 498 (a dramatic irony if he does not yet know she is his mother: compare the likely hostility of Zethus towards his unrecognized mother in Antiope).

Brief fragments: none. Other proposed ascriptions: Melanippe F 498, 501–5, 507, 511 (see notes to the translations below).

A lower date of 412 is suggested by the coincidence of F 507.1 with a line from Eupolis' Demes (produced in that year) and by possible imitations in Aristophanes' Women at the Thesmophoria of 411 (vv. 531–2, 785ff.). The evidence of metrical resolutions allows a date as early as 426, and Nafissi sees a political context for the play in the mid-420s (cf. test. iib with note). On the other hand, its romantic plot and (presumably) happy ending seem to align it with such plays as Antiope, Hypsipyle, Ion and Sophocles' second Tyro and suggest a date closer to 412.

The play seems to have had little or no impact in later poetry and art.

Bibliography: see p. 567.

ΜΕΛΑΝΙΠΠΗ Η ΔΕΣΜΩΤΙΣ

test. iib (= F 496 N)

ὠνομάσθη δ᾽ ἡ Σῖρις, ὡς μὲν Τίμαιός φησιν καὶ Εὐρι-
πίδης ἐν Δεσμώτιδι Μελανίππῃ, ἀπὸ γυναικός τινος
Σίριδος, ὡς δ᾽ Ἀρχίλοχος, ἀπὸ ποταμοῦ.

Athenaeus 12.523d

*489

τὸν δ᾽ ἀμφὶ βοῦς ῥιφθέντα Βοιωτὸν καλεῖν

Stephanus of Byzantium, 'Βοιωτία' (p. 173 Meineke)

MELANIPPE CAPTIVE

test. iib (= F 496 N)

Siris (the city) was named after a woman called Siris according to Timaeus and Euripides in *Melanippe Captive*, but according to Archilochus, after a river.[1]

[1] Siris was probably the name of king Metapontus' wife in Euripides' play (rather than Theano as in Hyginus, *Fab*. 186); she is so identified in Schol. on Dionysius Periegetes 461. A Greek settlement at Siris (by the river of the same name) was destroyed and annexed by Achaeans from neighbouring cities including Metapontium in the early 6th century, and refounded as Heraclea in 433. The god's speech at the end of Euripides' play may have established a connection between the dead woman, the river and the future city (cf. *Antiope* F 223.80–5). On the possible political implications of this and of Metapontus' marriage with Melanippe see now Giacometti and Nafissi.

*489

. . . and to call the other Boeotus, as having been thrown amongst oxen.[1]

[1] This connects Boeotus' name with the Greek *bo-* = 'ox', since Melanippe's sons were protected by oxen in a stable (cf. *Mel. Wise* test. i.12–14, iia.3). The etymology was probably given in the prologue of *Mel. Captive* and preceded by an etymology of Aeolus' name (cf. *Alexander* F 42d, *Antiope* F 181–2).

490

σὺν τῷ θεῷ χρὴ τοὺς σοφοὺς ἀναστρέφειν
βουλεύματ᾽ αἰεὶ πρὸς τὸ χρησιμώτερον.

Orion 5.3 Haffner

491

ἴστω δ᾽ ἄφρων ὢν ὅστις ἄτεκνος ὢν τὸ πρὶν
παῖδας θυραίους εἰς δόμους ἐκτήσατο,
τὴν μοῖραν εἰς τὸ μὴ χρεὼν παραστρέφων·
ᾧ γὰρ θεοὶ διδῶσι μὴ φῦναι τέκνα,
5 οὐ χρὴ μάχεσθαι πρὸς τὸ θεῖον, ἀλλ᾽ ἐᾶν.

Stobaeus 4.24.26

5 μάχεσθαι Conington: γλεῖσθαι Stob. mss. SM: τλεῖσθαι
ms. A

492

ἀνδρῶν δὲ πολλοὶ τοῦ γέλωτος οὕνεκα
ἀσκοῦσι χάριτας κερτόμους· ἐγὼ δέ πως
μισῶ γελοίους, οἵτινες τήτῃ σοφῶν
ἀχάλιν᾽ ἔχουσι στόματα, κἀς ἀνδρῶν μὲν οὐ
5 τελοῦσιν ἀριθμόν, ἐν γέλωτι δ᾽ εὐπρεπεῖς.

Athenaeus 14.613d (with F 494.9–10a subjoined)

490

Wise people should always heed the gods' will and redirect their plans towards what is more beneficial.

491

A man who has been childless and then has adopted the children of others into his home, distorting his destined lot into what should not be, should realise he is a fool. A man who is destined by the gods to be childless should not fight their will but should let it be so.[1]

---

[1] Against adoption see also *Erechtheus* F 359.

492

Many men practise ingratiating mockery for a joke, but I am inclined to despise these jokers who keep their mouths unbridled for want of wise things to say; they may be conspicuous for joking, but they do not count as men.[1]

---

[1] Cf. *Erechtheus* F 362.21–3.

493

ἄλγιστόν ἐστι θῆλυ μισηθὲν γένος·
αἱ γὰρ σφαλεῖσαι ταῖσιν οὐκ ἐσφαλμέναις
αἶσχος γυναιξί, καὶ κεκοίνωνται ψόγον
ταῖς οὐ κακαῖσιν αἱ κακαί· τὰ δ᾽ εἰς γάμους
5 οὐδὲν δοκοῦσιν ὑγιὲς ἀνδράσιν φρονεῖν.

Stobaeus 4.22.86

494

⟨ΜΕΛΑΝΙΠΠΗ?⟩

μάτην ἄρ᾽ ἐς γυναῖκας ἐξ ἀνδρῶν ψόγος
ψάλλει κενὸν τόξευμα καὶ λέγει κακῶς·
αἱ δ᾽ εἰσ᾽ ἀμείνους ἀρσένων, δείξω δ᾽ ἐγώ.
          ]ι ξυμβόλαι᾽ ἀμάρτυρα
5   ]‚‚ κοὺκ ἀρνούμεναι
με[   ]χο[ ] ἀλλήλας πόνους
κη[   ]δε[ ]θ[‚‚] αἰσχ[ύ]νην φέρει
…]αν‚[……]το[‚‚]ωτος ἐκβαλεῖ γυνή.
νέμουσι δ᾽ οἴκους καὶ τὰ ναυστολούμενα
10 ἔ[σω] δόμων σῴζουσιν, οὐδ᾽ ἐρημίᾳ
γυναικὸς οἶκος εὐπινὴς οὐδ᾽ ὄλβιος.

P. Berlin 9772, ed. U. von Wilamowitz and W. Schubart
(1907), cols. iii.4–v.1; see also Page, *GLP* 108–15 (no. 13(a)); Van
Looy (1964), 256–71 and in ed. Budé VIII.2.385–7; R. Seider,
Palaeographie der gr. Papyri II (Stuttgart, 1970), 49–50 with Pl. 5;
Diggle, *TrGFS* 123–4.   Vv. 1–3: Anonymous *Life of Euripides*
IV.2 (see *TrGF* 5.51); vv. 5–16: Satyrus, *Life of Euripides*, P. Oxy.

493

Hatred of womankind is a most grievous thing. Those who
have fallen bring disgrace on those who have not, and the
bad ones share their censure with the good; and where
marriage is concerned men think they have no integrity at
all.

494
⟨MELANIPPE?⟩

Vainly does censure from men twang an idle bowshot at
women and denounce them. In fact they are better than
men, as I shall demonstrate . . . contracts without witnesses
. . . and not reneging[1] . . . (they do not bring?) hardships 5
(upon?) one another . . . brings disgrace . . . a woman will
expel(?) . . . They manage households, and save what is
brought by sea within the home, and no house deprived of 10
a woman can be tidy and prosperous.

[1] Women fulfil obligations and repay loans to each other with-
out needing formal contracts. The review of this and other female
virtues in vv. 4–21 is imitated in Aristophanes, *Assemblywomen*
441–54: see J. Butrica, *CQ* 51 (2001), 610–3.

1176 fr. 39 col. XI; vv. 9–10 (νέμουσι . . . σῴζουσι): Athenaeus
14.613d (= F 492.6–7 N); vv. 27–9 (= F 494 N): Porphyry fr. 409f
Smith (in Eusebius, *Preparation for the Gospel* 10.3.19); Stobae-
us 4.22.78.

7 φέρει P. Berl.: ἔχε[ι P. Oxy.

ἃ δ᾽ εἰς θεοὺς αὖ—πρῶτα γὰρ κρίνω τάδε—
μέρος μέγιστον ἔχομεν· ἐν Φοίβου τε γὰρ
δόμοις προφητεύουσι Λοξίου φρένα
15 γυναῖκες, ἀμφὶ δ᾽ ἁγνὰ Δωδώνη‹ς› βάθρα
φηγῷ παρ᾽ ἱερᾷ θῆλυ τὰ[ς] Διὸς φρένας
γένος πορεύει τοῖς θέλουσιν Ἑλλάδος.
ἃ δ᾽ εἴς τε Μοίρας τάς τ᾽ ἀνωνύμους θεὰς
ἱερὰ τελεῖται, ταῦτ᾽ ἐν ἀνδράσιν μὲν οὐ‹χ›
20 ὅσια καθέστηκ᾽, ἐν γυναιξὶ δ᾽ αὔξεται
ἅπαντα. ταύτῃ τἀν θεοῖς ἔχει δίκη
θήλεια. πῶς οὖν χρὴ γυναικεῖον γένος
κακῶς ἀκούειν; οὐχὶ παύσεται ψόγος
μάταιος ἀνδρῶν †οἵ τ᾽ ἄγαν ἡγούμενοι†
25 ψέγειν γυναῖκας, εἰ μί᾽ ηὑρέθη κακή,
πάσας ὁμοίως; διοριῶ [δ᾽ ἐ]γὼ λόγῳ·
τῆς μὲν κακῆς κάκιον οὐδὲν γίγνεται
γυναικός, ἐσθλῆς δ᾽ οὐδὲν εἰς ὑπερβολὴν
πέφυκ᾽ ἄμεινον· διαφέρουσι δ᾽ αἱ φύσεις.

12 ἃ δ᾽ εἰς θεοὺς P. Berl.: τὰ δ᾽ ἐν θε[ο]ὶ[ς] P. Oxy.
14 δόμοις P. Berl.: χρησμο[ὶ]ς P. Oxy.   21 δίκη Cropp:
δίκης P. Berl.

596

Now as for dealings with the gods, which I consider of prime importance, we have a very great role in them. Women proclaim Loxias' mind in Phoebus' halls, and by Dodona's holy foundations, beside the sacred oak, woman- 15 kind conveys the thoughts of Zeus to those Greeks who want to know it.[2] Those rituals, too, which are performed for the Fates and the Nameless Goddesses[3] are not open to men, but are promoted by women entirely. That is how the 20 rights of women stand[4] in dealings with the gods.

Why then should womankind be denigrated? Will the vain censures of men not cease †and those excessively thinking† if just one is found to be bad, to condemn all 25 women alike? For my part I will make a distinction: on the one hand nothing is worse than a bad woman, but on the other nothing excels a good one in goodness. The natures of each are different.[5]

[2] Oracles at Delphi and Dodona were delivered respectively by the Pythia and the three priestesses ('Doves') of Zeus; on the latter see F 1021 with note.   [3] The *Semnai Theai* or August God-desses (in their malevolent form, Erinyes or Furies) are similarly described in *Iphigenia in Tauris* 944 and Sophocles, *Oedipus at Colonus* 128–33, and linked with Fate(s) in Aeschylus, *Seven against Thebes* 975–7, *Eumenides* 961–2 etc. They are 'nameless' because it is dangerous to name them: see A. Henrichs in Hofmann–Harder, *Fragmenta Dramatica* 169–79 and *ICS* 19 (1994), 37–8.   [4] In the papyrus, 'That is how women stand in respect of rights . . .'; but the Fem. Sing. adjective θήλεια can hardly mean 'women'.   [5] For the thought in the last few lines cf. *Protesilaus* F 657.

EURIPIDES

495

<ΑΓΓΕΛΟΣ>

'τίς ἦν ὁ . .[c. 12 letters μ]εθεὶς ἐμοί;'
ὡς δ' οὐκ ἐφαινόμεσθα, σῖγα δ' εἴχομεν,
πρόσω πρὸς αὐτὸν πάλιν ὑποστρέψας πόδα
χωρεῖ δρομαίαν, θῆρ' ἐλεῖν πρόθυμος ὤν,
5 βοᾷ δέ· κἂν τῷδ' ἐξεφαινόμεσθα δή,
ὀρθοσταδὸν λόγχαισ' ἐπείγοντες φόν[ον.
τὼ δ' εἰσιδόντε δίπτυχον θείοιν κάρ[α
ᾔσθησαν, εἶπόν θ'· Εἶα συλλάβεσθ' ἄγρα[ς,
καιρὸν γὰρ ἥκετ' '—οὐδ' ὑπώπτευον [δόλον,
10 φίλων προσώπων εἰσορῶντες ὄ[μματα.
οἱ δ' εἰς τὸν αὐτὸν πίτυλον ἤπειγ[ον δορός,
πέτροι τ' ἐχώρουν χερμάδες θ' ἡ[μῶν πάρα
ἐκεῖθεν, οἱ δ' ἐκεῖθεν· ὡς δ' ἦε[ι μάχη
σιγῇ τ' ἀφ' ἡμῶν, γνωρίσαντ[ε(ς)
15 λέγουσι· Μητρὸς ὦ κασίγνη[τοι φίλης,
τί δρᾶτ'; ἀποκτείνοντες ο[ὓς ἥκιστα χρῆν
φωρᾶσθε. πρὸς θεῶν δρᾶτ[ε μηδαμῶς τάδε.'
σὼ δ' αὐταδέλφω χερμ[άδ-

P. Berlin 5514, ed. F. Blass, *RhM* 35 (1880), 290–7; see also H.
Weil, *Revue de Philologie* 4 (1880), 121–4; Wilamowitz in *Berliner
Klassikertexte* V.2.84–7; Page, *GLP* 114–7 (no. 13(b)); Van Looy
(1964), 276–92 and in ed. Budé VIII.2.389–91; Diggle, *TrGFS*
124–6.   Vv. 40–3: Stobaeus 4.29.11.

1 ὁ τὰ[ργὸν τόδε βέλος μ]εθεὶς Weil and (τὰ[ργὸν) Wilamo-
witz   14 γνωρίσαντ[ε δὴ τὸ πᾶν Blass   18 χερμ[άδων
ἔσχον βολάς Diggle

495

⟨MESSENGER⟩

'Who was it who let fly . . . for me?'[1] But as we did not show
ourselves but kept silent, he turned back and ran towards
him, eager to take the beast, and gave a shout; but now
we did show ourselves, standing up and brandishing our 5
spears, intent on bloodshed. The twins, catching sight of
their two uncles, were glad and said, 'Hey there, join the
hunt, you're just in time', suspecting no (treachery) as they
saw the faces of friends. But they pressed on with the at- 10
tack (with their spears), and rocks and boulders flew (from
us) on either quarter; and as (the fighting) went on in si-
lence on our side, they realised . . .[2] and said, 'Brothers of
(our dear) mother, what are you doing? You are caught in 15
the act, trying to kill (those you should least kill). For the
gods' sake, (do not) do (this)! But your two brothers . . .

---

1 'who let fly this ineffective missile', Weil and Wilamowitz.
The Queen's brothers and their companions have lain in wait for
Melanippe's sons as they hunt a boar. Probably one of them has
shot an arrow or thrown a spear from cover, narrowly missing one
of the twins. After pausing and receiving no response to his chal-
lenge, the twin now advances on the thicket which he thinks hides
the boar but in fact hides some of the ambushers.   2 Blass
suggested 'they realised the whole of it'.

λέγουσί θ᾽ ὡς ἔφυσα[ν ἐκ δούλης
20 κοὐ δεῖ τυρανν[
πρεσβεῖ᾽ ἔχοντ[ας
κἀπεὶ τάδ᾽ εἰσή[κουσαν
ο]ὐ λῆμ᾽ ἔχο[

remains of two lines, then some lines from foot of page
missing, then:

26 ἔσφηλέ τ᾽ εἰς γῆν .[c. 10 letters] λετο·
ἡμῶν δ᾽ ἐχώρει κωφὰ πρὸς γαῖαν βέλη.
δ]υοῖν δ᾽ ἀδελφοῖν σοῖν τὸν αὖ νεώτερον
λό]γχῃ πλατείᾳ συοφόνῳ δι᾽ ἥπατος
30 παίσ]ας ἔδωκε νερτέροις καλὸν νεκρόν
.....].ος, ὅσπερ τὸν πρὶν ἔκτεινεν βαλών.
κἀντεῦ]θεν ἡμεῖς οἱ λελειμμένοι φίλων
κοῦφον] πόδ᾽ ἄλλος ἄλλοσ᾽ εἴχομεν φυγῇ.
εἶδον δὲ τ]ὸν μὲν ὄρεος ὑλίμῳ φόβῃ
35 κρυφθέν]τα, τὸν δὲ πευκίνων ὄζων ἔπι·
οἱ δ᾽ εἰς φάρ]αγγ᾽ ἔδυνον, οἱ δ᾽ ὑπ᾽ εὐσκίους
θάμνους κα]θῖζον. τὼ δ᾽ ὁρῶντ᾽ οὐκ ἠξίουν
δούλους φονε]ύειν φασγάνοις ἐλευθέροις.

19 ἐκ δούλης ποθέν Blass (νόθοι Nauck, τινός Van Looy)
20 τύρανν[α σκῆπτρα καὶ θρόνους κρατεῖν (e.g.) Weil (λαβεῖν
Wecklein)   21 ἔχοντ[ας δυσγενεῖς τῶν εὐγενῶν (e.g.)
Weil   23 ο]ὐ λῆμ᾽ ἔχο[ντες δοῦλον, ἀλλ᾽ ἐλεύθερον
Diggle   26 τ[ὸν βίον τ᾽ ἀ]φ[εί]λετο Blass (κ[αὶ πνοὰς
Weil)   30 καλὸν νεκρόν P. Berl.: καλὸν γέρας Nauck:
ἄλλον νεκρόν Diggle

rock(s), and said that they were born (from a . . . slave woman) and should not . . . royal . . . having precedence . . .[3]   20
And when they (heard) this . . . (not) hav(ing) a . . . spirit
. . .[4] *(remains of two lines, then some lines missing)* . . .
felled (him) to the ground . . .[5] Our missiles meanwhile   25
went vainly to the ground. And next . . . who had hit and
killed the first now (struck) the younger of your two broth-
ers through the liver with a broad boar-spear, and so deliv-
ered a fine corpse[6] to the powers below.   31

(Then) we who remained of their companions set off
(nimbly) fleeing in various directions. One man (I saw con-
cealed) in mountain-brush, and another perching on the
branches of a pine; (others) slipped (into) a ravine, while   35
others again crouched under shady (bushes). The twins
saw them but did not deign to (kill slaves) with free men's
swords.

3 With the supplements listed in the apparatus opposite (vv.
18–21): 'But your two brothers (restrained the) rock-(throwing),
and said that they were born (from a slave woman somewhere
[Blass] *or* bastards born from a slave woman [Nauck]), and should
not (possess [Weil] *or* take [Wecklein]) royal (sceptres, ill-born
men) having precedence (over well-born).'   4 Diggle sug-
gests '(not) hav(ing) a (slavish) spirit (but a free one)'.
5 '(and took away his life [Blass] *or* breath [Weil]').
6 Perhaps to be corrected: 'a fine offering' (Nauck) or 'another
corpse' (Diggle).

c. 12 letters σ]ῶν κασιγνήτων κλύεις.

40 ἐγὼ μὲν ⟨οὖν⟩ οὐκ οἶδ᾽ ὅτῳ σκοπεῖν χρεὼν
    τὴν εὐγένειαν. τοὺς γὰρ ἀνδρείους φύσιν
    καὶ τοὺς δικαίους τῶν κενῶν δοξασμάτων,
    κἂν ὦσι δούλων, εὐγενεστέρους λέγω.
    Ends of seven more lines (44–6 Chorus?, 47–50 Queen?)

39 μόρον τοιοῦτον σ]ῶν Nauck

(496 N = test. iib above)

... (of) your brothers ... you have heard.[7] For my part I
do not know how we should assess nobility. For I declare   40
that those who are brave and just by nature, though they be
born from slaves, are nobler than those who are mere
empty appearances.[8]

Ends of seven more lines (44–6 Chorus?, 47–50 Queen?)

[7] '(Such was the death of) your brothers that you have heard',
Nauck.   [8] For the thought cf. F 511 below, *Phrixus* F 831,
Ion 854–6, *Helen* 728–31; 'mere appearances' contrasted with
natural endowments also in *Erechtheus* F 359.2.

(496 N = test. iib above)

ΜΕΛΑΝΙΠΠΗ Η ΣΟΦΗ
or Η ΔΕΣΜΩΤΙΣ

497

τείσασθε τήνδε· καὶ γὰρ ἐντεῦθεν νοσεῖ
τὰ τῶν γυναικῶν· οἱ μὲν ἢ παίδων πέρι
ἢ συγγενείας οὕνεκ᾽ οὐκ ἀπώλεσαν
κακὴν λαβόντες· εἶτα τοῦτο τἄδικον
5 πολλαῖς ὑπερρύηκε καὶ χωρεῖ πρόσω,
ὥστ᾽ ἐξίτηλος ἀρετὴ καθίσταται.

Stobaeus 4.23.6

498

πλὴν τῆς τεκούσης θῆλυ πᾶν μισῶ γένος.

Stobaeus 4.22.146; cf. [Menander], *Monostichs* 665 Jaekel

(499 N = 494.1–3 above)

500

ὅστις δ᾽ ἄμικτον πατέρ᾽ ἔχει νεανίας
στυγνόν τ᾽ ἐν οἴκοις, μεγάλα κέκτηται κακά.

Stobaeus 4.26.3

MELANIPPE WISE
or CAPTIVE

497

Punish her! It is this that leads women to vice: some men
do not get rid of a woman when they find she is bad, either
considering their children or for the sake of a family con-
nection; then her wrongdoing overflows to many others
and progresses, so their virtue vanishes entirely.[1]

1 *Mel. Captive* F 493 and 494.22–9 protest against this kind
of prejudice, but this fragment has been plausibly attributed to
Hellen advising Aeolus to punish his daughter in *Mel. Wise*.

498

Except for my mother I hate all womankind.[1]

1 Probably from the attack on women in *Mel. Captive* to which
F 493–4 respond: see Introduction above.

(499 N = 494.1–3 above)

500

A young man who has an unsociable, sullen father in his
house possesses many troubles.[1]

1 Possibly Aeolus referring to his father Hellen in *Mel. Wise*;
cf. F 508–10 below.

501

γάμους δ᾽ ὅσοι σπεύδουσι μὴ πεπρωμένους,
μάτην πονοῦσιν· ἡ δὲ †τῷ χρεὼν πόσει
μένουσα† κἀσπούδαστος ἦλθεν εἰς δόμους.

Stobaeus 4.22.91

2–3 ἡ δ᾽ ὅτῳ χρεὼν πόσει μέλουσα Collard (μέλουσα West)

502

ὅσοι γαμοῦσι δ᾽ ἢ γένει κρείσσους γάμους
ἢ πολλὰ χρήματ᾽, οὐκ ἐπίστανται γαμεῖν·
τὰ τῆς γυναικὸς γὰρ κρατοῦντ᾽ ἐν δώμασιν
δουλοῖ τὸν ἄνδρα, κοὐκέτ᾽ ἔστ᾽ ἐλεύθερος.
5 πλοῦτος δ᾽ ἐπακτὸς ἐκ γυναικείων γάμων
ἀνόνητος· αἱ γὰρ διαλύσεις ⟨οὐ⟩ ῥᾴδιαι.

Stobaeus 4.22.94

503

⟨ΧΟΡΟΣ⟩
μετρίων λέκτρων, μετρίων δὲ γάμων
μετὰ σωφροσύνης
κῦρσαι θνητοῖσιν ἄριστον.

Stobaeus 4.22.132

504

ὦ τέκνον, ἀνθρώποισιν ἔστιν οἷς βίος
ὁ σμικρὸς εὐκρὰς ἐγένεθ᾽, οἷς δ᾽ ὄγκος κακόν.

Stobaeus 4.31.93

501

People who pursue undestined marriages are wasting their efforts; the woman †who remains for her proper husband†[1] comes to his house even without being pursued.

[1] A rough translation of the incoherent phrase transmitted in Stobaeus; Collard suggests 'the woman who is cared for by the husband who ought to care for her'. F 501–3, all reflecting on inappropriate marriages, may have been comments on the marriage of Metapontus and his wilful queen in *Mel. Captive.*

502

Men who marry wives above their rank, or marry great wealth, do not know how to make a marriage. The wife's interests prevail in the household and make a slave of the husband, and he is no longer free. Wealth acquired from marriage with a woman is unprofitable; for divorces are   5
(not) easy.[1]

[1] The husband 'enslaved' by his wife's dowry: cf. *Phaethon* 158–9. Marrying above oneself: F 503 below, *Antiope* F 214, *Electra* 932–7.

503

<CHORUS>

Ordinary unions, and ordinary wives with self-discipline, are best for mortals to find.[1]

[1] See on F 501 and 502 above. These lines may well come from the play's closing choral anapaests.

504

For some people, child, a modest living is appropriate,[1] and for some opulence is a bad thing.

[1] Literally 'well blended', as in *Antiope* F 197. This comment was perhaps made by Melanippe to one of her sons (enjoying a royal lifestyle) in *Mel. Captive.*

505

τὰ προσπεσόντα δ' ὅστις εὖ φέρει βροτῶν,
ἄριστος εἶναι σωφρονεῖν τ' ἐμοὶ δοκεῖ.

Stobaeus 4.44.55; [Plutarch], *Moralia* 116f

1–2 τὰ προσπεσόντα . . . ἄριστος εἶναι . . . [Plut.]: τὰ
τυγχάνοντα . . . | σοφὸν νομίζω . . . Stob.

506

δοκεῖτε πηδᾶν τἀδικήματ' εἰς θεοὺς
πτεροῖσι, κἄπειτ' ἐν Διὸς δέλτου πτυχαῖς
γράφειν τιν' αὐτά, Ζῆνα δ' εἰσορῶντά νιν
θνητοῖς δικάζειν; οὐδ' ὁ πᾶς ἂν οὐρανὸς
5 Διὸς γράφοντος τὰς βροτῶν ἁμαρτίας
ἐξαρκέσειεν, οὐδ' ἐκεῖνος ἂν σκοπῶν
πέμπειν ἑκάστῳ ζημίαν· ἀλλ' ἡ Δίκη
ἐνταῦθά πού 'στιν ἐγγύς, εἰ βούλεσθ' ὁρᾶν.

Stobaeus 1.3.14a

507

τί τοὺς θανόντας οὐκ ἐᾷς τεθνηκέναι
καὶ τἀκχυθέντα συλλέγεις ἀλγήματα;

Stobaeus 4.56.16; v. 1 = Eupolis, *Demes* F 99.102 *PCG*

505

The man who bears his fortunes well seems to me to be
excellent and self-disciplined.[1]

[1] Stobaeus has a banal alternative: 'The man who bears events
well I consider wise, and he seems to me to be self-disciplined.'

506

You think crimes leap up to the gods on wings, and some-
one writes them on Zeus's folded tablet, and Zeus looks at
them and delivers justice to men?[1] Even the whole sky
would not suffice for Zeus to write men's sins on it, nor   5
could he study them and send punishment for each of
them. In fact Justice is somewhere here close by, if you are
willing to see her.[2]

[1] An old belief reflecting the centralized administrative re-
cord-keeping of the ancient Near East, and recommended in Aes-
chylus F 281a (the 'Dikê fragment'): cf. M. L. West, *The East Face
of Helicon* (Oxford, 1997), 561–2.   [2] Justice, then, is not an
anthropomorphic deity who roams the world and reports human
wrongs to Zeus (Hesiod, *Works and Days* 220–4), but a matter
for human comprehension and judgement. This assertion is usu-
ally ascribed to Melanippe's rationalistic discourse in *Mel. Wise*;
Wilamowitz preferred Hippo correcting Aeolus at the end of that
play.

507

Why do you not let those who have died be dead? Why do
you gather up griefs that are already spilled?[1]

[1] Usually ascribed to someone consoling Melanippe (thinking
her sons long dead) in *Mel. Captive*; cf. *Alexander* F 46.5.

508

παλαιὸς αἶνος· ἔργα μὲν νεωτέρων,
βουλαὶ δ' ἔχουσι τῶν γεραιτέρων κράτος.

Stobaeus 4.50.12

509

τί δ' ἄλλο; φωνὴ καὶ σκιὰ γέρων ἀνήρ.

Stobaeus 4.50.57

510

παπαῖ, νέος καὶ σκαιὸς οἷός ἐστ' ἀνήρ.

Stob. 4.11.7

511

δοῦλον γὰρ ἐσθλὸν τοὔνομ' οὐ διαφθερεῖ,
πολλοὶ δ' ἀμείνους εἰσὶ τῶν ἐλευθέρων.

Stobaeus 4.19.38; P. Berlin 21144.6–7 (a few letters in each line)

512

ἀργὸς πολίτης κεῖνος, ὡς κακός γ' ἀνήρ.

Stobaeus 3.30.11

513

ἀλάστορας ⟨   ⟩ οὐκ ἐτόλμησεν κτανεῖν.

Erotian a 47

508

It's an old saying: the young are strong in action, but the old are strong in counsel.[1]

[1] Similarly *Bellerophon* F 291, *Peleus* F 619; cf. Homer, *Iliad* 4.323–5. This and F 509–10 may be from a dispute between Aeolus and Hellen (see also F 500).

509

What else? An old man is but voice and shadow.[1]

[1] Cf. *Aeolus* F 25 with note.

510

Whew, what a young, gauche kind of man he is!

511

The name of slave will not corrupt one who is good; many slaves are better men than those who are free.[1]

[1] Probably from *Melanippe Captive*: cf. F 495.40–3 above, with note.

512

That man is a useless citizen, for he is a worthless man.[1]

[1] Cf. *Antiope* F 187.

513

He did not dare to kill murderers.[1]

[1] Erotian (or his source) gives the sense here as 'murderers', but the reference may have been to suppliants seeking refuge after committing a murder, like Orestes in Aeschylus, *Eumenides* 236.

MELEAGER

H. Van Looy in ed. Budé VIII.2.397–425.

Webster 233–6, 306; Trendall–Webster III.3.37–40; *LIMC* I.i.578–80 'Althaia', II.i.940–50 'Atalante', VI.i.414–35 'Meleagros'; Gantz 328–39; P. Grossardt, *Die Erzählung von Meleagros* (Leiden, 2001), 88–95.

The play concerned the ancient story of the hero Meleager and his death following the hunt for the Calydonian boar. He was a son of king Oeneus of Calydon in Aetolia (the subject of Oeneus*) and his niece Althaea, or of Althaea and the god Ares (see on test. iiia below). Oeneus insulted Artemis by failing to recognize her in his harvest sacrifices; Artemis retaliated by sending a monstrous boar to ravage his lands, and Meleager assembled a band of heroes to confront and kill the boar; a quarrel ensued over the awarding of the boar's hide as a trophy, in which Meleager killed his mother's brothers, the sons of Thestius; and Althaea, valuing her birth family over her marriage family, avenged them by bringing about her son's death. The oldest extant version of this story in Homer's* Iliad *(9.529–605) is heavily adapted to suit the circumstances of Achilles' withdrawal from the fighting at Troy and Phoenix's attempt to persuade him to relent: thus Althaea curses Meleager after he has killed her brothers in battle, Meleager withdraws from* *the fighting in anger at the curse, and relents (persuaded by his wife Cleopatra) only when he must do so in order to save his besieged city and home. His death resulting from the curse is implied, and other epics ([Hesiod] F 25.9–13 and the* Minyas: *cf. Pausanias 10.31.2) seem to have followed the logic of this account by having him killed in battle by Apollo (who also had a hand in killing Achilles). But in an alternative account Althaea was told by the Fates at Meleager's birth that he would live as long as a log that they placed on the hearth; she retrieved and stored the log, but returned it to the fire when she resolved to kill her son. This may well be an older version of the story, though first attested only in the 5th century (Phrynichus'* Women of Pleuron *F 6, Aeschylus'* Libation Bearers *602–12, and especially Bacchylides 5.93–154, possibly anticipated in Stesichorus' mid-6th c.* Boar Hunters*).*

By the early 6th century, if not long before, the boar hunters included the Arcadian Atalanta, a devotee of Artemis. A common feature in later accounts (e.g. Ovid, Metamorphoses *8.270–525, Diodorus 4.34, Apollodorus 1.8.2–3, Hyginus,* Fab. *174) is that Meleager loved Atalanta and, on being awarded the boar's hide after killing it, insisted on passing it to her because she had been the first to wound it; his uncles then seized the hide for themselves, claiming precedence as his nearest kin, and thus provoked the quarrel that led to their deaths. Euripides seems to have popularized, if not invented, this scenario, and the fragments show strong signs of it.*

The play will have been set at Oeneus' palace in Calydon, with probably a chorus of Althaea's friends or servants. F 515–6 are alternative openings for the prologue speech (see notes to these), and test. iiia (below) and

*F 517 are best connected with it also (see note on F 517).
F 518 and 519 suggest an early scene in which Meleager
overrules his mother's fears about his attempting the hunt.
F 520–8 contain arguments on the familiar Euripidean
themes of sex, marriage, heredity and women's social roles:
probably Meleager proclaims his admiration for Atalanta
(F 520, 526–7), Althaea attacks her unwomanly conduct
(F 521–2), Atalanta insists on her virginal way of life
(F 524–5), and Althaea condemns her eloquence (F 528). A
lengthy three-way debate seems likely, but its exact context
and shape cannot be determined. Presumably the hunters
had gathered at Calydon, but it seems unlikely that others
had roles in the play or that (for example) the Arcadians
Cepheus and Ancaeus spoke against Atalanta as in Apol-
lodorus (cf. Grossardt 89). F 530–531a belong to a report
of the hunt itself, probably delivered to Oeneus; the quarrel
and killing of the Thestiads must have been reported here,
or in a subsequent speech if success and disaster were sepa-
rated as in the report speeches of* Phoenician Women *(for a
comparable report see* Melanippe Captive *F 495; less likely
is Webster's suggestion that Meleager returned triumphant
to the palace and debated his attachment to Atalanta with
his mother between the hunt and the conflict over the
hide). After this came very probably scenes of Althaea
making her fatal decision (see below on Accius), her suicide
announced (perhaps by the old woman—her Nurse?—
who speaks F 533), the dying Meleager returning and ex-
piring (F 535; similarities with* Hippolytus*), and a god
passing judgment on the events and predicting the family's
future (F 537). The remaining fragments cannot be placed
with any precision, but F 536 clearly belongs near the end;
see also the notes on F 528a, 532, 534. Apollodorus' report*

that Meleager was married to Cleopatra but wanted to have a child by Atalanta is sometimes attributed to Euripides but is surely due to later mythographic syncretism (the merging of related stories with each other). The prediction in F 537 of the death of Tydeus, Oeneus' younger son (usually by a second wife: see Introduction to Oeneus), need not suggest that he had a part in the play, and his appearance in the Apulian vase painting of Meleager's death (see below) may again be due to syncretism.

Brief fragments: F 538 'gods facing the sun' (i.e. outdoor images); F 539 'he consecrated (for sacrifice)'. Other ascriptions: F 971; adesp. F 188 'O Zeus, grant that I may strike down the boar'; adesp. F 632 (damaged papyrus text mentioning a beast's hide and Atalanta = Page, GLP no. 27). See also on adesp. F 625 under Oeneus, other ascriptions.

Accius' Latin Meleager (2nd c. B.C.) may well have followed Euripides. Its brief fragments feature the ravages and the hunting of the boar (frs. 1, 3–5 Dangel), perhaps Atalanta criticizing marriage (fr. 2), Meleager making and justifying his award to Atalanta (probably reported: frs. 6, 8), Althaea hearing of her brothers' deaths and deciding to burn the log (frs. 10–13), Meleager's slow death (frs. 14–16), and perhaps Althaea deciding that she must kill herself (fr. 7). Frs. 11–13 show Althaea, like Medea, reaching her fatal decision in an emotionally conflicted speech, as she does also in Ovid; Euripides' play may have been a model for both.

A date not earlier than 418, and probably some years later, is suggested by the 'free' style of metrical resolutions in the trimeter fragments, the trochaic tetrameter in F 536, and the quotations from Meleager in Aristophanes'

Frogs *of 405* B.C. *(F 516, 528a, 531). Sophocles'* Meleager *(F 401–6) was probably earlier, and a Scholion on* Iliad *9.575 implies that it was based on the Homeric account (it may have included the suicide of Cleopatra as well as Althaea, as in Apollodorus). Phrynichus'* Women of Pleuron *(above) seems to have concerned events later than Althaea's death, and Aeschylus'* Atalanta *(no fragments) may have been about the heroine's famous running race against her suitor Hippomenes. Fourth-century tragedies by Antiphon (F 1b–2) and Sosiphanes (F 1) are almost wholly lost, as are comedies by Philetaerus, Antiphanes and others. On Accius and Ovid see above. In art, Meleager's love for Atalanta is first suggested in four vases by the Meleager Painter (early 4th c.,* LIMC *'Meleager' nos. 37–40: cf. Trendall–Webster III.3.37–8, Todisco A 74), perhaps inspired by Euripides. Two later 4th c. Apulian vases show him presenting her with the hide (*LIMC *no. 41 = Trendall–Webster III.3.39, Todisco Ap 171a) and his death (*LIMC *no. 42 = Trendall–Webster III.3.40, Todisco Ap 106, Taplin no. 69); these have tragic features but need not reflect Euripides exactly (see above on Tydeus). The story as a whole was much exploited in Greek, Etruscan and Roman art, and again in literature, art and music since the Renaissance (*OGCMA *II.653–8).*

ΜΕΛΕΑΓΡΟΣ

test. iiia

Ἄρης· Ἀλθαίᾳ συνῆλθε καὶ Μελέαγρον ποιήσας <
>, ὡς Εὐριπίδης ἐν Μελεάγρῳ,

[Plutarch], *Moralia* 312a

515

Καλυδὼν μὲν ἥδε γαῖα, Πελοπίας χθονὸς
ἐν ἀντιπόρθμοις πεδί᾽ ἔχουσ᾽ εὐδαίμονα·
Οἰνεὺς δ᾽ ἀνάσσει τῆσδε γῆς Αἰτωλίας,
Πορθάονος παῖς, ὅς ποτ᾽ Ἀλθαίαν γαμεῖ,
5 Λήδας ὅμαιμον, Θεστίου δὲ παρθένον.

Aristotle, *Rhetoric* 1409b8, with anonymous commentary ed. H. Rabe, *CAG* XXI.2, pp. 195.27ff. and 197.3ff.; vv. 1–2: Praxiphanes fr. 13 Wehrli, Lucian 17.25; v. 1: Schol. on Aristophanes, *Frogs* 1238

MELEAGER

test. iiia

Ares: lay with Althaea, and after begetting Meleager ⟨   ⟩, as
Euripides (says) in *Meleager*.[1]

[1] For Ares as Meleager's true father cf. Ovid, *Metamorphoses*
8.437, Apollodorus 1.8.2, Hyginus, *Fab*. 171.

515

This land is Calydon; its prosperous plains lie across the
strait from Pelops' country. Oeneus rules over this Aeto-
lian land, Porthaon's son, who in bygone days married
Althaea, Leda's sister and daughter of Thestius.[1]

[1] Althaea's mother was her husband's half-sister. The scholia
on Aristophanes, *Frogs* 1238 indicate that in the text known to Al-
exandrian scholars these were the opening lines of the play and F
516 followed several lines later. But in *Frogs* itself F 516 is quoted
as the opening of the play (see below). Fritzsche's suggestion
that F 515 was added to the text for a revival of the play so as to
mitigate the comic effect of the original opening is accepted by
Kannicht; against this see e.g. Scullion 2006 (see bibliography for
Archelaus), 192. Euripides or a later reviser may simply have pro-
vided a more elaborate and informative prologue for the text that
went into general circulation.

516

Οἰνεύς ποτ' ἐκ γῆς πολύμετρον λαβὼν στάχυν
θύων ἀπαρχὰς . . .

Aristophanes, *Frogs* 1240–1 with Schol.

517

Μελέαγρε, μελέαν γάρ ποτ' ἀγρεύεις ἄγραν . . .

Etymologicum Magnum p. 576.30 Gaisford; cf. Proclus, *Commentary on Plato's Cratylus* 85

518

⟨ΜΕΛΕΑΓΡΟΣ⟩

καὶ κτῆμα δ', ὦ τεκοῦσα, κάλλιστον τόδε,
πλούτου δὲ κρεῖσσον· τοῦ μὲν ὠκεῖα πτέρυξ,
παῖδες δὲ χρηστοί, κἂν θάνωσι, δώμασιν
καλόν τι θησαύρισμα τοῖς τεκοῦσί τε
5 ἀνάθημα βιότου, κοὔποτ' ἐκλείπει δόμους.

Stobaeus 4.24.2

519

⟨ΜΕΛΕΑΓΡΟΣ?⟩

δειλοὶ γὰρ ἄνδρες οὐκ ἔχουσιν ἐν μάχῃ
ἀριθμόν, ἀλλ' ἄπεισι κἂν παρῶσ' ὅμως.

Stobaeus 3.8.3

516

Oeneus once took an abundant harvest from the land, and in sacrificing the first fruits . . .

1 This is one of the Euripidean prologue openings subverted by Aristophanes in *Frogs* 1198ff. with the conclusion 'lost his little oil jar': cf. *Stheneboea* F 661, *Hypsipyle* F 752, *Phrixus B* F 819, and F 846 (ascribed to *Archelaus* in the Aristophanic scholia); and see on F 515 above. The original text must have referred to Oeneus' failure to sacrifice to Artemis.

517

Meleager—malign indeed is the chase you've chosen . . .[1]

1 The translation attempts to reflect the Greek text's double etymological play on the name Meleager (*mele-* 'wretched, ill-fated', *agr-* 'chase, hunt'). The Greek present-tense verb is probably 'prophetic' (lit. 'the hunt you (will) hunt') and spoken by a god (Artemis?) in the prologue speech.

518

⟨MELEAGER⟩

Moreover, mother, this is a very fine possession, more valuable than wealth; for wealth flies quickly away, but good sons, even if they die, are a glorious treasure for their family and an ornament to their parents' lives, and this never leaves their house.[1]

1 Meleager consoles his mother for his possible death in the boar hunt: cf. *Erechtheus* F 360.28–37, *Temenidae* F 734, and for the actual loss of sons in battle, Thucydides 2.44.4.

519

⟨MELEAGER?⟩

Men who are cowards count for nothing in battle; even if present, they are absent none the less.

520

⟨ΜΕΛΕΑΓΡΟΣ?⟩

ἡγησάμην οὖν, εἰ παραζεύξειέ τις
χρηστῷ πονηρὸν λέκτρον, οὐκ ἂν εὐτεκνεῖν,
ἐσθλοῖν δ᾽ ἀπ᾽ ἀμφοῖν ἐσθλὸν ἂν φῦναι γόνον.

Stobaeus 4.22.131

521

⟨ΑΛΘΑΙΑ?⟩

ἔνδον μένουσαν τὴν γυναῖκ᾽ εἶναι χρεὼν
ἐσθλήν, θύρασι δ᾽ ἀξίαν τοῦ μηδενός.

Stobaeus 4.23.12

522

⟨ΑΛΘΑΙΑ?⟩

. . .

εἰ κερκίδων μὲν ἀνδράσιν μέλοι πόνος,
γυναιξὶ δ᾽ ὅπλων ἐμπέσοιεν ἡδοναί·
ἐκ τῆς ἐπιστήμης γὰρ ἐκπεπτωκότες
κεῖνοί τ᾽ ἂν οὐδὲν εἶεν οὔθ᾽ ἡμεῖς ἔτι.

Stobaeus 4.22.188

4 ἡμεῖς Stob. ms. Voss. and most editors: ὑμεῖς Stob. mss.
SMA

(523 N = 528a below)

520
⟨MELEAGER?⟩

So I reckoned, if one joined an inferior spouse with a man
of worth, one would not get good children—but if both
were good, their offspring would be good also.[1]

[1] Moral character inherited: cf. F 527 below, and on *Alcmeon
in Corinth* F 75.

521
⟨ALTHAEA?⟩

A wife who stays at home is certain to be a good one, and
one who spends time out of doors is certain to be worth-
less.[1]

[1] A widespread prejudice in Greek society, e.g. F 927,
Children of Heracles 474–7, *Trojan Women* 647–50; Xenophon,
Oeconomicus 7.30.

522
⟨ALTHAEA?⟩

. . . if men concerned themselves with the labour of weav-
ing, and women were overcome by the joys of armed fight-
ing; cast out from their proper sphere of knowledge, they
would be good for nothing, and so would we.[1]

[1] 'We' is more likely than 'You' (as in the main mss. of
Stobaeus) and suits the attribution to Althaea. For the notion of
male-female role reversals cf. Herodotus 2.35, Sophocles,
Oedipus at Colonus 337–45.

(523 N = 528a below)

524

⟨ΑΤΑΛΑΝΤΗ?⟩

ἡ γὰρ Κύπρις πέφυκε τῷ σκότῳ φίλη,
τὸ φῶς δ᾽ ἀνάγκην προστίθησι σωφρονεῖν.

Stobaeus 4.20.50

525

⟨ΑΤΑΛΑΝΤΗ⟩

εἰ δ᾽ εἰς γάμους ἔλθοιμ᾽—ὃ μὴ τύχοι ποτέ—
τῶν ἐν δόμοισιν ἡμερευουσῶν ἀεὶ
βελτίον᾽ ἂν τέκοιμι σώμασιν τέκνα·
ἐκ γὰρ πατρὸς καὶ μητρὸς ὅστις ἐκπονεῖ
5 σκληρὰς διαίτας οἱ γόνοι βελτίονες.

Stobaeus 4.22.96; vv. 4–5: Stobaeus 2.31.21; Clement of Alexandria, *Miscellanies* 6.2.9.1

3 σώμασιν Musgrave: δώματι Stob.   4 ὅστις ἐκπονεῖ
Stob.: ἐκπονουμένων Clem.

526

⟨ΜΕΛΕΑΓΡΟΣ?⟩

τό τοι κράτιστον, †κἂν γυνὴ κράτιστον ᾖ,†
τοῦτ᾽ ἔστ⟨ιν⟩ ἀρετή· τὸ δ᾽ ὄνομ᾽ †οὐ διαφέρει.†

Orion 7.1 Haffner

1 κἂν γονῇ (Conington) κακός τις ᾖ Gomperz: κἂν γένος
κάκιστον ᾖ Collard   2 οὐ διαφθερεῖ Meineke and others

524
⟨ATALANTA?⟩

Cypris is fond of darkness, while daylight imposes a need
for modest behaviour.

525
⟨ATALANTA⟩

And if I embarked on marriage—which I hope may never
happen!—I would bear physically stronger children than
women who spend all their days at home. A father and
mother who toil at strenuous activities will have children
who are stronger.

526
⟨MELEAGER?⟩

The most important thing, †even if a woman is the most
important thing,† is excellence; the name †makes no dif-
ference.†[1]

1 Text confused; the sense may have been that a woman's ex-
cellence (such as Atalanta's) should not be dismissed merely
because she is a woman (but the point becomes different with
Gomperz's 'even if a person is low in birth', or Collard's 'even if
one's birth is very low'). In v. 2 the Greek 'makes no difference' is
unmetrical, and Meineke's 'will not destroy it (i.e. its possessor's
excellence)' may be correct: for such phrasing cf. *Eurystheus* F
377, *Melanippe* F 511.

527

⟨ΜΕΛΕΑΓΡΟΣ?⟩

μόνον δ' ἂν αὐτὰ χρημάτων οὐκ ἂν λάβοις,
γενναιότητα κἀρετήν· καλὸς δέ τις
κἂν ἐκ πονηρῶν σωμάτων γένοιτο παῖς.

Stobaeus 4.29.31

528

⟨ΑΛΘΑΙΑ?⟩

μισῶ γυναῖκα ⟨πᾶσαν⟩—ἐκ πασῶν δὲ σέ—
ἥτις πονηρὰ τἄργ' ἔχουσ' ⟨εἶτ'⟩ εὖ λέγει.

Stobaeus 4.22.190

1 ⟨πᾶσαν⟩ Nauck   2 ⟨εἶτ'⟩ Dobree   λέγει, and punc-
tuation in v. 1 as printed, West: λέγεις Stob.

528a (= 523 N)

κερκίδος ἀοιδοῦ μελέτας

Aristophanes, *Frogs* 1316 with Schol.

529

ὡς ἡδὺ δούλοις δεσπότας χρηστοὺς λαβεῖν,
καὶ δεσπόταισι δοῦλον εὐμενῆ δόμοις.

Stobaeus 4.19.3; ascribed to Philemon in P. Schu-
bart 28 (= [Menander], *Monostichs* Pap. XIX Jaekel), 9–11;
v. 1 ~ [Menander], *Monostichs* 858 Jaekel

527

⟨MELEAGER?⟩

They are the only things you cannot get for money—nobility and virtue; whereas a handsome son can be produced from bodies that are inferior.[1]

> [1] The argument is rhetorically compressed: nobility and virtue cannot be acquired through wealth, nor can they be inherited from inferior parents (as handsomeness can); thus only noble and virtuous parents can produce noble and virtuous children: cf. F 520 with note.

528

⟨ALTHAEA?⟩

I detest every woman—and you above all of them—who has done wicked deeds and then defends them with fine words.[1]

> [1] Cf. *Palamedes* F 583. West's reading and punctuation improve on Stobaeus' 'I detest every woman, and especially you whose actions are wicked, etc.'

528a (= 523 N)

. . . work of the singing shuttle . . . [1]

> [1] Included by the Aristophanic Aeschylus in his pastiche of Euripidean lyric, *Frogs* 1309–22. The shuttle's 'song' is the twanging sound made as a weaver passes it through the warp-threads of a loom.

529

How pleasing it is for slaves to have good masters, and for masters a slave who is friendly to their family.

530

⟨ΑΓΓΕΛΟΣ⟩

Τελαμὼν δὲ χρυσοῦν αἰετὸν πέλτης ἔπι
πρόβλημα θηρός, βότρυσι δ' ἔστεψεν κάρα,
Σαλαμῖνα κοσμῶν πατρίδα τὴν εὐάμπελον·
Κύπριδος δὲ μίσημ', Ἀρκὰς Ἀταλάντη, κύνας
5 καὶ τόξ' ἔχουσα· πελέκεως δὲ δίστομον
γέννυν ἔπαλλ' Ἀγκαῖος· οἱ δὲ Θεστίου
παῖδες τὸ λαιὸν ἴχνος ἀνάρβυλοι ποδός,
τὸ δ' ἐν πεδίλοις, ὡς ἐλαφρίζον γόνυ
ἔχοιεν, ὃς δὴ πᾶσιν Αἰτωλοῖς νόμος.

Macrobius, *Saturnalia* 5.18.17 (vv. 7–9 τὸ λαιὸν . . . ἔχοιεν = Aristotle fr. 74 Rose)

531 + 531a

⟨ΑΓΓΕΛΟΣ⟩

531 σιδηροβριθές τ' ἔλαβε δεξιᾷ ξύλον . . .
(*a line intervening?*)
531a . . . δίμορφον ὤλεσεν Μίνω γόνον.

F 531: Aristophanes, *Frogs* 1402 with Schol. F 531a: Photius, *Lexicon* δ 389 Theodoridis

532

τοὺς ζῶντας εὖ δρᾶν· κατθανὼν δὲ πᾶς ἀνὴρ
γῆ καὶ σκιά· τὸ μηδὲν εἰς οὐδὲν ῥέπει.

Stobaeus 4.34.4 and 4.53.25

MELEAGER

530

<MESSENGER>

. . . and Telamon (having) on his shield a golden eagle to confront the boar—he had wreathed his head with grapes to honour his homeland of Salamis with its fine vines; and Cypris' bugbear, Arcadian Atalanta, with hounds and bow, and Ancaeus brandishing his double-bladed axe, and Thestius' sons, each with his left foot unshod while the other was sandalled, so the knee should carry less weight, as is the custom for all the Aetolians.[1]

[1] All these figures were traditionally amongst the hunters of the Calydonian boar. Telamon of Salamis was the father of Ajax. Ancaeus was traditionally one of the boar's victims. For the sons of Thestius see Introduction above. Aristotle fr. 74 (cited by Macrobius, the source of our fragment) contradicted Euripides by asserting that the Aetolians kept the right foot bare, not the left.

531 + 531a

<MESSENGER>

He took in his right hand the iron-weighted club . . . (with which?) he had killed the hybrid son of Minos.[1]

[1] F 531 and 531a could be adjacent lines. Theseus killed the Minotaur with the club taken from the giant Periphetes whom he killed at Epidaurus on his journey from Troezen to Athens.

532

Do good to the living—once dead, every man is earth and shadow; what is nothing counts for nothing.[1]

[1] Possibly from the same speech as F 533.

533

τερπνὸν τὸ φῶς τόδ', ὁ δ' ὑπὸ γῆς Ἅιδου σκότος
οὐδ' εἰς ὄνειρον ἡδὺς ἀνθρώποις μολεῖν·
ἐγὼ μὲν οὖν γεγῶσα τηλικήδ' ὅμως
ἀπέπτυσ' αὐτὸ κοὔποτ' εὔχομαι θανεῖν.

Stobaeus 4.52.13

1 so Nauck (γῆς Osann): τερπνὸν τὸ φῶς μοι τόδ' ὑπὸ γῆν
δι' ἄδου σκότος Stob. (τὸ δ' ὑπὸ γῆν Ἅιδου σκότος Grotius)
2 ἡδὺς ἀνθρώποις Nauck: οὐδ' εἰς ἀνθρώπους Stob.

534

τὸ μὲν γὰρ ἐν φῷ, τὸ δὲ κατὰ σκότον κακόν.

Etymologicum Genuinum mss. AB, 'φῷ' (= *Etym. Magnum*
p. 803.45 Gaisford)

535

⟨ΜΕΛΕΑΓΡΟΣ?⟩
ὁρᾷς σὺ νῦν δή μ' ὡς ἐπράϋνας, Τύχη.

Photius, *Lexicon* 'νυνδή' (I.451.18 Naber) = Suda ν 603

536

φεῦ, τὰ τῶν εὐδαιμονούντων ὡς ταχὺ στρέφει θεός.

Stobaeus 4.41.46

537

εἰς ἀνδροβρῶτας ἡδονὰς ἀφίξεται
κάρηνα πυρσαῖς γένυσι Μελανίππου σπάσας.

Schol. on Pindar, *Nemeans* 10.7 (10.12b Drachmann)

533

This light of day is a joy, but the darkness of Hades beneath the earth is unpleasant for mortals to enter even in their dreams. Old as I am, I spurn it and I pray that I may never die.[1]

1 In vv. 1–2 Stobaeus' text is unmetrical and gives confused sense; for the thought cf. *Iphigenia at Aulis* 1250–2. The wording in v. 3 makes it clear that the speaker is female, perhaps Althaea's nurse reacting to her suicide.

534

For the one evil is in daylight, the other in darkness.[1]

1 Less likely, 'For the one is in daylight, while the other is an evil in darkness'. The point might be connected with either F 533 or F 524.

535

⟨MELEAGER?⟩

You see how you have just now tamed me, Fortune!

536

Ah, how quickly God upsets the fortunes of the prosperous!

537

He will come to cannibal pleasures and tear the head of Melanippus with gore-red jaws.[1]

1 Tydeus ate the brains of Melanippus after killing him in the assault of the Seven on Thebes, and so was deprived of his chance of immortality by Athena. The prediction will have come from a god (Athena herself?) at the end of the play (see Introduction).

INDEX

Both names and references are included. Play-titles or their obvious abbreviations refer to the introductions and/or testimonia for a play; references in the form '(t. ii)' are to a specific testimonium. Numbers refer to fragments; double numbers (370.3) indicate verses within the longer fragments. Fragments placed out of numerical sequence or listed as 'brief' in a play-introduction are accompanied by the name of the play to which they belong, e.g.: 1132 (*Danae*); 514 (*Mel.W.* brief).

Abas: 228a.5

Achelous: *Alcm.Ps.*

Acrisius: *Danae*; 228a.8; 316; 1132 (*Danae*)

Acropolis of Athens: 370.3; 481.10

Adonis: 514 (*Mel.W.* brief)

Aegeae, in Macedonia: *Arch.*

Aegeus: *Aegeus*; 386b.10

Aegisthus: *Thyestes?*

Aeolia: 481.3–6

Aeolian Isles: *Aeolus*; *Mel.C.*

Aeolus, ruler of Aeolian Isles: *Aeolus*; 13a–41

Aeolus, son of Hellen: *Mel.W.*; 481.2, 14; 485; 500?; 510?

Aeolus, son of Melanippe: *Mel.W.*; *Mel.C.*; 489; 495

Aerope: *Thyestes*; *Cret.W.*; 466

Aethēr. See Heaven

Aetolia, Aetolians: *Cresph.* (t. ii); *Meleager*; 515; 530

Agamemnon: *Cret.W.*

Aidōs (Shame): 436

Alcaeus: 228a.13

Alcmene: *Alcmene*; *Licymn.*; 87b; 88a; 228a.14, 15

Alcmeon: *Alcm.Ps.*; *Alcm.C.*; 65–87

Aleus: *Auge*; 268

Alexander (Paris): *Alex.*; 41a–62i

Alope: *Alope*; 106–111

Alphesiboea. See Arsinoe

Althaea: *Meleager*; 515; 518; 521–522?; 528?

Amphiaraus: *Alcm.Ps.*

Amphilochus: *Alcm.C.*; 73a; 75

Amphion: *Antiope*; 179–223

Amphitryon: *Alcmene*; *Licymn.*; 87b; 89

Ancaeus: *Meleager*; 530

INDEX

Andromeda: *Andromeda*; *Danae*; 114–145; 228a.11

Antaeus: *Busiris*

Antenor: *Alcmene?*

Anticlea: *Autolycus*

Antigone: *Antigone*; 161; 166?

Antiope: *Antiope*; 179–223

Aphrodite: 26; 472c?. *See also* Cypris

Apollo: *Alcm.C.*; *Arch.*; 73a; 190; 245; 472b.3–7; 477. *See also* Loxias; Paian; Phoebus

Arcadia: *Auge*; 530

Archelaus: *Arch.*; 228–264

Ares: *Meleager* (t. iiia); 223.82, 112

Argeus: *Licymn.*

Argos, Amphilochian: *Alcm.C.*

Argos, Argives: *Alcm.Ps.*; *Alcm.C.*; *Andromeda*; *Arch.*; *Bell.*; *Danae*; *Cret.W*; 70; 124; 228; 228a.13, 18; 305; 1132.5, 23 (*Danae*)

Ariadne: *Theseus*; 387?

Aristomachus: *Cresph.* (t. ii)

Arsinoe (or Alphesiboea): *Alcm.Ps.*; 72

Artemis: *Hipp.V.*; *Mel.W.* (t. vb); *Meleager*; 472b.8; 516

Asopus, R.: 223.55; 481.3

Asterius: *Cretans* (t. iiia)

Atalanta: *Meleager*; 524; 525; 530

Athamas: *Ino*; 399; 421?

Athena: *Aeolus?*; *Andromeda* (t. iiia (a)); *Erech.*; *Theseus*; 1132.hyp. (*Danae*); 351; 360.49; 369.4; 370.55–118; 388?; 537. *See also* Pallas

Athena Alea: *Auge*; 264a; 266

Athena Polias: 370.94–96

Athens: *Aegeus*; *Alope*; *Erech.*; *Theseus*; 360.5–12, 50–55; 481.9. *See also* Cecropia

Atlantic Ocean: 145

Atreus: *Thyestes*; *Cret.W.*; 396; 397b; 465

Attica: *Erech.*

Auge: *Auge*; 266; 271–271b

Autolycus: *Autolycus*

Bacchus (title of Dionysus): 477

Bellerophon: *Bell.*; 285–312

Boeotia: *Antiope*; *Mel.W.*; 481.3–6

Boeotus: *Mel.W.*; *Mel.C.*; 489; 495; 498?

Busiris: *Busiris*

Cadmus: [*Cadmus*]; 223.55, 79, 86, 99, 108

Callirhoe: *Alcm.Ps.*

Calydon: *Meleager*; 515

Calydonian Boar: *Meleager*

Canace: *Aeolus*

Capaneus: 159

Cassandra: *Alex.*; 46.11?; 62f–h

Cassiepeia: *Andromeda*; 141?

Catreus: *Cret.W.*; 465?; 466

Cecropia, Cecrops' land (= Attica): 481.10

Cecrops, younger: *Erech.?*

Centaurs: *Ixion*

Cepheus: *Andromeda*; 120; 138a?; 141?; 228a.11

Cephisus: *Erech.* (t. ii); 370.63

Cerberus: *Eurysth.*

Cercyon: *Alope*; 109–111

INDEX

Cetus. *See* Sea monster
Chalybeans: 472.6
Chione: *Erech.* (t. ii); 349
Chiron: *Mel.W.*; 481.13
Cisseus: *Arch.*; 229–230; 231; 263?
Cithaeron, Mt.: *Antiope*
Clymene: *Cret.W.*; 466
Cocalus: *Cretans* (t. iiia)
Corinth: *Alcm.C.*; *Bell.*; 74
Corycian mountain: 481.19
Creon, of Corinth: *Alcm.C.*; 75; 76
Creon, of Thebes: *Antigone*; 171; 172
Cresphontes, father: *Cresph.*; 448a.17–24, 71–2, 78; 451
Cresphontes, son: *Cresph.*; 448a; 450; 453
Crete, Cretans: *Theseus*; *Cret.W.*; *Cretans*; 381; 471a; 472.3; 472c; 472f
Cretheus: *Mel.W.*?
Creusa: 481.9–11
Curetes: 472.14
Cypris (title of Aphrodite): 162; 324; 331; 340; 388; 428; 524; 530. *See also* Aphrodite

Daedalus: *Cretans*; *Theseus*; 372; 988 (*Cretans*)
Danaans: 228
Danae: *Danae*; *Dictys*; 228a.8, 9; 323; 1132 (*Danae*); 332; 342
Danaids: 228
Danaus: 228
Deio (Demeter): 370.34, 109
Deiphobus: *Alex.*; 62a, b, d

Delphi, Delphic oracle: *Alcm.Ps.*; *Erech*; 1132.7 (*Danae*); 472b?
Demeter: 370.102. *See also* Deio
Dictys: *Dictys*; 332; 342
Dione: 177; 228a.22
Dionysus: *Antigone*; *Antiope*; *Ino*; *Theseus*; 175 (*Antiope*); 177; 178; 179; 203. *See also* Bacchus; Zagreus
Dirce: *Antiope*; 175 (*Antiope*); 221; 223.6, 60–64, 80–85, 111–115
Discord (Stasis): 453.20
Dodona: 228a.20; 367; 494.15

Earth (Gaia; Gē): 24b; 61b; 86; 154; 182a; 195; 223.94; 316; 370.45; 415; 953f.12 (*Hipp.V.*); [448]; 1004 (*Cretans*); 484; 533
Echinades, isles: *Alcmene*; 87b
Echo: *Andromeda*; 114; 118
Egypt: *Busiris*; 228n
Electryon: *Alcmene*; *Licymn.*; 89; 228a.15
Eleusis: *Alope*; *Erech.*
Eleutherae: *Antiope*; 179; 175 (*Antiope*)
Enipeus, R.: 14
Epeus: *Epeus*
Epigoni: *Alcm.Ps.*
Epopeus: *Antiope*
Erechtheids: *Erech.*; 358; 360; 370.65–89
Erechtheum: 370.90–91
Erechtheus: *Erech.*; 349–370; 481.10

635

Erinyes. *See* Furies
Eriphyle: *Alcm.Ps.*; 71
Eros (Love): *Cretans* (introd.
    n.); 136; 269; 430
Eteocles: *Antigone*
Ethiopia, Ethiopians:
    Andromeda; 147; 228;
    228a.11; 349
Eumolpus: *Erech.*; 360.48;
    370.15?, 100
Europa: 472.1
Europe: 381
Eurystheus: *Eurysth.*; 89

Fame (Eukleia): 474
Fates (Moirae): *Meleager*;
    494.18
Fortune (Tychē): 535
Furies (Erinyes): *Alcm.Ps.*

Gaia; Gē. *See* Earth
Glaucetes: 122
Glaucus, son of Bellerophon:
    Bell.?
Gorgon: *Andromeda*; *Danae*;
    Dictys; 124; 228a.10; 351;
    360.46
Greece, Greeks: 282.1, 13, 25;
    370.73; 494.17; 1132.5, 26
    (*Danae*). *See also* Hellas;
    Danaans

Hades: *Eurysth.*; 77 (*Alcm.Cor.*
    brief); 120; 332; 370.71; 371;
    448a.57; 465; 533
Haemon: *Antigone*; 161–167
Harmonia, necklace of:
    Alcm.Ps.; 70; 79

Heaven, Sky (Aethēr; Olympus;
    Ouranos): 114; 124; 182a;
    223.11; 228a.{4}; 286.1; 308;
    309a; 330; 370.72, 99; 443;
    [448]; 1004 (*Cretans*); 484;
    487; 506
Hector: *Alex.*; 62a, b
Hecuba: Alex.; 45; 46; 62; 62b–
    d; 62h
Helicon, Mt.: *Mel.W.* (t. vb)
Hellas: 228. *See also* Greece
Hellen: *Mel.W.*; 481.2, 7; 500?;
    509?
Helloi or Selloi: 367
Hera: *Ino*; *Ixion*; *Lamia*; 89
Heracles: *Alcmene*; *Auge*; *Arch.*;
    Busiris; *Eurysth.*; *Licymn.*;
    89; 175 (*Antiope*); 228a.16,
    18, 23; 260?; 268; 272–272b;
    371; 373; 379a; 450; 473?
Heraclidae: *Cresph.*; 448a.16
Hermes: *Alcmene*; *Antiope*;
    Autolycus A and B; *Danae*;
    24a; 190; 223.67–116; 1132
    (*Danae*); 370.113
Hippo or Hippē: *Mel.W.*;
    481.13–22; 483; 484
Hippocrene: *Mel.W.* (t. vb)
Hippodamia: *Dictys*
Hippolytus: *Hipp.V.*; 446
Hippothoon or Hippothous:
    Alope
Horse (constellation): *Mel.W.* (t.
    vb)
Hyacinthids: *Erech.*; 370.73–89
Hyades: 370.107
Hydra, Lernaean: 373
Hyllus: 228a.17

INDEX

Icarian Sea: *Cretans* (t. iiia)
Icarus: *Cretans*; 472g
Ida, Mt.: 472.10; 472f
Ilium. *See* Troy
Inachus: 228
Ino: *Ino*; 398; 399; 413
Iobates: *Bell.*
Ion: *Erech.?*; 481.11
Iphicles: *Alcmene*
Isander: *Bell.?*
Ismenus, R.: 223.87
Ixion: *Ixion*; 424

Jupiter. *See* Zeus
Justice: 151; 222; 223.57–58;
    255; 486; 506

Kentauros: *Ixion*
Kerykes (Heralds): 370.114

Labyrinth: *Theseus*; *Cretans*
Lamia: *Lamia*; 472m
Laomedon: *Licymn.*
Learchus: *Ino*
Leda: 515
Leto: 472b.3
Leucothea (White Goddess): *Ino*
Libya, Libyans: *Lamia*; 370.8;
    472m
Licymnius: *Licymn.*
Lityerses: *Theristae?*
Love: 269. *See also* Eros; Aph-
    rodite; Cypris
Loxias (title of Apollo): 1132.17
    (*Danae*); 455; 494.14
Lycia: *Bell.*; 472b.2
Lycus: *Antiope*; 223
Lynceus: 228a.4

Macareus: *Aeolus*; 13a–41
Macedonia: *Arch.*
Maeon: *Antigone*
Maia: 223.69
Manto: *Alcm.C.*; 73a
Marathon, Bull of: *Aegeus*;
    386b?
Medea: *Aegeus*
Medusa. *See* Gorgon
Megapenthes: *Bell.?*; 304a?
Megara (city): *Alope*
Melanippe: *Mel.W.*; *Mel.C.*;
    481–5; 494; 497?; 498?; 507?
Melanippus: 537
Meleager: *Meleager*; 517–520;
    526?; 527?; 535?
Melicertes/Palaemon: *Ino*
Menelaus: *Cret.W.*
Merope, mother of
    Cresphontes: *Cresph.*;
    448a.30, 70; 451; 453.13;
    454–456; 458
Merope, wife of Creon of Cor-
    inth: *Alcm.C.*
Messenia: *Cresph.*; 448a.19
Metapontium: *Mel.C.*
Metapontus: *Mel.C.*
Minos: *Cretans*; *Theseus*; 386c;
    472b.29–41; 472e; 472f; 988
    (*Cretans*); 531–531a
Minotaur: *Cretans*; *Theseus*;
    472a; 472b.29–41; 531–531a
Moirae. *See* Fates
Mopsus: 73a
Mountain Mother (Rhea): 472.13
Mycenae: *Andromeda*;
    Eurysth.; *Thyestes*; 228a.14
Mysia: *Auge*; 476

Nameless Goddesses: 494.18
Nauplius: *Auge*; *Cret.W.*; 466
Naxos: *Theseus*
Neptune. *See* Poseidon
Nereids: *Andromeda*; 1132.hyp.
  (*Danae*)
Night: 114
Nile, R.: *Busiris*; 228
Niobe: 223.100–102; 455
Nycteus: *Antiope*; 223.42

Oedipus: *Antigone*; 70; 157–8
Oeneus: *Meleager*; 515;
  516
Oenoe: 179
Oenomaus: *Dictys*
Olympus. *See* Heaven
Ouranos. *See* Heaven

Paian (title of Apollo):
  370.5
Palaemon. *See* Melicertes
Pallas Athena: 360.49; 370.3
Panactus: 12 (*Aegeus* brief)
Panathenaea: 370.79–80?
Pandion: 448a.82?
Paris. *See* Alexander
Parnassus, Mt.: *Ino. See also*
  Corycian mountain
Parthenion, Mt.: *Auge*
Parthenon: 369
Pasiphae: *Cretans*; 472b.38–9;
  472e
Peace: 453
Pegasus: *Bell.*; *Mel.W.* (t. vb);
  306–309a; 312
Pelasgians: 228
Pelopia: *Thyestes*?

Pelops: 515
Peneus, R.: 481.3
Penia. *See* Poverty
Persephone: *Erech.* (introd. n.);
  63 (*Alex.* brief)
Perseus: *Alcmene*; *Andromeda*;
  Danae; *Dictys*; 124–147;
  228a.12; 1132.hyp., 14
  (*Danae*); 344
Phaedra: *Hipp.V.*; 430; 433; 434
Phegeus: *Alcm.Ps.*; 71; 72
Phineus: *Andromeda*
Phlegyas: 424
Phoebus (title of Apollo): 245;
  1132.7 (*Danae*); 494.13
Phoenicia: 472.1
Phrygians: 223.102
Pirithous: *Eurysth.*
Pisa: 14
Pleiads: 124
Pleisthenes: *Cret.W.*
Polydectes: *Dictys*
Polynices: *Alcm.Ps.*; *Antigone*;
  168?; 176
Polyphontes: *Cresph.*; 448a.16–
  24; 452; 453.3–9
Porthaon: 515
Poseidon: *Alope*; *Andromeda*;
  Busiris; *Cretans*; *Dictys*;
  Erech.; *Hipp.V.* (t. iib?);
  Mel.W.; *Mel.C.*; 106; 107;
  349; 370.49, 55, 92–94; 386b;
  472e.26; 481
Poverty (Penia): 248
Praxithea: *Erech.*; 351; 360;
  360a; 370
Priam: *Alex.*; 46; 48; 60; 61a;
  61d.13; 62d

INDEX

Procne: 448a.82–86
Proetus: *Bell.*; 228a.6
Psophis: *Alcm.Ps.*
Pytho. *See* Delphi

Rhea. *See* Mountain Mother
Rhodes: *Licymn.*?

Salamis: 530
Salmone: 14
Salmoneus: 14
Sea-monster (Cetus):
    Andromeda; 115a; 145
Selloi. *See* Helloi
Seriphos: *Andromeda*; *Danae*;
    Dictys; 330b; 1132.hyp.
    (*Danae*)
Seven against Thebes: *Alcm. Ps.*
Shame. *See* Aidōs
Sibyl (Delphic): *Lamia*?
Sicily: *Cretans* (t. iiia)
Sicyon: *Antiope*
Silenus: *Eurysth.*; 282a; 373
Sirens: 116
Siris: *Mel.C.*; 495.15
Sisyphus: *Autolycus*
Sky. *See* Heaven
Sphinx: 178
Stheneboea: *Bell.*; 304a
Sthenelus: 89; 228a.13
Strife (Eris): 453.21
Syleus: *Theristae*?

Tantalus: 223.102
Taphians or Teleboans:
    Alcmene; *Licymn.*; 87b
Tegea: *Auge*
Telamon: 530

Teleboans. *See* Taphians
Telephontes: *Cresph.* (t. ii)
Telephus: *Auge*; 271b?
Temenus: *Arch.*; 228a.20, 22
Teuthrania: 476
Teuthras: *Auge*
Thebes, Thebans: *Alcm.Ps.*;
    Alcmene; *Antigone*; *Licymn.*;
    69; 87b; 178; 223.78–116
Themisto: *Ino*; 411; 415
Theseus: *Aegeus*; *Alope*;
    Eurysth.; *Hipp.V.*; *Theseus*;
    10; 11a; 260?; 379a?; 386b.11;
    386c; 439; 440; 953f
    (*Hipp.V.*); 531 + 531a
Thessaly, Thessalians: *Ino*;
    Hipp.V. (t. iib); *Mel.W*; 422;
    481.3–6
Thestius: 515
Thestius, sons of: *Meleager*;
    530
Thrace, Thracians: *Arch.*;
    Erech.; 360.48; 366?; 369;
    370.13
Thyestes: *Thyestes*; *Cret.W.*;
    396; 462?
Time: 222; 303
Tiresias: *Alcmene*; *Alcm.C.*
Tisiphone, daughter of
    Alcmeon: *Alcm.C.*; 73a
Tlepolemus: *Licymn.*
Toil (Ponos): 474
Triopas: *Aeolus*
Troezen: *Hipp.V.* (t. iib)
Trojan Horse: *Epeus*
Troy (Ilium): *Alex.*; *Licymn.*;
    41a
Tychē. *See* Fortune

Tydeus: 537
Tyro: 14

Xuthus: *Erech.*?; 481.9

Zagreus (Dionysus): 472.11
Zethus: *Antiope*; 179–223
Zeus: *Alcmene*; *Alope*; *Antiope*;
   Bell.; *Busiris*; *Danae*; *Dictys*;

Thyestes; *Ixion*; *Cretans*;
Lamia; 88; 89; 107; 151; 208;
210; 223.2–3, 11–14, 70–77,
96–111; 228a.15, 24; 312;
1132.hyp., 27, 46 (*Danae*);
336; 370.99; 388; 397b;
448a.71; 472.2, 10; 480;
481.1, 16; 487; 494.16; 506